A FIERCE, WILD JOY

A Fierce, Wild Joy

The Civil War Letters of Colonel Edward J. Wood, 48th Indiana Volunteer Infantry Regiment

Edited by Stephen E. Towne

Voices of the Civil War
Peter S. Carmichael, Series Editor

The University of Tennessee Press • Knoxville

Frontispiece. Wartime photo of Edward J. Wood, in either his major or lieutenant colonel uniform. Courtesy of Dr. Daniel Wood.

The Voices of the Civil War series makes available a variety of primary source materials that illuminate issues on the battlefield, the home front, and the western front, as well as other aspects of this historic era. The series contextualizes the personal accounts within the framework of the latest scholarship and expands established knowledge by offering new perspectives, new materials, and new voices.

The letters in this volume can be found in the Edward Jesup Wood Papers M 0794 Collection, Indiana Historical Society.

This book is printed on acid-free paper.

Wood, Edward J. (Edward Jesup), 1834–1873.
A fierce, wild joy: the Civil War letters of Colonel Edward J. Wood, 48th Indiana Volunteer Infantry Regiment / edited by Stephen E. Towne.—1st ed.
        p. cm.—(Voices of the Civil War)
"The letters in this volume can be found in the Edward Jesup Wood Papers M 0794 Collection, Indiana Historical Society"—T.p. verso.

Includes bibliographical references and index.

ISBN-13: 978-1-57233-599-8 (hardcover: alk. paper)
ISBN-10: 1-57233-599-8 (hardcover: alk. paper)

  1. Wood, Edward J. (Edward Jesup), 1834–1873—Correspondence.
  2. United States. Army. Indiana Infantry Regiment, 48th (1862–1865)
  3. United States. Army.—Officers—Correspondence.
  4. Abolitionists—United States—Correspondence.
  5. Southwest, Old—History—Civil War, 1861–1865—Personal narratives.
  6. Southwest, Old—History—Civil War, 1861–1865—Campaigns.
  7. Alabama—History—Civil War, 1861–1865—Campaigns.
  8. Georgia—History—Civil War, 1861–1865—Campaigns.
  9. United States—History—Civil War, 1861–1865—Personal narratives.
  10. United States—History—Civil War, 1861–1865—Campaigns.
  I. Towne, Stephen E., 1961–
  II. Indiana Historical Society.
  III. Title.

E506.548th .W66 2007
973.7'80922—dc22
[B]   2007015655

CONTENTS

Figures

Maps

Foreword

Edward J. Wood was no ordinary Hoosier. Born of a Connecticut Yankee father, Wood graduated from Dartmouth, where he was noted for his translations of Livy and his studies in civil engineering. Living among the eastern elite during his formative years instilled in Wood a deep commitment to hierarchy as a natural order of the world, even though he also believed in republicanism and abolition. He possessed both egalitarian and reactionary tendencies. Wood exhibited a contradictory consciousness that can be found in any individual, past or present. These tensions signify larger ideological fault lines that crisscross every society. Service as an officer in the 48th Indiana Infantry deepened his belief in the inequality of man and sharpened his contempt for those whom he deemed inferior. "What *is* to be the end of all this turmoil," Wood wrote from the field, "and *when* it is to come, are questions of intense interest to the whole country, & most especially the soldiers. I don't think the privates worry much about it—they never do about anything—Uncle Sam feeds & clothes them, & they obey orders & ask no questions—but to the intelligent officer, who has time and brains to think, this suspense is at times agonizing."

His low opinion of the rank and file must have originated within the volatile, brutal conditions on the front lines, where the daily struggle of survival fractured military relationships that officers believed should be defined by deference and obedience. Wood's letters speak to the turmoil inside a Civil War regiment, leading him to contradict his rather smug observation that his men were docile and well behaved. He was particularly outraged by the monopoly of sutlers, who charged exorbitant rates to all soldiers while the men survived off insufficient and irregular army supplies. "I believe if the Gov't would only abolish the monopoly of Sutlers," Wood wrote indignantly, "and throw open the trade of the army to competition some men would be found, who would be willing to furnish the soldiers such comforts at reasonable rates." The ordinary soldier, who Wood claimed was an unthinking brute, would not wait for the sutler to lower prices; nor would they stand by until the army commissary became efficient. The buck private took matters into his own hands and raided Southern farms. This was not an act of vandalism in Wood's eyes, but a blow against the Confederacy's ability to wage war. The men who supposedly obeyed orders without a murmur of discontent were not so passive in Wood's opinion when it came to waging war against Southern civilians.

Wood could not understand, furthermore, why some Union officers protected the property of rebellious citizens when their farms produced bounty for desperately hungry Federal soldiers. For a man who had a deep respect for the social order, he quickly jettisoned those conservative views to embrace a hard war of revolutionary fury. Rather than chastise Wood for his lack of consistency, one can find in *A Fierce, Wild Joy* how war compels individuals to reevaluate their most basic assumptions. Those moments when historical figures rework long-held ideas are singular opportunities to recover the fluid complexities of people trying to make sense of their unpredictable existence.

Trying to understand the inner world of any historical figure is a humbling experience, as the deeper we probe into the recesses of an individual's mind, the more complicated and confusing becomes the journey. Wood's wartime letters are filled with the most loving sentiments to his wife and child, and the most patriotic declarations of love for home and country. Combat did not seem to leave a sickening residue that enshrouded Wood in a deep state of depression. The brutality of soldiering did not seem to turn him against his fellow man as an inherently depraved and irredeemable creature. In fact, a surprising optimism pervades his letters to his wife, a hopefulness that animates his words, even in the midst of such vast destruction and death. His wartime letters speak of a better world that awaited him, his family, and his nation. In 1873, during a trip to Michigan, Wood locked himself in his hotel room, removed a revolver from his clothes, put the gun to his temple, and pulled the trigger. Alcohol was suspected as the cause of Wood's depression and suicide, and it appears that he had, for many years, battled his dependency on liquor. Surprisingly, his letters reveal nothing about the inner demons that caused him to escape through drink. In *A Fierce, Wild Joy* we must remember that soldiers had many personalities, sharing different sides of themselves and the conflict, depending on the audience. This important volume contains the sincere and devoted writings of a man who was consumed with love for his wife and child while also trying to shield his family from a dark, volatile world that he could neither escape nor convey.

PETER S. CARMICHAEL
UNIVERSITY OF NORTH CAROLINA AT GREENSBORO

PREFACE

This book is the result of a meeting which occurred in April 1998 between an intrigued descendent/researcher and a reference archivist. At that time, Dr. Daniel Wood, an endocrinologist residing in Maine, traveled to Indiana to learn about his great-grand-father, Edward Jesup Wood, an officer who commanded an Indiana regiment in the American Civil War. After stops at the Indiana Historical Society and the Indiana State Library, where he investigated the service of the regiment, Dr. Wood was encouraged to visit the Indiana State Archives (where I worked at the time) and speak to me. I had developed a small reputation among my archivist and librarian colleagues as the "go to" person to find information on obscure Civil War arcana relative to Indiana soldiers and political figures. I enjoyed helping researchers ferret out records and information to serve their needs.

Dr. Wood introduced himself and revealed what he was looking for. He showed me a spiral-bound set of his transcriptions of the Civil War letters of E. J. Wood and asked me if I could help him. I certainly could! I knew well who Colonel Wood was. At that time I had been for several years researching the Civil War career of an Indiana general, Milo S. Hascall, who had distinguished himself by suppressing Indiana newspapers and political speech during a short period when he commanded the military district of Indiana. Hascall and Wood were both from Goshen, a small town in northern Indiana. The two men were good friends. Dr. Wood showed me references in his ancestor's letters to Hascall as well as to other personages, places, and events that I knew well as a result of having dug through Goshen's old newspapers, records, and other sources. I was able to answer on the spot a number of questions arising from the letters. We went to lunch, where we continued our discussion and, as I perused the letters at greater length, came to recognize their significance and interest. Dr. Wood indicated that he was interested in perhaps publishing the letters. I encouraged him, and, even based on my brief acquaintance with them, spoke warmly of their usefulness to Civil War scholarship. He then asked if I would be interested in the project. Yes, indeed, I was.

Since then Dan Wood and I have cooperated to prepare this edition. Work, family, play, and other aspects of life have intervened at times to delay research and writing, but the effort continued. In the summer of 2002 I spent a delightful weekend in Maine at the home of Dan and Linda Wood, where we dug deeply into the family records and lore to get a greater understanding of E. J. Wood's family, and where this son of the Midwest feasted on freshly caught lobster for the first time. Above all things, I am grateful to the Woods for allowing me this opportunity to explore the Civil War experience of their ancestor.

I would also like to thank many colleagues at various archives and libraries who have assisted me in my research. These include my friends at the Indiana State Archives Alan F. January and Vicki Casteel, Darrol Pierson at the Indiana State Library, Randy Bixby, formerly of the Indiana State Library but now at Southern Illinois University at Carbondale, and Glenn L. McMullen and Susan Sutton of the Indiana Historical Society. DeAnne Blanton of the National Archives helped me grasp the U.S. Army records in Washington, D.C. Sarah I. Hartwell of the Rauner Special Collections Library at Dartmouth College provided information on several of Wood's classmates and other college-related matters. Mark Jaeger at Purdue University was an important sounding board for ideas about Wood's life and service, as well as a good friend. I would like to give special thanks to Jim Ogden of the Chickamauga and Chattanooga National Military Park, who kindly read Wood's letters written during the Chattanooga campaign in 1863, explained the details of the role of the 48th Indiana at Missionary Ridge during a tour of the Chattanooga battlefield, and who encouraged me to submit this manuscript to the University of Tennessee Press for publication.

INTRODUCTION

I

In 1861 rebellion and attack propelled hundreds of thousands of young men and women to defend the United States. They responded to the call to arms in an emergency, committed to the preservation of constitutional government and republican institutions. Their backgrounds were diverse, and their experiences during the ensuing warfare were likewise varied. Sensing intuitively that the Civil War was to be the seminal experience of the country and their lives, many, if not most, recorded their observations in one way or another. The writing of diaries and letters flourished.

Like thousands of other participants, Edward Jesup Wood recorded his experiences and thoughts in letters written to family and friends. His letters recount the pain of separation from wife and child, the anticipation of the collision of armies, the adrenaline-charged ferocity of battle, the exaltation of victory, the impatience with slow progress and setbacks, the comradeship found in war, and the revulsion from the scenes of carnage and death. These themes are commonplace in the personal writings of Civil War participants. But seldom are the themes recounted so well, so cogently, so insightfully as in these letters. Wood possessed an uncommon gift of conversation through letter writing, an ability "to talk on paper" for which he seems partially to have been aware but characteristically modest in asserting. Nonetheless, he was self-conscious enough of the moment and the momentousness of the great conflict to conceive of his letters as a "sort of journal," a record of his actions, thoughts, "trifles," and desires.

Edward Jesup Wood's extraordinary life was the product of the most turbulent period in U.S. history. Born of a Connecticut Yankee father and Florida planter mother in the South, taken from his mother, raised in New England, and educated to be an abolitionist, he fought during the war against his (half) brother, an officer in the Rebel service, yet feared for the safety of his southern relatives in Georgia and Florida when Federal forces invaded those states. Returning home to Indiana, he entered politics and won office and honors. But his life ended abruptly and sadly, a victim of either an accident or suicide while still a young man. The details of Wood's life provide a fascinating picture of the American experience in the middle of the nineteenth century.

Edward Jesup Wood was born at Marianna, in the panhandle of Florida, on August 2, 1834. He was the son of Elizur Wood, a Connecticut-born steamboat captain, and Marie Gautier Wood, a member of a plantation-owning and slave-owning family of Marianna, Florida. Elizur Wood came from an established family that settled in the Massachusetts Bay colony in the 1630s. Elizur's grandfather, Samuel Wood, a Harvard College graduate of 1745, served as a pastor in the Congregational Church in Union, Connecticut. Later, he returned to Massachusetts and still later served a church in Nova Scotia. In 1772 he returned to Connecticut. There he served in a Connecticut militia regiment in the war for independence, was captured at Fort Washington in New York, and died in 1777 in a British prison hulk in New York harbor.

Samuel Wood's youngest child, Elizur, married Eleanor Jesup, the daughter of a Yale College–educated physician, in 1793, and settled in Green's Farms, Connecticut. Elizur died in 1814, but not before fathering sons of his own. Elizur *fils* was born in 1798 in Westport, Connecticut. In the 1820s he and two of his brothers ventured to western Florida, recently ceded to the United States from Spain. There Elizur entered the steamboat business on the Apalachicola River, which flows from southern Georgia to the Gulf of Mexico, and participated in efforts to combat the Seminole Indian insurgency on this southern frontier. In a letter of 1829 he wrote that northerners believed it "certain death" to pass a summer in the South. Perhaps that is true in places like New Orleans, Mobile, or Savannah, he surmised, "but this part of Georgia is as healthy as any part of the eastern or northern states."[1]

Elizur Wood married Marie Elizabeth Gautier on October 3, 1832. Marie was the fourteen-year-old daughter of Peter (Pierre) Gautier, the son of a French Protestant pastor from Nimes, a town in the south of France near the Mediterranean Sea. Pierre Gautier and two brothers left England for North Carolina in the 1790s. Marie was born in Monticello, Georgia, and moved with her family to western Florida in the 1820s where they soon became established slave-owning plantation farmers in Marianna, near the Georgia border on the nearby Chippola River.

The married couple resided in Apalachicola, Florida, during their marriage, and their three children were born there. Edward Jesup Wood was the firstborn issue of the marriage. He was followed by brother William ("Willie") Wood, born in 1837, and sister Fannie Gautier Wood, born in 1839, about whom little is known and who probably died in 1843. While visiting his mother, Eleanor Jesup Wood, Elizur Wood became ill and died in her home in New York City on August 24, 1840, leaving a widow and two young sons in Florida.

Introduction

Wood family history of the events that followed is confused and incomplete, based on hazy accounts. Marie Wood, a twenty-two-year-old widow alone with three young children in Apalachicola, was distraught at the death of her husband. In a poem penned soon after word reached her of his death, she wrote:

> 'Tis true that he died in his native land,
> And his sorrows were soothed by his sister's hand,
> But the one that loved best, that noble heart,
> Was forced with anguish from him to part.
>
> Oh many a pang will this widowed heart feel,
> When my fatherless children beside me shall kneel,
> Tho we wander as strangers a few years of pain,
> May we there meet as best friends in Heaven again.[2]

Eleanor Jesup Wood, her mother-in-law, pressed the grieving widow that it would be wise to send the two boys (but not Fannie) to live with her, perhaps temporarily, in New York City. According to family history, Elizur's will specified that his sons were to be educated in the North. Perhaps the grandmother held out the promise of financial support and educations for the boys, though she, a widow herself, does not appear to have had substantial means at her disposal. According to Marie's daughter from a subsequent marriage, "[t]he picture that was drawn to her was untold wealth or abject poverty to herself & boys—she gave the children up little suspecting the villainous scheme." Marie was "so unsuspecting, and took everyone at their word." Eleanor Jesup Wood evidently persuaded the young mother to send the boys to live with her, their paternal grandmother, in New York City with the understanding that they would not be separated from their mother permanently. However, the "tyrannical grandmother" had other plans, and made provision for keeping the boys from their mother. Eleanor Jesup Wood herself died suddenly in 1842, but succeeded in keeping the boys in the North. A Wall Street attorney, Thomas Denny, was put in charge of the boys' financial support and education and managed a trust left by their grandmother. While she corresponded with her boys, Marie Gautier Wood probably never saw her younger son Willie again, though it is possible that she saw Edward once in 1851 or 1852 when he visited Savannah, Georgia. Wrote Marie's daughter to Edward's daughter, "[h]er separation of your father & brother Willie was her greatest grief."[3] From evidence in surviving family correspondence, Edward found family affection and comfort in the household of his aunt Juliet Wood Mackie, younger sister of his father Elizur. Her children Mary and John Walter Mackie were probably Edward's closest relations. During the Civil War his letters speak eloquently of his great affection for his cousins, and John Walter Mackie's death in 1868 was a severe blow to Wood.[4]

Willie was mentally handicapped, and did not receive extensive schooling. In time he was sent to live on the farm of a Mr. Houghton in upstate Ogdensburg, New York, where he lived happily until his death in 1889. Edward, however, was sent to a succession of private schools and tutors. The boy was enrolled in schools in Connecticut, first in Deacon Hyde's School for Small Boys in Green's Farms, and subsequently he prepped at the academy in Woodstock with James Willis Patterson, a future U.S. senator but then merely a Dartmouth College graduate. Little is known of Wood's schooling or of his childhood experiences. Patterson evidently encouraged him to enroll at Dartmouth, and Mr. Denny made the requisite arrangements for tuition, board, and books.[5] He matriculated at the New Hampshire college in 1849 at the age of fifteen.

Wood succeeded at Dartmouth, and made a reputation for himself as a fine scholar, noteworthy for his "brilliant" translations of Livy. As reported in the *Class Memorial* in later years, "[t]hough among the youngest, he was one of the best translators in the class."[6] He also studied civil engineering, an effort that stood him in good stead during his service in the Civil War. While at Dartmouth, Wood affected strong friendships that were to last the rest of his life. He was particularly close to Redfield Proctor, a future secretary of war in the Benjamin Harrison administration and U.S. senator for Vermont. Proctor and Wood corresponded during the war. Wood in 1863 also wrote of visiting his classmate Charlie Blood in St. Louis, Missouri, and touring the new botanical gardens there. His Dartmouth College experience and the friends he made there clearly were of great importance to him in later years.

Wood graduated from Dartmouth in 1853 at the age of eighteen, possessed of an excellent education, a rare attainment for any young man in America in the mid-nineteenth century. He put his civil engineering studies to practical use by promptly contracting to supervise the construction of a fifteen-mile section of railroad line of the Michigan Southern and Northern Indiana Railroad, part of the line under construction between Toledo, Ohio, and Goshen, Indiana. This project brought him to Goshen, a small town in Elkhart County in the far northern part of the state. Wood would later voice chagrin at his decision to go west in search of employment rather than look for work in New York City. While in the army in 1862 he would write to his wife, "Confidence & assurance are the main stock in trade in most businesses & if I had had more in my younger days I never would have turned westward" (see letter number 19 of July 3, 1862). The railroad boom had reached Indiana by then, and railroad construction was in full swing all over the state. Fortunes were to be made in railroading, and taking part in the boom would have been a natural impulse in 1853 for a young man of talent. Wood worked on the railroad until the line was finished in 1857.

While in Goshen, Wood by 1856 entered into the political life of the community. Politics at all levels—local, state, and national—in mid-nineteenth-century America was a seething cauldron fueled by the differing views of the role of chattel slavery in American society. Antislavery politics were on the rise in Indiana and elsewhere, and a new political party, known then in Indiana as the People's Party but later to be called the Republican Party, was born as the champion of abolition and the halt to extension of slavery into the western territories. The upstart party challenged the then comfortably ensconced Democratic Party in the statehouse in Indianapolis and the national capital in Washington, D.C. Oliver P. Morton, a young, dynamic attorney from Wayne County in eastern Indiana, ran for governor on the People's Party ticket. The party's presidential champion was the famous western explorer John C. Frémont, a noted abolitionist.

Wood entered the campaign as a speaker against the extension of slavery into Kansas territory, and attacked slavery as the national scourge. In a surviving text from a speech he gave in June 1856, Wood assailed the Democratic Party's support for slavery in Kansas, and asserted that in the upcoming presidential race "there will be but this one all-absorbing issue, freedom or slavery in the territories." Later, when Frémont obtained the party nomination, he wrote a multiverse campaign song, "Freedom & Frémont," which began:

> Oh we come down to Elkhart to help the people start
> The Fremont ball a-rolling
> And we'll never let it stop, till the last foe shall drop
> And the people all their votes all polling

> **Chorus**
> So take off your coats & roll up your sleeves
> Pitch in for Freedom in Kansas
> Take off your coats & roll up your sleeves
> Freedom & Fremont will beat 'em I believe.[7]

In 1857, perhaps encouraged by his reception as a stump speaker and still only twenty-three years old, Wood made a career change, entering the law office of Joseph H. Mather, a prominent local Republican attorney and politician. There he studied the law under Mather's tutelage, a common method for legal education at that time. Mather died in 1859, but by that time Wood had begun to practice law in a small way. He then entered the law office of Edward W. Metcalfe, the judge of the Court of Common Pleas for the county, and served as the junior partner. He also ran for elective office and won the county surveyorship in Elkhart County on the Republican Party ticket. He continued to practice law with Metcalfe and hired a deputy to undertake the duties of the county surveyor's office.

Also in that year, on October 25, Wood married Jane Augusta Williams in Syracuse, New York. Sources provide neither clues nor suggestions about where, when, or how the two met. Jane was the daughter of Coddington Billings Williams and Sarah Smith Williams, both of whom were born in Connecticut. Coddington Williams was a prominent and prosperous salt merchant in Salina, now part of Syracuse. Sarah Williams bore nine children, of whom Jane was the seventh. She was born in Syracuse on October 25, 1835 (she was thus wedded on her twenty-fourth birthday). Little is known of her education, but she clearly was an intelligent and capable woman. Though occasionally he assumed a patronizing tone in his letters, Wood clearly respected Jane's intelligence and, during the years of separation, rather than dictating from afar, deferred to her decisions. References show the young couple read the novels of the day and the periodical press together. The letters also suggest that Jane, whom Edward usually in his letters called Jennie or Jeanie, was familiar with the poetry that he quoted so frequently. Photos of her show a very pretty young woman, stylishly dressed and coiffed.

It is unfortunate that none of Jane's letters to her husband during the war has survived. But Edward's letters to his wife show the couple's unflagging affection and devotion, with no trace of anger, bitterness, or argumentativeness during their long and painful separations. Edward's frequent declarations of his desire to be with her, to "clasp her in [his] arms," demonstrate deep affection and devotion and were no doubt reciprocated. In an era when private letters were commonly read aloud to family members or friends either whole or in part, it is understandable that there are no more ardent or intimate expressions of love and longing in his letters, but his hints of his desire to return to her "good bed" and sleep with his wife reveal his sexual ardor.[8] From Edward's replies to his wife's frequent requests for him to leave the service and return to her, a clear picture emerges of a young woman who suffered from separation from her husband, chafed at living cooped up together in the same house with parents or siblings, and longed for the independence from extended family that married life afforded.

Jane and Edward established their household in Goshen, where Edward continued to practice law in a second-floor office over the Republican newspaper overlooking the courthouse and participate in county politics. However, any plans they might have had for quiet, peaceful domesticity collapsed quickly. The 1860 elections, with the divisive victory of Illinois

Republican Abraham Lincoln in the presidential contest, brought national political conflict and crisis to the forefront in every locale in the country. Southern slave owners, threatened by the prospect of an avowed abolitionist in the White House, agitated for the secession of the southern slave states from the national union. Efforts at compromise failed in early 1861, and war began on April 12, 1861, when South Carolinian military forces bombarded a U.S. facility, Fort Sumter, in Charleston harbor.

War fever was high in Goshen, as in other communities throughout the North and South. Almost immediately the town offered companies of volunteers to the Federal cause, and men departed for rendezvous camps in Indianapolis and "the seat of war" soon thereafter. Wood noted in one of his wartime letters that he had wished to volunteer his services immediately on the news of hostilities. But in April 1861 Jane was eight months

Jane Wood. Courtesy of Daniel Wood.

pregnant with their first child, Marie (or Mary) Gautier Wood, who was born May 18, 1861, in Goshen. Sentiment was universal that the Southern rebellion would be quashed quickly, and President Lincoln's initial call for seventy-five thousand men for three months' service would be sufficient. Wood probably thought that he would miss the opportunity to strike a blow against disunion. But Union fortunes took a bad turn starting at the first battle of Bull Run in July. Additional troops would be necessary to uphold the national Union and put down the "unholy" rebellion.

In September 1861 local Republican political leader Erastus Winter Hewitt Ellis secured a promise from Governor Oliver P. Morton to site a rendezvous camp at Goshen in the third wave of recruiting of volunteer regiments for the war effort. The camp would serve as the training camp for one of the regiments to be formed in the ninth and tenth congressional districts in northern Indiana. Ellis was named the commandant of the camp, which soon sported the appellation "Camp Ellis." Norman Eddy, a fifty-one-year-old attorney and former Democratic U.S. representative from nearby South Bend, Indiana, was named as the regiment's commander. In November recruiting began in earnest for the unit designated the "48th Indiana Volunteer Infantry" regiment. Also in that month advertisements appeared in Goshen's Democratic and Republican newspapers that Edward J. Wood was organizing a company for the 48th Indiana, and that his recruiting office was located over Hascall, Alderman & Brown's store in the Hascall block of downtown Goshen.[9]

Wood's strong patriotism and sense of duty propelled him to put himself forward and volunteer for service. However, no evidence exists to suggest that he entertained the idea of serving as a private soldier. E. W. H. Ellis, who took the leading hand with Governor Morton in recommending suitable men to be officers for the regiment, probably pushed him to volunteer as an officer in the regiment. With two War Democrats tabbed for the top two appointments in the regiment in an effort to achieve bipartisan support for the regiment and boost recruiting, Ellis may have endeavored to appoint talented and reliable local Republicans to the other commissioned positions.[10] As his letters written in the course of the war show, Wood expressed modest notions of his leadership qualities. But he grew in the position, and with his promotions ultimately to command of the regiment, he showed skill, ability, and careful stewardship of first his company and then the regiment.

With Marie six months old and Jane recovered from her pregnancy, Wood's sense of national duty took precedence over familial responsibility. We do not know Jane's attitude to Edward's decision to volunteer. Jane and Marie were sent east to Syracuse to live with her parents, and Wood turned his attentions to recruiting for his company. His frequent references to the

Erastus Winter Hewitt Ellis, a Goshen political leader who organized the 48th Indiana. Courtesy of Daniel Wood.

pain of separation from his daughter, "Mamie," show him to have been a doting father in absentia. He offered advice to Jane on weaning, allowing Marie to play outside and get dirty, and was anxious when he heard that she was ill. During the three furloughs while in service Wood had the opportunity to play and become acquainted with his toddler daughter, showing him to be her play partner at these times, indicative of a growing middle-class phenomenon of the father as close and tender to his offspring, as friend and playmate rather than distant disciplinarian. He lamented missing the opportunity to witness Marie's maturation from infant to toddler. He frequently remarked in his letters on his wish to "toss her up high, and roly-loly her & have a regular frolic" when he arrives home.[11] It is at the point when the family separated, in January 1862, that the letters begin. The ninety letters printed here cover the next three years of their lives.

II

Edward Jesup Wood was an excellent writer. He wrote with style and verve, always with an aim to entertain his faraway wife. His letters are full of vivid images, employing a wide descriptive vocabulary to recount his life and his surroundings. He consciously painted word pictures to convey the sights, sounds, smells, and textures of campaigning "in the tented field." A letter written during the siege of Vicksburg in June 1863 serves as an example of his efforts "to re-produc[e] the picture": "Seated under an ample, thickly-shaded a[r]bor, in front of our neat, white tents, with a cooling breeze wafting the hidden perfumes of many flowers & the soft music of innumerable birds—even the sharp, constant *crack* of the sharpshooters in our front, and the continual *boom* of cannon of every size, far & near, are not enough to disturb the deep tranquility of the hour & the scene." An avid reader of the prose and poetry of his age, Wood infused into his letters the cadences of the heroic verses he knew from memory. His quotations from Byron, Longfellow, Lowell, and others often blended into his own writing. At times, he mocked the grandiloquent style of much of Victorian patriotic fluff. Whether recounting battle scenes or the misadventures of his runaway horse or the regimental cow, Wood wrote with both wit and precision. He always conveyed his meaning clearly and directly.

Wood expressed himself always as an ardent patriot, determined to subdue the rebellion that threatened to destroy the republic. Early in the war, when most believed the conflict would end quickly, he champed to get in a fight, to strike a blow for the Union. Later, having experienced the horrors of battle, his eagerness for fighting subsided. But his zeal to see the rebellion crushed did not abate. Two years into the war, during a long and grueling march toward an anticipated battlefield, he could write, "I feel the natural ardor of a soldier & a patriot, . . . and all merely personal things are for the moment lost sight of." Such expressions, along with notions of personal honor, served as reminders to his wife about why he was in the army and why he would not try to shirk his duty and resign or seek a medical discharge. "I don't like to resign while I am well & able for the service as I am now. . . ." Though a Republican and abolitionist, Wood's patriotism transcended partisan politics to allow him to criticize the Lincoln administration's policies. Perhaps because Jane did not enjoy political tirades, he expressed few purely political comments to his wife, a somewhat uncommon trait for a member of the political ruling classes of his day. In the summer of 1862, he voiced his disgust with the army's policy of guarding the private property of Southerners while the soldiers suffered from lack of decent food. "I am glad to say such nonsense is about 'played out,' and on the last march the boys foraged quite extensively." Shortly thereafter, with the first call for a draft of troops for the Federal army, Wood could comment that the "North has just commenced to get in earnest, & has for the first time put forth an effort." In the following year, perhaps reflecting the increased radicalization of the army and its growing disillusionment with civilian society, Wood launched into a rare tirade regarding the mismanaged Federal draft. "The weakness of the Administration affords most cause for alarm. . . . It is almost incredible that the affairs of a nation should be managed with so little fore-sight. . . . It is most disheartening." The "imbecility of the Administration" was to blame. At the end of this, his most vituperative rant, Wood remem-bered to whom he was writing and attempted an apology: "Well I'm afraid I've bored you with this long disquisition, but it's hard to stop or condense when I get started on this theme." His comment suggests that he and his fellow officers in their idle hours frequently vented themselves on the war's political vicissitudes, but he rarely did so with his wife.[12]

Wood's motivations to enter the army and subdue the rebellion rested on his self-described patriotism, a term he uses several times in his letters but does not explain. It was his duty to fight to preserve the Federal union against rebels intent on protecting slavery and willing to destroy the coun-try in the process. However, though he was a Republican and abolitionist, he hardly mentions slaves and slavery in his letters. Wood shared with other Union soldiers the ardent desire to quell the rebellion but, unlike many Northern soldiers, makes no reference to abolishing slavery in the letters to his wife. Significantly, his sole reference to eliminating slavery comes in his letter of July 4, 1862, for publication in the Goshen *Times*. There, he wrote of fighting for "eternal right," that "Slavery and Rebellion, its outgrowth, are henceforth powerless for evil in the land." Should the Federal armies fail to restore the Union, the result would be "too sickening and disheartening to contemplate."[13] Wood acknowledged his patriotism, however defined, to be his driving force. Yet that patriotism was not limitless. His duty to his family also called him. At one time, not long into his commission, he wrote his wife, "It will require a fresh installment of patriotism to keep me away from [wife and child] many months longer." And later, in 1864, he wrote his wife, "my patriotism, of which you are pleased to think I have a large share, would ooze rapidly away" and he'd leave the service by any means should she become seriously ill.[14]

Wood's letters reflect his status as an officer and a member of the educated eastern middle class. If the letters serve as accurate reflections, Wood had little connection or interaction with the enlisted men in either his company or the regiment. "The boys," "the men," "my company," and "the regiment," are the ways in which the collective persona of his unit was expressed. The names of individual soldiers are never mentioned, even when during a disagreeable march without their supplies Captain Wood had to mess with a squad from his company. They appear as an almost faceless, unthinking, obedient mass, as in one passage he patronizingly wrote: "What *is* to be the end of all this turmoil and *when* it is to come, are questions of intense interest to the whole country, & most especially the soldiers. I don't think the privates worry much about it—they never do about anything—Uncle Sam feeds & clothes them, & they obey orders & ask no questions—but to the intelligent officer, who has time and brains to think, this suspense is at times, agonizing." Wood was bound by military regulations from fraternizing with the men in the ranks, a wise precaution meant to preserve unit discipline and morale. Nonetheless, given his obvious solicitousness for the well-being of his troops, this attitude is remarkable. The one exception was "Tommy" Donohue, Wood's servant and cook for a while in 1862, for whom he expressed real friendship and devotion. Again, it may be a reflection of Jane Wood's unfamiliarity with and lack of regard for the rustic farmers and tradesmen who filled the ranks of the 48th that he refrained from noting their names. Wood's letters make clear that Jane disliked Goshen and the rough, western ways of its "Hoosiers." But it appears Wood held somewhat a patrician's disdain for the common man.[15]

Wood inhabited the world of officers and those whose tastes were refined by education and social status. He was comfortable rubbing elbows with the "Generals & big bugs" in camp. The letters recount meetings to discuss tactics and strategy, and other times convivial gatherings with prominent officers, some of whom enjoyed the rare social distinction of a West Point education. One such West Pointer, Brigadier General Milo S. Hascall, a friend from Goshen whom Wood occasionally encountered in the field, kissed Mamie's photo in uncle-like delight. While occupying northern Alabama in 1864, Wood enjoyed a lighthearted fishing trip and fish fry with Brigadier General Marcellus M. Crocker, another West Pointer. He recounted to his wife meeting and being commended by Major General William T. Sherman when serving at Paducah, Kentucky, in the spring of 1862. But he omitted to mention that he succeeded in extracting a notable confession from Sherman in a relaxed moment, an exchange recorded in a letter home by regimental Adjutant Edward P. Stanfield (a Princeton University man himself). According to Stanfield, General Sherman encountered Wood in Atlanta shortly after the fall of that city in September 1864. Wood told him he remembered him at Paducah criticizing the generalship of, among others, Ulysses S. Grant: "[h]e didn't think Grant was much of a general." Later, during the Vicksburg siege on a visit to the 48th in the trenches, Sherman remarked that "Grant was a great general and that this campaign surpassed all others." When confronted by Wood with his early criticism of Grant, Sherman replied, "I don't remember saying that, but I know I thought so at the time."[16]

Wood developed close attachments to fellow officers in his regiment and those with which his regiment was brigaded. They formed a group that provided friendship and emotional support that he appears to have leaned on heavily. He confessed in a letter not liking to be alone, and when several of his officers obtained short furloughs and left him behind in camp, he complained of being "absolutely alone" and "dismally blue." When his regiment was sent away under a subordinate's command to shepherd a herd of cattle to Sherman's army in Georgia while he was detailed on court-martial duty, Wood was despondent. He sought out companionship in different quarters. He rejoiced in the comradeship of the fellow officers who served with him on a court martial. He noted approvingly that many, if not most, in the Federal officer corps were Masons, an association that Wood valued and venerated. He became a close friend with Colonel Jesse I. Alexander of the 59th Indiana Volunteer Infantry regiment, with which the 48th Indiana was brigaded for much of the war. Several wives of the officers of the 59th ventured south to stay with their husbands, and Wood enjoyed their society (though apparently not too much to incur jealous comments from Jane). He befriended the civilians with whom he occasionally boarded. In sum, Wood craved society and social interaction, and the army provided plenty of both. It can be conjectured that his orphaned childhood, shuttled from boarding school to boarding school, cut off from almost all family, propelled him to combat loneliness and seek emotional comfort in the groups surrounding him.

Wood enjoyed army life. His letters betray a delight in the social life of camp and march, but also show his satisfaction with the order, neatness, and regularity that the army provided. His descriptions of camp routine—white gloves on parade; cooking; "neat white tents" arranged in grids; campgrounds swept clean, decorated, and improved with substantial buildings—are frequent. The Bedouin existence of living in tents is preferable to domestic life in houses, he noted at one point. He has put on weight, he proudly added. Such are his expressions of happiness in military life that the reader suspects that some of his protestations of his desire to quit the army were meant to please and pacify Jane. His accounts of the military bureaucracy holding him in the service are difficult to take at full value, given the ability of many officers readily to resign their commissions. His story of the lieutenant pining away and dying for lack of proper paperwork to allow him to go home is suspect; no lieutenant from the 48th Indiana died during the period in question.

That is not to say that Wood enjoyed war. While initially, in a desire to prove his patriotism and manhood, he eagerly looked forward to the experience of battle, and when he had the adrenaline-charged experience described it rapturously ("a fierce wild joy exhilarated & filled me"), he later expressed his dislike of war's horror. Describing the scene after the battle of Champion Hill he wrote: "and as night fell and our victorious hosts passed over the battle field, after the vanquished foe the ground thickly strewn with dead & dying, revealed the terrible nature of the struggle. I did not go over the battlefield only where my duty called me, as I have no penchant for such horrors. I was told that I did not see the worst portions of it, but I saw enough, & the recollection of which will suffice to send a chill thro' me to my latest day." Still later, he voiced the veteran's desire to escape from the carnage, destruction, and death. The 48th expressed general satisfaction that they were detailed to guarding railroad lines and avoided frontline service in the bloody Atlanta campaign. "The duty is rather heavy," he wrote, "but the boys are so gratified with the idea of spending the summer in the delightful town of Huntsville, that they don't complain."

Wood reassured his wife frequently that a providential God would protect and preserve them during the war's hardships and dangers. "God rules over all, and hard and dark His ways may seem, He means that we should walk in them for His purposes, and for our own good." Later, he wrote, "You must trust in the good God, who has preserved me thus far, that I shall come out unharmed." Wood, a good Episcopalian, related occasionally hearing a sermon in camp or attending a church service in a southern town. He quoted scripture several times in his letters, apparently from memory.

Many other themes and threads are to be found in Wood's rich letters. Throughout, however, the central theme is the war for the Union and the suppression of the rebellion. Wood wrote his letters to his wife as a form of journal, recounting the everyday details of campaigning, but giving greatest importance to military issues. Battle descriptions form the core of his account, much like official after-action reports submitted up the chain of command. As he became more comfortable and grew in his increasingly important role in the regiment (Wood assumed effective command of the regiment in May 1863, in the middle of the Vicksburg campaign, as Colonel Eddy was wounded and unable to command), Wood came to grasp more fully both the tactical and strategic significance of events. Tactically, his cool thinking while stuck on the side of the Rebel works during the frontal assault on Vicksburg on May 22, 1863, probably saved heavy casualties in his regiment. Later, he rightly saw the big, strategic picture during the long march to the relief of Chattanooga in October 1863. "It is the grandest military movement of the war," he wrote, "like movements on a chess-board, everything else has become subordinate to this grand attack on the enemy's centre at Chattanooga, which is in reality the Key to the whole position." Should Union forces be successful there, "we [will be] in position to knock loudly at the back-doors of Charleston and Richmond." Wood's skill as a soldier grew, and he took modest satisfaction in his personal accomplishment as a good officer who cared for his men as best he could. He also expressed some pride in the progress of his regiment and the individual soldiers who formed it. After the regiment built "uniform regular barracks" at a new camp in Georgia in July 1864, replacing the "board shanties" that had preceded them, he wrote:

> It is a great pleasure to me to see how the Regiment has improved in this respect—if I have never been of any other advantage to them I can fairly claim that I have educated them to appreciate the value of neatness & cleanliness. I say educated them to it, for it has not been accomplished without persistent efforts, and now they have acquired habits of good order & neatness, it is no trouble at all to keep them up to the mark. . . . I superintended the erection of one set of quarters, and without an order or a word, except of advice when it was asked, the other companies built them to correspond.

Seen as a symbol of efficiency and good order in the regiment, this trait was manifest on the battlefield and on the march. Wood and his subordinates became an effective fighting team, all the parts of which fulfilled their assigned roles with efficiency and zeal.

Wood's letters depict battles and marches in the western theater of the war. The 48th Indiana participated in the battles of Iuka and Corinth in the fall of 1862 (though Wood was "chagrined" to miss the regiment's first battle while temporarily detached on provost duty. "However," he wrote, "I am consoled by the reflection, that I was doing my duty here under orders, and no one can impute any bad motive to me, in being away"), the long Vicksburg campaign, the march to relieve Chattanooga and the battle of Missionary Ridge, the Atlanta campaign, and the March to the Sea at Savannah. He vividly reports the battles in which the 48th participated. It was a war of movement, of long marches in stifling heat and dust or in freezing rain, of bivouacking without shelter or even blankets for warmth and dryness. It was a war of long encampments, of hot summer days of boredom and lassitude or of shivering cold and snow, huddled in a tent or makeshift barracks. Wood records it all.

While Wood was better educated than most Americans of his day, he shared the relaxed orthography and punctuation habits generally exhibited in the era's personal writings. He consistently misspelled certain words, for example, "beleive" and "abscence." He often neglected to use periods, opting to leave blank space or dashes to indicate the ends of sentences. Excessive commas litter his sentences. Indentation at the start of new paragraphs was generally apparent but sometimes not. His handwriting was usually quite clear, and few words are illegible. However, where a word could not be clearly identified I give my best guess in brackets with a question mark. I have retained all of Wood's idiosyncrasies of spelling and punctuation as they generally do not detract from understanding his meaning. I have not followed the example of some Civil War editorial efforts and excised any of his lamentations of separation and absence. To do so would be to destroy a central thematic thread of the letters, as well as to ignore the pain that combatants and loved ones alike endured.

CHAPTER 1

The War Is to Be of Short Duration

Organizing in Goshen, January–February 1862

Edward J. Wood undertook the task of recruiting his company. There was no guarantee that he would obtain all the men necessary to fill a company, and many a recruiter failed to attract volunteers. The U.S. Army lacked any coordinated recruitment policy in the first months of the rebellion. Much was left to political leadership in each Northern state as to the methods for filling the calls for troops. In Indiana, Governor Oliver P. Morton instituted a system of assigning one volunteer infantry regiment to be raised in each congressional district in the state. Most of the districts contained roughly ten counties, and each county would be responsible for filling a company for a ten-company volunteer infantry regiment. However, in times of pressing need more than one regiment per district was expected. Competition for recruits was often fierce. In Wood's case, Elkhart County and its neighbors were swept thoroughly by recruiters from other companies of the 48th Indiana. Recruiters from the 44th Indiana Volunteer Infantry regiment also scoured the county at the same time. Wood received no official funds for recruiting purposes, and paid his expenses from his own pocket (he was to complain later that the federal and state authorities owed him pay for his time recruiting his company). Part of those expenses often included treating the recruits and potential recruits to transportation, lodging, food, and liquor. Indeed, many recruiters spent generously on alcoholic beverages to entice men and boys to volunteer.[1]

While busy recruiting his company up to required strength, Wood had both to learn the soldier's trade and to teach it to his company. Officers and enlisted men both began to drill assiduously on the parade ground, marching, maneuvering, and marching some more. Great store was placed in *Hardee's Tactics*, the standard manual for battlefield maneuvers and employed by both Federal and Rebel forces.

LETTER 1
Camp Ellis[2]
Jan'y 16th, 1862

My Dear wife,

I wrote you a hurried scrawl a few days ago, and this is the first time I have had since to write a line. I started last Saturday on a recruiting trip with 'Gus Crane[3] over into La Grange County, and was gone several days, and since my return I have been very busy indeed. We had a pretty hard time of it. The weather was intensely cold and blustering, but I think I am fast getting toughened to exposure & am still feeling quite well. Mr Crane was very kind as usual. He took his own horses, & spent his whole time for four days helping me to get men. We did not have very good success, as a recruiting officer from the 44th Regt. had just been back there and taken away a good many men—still our company is fast filling up.[4] I think it will be full in a few days, then we will have our election & as I beleive I wrote you there is not doubt of my success.[5] I have become much attached to my men & I think they have confidence in me. Our Regt is composed of much better material than many of those that went earlier. The young boys & the loose floating population generally went among the first, and now the recruits are mostly solid farmer boys, and men of family.[6]

To-day I have been the officer of the day, & till tomorrow morning at 9 o'clock am second in authority, only to the Colonel, & indeed tonight I am in sole charge of the camp—the Col, Lt Col, & Major all being away. A part of my duties is to make the "grand rounds" of the guards at least once after 12 o'clock at night, and it is to that fact that you are indebted for this letter, for although it was nearly that time when I was freed from other duties I did not know how soon again I might have a chance to have a quiet halfhour's chat with my little wifey.

Your letter and the picture came safely to hand and you cannot tell how much I prize it—It is not a good one of you, but the baby's is remarkably good for so young a child, & it is almost impossible to have them both perfect. The p[r]ecious little dear! What would not her papa give to hug his babies tonight. You must have another taken before a great while to try to get a better one of yourself. In about two weeks, I shall have my soldier clothes, & then I will have a picture taken for you. "Grand rounds!" I am glad you got the letter with the money enclosed.–Tho' the amount was so small, I thought it might save you from inconvenience till I could send more, but it was so long on the way, I had given it up as lost.

I am in hopes next week to send you more.

I saw Nettie Bissell[7] in town the other day & reminded her of her promise to write you. She inquired very particularly about you & the baby & promised to write soon. Ed. Kerstetter was at home on furlough a few days, and Milo wrote offering me a captaincy in his Regt![8] It is a good time to offer to help one, when they don't need any assistance

I have got the company without any great outside help & in spite of a good deal of opposition from the same kind friends, who carried such charitable reports to Father.

I think it is a sufficient answer to all their vile aspersions that I have been able almost unaided and without the use of money to raise a company where so many have been raised, and have now nearly a hundred men, who are willing to risk their lives, with me as their captain—There are 4 companies from this county in this Regt & you may be sure it has been no easy matter to get men, but I had staked my reputation & everything else in the endeavor, & have worked night and day, till it is accomplished.

You do not write me about your health—you look thinner in the picture. I hope you have got rid of that terrible cough. You must be prudent and not expose yourself to taking cold. I should think, with quiet & rest, you must get over that cough. How soon will you wean the baby & do you give her any other food. I should think you could feed her considerably now, and you be stronger for it. She must be a great load—16 pounds! You must not tax your strength too much with her.

I do not know where our Regt will go—tho' probably to Kentucky—we have now 875 men in camp & are liable to receive marching orders any day. Tho I hardly think we shall leave before the 1st Feb'y. Well I must say Good-night or rather Good morning for it is well into the "wee small hours." Write often Jeanie, and tell me all about yourself and our darling, and may God bless & keep you safely is the prayer of your husband

Edward

LETTER 2

Goshen Ind. Jan'y 23rd/62

My dear wife,

I came down from camp tonight on purpose to get a letter from you and was not disappointed. I was very glad to hear you were so well, and tho' I haven't time to write much of a letter, thought I would not let the chance slip, of telling you that I am well and in better spirits than ever.

You will see by the paper I send that I am elected Captain by an unanimous vote, and that our company is nearly full. There is the utmost harmony & good feeling prevailing, and if we ever have a chance at the rebels, you will hear a good account of Capt. Wood's Co. I shall never rashly expose myself or my men, but I do feel as if I would like to strike a stout blow or two, in this finishing off, of the rebellion. For in my opinion the war is to be of short duration, and this monster of rebellion throttled, if not completely strangled within the next three months. I don't apprehend we will be discharged from the service within that time, but the worst fighting will be over. We shall probably be put under marching orders by the 1st next month, but may not leave before the 10th I don't know our destination positively, but think it will be Ky.

You cannot feel more keenly than I do—when I have time for reflection—the pangs of separation. But my dear girl you must keep up a brave heart for the sake of your soldier boy. I know it is much harder for you to bear than for me—not that I love you and our precious babe any less—but you are more alone, without active employment for the mind, while I have been constantly engaged, with plenty of work for both mind and body. Work was the curse pronounced upon man, but it is after all, the divine panacea for all sorrow.

You must not allow yourself to brood over the sorrow of our separation, but by taking as much outdoor exercise as you possibly can, by pleasant social intercourse with your friends, by taking daily doses of good reading, and above all by only thinking of your boy, as gone but for a short time soon to return to you enriched in health, & in the proud satisfaction of having done his duty. You must endeavor to keep your mind serene, and your own health and little Mary's will attest to good effects of this advice.

To-day I have been drilling over 7 hours, at 8 o'clock in officer's drill till 9½, then company drill till 12.m. Company drill again from 1 pm till 3½. Dress parade at 4. I have been away from camp so much recruiting, that I haven't had much chance to drill but tonight the Lt. Col & major complimented me on the fine appearance of my company on Dress parade—all owing to my steady work with them to day—

The sleighing is excellent here. I have not improved it only by way of business & but very little in that way. I was in hopes to take a ride before we left, but the chances now are very slim.

I have been writing this in Mr. Copeland's office,[9] who has been very kind to me in getting up the Company. Milo Hascall returned home sick—a few days since. I have not seen him, but understand he is about, & some uncharitable people suggest that another battle is imminent in Ky.

I send you enclosed $5.—it is all I can spare at present.—we have not been paid off, and may not be for two months, but when we are, I will send you enough, so that you can pay your board & other expenses—if this is not enough for present necessities write me, & I will send more at once. Direct here as usual, & write soon, all about yourself & our darling one—Papa's two babies!—God bless them and keep them safely is the prayer of your devoted Husband.

Edward

LETTER 3

My dear wife

I haven't heard from you since writing last week from Goshen, but tonight three of the usual occupants of our quarters are away, and the other two have retired unusually early, so I am left to a very unwonted quiet, and my thoughts naturally turn to my dear "loved ones at home"

I know how well I would like to look in on you and our sleeping babe, and I think you would like a peep at our snuggery—so here goes for a picture of it, as well as I can draw it. You have seen the long rows of sheds that ornament the Fair Ground—well, in one of the two in the centre of the grounds outside of the track, at the west end of said shed, has your husband domiciled for the past two months. Here is a cross-section of the premises.— the first of the apartments on the left—being exactly twelve feet square on the floor, with a tendency to expansion in hight as the ceiling approaches the ridge pole—is the Captain's Head Quarters. The other—ignoble contrast! is the Kitchen, whence oftimes emanate most unsavory odors, penetrating even the sacred precincts aforesaid, and driving the inmates thereof to the verge of despair—and the door.

But aside from such trifling annoyances, within it is very comfortable. Three tier of bunks—each accomodating two, with space between them for very limited perpendicular movement, but amply wide and provided with good straw ticks well filled, occupy one corner of the room. Three chairs and a permanent bench [form?] the bunks to the other side of the room, form the sitting accomodations—my old office desk and lamp that lights up the pictorially-papered walls, help to make it cheerful and liveable

Wood's drawing of his quarters at Camp Ellis, January 29, 1862. Courtesy of the Indiana Historical Society.

Above are ranged s[h]elves on two sides of the room, upon which are neatly piled the clothing etc for the company not yet distributed. A good box stove with its cheerful roar and kindly heat, completes the furniture of our rude apartment—rude but pleasant as you must admit, and one which I should be loth to leave, but for the prospect of more active service. Within ten days, we shall probably move southward—stopping at Indianapolis a week or so, and thence probably to Bardstown KY, where we will be in a camp of instruction, until the exigencies of the service may need us.[10] We already show considerable proficiency in drill, but the efforts of all the officers have been directed so much toward recruiting that we have really learned but little of the duty of a soldier. Recruiting goes very slowly, we number now 93.—lacking only eight of a full company. I hope to get them this week. Our 1st Lieut. Mr. Fisher of Ligonier, is a fine gentleman and a very capable man—he has done a great deal for the Company & is a great acquisition to it. Geo. Gibbons our 2nd Lieut.[11] you know, he has been very serviceable in drilling the men & is well liked by them all.

Now isn't this a regular Camp letter! & I haven't done yet. Tomorrow I expect to get my uniform, & next week to have the picture taken, with "buttons all over me"

I hope you got my last with $5. enclosed. I will send you more as soon as possible. My expenses have been very heavy for recruiting purposes, & for uniform, sword, sach & belt, & other necessary outfit, it will take all I can raise. I shall expect a letter from you tomorrow (Thursday) night. I haven't been disappointed yet, & hope I shan't be. I may not be able to answer it at once, as I am going away Friday, to be gone till Monday or Tuesday, but you must not let that prevent you from writing. Keep a good heart, my dear one. Kiss papa's darling a thousand times for him—I wouldn't begrudge my Captaincy just to kiss my babies once—but Goodnight dearest—God Keep watch & [ward] over you and our Mary, & hasten the day when the same rooftree shall shelter us is the prayer of

Your husband

Edward

[*Envelope endorsed:* "Mrs Edward J. Wood, care Jas. S. Gillespie[12] Esq, Syracuse New York"]

LETTER 4

Goshen Ind Feb 6th 1862

My dear wife,

We have just rec'd marching orders, & leave tomorrow morning at 9 o'clock. Our destination is still uncertain, but the probabilites are that we will go to Cairo—whence there it is all uncertain

You shall hear from me as soon as we reach our destination

Our orders were rec'd tonight very unexpectedly, and you may imagine I have my hands full. I have snatched this moment to write you a line

This afternoon I was presented with a sash & sword by the Masonic brethren. Dr Foster[13] presented it & I was so overpowered that it was almost impossible for me to reply, but I made a stagger at it and I am pleased that the impression left was satisfactory to myself

But a moment is left my dear wife, & you may be sure whatever may be our fortune, and whatever may be the event of war, you may be sure that you have ever the best love of Your Husband

E. J. Wood

I expected a letter tonight. Let me hear from you as soon as I write—

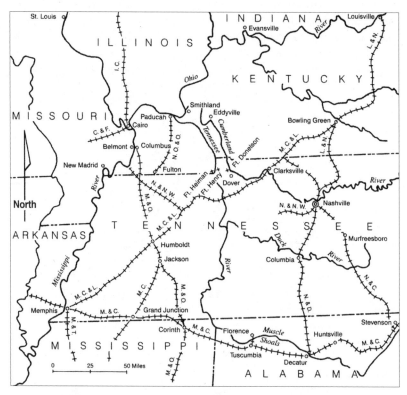

The Western Theater, 1861–1862. From Benjamin Franklin Cooling, Forts Henry and Donelson: Key to the Confederate Heartland *(Knoxville, 1987).*

CHAPTER 2

The Provost Marshal Is Almost a Military Dictator

Policing Paducah, Kentucky, February–April 1862

The 48th Indiana left Goshen on February 7 by train en route to Cairo, Illinois, where the Ohio and Mississippi rivers meet. Wood's disgusted description of the town—below river level and protected by levees—was echoed by many observers. The town's location made it an important transportation center for Union military forces in the west. The regiment soon boarded a riverboat and steamed about forty miles up the Ohio River to Paducah, Kentucky. There the regiment formed the garrison for the town as Union forces collected and organized for expeditions into the interior of the Rebel-controlled South.

Located at the mouth of the navigable Tennessee River, Paducah served as entrance to a large section of Kentucky, Tennessee, and Alabama. The Cumberland River, a major conduit through Kentucky and Tennessee, likewise emptied into the Ohio a short distance from the Tennessee, and Federal and Rebel leaders knew that control of the two rivers meant control of the middle of the Confederacy. Union naval and army forces advanced up both rivers in early February 1862, seizing Fort Henry on the Tennessee River, and soon thereafter attacking the large Rebel force at Fort Donelson on the Cumberland. The Federal victory at Fort Donelson afforded control of Kentucky and much of Tennessee to the Union, and dealt a major blow to Rebel fortunes early in the conflict.[1]

During the initial advances up the rivers, the much-chagrined 48th Indiana was left behind in Paducah in charge of the town's defenses. Wood was appointed provost marshal of the town, a position that gave him supreme authority over Paducah. In the absence of absconded town officials, he superintended the policing, sanitation, and security of the town, no small effort when thousands of troops are stationed there or passing through. An important part of his job was the suppression of Rebel sympathizers in and around

Paducah. In the absence of hard and fast military policy, local commanders improvised their methods for controlling anti-Union sentiment.

LETTER 5

Paducah Ky. Feb'y 12/62

My dear wife,

I wrote you a hurried scrawl the night before we left Camp Ellis, when we knew nothing of our destination. We left Friday the 7th about noon, amid the largest crowd I ever saw assembled in Goshen on such short notice, & altho my hardest trial of parting had been undergone I could not help feeling badly at leaving a place with which I had become so much identified. We went straight thro' to Cairo Ill. without change of cars, arriving there about 2pm of Saturday.—that night we staid in the cars, and the next morning marched over to our barracks. Such another looking town you never saw! For miles before we came to the city, the R.Rd runs on trestlework supported by piles, thro' a most dismal looking country—at this time of high water entirely overflowed—& the city itself is only saved from the same fate by its huge levees—the town being 15 feet below the river in an usual stage of water. Cairo mud has passed into a proverb, and we certainly saw it in it's height of muddy excellence. It is a yellowish clay of just the right consistency to let you in knee deep, and then hang on with a double suction power that well nigh prevent all further locomotion. We were all overjoyed when the order came about 12 o'clock Sunday night, to take boat for this place. We embarked at once, reaching here about 4 P.M. Monday—The trip up the river (Ohio) was delightful.[2] We did not leave Cairo till daylight, so we had all the benefit of the scenery.—there is nothing grand about it but the stately motion of our splendid packet, the broad majestic river, the beautiful blue sky, flecked with snow white clouds, & the warm springlike atmosphere, all contributed to make the trip a very pleasant one. There was another besides our Regt—the 32nd Ill—but the immense steamer carried them so easily, that there was not even the inconvenience of being crowded

Arrived here, we had some delay in getting quarters, but the first night slept in a large tobacco-factory or warehouse & yesterday succeeded in getting into our new camp. It is beautifully situated on a bluff of the Ohio, about a mile from the center of town. Paducah is a fine town, & has many superior residences. It contained a great deal of wealth, before the breaking out of the rebellion, but most of the more wealthy & influential citizens were *secesh* & have fled at the approach of the Union army, leaving their splendid houses, & in many cases, everything else. Many of these houses are occupied by the Govt for hospitals & for storing provisions for the army. I can assure you, one of the saddest sight[s] I have seen in a long time was when I stood in one of these dwellings, saw where the movable valuables had been hastily snatched up, the secretary of rosewood & of costly finish turned over & letters of every kind & description, but denoting intelligence & refinement, scattered promiscuously over the floor. War *is* terrible & this picture is one of the least terrible of its realities—We are at the mouth of the Tennessee river up which about 70 miles is Fort Henry, the capture of which you have doubtless read in the paper.[3] This place is being made headquarters for storing all the stores for the great expeditions, going up the Tennessee & Cumberland rivers. If you will take the map & look along up these rivers 70 to 100 miles you will see that it is about half way between Columbus Ky, on the Mississippi & Bowling Green in the interior, both of which places are strongly fortified by the rebels. I think these expeditions—one of which went up the Cumberland, this morning consisted of 5 Gunboats & 11,000 troops—are destined to operate against both the named places, & I only hope we may soon join them, as it is we shall probably be here some time, guarding the town, which is no small job.[4] I have not yet been detailed for picket duty but expect to be in a few days. I need not assure after this long letter that I am well. I have written very hurriedly at the St Francis House in town. Lt. Col. Hascall[5] at my side & both writing by steam to get back to camp by 9 o'clock. I will write whenever I have a chance & my darling one you must not fail to write immediately telling me all about yourself and our precious little one I have worried about her & shant be easy till I hear she is quite well. Tell me all about yourself & Mary. I will write you again in a few days, if possible. Goodnight dearest papa wishes he could kiss his darlings goodnight—but the precious picture is a great comfort. I had a large ambrotype in frame taken for you, but the day before I left, the boys in the Lodge gave me a sword & wanted that to hang in the room & I gave it to them. I will have a photograph taken soon. God bless you my dearest, Your Husband Edward

[In margin: "Direct to Capt E. J. Wood. Co I. 48th Regt Ind Vols. Paducah Ky"]

LETTER 6

In my tent. Camp Smith
Paducah, Ky. Feby 19th 1862

My dear wife,

I wrote you about a week since shortly after our arrival here and since then have rec'd your last letter directed to Goshen of date Feb 6th—that is the enclosure, or second letter—if the first one had been mailed at once I would have got it before leaving Goshen. We left Friday the 7th & your letter reached me Saturday the 15th by private hand from Goshen.

I was very sorry to hear that you & the baby had been so poorly—and should indeed have been in distress, if your second letter had not assured me of your improved health, so the delay was for the best after all. You can't know how glad the bare sight of your loved & familiar handwriting made the heart of this lonesome fellow that night, and how I was the envy of the whole camp eager for news from home, with my two precious sheets, breathing of home and love for the absent soldier boy.

No wonder the poor soldiers write letters! it is almost their only solace, & when wearied with marching & drill & all the endless routine of a soldier's duties, they think of their dear ones and all the kindly comforts of home

I hardly recollect what I wrote you in my last, & indeed my head was so full of the novelties of the situation, & I wrote in such a hurry that I doubt much whether I gave you any very distinct ideas whatever. I believe I told you to look at the map, in Harper's Weekly for this week. Feb 22nd you will find one, that will give you a very good idea of our position in reference to the recent exciting scenes on the Tennessee & Cumberland rivers. We should have been in both the engagements at Forts Henry and Donelson,[6] but for a

Lieutenant Colonel Melvin B. Hascall, 48th Indiana. Courtesy of Daniel Wood.

The Provost Marshal Is Almost a Military Dictator

delay on the part of the authorities at Indianapolis in shipping us our arms & tents. These failed to meet us at Cairo, as expected & we were detained here, & have been doing garrison & fatigue duty at this point every since.

Our arms & tents have reached us, the latter of the Sibley pattern—a fine one—& the arms for the four flanking companies—that is the two on the right & the two on the left of the regiment are Enfield rifles, the others are inferior. Our Co. I is the next Co. to the extreme left & has the Enfields[7]

The weather has been extremely bad since I last wrote. That night a severe snowstorm with a cold piercing wind from the north set in & after the recent mild weather our men, in old tents, without flooring or straw, suffered terribly As a consequence, all the men in the Regt have severe colds & some are quite sick. Twenty in my Co. are down, & I don't think the per cent is larger than in the other Cos. Today a cold rain has poured down steadily, & tonight the wind is raising a gale.—But I sit in my tent secure—well, thank God! & as contented as it is possible for a *man* to be with such a dear wife & little one, so many miles away.

My tent is what is called a *wall* tent, that is, the canvass that forms the roof does not come directly to the ground, but has straight sides about 4 ft high. It is 10 ft square in the inside & 8 ft high in the centre, so you see I have quite a little room. We are encamped on an old camp ground, where chimneys had been built, & the back of my tent is set directly in front of one of these—by ripping up one breadth of canvass, I have the benefit of a good fireplace, in front of whose roaring blaze seated on a camp stool, this "epistle of Edward to the dearly beloved" is being indited

The surroundings & accompaniments are certainly unique—while the wind whistles a shrill treble an army of snorers within hearing put in the bass with tremendous effect. Inside the tent, the most prominent object just at present is doubtless the subscribed seating as aforesaid before his pine table, manufactured from *secesh* lumber by his carpenter Joe, on which table, besides writing materials, are his candle & very *extempore* candlestick the dear wife's last letter unfolded, the recently used thread, needle & wax, the "Army Regulations" & "Hardee's Tactics,"[8] a cup of water, combs brushes & pipes & last but *not* least, the *plug* of "natural leaf." To the right, is our bunk where Gibbons is quietly sleeping—at the foot my trunk open, on one of the poles hangs G's looking glass—vain man!—on the other swords sashes etc.—from the ridge pole is suspended another pole, upon which hangs sundry articles of clothing towels, pistols, etc., etc. In a small tent in the rear is our servant with stores, cooking utensils etc., all save the frying pan which elegantly festooned by the dishcloth, hangs over our fireplace in lieu of mantel piece ornaments—There I think you can make a drawing of the premises from the description. My fire burns low & the sheet runs short. I shall expect a letter from you this week & will always write when possible I do hope you are both entirely well by this time. I know you will be prudent, but I can't help feeling anxious about you, whenever I don't hear often—It is two weeks now since the date of your last. I know the baby must be a great care, & when you are not well yourself it is hard work to write. We may be here for some time, & I hope you will write once a week, if it is but a few lines to let me know how you are. I hardly think it will be possible for me to leave here, at least not for two or three months—if we should stay here that long it might be possible I'm afraid I can't send the photograph until after payday & when that will be is hard telling. Officers have to furnish themselves with everything board included & everything is very high here. Goodnight my dearest. Kiss our darling daughter & pray Heaven with me, that we may soon meet again. Love and kind regards to all Your Husband Edward

LETTER 7

St Francis Hotel
Paducah Ky. March 8th 1862

My dear wife,

I know how anxiously you have been looking for a letter for the last few days, and you shall not wait longer than it takes Uncle Sam to carry this to you.

I have felt every day for the last two weeks that I ought to write & have commenced once or twice, but every time have been broken off, and it is by outright robbery that I get the time to write to you tonight. but your dear welcome letter of the 27th ult. was recd today, & I have left the office & every thing else to take care of itself & determined to write to you at all hazards.

For you must know that since last I wrote you, our duties have been very much changed & I have filled the very responsible position of Provost Marshal of this city. Two weeks ago today I was appointed & our Company was detailed as Provost's Guard, & since then besides being busy all the day I have scarcely had a night's quiet rest. The duties were new & onerous but I have the consolation of knowing that I have been "equal to the emergency" & no one of the citizens or of the military have made complaint of my administration

The Provost Marshal is almost a military dictator, his word is law as far as all municipal regulations are concerned & it requires close attention & a cool clear head, to decide all the various matters presented. I am astonished when I think of the vast amount of work I have done in the last two weeks—with the whole of the city police under charge—some two hundred political prisoners—besides a hospital full of sick & wounded prisoners of war from Fts Henry & Donelson—no man allowed to pass the pickets without a pass from the Provost & no article of merchandise, unless there is a bill of it made & endorsed "Approved. E. J. Wood Provost Marshal"—I say I am astonished when I think that I have actually done all this & done it in a satisfactory manner. I have also collected from Secession sympathizers over $1000 tax & paid it out for the benefit & support of Union Refugees— the payments ranging from $2.00 to $25. & that duty is a small item in the duties of the office. Do you wonder that I haven't had time to write, or that I write a miserable, hurried hand now?

Captain Edward J. Wood, 1862. Courtesy of Daniel Wood.

With all the responsibility work & hurry of the office, there have been some pleasant things connected with it—when one is in power he necessarily makes friends (sad comment on humanity, but too true) & I have made many pleasant friends—that is, those who try to do everything for me & I never could stop to inquire whether a man's motives were mercenary when he seemed to be anxious to oblige me. For instance, here at this hotel, as soon as I was installed in office, the landlord called, said he should be glad to have me make his house my home & has been indefatigable since to have every thing provided for my comfort.

Wednesday the 12th—I commenced this last Saturday as you will see, but was interrupted just here, & I haven't had time since till tonight to resume. I am very sorry, for I know you will be uneasy before this reaches you. My health has not been so good within the last few days—but is now completely restored. It was only one of my periodic attacks of a day or two's sickness, which you know I am subject to, & has quite passed away & I am well again. I kept my room one day & the quiet & rest that I needed cured me up. The people of the house were very kind to me—the landlady sent me a dish of oysters, & very fine they tasted I assure you.

There is some talk of our being relieved from Provost duty, as the Col. is anxious to have the company back with the Regt so they can have the benefit of drill & instruction. I shall not be sorry for it, tho' I shall be leaving very comfortable quarters for tent life again. Most of the troops here have gone up the Tennessee on an expedition supposed to be directed against Memphis, and the town is much more quiet & the duties of Provost, consequently lighter.[9]

Genl Sherman[10] who was in command here, paid the 48th a high compliment when he said they were the only Regt in whose hands he could trust the safe keeping of the town.—& what he told Col Hascall about the boy that did the Provost business, it wouldn't be modest to repeat. Our Regt is the only infantry left here, & is much divided up. 4 Cos being in the Fort, (Anderson) and one doing guard duty at the wharfboat, the other 4 besides ours, being in camp. This disposition of the Regt indicates that we shall remain here some time, but soldiers are always subject to orders, and a day may see us on our way hundreds of miles up the river. The weather has been very changeable a great deal of rain has fallen, & the Ohio is very full. The town is admirably situated for drainage, and the soil dries very quickly—so that tho' the streets may be rivers at night, in the morning they are dry, & by the next day, dusty. Yesterday & today have been delightful spring days & the bluebirds have shown their appreciation of the fine weather in amazing numbers. I heard a faint solitary twitter from one adventurous straggler three weeks ago, but main body of the army didn't arrive till yesterday.

I have had two pictures taken—both cheap things & neither very good—but I will send them with this, & perhaps they will be better than none, till I can send a better one. They are both in one case, pry out the top one & take choice—if there is any.

Oh! a man in the office the other day after a pass happened to say something about Salt Point, & when I told him I married my wife there & your name he seemed to be well acquainted with the whole family & named over all the older girls by the first names, said he lived near Father's & went to school with the girls. His name is E. D. Richmond—I found out afterwards not a very reputable character—a showman etc.—but it really seemed good at the time, to find any one that had ever lived in the Saline region & knew even by name any of the Saltpointers.[11]

You can't tell my dear one, how often and how anxiously I think of my precious treasures at home. I do not dare to let myself indulge in the longing vein often, but the day I spent in my room, with yours & Mary's picture & your last letter, full of her cunning tricks, I could not help feeling that it was downright cruel—the fate that kept me from you, & that night I had a sick man's bad dream, & so and so and so. I was homesick—that's the long & short of it.

But when the bile was worked off, appetite & digestion good, the clear head & willing heart asserted their supremacy & I am left feeling that the sacrifice was one that should have been made & all the conditions of it should be accepted without murmuring. I feel sometimes chagrined that we should have been fastened down here, & lost all chance of military distinction, but then that would never have been a powerful enough inducement for me to enlist & altho' very desirable for a soldier, I am content to do my duty in this struggle, wherever I be most useful.

I found this evening in an old Harper a cut of the Provost's office in St Louis, & have cut it out as a fair representation of ours in the number & variety of its customers.

I shall expect to hear from you this week & do hope you & the darling little one are both well. I have been a very regular correspondent before & will try not to have so long an interval again. You mustn't worry tho' if you don't always hear, for sometimes it is among the impossibilities to write often my darling. I am always satisfied for a week when I get word that you are well & enjoying yourself as well as possible

And now goodnight my precious pets—Papa sends a thousand kisses to his darlings, & a thousand wishes that he had them in his arms tonight

Excuse the looks of this page, one of the blots was already on & the other two my pen dropped accidentally. Be sure to write soon & believe me as ever Your Husband

Edward

LETTER 8

Paducah. March 17th/62

My dear wife,

I know a letter is always welcome, no matter how brief it may be, & while sitting by this open window looking out upon the broad expanse of the Ohio, waiting to fill an appointment, I have taken my pen to chat it may be five minutes & it may be half an hour.

I was afraid my last might leave you feeling uneasy about my health, but indeed I am quite well feeling stronger & better for the little renovation I went through with when I was sick a day or two.

Your dear welcome letter of the 6th was read Saturday & has been read again & again The dear precious little one! When I dare trust myself to think of her cunning ways I am impelled to do anything to be able to see her.

But duty must be performed & sacrifices must be made & while we all are well our sacrifices are as nothing to those of the widowed & fatherless ones whom cruel war has deprived of their all. We must bear with brave hearts this separation & all the evils incident to it, trusting that a kind Providence will order things for the best.

There is nothing of special interest here. The soldiers have mostly gone up the Tennessee river & the town very quiet. A great battle is expected in a few days. Troops are constantly being moved up the river—there must be nearly 100,000 now on *steamboats* up the river ready to be moved as soon as it is determined where the attack is to be made, or to be landed rather where & when the generals may direct. I was told yesterday that there were 120 steamboats loaded with troops within 50 miles of each other on the Tennessee river.

I sent the pictures but a day or two after my last letter, write me if you like either of them & which.

I will have a photograph taken when we get pay—which time seems to be at the end of a very indefinite period—The weather is delightfully warm. I have been writing in my shirt sleeves all the morning. Rather a contrast to your two feet of snow. I suppose you wont look for much settled weather before May

I think I would wean Mary then & she will soon be able to tottle about. You must consult your own health about it, but I think you would grow stronger & fleshier if you were to wean her—she is so large & must be such a burden to carry.

Kiss the dear one all over for her papa. Remember me kindly to all, & believe me always your loving Husband

Edward

LETTER 9

Paducah Ky.
March 30th 1862

My dear wife,

Yours of the 13th was received a week since and is the last letter I have had from you. I have been expecting another for the last week and was much disappointed at not getting one last night. Your last was 11 days coming & I am still in hopes there is one on the road for me, that will reach me in a few days—Only think it is 17 days since the date of your last and how many things might have happened in that time

I don't wonder you feel anxious when you don't hear from me for so long. I hope it will never so long again; as it was just after I got into this perplexing office of Provost. My predecessor had been in the office about seven months, was a superior man for the place, & was universally regretted by both military & civilians when he left.

In addition to a desire to do my duty in every situation, my pride would not suffer that disparaging comparison should be made between the old & the new Provost, if in my power to prevent.

Consequently, I bent my whole energies day & night to a personal discharge of all the duties of a new & onerous office until I was bound to stop a day or two & recruit, satisfied that I had got the machine in such order that it could "run itself" for a few days. You know if it hadn't been so I wouldn't have stopped

You can't think how many & kind friends I have made, and I never can be sufficiently grateful to them, nor can one appreciate, till thrown among strangers how strong the "mystic tie" that makes them brothers. Three-fourths of the officers of the army I have met with, are Masons and you may be sure, I enjoy our occasional re-unions, with more than ordinary zest.[12]

I have just read this page over and I am afraid you will think I have been more unwell than I have written you before—which I believe was very slight—and in fact the illness was so.—you know so well my constitution & habits that you know I have been unusually well, when I tell you that since the day of my enlistment to the time when I gave up for a day or two, I had not consulted a physician or taken a particle of medicine. I have been suffering for two or three weeks with a diarrhoea, consequent upon change of climate, water etc. & when I concluded that it must be checked and called on Companion Neglas,[13] Surgeon of the 6th Ill. Cavly—in two days he had it checked, and since then I have felt as well and strong as I every did in my life. So, my sweet one don't worry, as I know you have done, for the health of your boy, who means to take excellent care of himself and return to his darlings (a kind Providence permitting) before many months.

I am afraid we are located here for some time, for now that my pride is satisfied I am anxious to be rid of the drudgery of my position and go into the field, where laurels may be won as a soldier. In anticipation however of our staying here, I have, as a sanitary precaution, had a large force of contrabands[14] at work upon the streets, cleaning out the gutters & removing the filth, which seven months occupation by an army, without any municipal regulations has accumulated most enormously—

I have told you of the town and how beautifully it is situated—the last week of spring weather has unfolded it's charms wonderfully,—the green grass in the door yards, the lilacs bursting in to bloom and all nature preparing for her grand annual renovation have a charm that will always hold me, in spite of the "pomp & circumstance of glorious war."—for peace is sweet, & war is terrible[15]

To-day has been uncomfortably warm—I don't think they have any of Lowell's "Heaven's perfect days" in this latitude—you recollect the description & know the kind of day[16]

And this allusion makes me think of Tracy, who was writing to me the other day about a brother of his who had strayed off into the 12th Ind.[17] Asking me to do something for him by way of a recommendation for a position, and I am sorry to say I have not acknowledged the letter or tried to do anything for him I shall when I have the least time.

I sent you two Goshen papers the other day, but I think they were both before sad intelligence reached us that Col. Barron was dead, and Mart.

Brown so low with consumption that his recovery was considered doubtful. He was taken with spitting of blood and continued for several days spitting as high as a pint a day; and tho' he is reported as better he will probably never recover.[18] Col. Hascall, who was up the Tennessee river as aid to Genl Sherman has returned, and gone home, and I think may resign. I should be sorry to have him, for he has been a very good friend to me. Col. Barron continued to fail, as you know he has for some time past, until he died. I have not learned what has become of Mrs. B. and Gracie, but as Mrs. Bur[n]hans[19] was at the funeral I make no doubt she has returned with them to their home.

There is nothing else new in Goshen, except that my friend 'Gus Crane is married to Miss Case. Mrs. Weyburn's daughter, & has been made a Mason—two very desirable things that I am glad Augustus has done.[20]

And now what a chat all by myself, & for a wonder without an interruption, I have had with my little wifey, it is the very next best thing to seeing my dear ones and holding them in my arms, to sit down when I can feel that I can have the time to talk as near as possible on paper, as I would, were I with you

I have got a photograph taken (or given rather, for Provost Marshal is *deadhead* everywhere) that I am going to send along with this. It is a "powerful sight" *stiffer* than I am, & don't suit me, but the artist says it is excellent & friends have importuned me for it, so I am going to send you the best one of the batch.

I want you to have a better picture taken of yourself and Mary and send them to me. You know you kept the only of you I value, & I thought rightly for safe keeping, but I want a picture of my wife, and our dear child. Have them taken separately if you can as well but be guided by the artist & have a good picture. If none of those I have sent suit you, write me, & I will try again

I haven't affected the military paraphernalia much & have usually gone about in my fatigue coat.—if you want one with all the extras, I will rig up and have one taken.

We have not yet been paid, tho' we are expecting to be in a few days. I have however received remittances from Goshen & I enclose you $20 which I hope may be sufficient for the present. I know you need many things & am ashamed that you should have been so long unprovided I will send you more as soon as we are paid. I want to buy whatever you want for yourself or Mary first, & I will furnish you with enough to satisfy all the indebtedness you may incur by way of board, etc.

What of Myrna & Henry,[21] & Jas & Nellie—are you still pleasantly situated, write me all about it, for I am anxious to know.

Give my love to all, and Kiss that precious wonderful baby, when ever she calls for her unknown absent "papa." "Bless it's little heart," wouldn't papa tumble it all about, and squeeze it up close, if he could lay his hands on the precious bundle just for a moment

Goodnight my darlings, and may Heaven bless and protect you both is the constant thought & prayer of your devoted husband

Edward

Jennie, I am very sorry, but after mailing this, this morning, I had immediate need of money, & didn't know where else to get it, so I have opened this & taken the bill enclosed, will send it now as soon as possible

Your of the 21st is just rec'd and I reenclose the $20.00 I am sorry to hear Mary is sick take good care of her & yourself, & write soon. In great haste Edward

LETTER 10

Paducah April 7th 1862

My dear wife,

Your letter of the 23rd March was duly received, and I should have written you a good long letter yesterday—being Sunday—but for an ugly *stye* on my right eye, that made it almost impossible for me to do anything. Last night I gave it a good poultice of scraped *raw potatoes,* had it pricked this morning, and tonight it is feeling quite well again.

I am afraid this letter is going to prove a failure, as several of the officers of the 48th have come down from camp and have commenced a very animated chatting on all sides of me. Tonight is the first time I have undertaken to write in the office & I must break off now, with the promise to finish this when I can get to my room—I have sat the seige out.—all the boys have gone & I resume—

Nothing new of importance has occurred since I last wrote. I am still in the Provost's office & from all appearances likely to continue here for some time. The 48th boys are all proud of the distinction of having the Provost from the Regt and I think most of them are proud of the way in which the duties have been performed—Mr Day,[22] our sutler, has just returned from home and he tells me that every letter home from officers & soldiers is filled with praises of the Provost, & congratulations that he is from our Regt. This is very gratifying to me, & I knew it would be more so to my little wifey than any other beside in the wide world or I wouldn't have indulged in what to any one else would be egotism.

I think the great battle which is now daily imminent[23] up the Tennessee will be decisive of the contest in the section and regiments like ours not in the field will probably be mustered out of the service—All recruiting is stopped and the administration doubtless think they have men enough in the field to crush the rebellion.—of course, the next step will be to decrease the enormous expense of the war, by dispensing with all the forces not absolutely needed.[24] I shall be sorry for it, for however grateful to me would be the society of my dear ones, I enlisted, as you know I have wanted to from the commencement, to have a hand in the *fight,* and I shall feel as if we had come ingloriously if we should not have the privilege of helping to thrash the rebels out on some well fought field. But we are soldiers—subject to orders—and the sacrifices we have made in defence of the country must be forgotten in the gratification we shall feel that our country is no longer imperilled, and that the rebellion which threatened to destroy her, has sunk to such insignificance, that she can safely dispense with our services.

I am sorry you didn't get the pictures—they were cheap ones, but quite good. I don't see why they should have miscarried—they were directed just as plainly as my letters, the postage paid & everything straight I am in hope you will get them yet. I sent a photograph the last time I wrote, but am keeping another, for fear you may not get that. I want you to have one taken of that "blessed baby," just as soon as you conveniently can, and one of yourself too.—the one you sent of yourself is not good—& I want my wifey's picture to be *like her* & then it must be good.

It seems as strange to read of snow & snowing down in this sultry latitude, as it must be you to hear of our warm weather. I took a little horseback (!) jaunt yesterday up the Tennessee and was surprised to see the forest trees that fringe the river in full leaf.

I had been luxuriating for a week in the delicious odor of the peach & plum & cherry trees that fill the yards, but didn't think the trees would show such evidences of approaching summer.

One night last week we had a most terrific hurricane—you have doubtless seen notices of it in the papers—nearly every tin roof in the city was ripped off, and the roof of our building was lifted up bodisceously and carried several rods before it landed—several prisoners in the guard room were injured by falling bricks from the walls, but beyond that no casualty occurred—it happened about 4 o'clock in the morning & only lasted a few minutes or more would doubtless have been injured—You didn't mention getting the Goshen papers I sent—they were old but had several interesting items from here, & I hope you got them.

I am so glad you are so pleasantly situated, and everybody is so kind to you It has worried me more than anything else, for fear there might be something unpleasant about your situation & I believe I wrote to you the last time particularly to inquire. I hope you rec'd my letter mailed a week ago, as there was $20 enclosed—it is a small sum but perhaps will answer for present necessaries, until we are paid off—and that day can't be very far distant.

I think you ought to take more outdoor exercise—but I know how hard it is for you to leave *your* baby. (for I suppose you will claim exclusive proprietorship pretty soon) and how unwilling you are to seem to force the care of her upon any one. She will soon be a year old, & if you could get a little girl to help you take care of her, you would have much more freedom You will have a great deal to do this spring, in getting her into short clothes and doing your own sewing, & I think you ought to have some one to help you Try what you can do in that way—if you need some one to take care of the baby, or to sew, as may think best, or both, get them. If you had a girl, & then could get your sewing done, it would leave you much freer to take care of your own health.

I don't think it would be policy to nurse the baby thro' the warm summer months but you know better than I do, & must do as you think best. She is most old enough to begin to walk, but I suppose you won't put short clothes on her till warm weather

How many teeth has the darling got, and does she still grow to look like papa? And how many questions he could sit & write, if it did not send a heartache with each one, that he can't be with his treasures

It must be twelve o'clock and a hard day's work is before this boy for tomorrow, and I must close.

In addition to usual duties I have ten new secesh prisoners on hand for examination tomorrow. They are not men who have been in arms but are active sympathizers with rebellion, and the course we put them through, is to examine witnesses in each case, assess them from $100 to $500, for the benefit of Union refugees, administer the strongest kind of an oath of allegiance and then make them give bonds in the sum of $5,000 that they will keep it, and for their general good behavior. It is galling & humiliating in the extreme for some of these men who have been leaders to be thus brought under, but the effect is most excellent. They are humiliated enough to keep quiet, and the men who have been accustomed to look up to them become loyal very suddenly—[25]

But if I was to write all our performance, I should never stop. I shall expect a letter in a few days, for I know you will write as often as you get a letter & I hope you won't always wait for one.

Good night, my dear Jean, remember me with a brother's affection to Myra & Nellie for their kindness to you & believe me ever

Your devoted Husband
Edward

LETTER 11

Paducah April 21st 1862

My dear wife,

I suppose you will be worried again before this reaches you, but I have been very busy for the last two weeks and haven't had time to write even a scrawl.

I haven't time now to tell anything of what we have been doing, for our Regt is under marching orders for the Tennessee, and I have more than ten men ought to do tonight in closing up my affairs in the Provost office and getting the Company ready for moving. It is not unexpected. I have thought for several days, we should be ordered off, and have been shaping things accordingly—if it had not been for that I could not possibly have got ready to leave tomorrow. I am very glad of the change—Provost business had got be a sad bore, and I want to see something of actual service

You must not feel alarmed my dear Jeanie, because of the late disastrous battle—it cannot happen again that our forces should be so surprised and routed as they were on the first day's fight.[26] If we have another battle we shall certainly whip them, and without any such loss of life. Over 30,000 new troops have gone up in the last two days—in addition to the two magnificent armies under Buell & Grant, must make the number nearly or quite 200,000 men. The rebels have no sufficient force to stand against them, & we understand are already retreating

But let that be as it may I know my little girl's brave heart, that gave up her darling would not have him shrink from duty, tho' it calls him to the desperate battle-field. I know you will feel badly, but don't give way to despondency—Our efforts may only hasten the time when peace will come, and we can all meet again. I wish I had got the picture of you and Mary, but it will be forwarded I will write you even oftener than I have for camplife will give more leisure, and I do not anticipate any fighting for some time.

Both your last letters have been received and most gratefully read—especially of date April 6th such a dear good letter makes one half reconciled to absence

. I havent any idea what I have written for I have talked to over twenty men in this brief time, despite a locked door in my own private room. They would come in & I must attend to them. You must know I am greatly over-run with business & have only snatched what time I could to let you know of our intended movement. Direct your letters here as usual—they will be forwarded.

I hope your headache—(talking again) toothache I mean, and swelled face are entirely well. You *must* get your teeth fixed as soon as possible. How I wish I could see you and that darling little cherub—she has grown out of all knowledge of her papa—& I don't suppose her papa would know her—but I think he could pick her out in a *baby-show!* for she would certainly be the sweetest & prettiest in the lot.

I must say Goodby my dearest one. Keep a brave loving heart, and trust in that kind Providence that governs all thing for the best. Write to me often as usual, and send the picture if you haven't. We have not yet been paid—I was in hopes to have sent you home a package of pretty things from here, where we were, but now it can't be. Remember me to all, and kiss that precious one, ever so many times for papa—take good care of yourself and her, and write soon Goodby dearest and God bless my darlings.

Your Husband
E. J. Wood

LETTER 12

Paducah Ky
April 25, 1862

My dear wife

We are just going on board the boat for the Tennessee and I take one moment to let you know I am well and to enclose you $20.00. I don't know when I may have a chance of spending it again & I don't want to take it with me

Keep up good spirits my dearest I don't think there will be a battle where we are going—the chances seem to indicate that in the last few days—I sent Aunt Mackie one of my photographs—write to Mary if you have not, she would like to hear from you[27]

Kiss my darling pet, and may God watch over & protect us all is the prayer of your Husband

Edward

[*Envelope endorsed:* "Mrs. Edward J. Wood, Care E. B. Judson Esq, Syracuse, New York"][28]

CHAPTER 3

A Barren Sceptre in Our Gripe

The Advance on Corinth, Mississippi, April–June 1862

The 48th Indiana departed Paducah excited to at last be on the march and hoping to strike a blow for the Union. Wood's confident and cocky tone was common among Federal troops that had not yet seen action, notwithstanding the recent bloodletting at Fort Donelson and Shiloh. He and many others fully expected that soon "the rebellion will be dead and it must come before many months."

The massing of the huge Federal army of one hundred thousand men under Major General Henry W. Halleck that advanced south from Pittsburg Landing into northeastern Mississippi suggested that Union victory was imminent and sure. Rebel forces commanded by General P. G. T. Beauregard had fallen back to Corinth, Mississippi, intent on guarding the vital railroad crossroads there. Halleck, who superseded U. S. Grant in personal command on his arrival, was a cautious commander, worried of surprise attack from Rebel forces like that which almost destroyed the Federal army at Shiloh, and crept slowly toward the Rebel town, digging entrenchments regularly. Though skirmishes occurred frequently, no major fighting resulted. Beauregard, knowing his forces to be outnumbered, decided to evacuate the town. His ruse of keeping up a loud artillery exchange with just a few men while his army and its supplies entrained to the south to safety succeeded. Union forces seized Corinth on May 30 in a massive anticlimax. Halleck was satisfied with the capture of the railroad nexus, and dispersed his large army to various points without a vigorous pursuit of the Rebel army.[1]

Wood voiced the sentiments of many of the men in the ranks when, after long and tediously slow advances, no battle ensued. "I don't know how the Genls & big bugs felt," he wrote, "but it was a source of great mortification to the boys to find the bird flown and the nest yet warm." The hoped-for climactic battle failed to occur. Many Federal troops, including the 48th Indiana, settled down to occupation duty and rebuilding railroads.

LETTER 13

Steamer "L. M. Kennett"

Tennessee river, April 27, 1862

My dear wife,

At last we are off—bound Dixie-ward—we left Paducah this afternoon about 5 o'clock, and now at nearly midnight, while we are nearing Fort Henry—I embrace the opportunity that the quiet of the boat affords to write you a few lines

I have taken possession of the Captain's office, by his invitation, and have made myself quite at home. I don't think you know, but steamboating is my passion—I can't help it for it was born in me—my father was a steamboatman all his life—and I always experience a peculiar pleasure when I tread a deck, and feel the boat beneath me "walk the water, like a thing of life."[2] The day has been very beautiful and our final embarkation was attended with every omen of success. The whole regiment is safely on board, and I can safely say, as a body of men, they are rarely excelled

We left behind us an excellent reputation and we are determined to maintain it on the field. We are ordered to report to Maj. Genl. Pope,[3] at Amburg [Hamburg]—that wide place on the extreme left wing of the army. I don't apprehend that any fighting will be done where we are going, indeed we know already that the rebels are evacuating They expect to fall back, and let the climate do what they are unable to do with their arms but they will find themselves mistaken. We can stand the effects of the climate as our soldiers did in Mexico, better than the natives—I have got one hundred picked men, any one of whom can go into the harvest-field in July and kill off a dozen of the Southern chivalry at right down hard work under a burning sun. I know the material of the Southern army, and I know they are greatly mistaken when they think the Yankees can't stand the climate as well as they can.[4]

But enough of war & fighting I am sorry we are not to have a hand in cleaning the rebels out of Corinth, and am really disgusted at the prospect of having to follow them into the Gulf. I am in hopes tho' that McClellan's operations, on Richmond, and the extended line of coast attack, may force them to the centre, sooner than they have anticipated.[5]

Your letter of the 13th was received yesterday I have written you two or three scrawls, within the last few days, & I am afraid you will think this little better. We were paid for two months, just before leaving Paducah, and I sent you $20—a small sum but after paying all my debts—all I could spare. I am in hopes, we will be paid again after the 1st May, when I will send you more.

My dear Jeanie you must write as often as you can. You don't know how much good it does me to hear from you and how disappointed I am, when

A Barren Sceptre in Our Gripe

the mail for the 48th brings no tidings from my dear ones. I am surprised that Henry thinks of going to Pittsburgh. You are right in not indulging in any plans for the future. I can only say that I don't think we will ever settle in the West again. I know I can do better even in New York city, than to try the wooden country of Goshen any more.

The bell strikes that we are at Ft Henry, & I must off to send a telegraphic message, for some of my boys who are behind.

Goodnight my dearest, may God keep you and our babe safely is the prayer of your Husband

Edward

Monday night, April 28th 1862. We have just reached Pittsburgh Landing, the scene of the great battle and our Colonel has gone to report to Gen. Halleck.[6]—we may have to land here and I have opened my letter to add a word, before getting it ready to send back by the boat. Our trip has been a complete success & the Regt attracts the same attention and gets the same praise here, that it has had ever since we started. I *am* proud of it. Don't be alarmed, Jeanie, everything seems to promise a speedy termination of this war. We have just learned here that New Orleans is taken[7]—it is going just as I wrote you yesterday—when we have possession of all their principal seaports, and have penetrated into the interior as we must from this point, the rebellion will be dead and it must come before many months.

You must send me the picture as soon as possible—you don't know how I want to see the little cherub, and I have no good picture of you. I hadn't time to get one taken in full regimentals, so you will have to do for the present with those you have. I have been writing all day making out pay-rolls, & this is very scrawlly—

Goodbye again, dearest, write often—direct to Paducah as usual, & the letters will be forwarded Remember me with love to all
Your loving husband

Edward

LETTER 14

Camp near Corinth, Miss
Genl Pope's Division. May 7th 1862

My dear wife,

I wrote you on the boat that brought us up the river some ten days ago & since have not had time to write before. The first day we landed, Tuesday morning the 30th we marched out to our first camp five miles from the river The road was execrable owing to heavy rains, and the same cause made the little streams—five in number—that we had to cross unusually high—one was nearly breast deep and some of the companies made a detour for a better crossing place but Co. I came up in style & crossed where the foremost companies had An artist from Frank Leslie's paper[8] took a picture of us as we were crossing, but I learned afterwards that it was imperfect & could not be used. I am sorry for I would like to have had you seen it.

The men were all in excellent spirits, and made the march at quick time in little over an hour and then such a time of stripping & wringing out & hanging up to dry—it was a ludicrous sight. About night, the baggage train came up, fires were quickly lighted, camp kettles swung, tents pitched and we were ready for our first night's camping after a march. We stayed at this camp until last Saturday the 3rd without any incidents of importance where we were ordered to move forward and take up this position 7 miles in advance of our former one. The march was much easier than the other one, being through an undulating wooded country with a light soil, that had absorbed the rains and made the walking good Owing to the immense number of teams on the road however—for the whole division was moving—our wagons did not come up until morning, so we had a trial of camping without tents & on short rations. We cut poles & spread boughs on them for shelter & spread bark peeled from the trees for flooring & with huge fires in front it didn't go so bad. The next morning I was detailed as captain of the grand guard—the duties of which are so numerous that I can only refer you to the Army Regulations for them. We went out about five miles in advance of our column and were posted along a line about two miles in length covering a part of our front and flank. With the exception of picking up three stray *secesh* and visiting a farmhouse or two where we got some unwonted luxuries, such as butter, eggs, buttermilk, cornbread etc we had no adventures

Two nights lying out was a little much for me & I have been under the weather since Monday—day before yesterday—I took cold & had a fresh attack of diarrhoea—the cold is entirely well, but the diarrhoea still hangs to me. Tho' it is much better.

Yesterday the boys moved out about a mile, to repair the road and building some bridges that had been washed away by the heavy rain of the night before. I didn't feel much like engaging in such a glorious enterprise, so I have quietly remained behind these two beautiful days, wandering about the country as much as strength would permit, and all the while enjoying the clear blue sky and the delightful invigorating air—for so it certainly seems tho' it may be laden with deadly malaria. Tonight I learn the boys are to make another advance in the morning & I must up betimes to rejoin them You will probably read the details of the great battle we are about to engage in before this reaches you & I want you to understand our position Here is a rough diagram The dotted line represents roughly the position of our forces—we are on the extreme left under Genl Pope and you will see

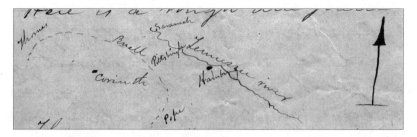

Wood's drawing of his troops' position at Corinth, May 7, 1862. Courtesy of the Indiana Historical Society.

are South of Corinth & not over ten miles distant. The attack will be made within the next two days and the conflict will be terrific and the result by no means certain. Beauregard[9] is a wily strategist and he has had our Generals completely fooled with the idea that the place was evacuated until tonight

I am inclined to think the battle of Pittsburg or Shiloh will sink into insignificance, in comparison with the magnitude of the coming engagement.

I know how alarmed and worried you are for my safety, but you must try not to indulge in such feelings. I am glad the enemy are to make a stand here, for in the event of our success, which I cannot doubt, the rebellion will be more speedily subdued, and we shall be saved from following them further South. You may be sure, my dear Jeanie, for your sake & for the sake of our precious one, I shall not rashly or unnecessarily expose myself The rest we must trust to that good God who doeth all things well. The sacrifice of the life of every man in this grand army, would be a cheap offering, if thereby harmony & enduring peace could be restored to our distracted country

Thursday morn, May 8th/62. Our camp is to be moved forward this morning and I take a little time before sunrise to finish this. I don't know when I am ever to hear from you again. We have got no letters since leaving Paducah & now if we move on & have a fight too, I reckon they'll never reach us

I was so in hopes our mail matter would find us before we left this camp—it has been forwarded from Paducah & is either "strayed or stolen" on the route—probably the former. I think you had better direct one letter to me as follows "Army of the Mississippi." "Genl Pope's division, Genl Buford's[10] Brigade. 48th Regt. Ind. Vol. *Near* Hamburgh Tenn." I would get James to direct it in a large envelope & I believe it would reach me—I sent you $20 from Paducah just before leaving which I hope you got. I would send you more now if I had any assurance that it would reach the confines of a civilized country in safety. I am in hopes I shall get the picture when our mail comes I want to see my dear ones so bad, since the comparative inaction of camplife I have thought of you constantly & I do long to see you and "clasp you to my bosom." I don't think it can be much longer, but you must not make any calculations on seeing me before the war is over, as a leave of absence is among the impossibilities. You must be a brave girl, tho' Jean, & keep up good courage. We are much better situated than many thousand poor families and we must thank God for present good, and hope for the best in the future. Kiss the darling pet for Papa remember me kindly to all, & remember always that you my dear wife, have the largest share of the love of your husband,

Edward

LETTER 15

Army of the Mississippi
Camp near Corinth, May 16th, 1862

My dear wife,

Your two letters, one of date April 18th & the other April 28th, were both received a few days since, in the first mail we have had since leaving Paducah. You can't tell how much good they did me, for they assured me of the continued good health of my darlings—Although I know you are so well situated, I always worry if I don't hear from you often—and it is the greatest consolation, when I hear that you are well, and that the precious babe is so hearty, & grows so finely. I could not stand it all, if it was not so.

I wrote you about a week since, but doubt whether the letter has got farther than the Landing—there has been an embargo laid on all communications from this army, for some time past, to prevent intelligence from reaching the enemy thro' the newspapers.—It has been a thorn in the side of the newsmongers, who have thus found their occupation gone, but they have been none the less industrious and we have been greatly amused by the telegraph news, manufactured at Paducah & Cairo in relation to the achievements & movements of Gen. Halleck's Army—There is but very little truth in all you may have seen in the papers in reference to matters in these parts

We have a hundred different rumors in camp every day, and some few of these are carried to the Landing & so down the river where they are repeated from mouth to mouth, until the large eared gentlemen of the press catch them, and telegraph them to Chicago & elsewhere as actual occurrences—probably in an hour after they are first repeated in camp they are contradicted and no one pays any attention to them.[11]

Tonight, for instance, it is confidently asserted for the twentieth time, that Corinth is evacuated, and right upon the heels of it we are ordered to march tomorrow morning at 4 o'clock, without baggage & with two days cooked rations in the men's haversacks. I don't think this looks much like evacuation, but apprehend as I wrote you before that we are on the eve of a great battle

But to resume my narrative where I left it about a week since, I was at the camp in the rear of the Regiment having staid behind because I didn't feel very well, and I had no idea we were advancing with any chance of a fight. But on Friday, a week ago today I came forward (or rather Thursday, it was,) to the new camp, five miles in advance, only to find that the Regt had advanced three miles further, without baggage and in light fighting order. It was too late for me to think of joining them, so I stopped at a farmhouse by the road side and slept delightfully in the loft, on a great pile of unginned cotton

But early in the evening, the artillery began to pour along on the retreat, and then the infantry streamed along nearly all night. I staid up long enough to find out that our Regt was among the number, and then turned in without any clue to the strange maneuvre. The next day however furnished one. A scouting party of cavalry and three regiments of infantry who occupied the same ground, were fired upon by batteries planted at close range and driven back with heavy loss and in great confusion—The long roll sounded in our camp, so after the cannonading opened, and we were marched out towards the scene of action. We met the scattered and wounded of the retreating regiments at every step, and the sight and their remarks, were anything but cheering to men expecting to go into action. The 48th faltered not, but marched coolly to the post assigned them to support a battery, the apprehension being that the enemy were about to commence a general attack. This however proved groundless and at night we were marched back to our camp.[12] The next day we had another alarm caused by the firing of our pickets upon a body of our own cavalry who approached at a rapid rate in a cloud of dust & who were mistaken for the enemy—This soon proved to be a false alarm & since then we have rested in peace—Upon the next day, Sunday while Col. Hascall & I were bathing about a half mile from camp, a message came to him, that Genl Hascall (Milo) was very sick & wanted to see him. He went over to his Milo's brigade[13]—about two miles, & returned, & in the evening we both went over & stayed all night. He was quite sick, but tonight is reported much better.

And by the way I must tell you that I have become a great horseback rider & enjoy it hugely. My position in Paducah forced me into it at first, & now I really pride myself on my riding & do enjoy it so much. Col. Hascall has two horses & one of them is generally at my disposal. I don't know when I have enjoyed anything as much as that evening gallop and the early morning return ride. Since Sunday, our camplife has been free from incidents. I suppose it is superfluous to add that I have been well, & am in fine health & spirits now.

We have an agreeable set of officers and a fine regiment of men—the more I get acquainted with them—of course with some exceptions—the better I like them—Camp life in the field has been with us so far, very much like our first experience at Paducah—except that the weather has very much mollified—We were encamped until today in an old cotton-field and the heat beat down terribly—Today we changed for the woods, & tomorrow we leave the camp behind—for we know not what. I have the same old wall-tent, with the *fly*—which is a great protection or convenience as you have a mind to use it. The fly is an extra cover that can be stretched above the tent or in front of it, there forming a verandah & it is in this capacity that it is most useful in this latitude. The inside of the tent accomodates Lieut. Gibbons & myself stretched upon cots, with some of the identical bed-clothes that started with us from Goshen (this *is* remarkable whether you believe it or not)—in addition we both have mattresses, & this with our camp stools and trunks make up the furniture of the *inside*.

But under the fly stretched in front, is our invaluable Tommy, with *his Kit*, consisting of the inexhaustible mess-chest, and himself more inexhaustible still in resources. He is an Irishman—English-bred—is Tommy Donahue[14] a railroad engineer by profession—escaped from Secessiondom within the last two months & enlisted with me at Paducah, and the cleverest, most faithful boy of twenty I ever saw. Praising don't spoil him, and he would die in an instant for his Captain. When I find such a true man I become attached to him, & the feeling is generally reciprocal.—he is a private in the ranks, but I have detailed him to take care especially of our things & treat him as a friend

I have just turned to look at a beautiful boquet of wild flowers, I gathered this afternoon. I wish you could see them and inhale their fragrance—there are many varieties new to me, & indeed a few nearly faded may-pinks are all that are familiar In my ramble too I found ripe strawberries of large size, and the usual delicious flavor—didn't I wish as I plucked the ripe clusters, that I could hold them up to my Jeanie's mouth, and see her eyes sparkle thanks as she tasted them. I believe I did gather a bunch of such clusters, with some such sort of a foolish notion, and then sate down on a bank, and greedily ate them all myself—wasn't it selfish?

I am looking for the pictures whenever we get a mail. I know you have sent them before this, and I do so want them.

Well, my dearie, I have written you a long letter, I find, by looking back at the paper marked over. I read Tommy the first about the newspaper rumors, & says he, "why you write just like you talk," & I only hope you may find all of it so. I can't talk on paper, for a thousand things that I would say to you my dear wife crowd into my mind and but a little is really said when

I cover a sheet. You know though, how truly I am yours, and how every act & thought of my life is tinged with the remembrance of you and our darling Mary—Write me often & tell me all about yourself & her. Remember me kindly to all, and believe me as ever

Your faithful husband Edward

I sent you $20 from Paducah just before starting—& $10 in my last. I hope they may both come to hand—.E.

LETTER 16

Army of the Mississippi
Camp near Corinth. May 24th 1862.

My dear wife,

I have just heard of a chance to send a line out of these woods, and tho' I have but a few minutes to write in, I embrace the precious opportunity. I have written you regularly about every week, but understand that an embargo has been laid on letters & none are suffered to go out from the army

I know how anxious you must be, if you have not heard from me for so long My last date from you is April 28th, just after you had heard that we had marching orders. I do hope you & the babe have continued as well as you were then. I was greatly disappointed yesterday, that I didn't get a letter—we had a large mail & I was sure there must be one for me

My health has been good with the exception of the diarrhoea—that is checked now and I hope will remain so

I sent you $20 from Paducah & $20 since we came up the river. I hope you have got it, or will get it

We are within 3 miles of Corinth, and very near the enemy, a battle may take place at any moment what the result will be the God of battles can only tell, we must put our trust in him my dear one, with the firmest reliance that he will order all things well

I have kept the messenger waiting now & must close. Goodnight my dearest may Heaven bless & protect you and our darling and soon restore you to the arms of your loving Husband

Edward

LETTER 17

Do send me some Postage stamps. I am entirely out, & can't get any—

Army of the Mississippi
Camp near Booneville. June 8th 1862

My dear wife,

I know how anxiously you must have been looking for a letter for a long time past, but I do assure you it has been among the impossibilities that I should have written you within the last two weeks. Your dear long letter with the pictures was rec'd two weeks ago tonight and I wanted to answer them right away but I was very tired & not feeling very well, so I waited till morning, but with the morning came the order to "fall in," for an advance, and it has been "fall in," "forward march!" "Halt!," repeated something less than a hundred times a day ever since

The first night we advanced about 4 miles—making considerable of a detour to our left—and there bivouaced for the night—On the morning of Tuesday, we advanced still further to within a mile of the enemy's outer works, our pickets being still in advance and constantly engaged in skirmishing. Here we threw up an entrenchment, just at the edge of the woods, capable of protecting the whole regiment Our General of Division Genl Schuyler Hamilton of New York,[15] complimented us highly on the character of our works—By the way, Seymour Burt,[16] Tracy's bosom friend, is aid to the General and I believe is chief of his staff. Tracy had been writing to him of me, so he called one day and introduced himself. I was considerably under the weather at the time, having had one of my bilious performances, and didn't feel much like entertaining him But he sat & chatted sometime about Tracy and Syracuse, & I found him a very pleasant fellow—he invited me very cordially to call on himself & the Genl but I haven't found time to do so yet.

But to resume, we lay Tuesday night in the woods, near our entrenchments, called several times by alarms, that proved to be false, but the next morning our heavy guns having got into position, it seemed as tho' the ball had opened in earnest. The big 30 pounder Parrott guns[17] were in our rear, and opened up a fire of the liveliest description on a rebel battery a mile in our front that replied with great spirit. As we lay in the woods between the two fires, we could hear the unearthly scream & shriek of the shells from both batteries as they passed over us. Occasionally one from the rebels fell short and exploded in the field in front of us or buried itself in the ground without exploding. The cannonading lasted nearly two hours, without any apparent results on either side, and with the exception of some sharp musketry firing from pickets, which called us under arms, was the last of excitement for that day. But on Thursday morning, our batteries opened to some purpose Among the first few shots, a shell stuck one of their large guns, dismounting it & killing or driving the gunners from their post. The rebels were distinctly seen afterwards by aid of a glass, forcing men at the point of the bayonet, to work the remaining guns.

There was considerable sharp skirmishing during the day, none of which however we participated in—The general result however of the day's work was to advance our lines with the batteries a half mile nearer. During the night there was great commotion in the enemy's camp and we could plainly see their signal lights from one end of their lines to the other.

A Barren Sceptre in Our Gripe

Directly in front of us they were remarkably busy with their R.Rd trains & signals, and we had every reason to believe they were strongly re-inforcing their right, which we under Genl Pope had been so pertinaciously pressing for the last few days. At last it seemed as if the great battle so long imminent could not be delayed another day. Our dispositions were all made, we had the utmost confidence in our Genl and it seemed as if he had infused some of his determination and resistlessness of purpose into his command. I have only barely seen Genl Pope, but the determined & persistent manner in which he has continually forced back the rebels at every point, is the wonder and admiration of every officer in his command

Whatever might be the condition of the enemy, he was not going to wait for an attack, so at day-break on Friday morning, our batteries opened as vigorously as every, but without eliciting any reply. After an hour of this work I think the Genl began to mistrust the true condition of affairs, for soon he & his body-guard went galloping by at a furious rate, and in an hour after, the stars & stripes floated from the Courthouse of Corinth

The enemy had incontinently fled, and no one knew whither, the main body of their army had been gone for two days, and the few left behind who had been fighting us so gallantly to cover the retreat of their comrades, had left in the night, taking with them their cannon & everything of value, & destroying what they could not carry. The victory for which we had been so long preparing, & for which we had gathered so magnificent an army, proved but a "barren sceptre in our gripe"[18]—we had Corinth a miserable collection of houses, and heaps of destroyed property with more than the usual amount of filth, & that was all. No prisoners, no stores, no ammunition or implements of war, no information, nothing only Corinth. I don't know how the Genls, & big bugs felt, but it was a source of great mortification to the boys to find the bird flown and the nest yet warm, but no other sign or indication of the late inmates. Their fortifications proved to be of quite a formidable character, but nothing could have withstood the terrible attack we were prepared to make with our artillery along the whole line.[19] Well we lay uncertain of our destination till nearly night, when orders came for our whole brigade to "fall in," & we took up our line of march, going very slowly & marching until 11 o'clock at night Here we rested the next day Saturday, and upon Sunday, our tents & baggage came up from our old camp which we had left on the preceeding Monday—The luxury of a wash & clean clothes, and a tent with a cot to sleep on, was duly appreciated after a week's bivouac in the woods, and we were hoping for a day or two's rest, but Sunday night, the order was to have two days rations cooked & be ready for an early start in the morning. So on we pushed Southward again—two divisions of our army being yet in advance of us,—we made about ten miles the first day, and the same distance the next, when we were halted some 30 miles south of Corinth, on the Mobile road. Here we have lain ever since with no enemy that I can hear of within 50 miles of us. Our advance guard is fully that distance ahead & tho' they have come up with the rear-guard of the enemy several times, they have never been able to engage them The fact is they run like fury, & thro' every town the inhabitants say they were going it on the "double quick." Our pursuit has been so deliberate, that it cannot amount to anything. Why we were stopped here and what our final destination may be, no one knows. Our tents and baggage have just come up again, and we have a chance to make ourselves comfortable again, but we have learned from experience that this but betokens a change. At least, when ever we get comfortably settled, I always consider it ominous of a change, so I have seized this first night under a tent, to scratch you a hurried account of our last two weeks.

I have written very rapidly & tried to condense it as much as possible, but I find I have travelled over a great deal of paper. I hope it may be interesting My health has not been as good as it might be. My bowels trouble me a good deal, for several days they will be as regular as can be, and then all at once I will have a run of diarrhoea I try to be very careful in my diet, & some times I am wholly at a loss to account for the cause of such sudden changes. Otherwise I am, "as well as could be expected."

The dear little cherub's picture! it is the cunningest thing in the world—everyone admires it so much. Milo Hascall said it looked good enough to eat, and he actually kissed the little sweet. May be papa hasn't kissed them both many times. I didn't like yours at first it is so solemn-choly—but it is the best I've got & it looks like you but with such a sad expression I hope you don't wear that look habitually it would make me crazy if I thought you felt always as bad as that looks. I have cut it down to the oval shape of the photograph & carry them both continually—Jeanie, I can't write to Father, till I can send him some money—I have 3 mo's wages due now. I have been paid for 2 mo's only—from 1st Jan'y to 1st March. I have 3 mo's due from the U.S. since 1st March, and 2 mo's due from 1st Nov. to 1st Jan'y due from the State of Indiana. We were greatly disappointed at Paducah, in not getting pay from the date when we were commissioned Nov 1st, but instead of that, we only got pay from the time when we were mustered into the U.S. service Jan'y 1st[20] My two months pay when I expected to get four was barely sufficient to pay my debts for my outfit & my board in Paducah, and leave me a small sum to get along on until next pay-day—for an officer has to buy every thing and prices here are enormous, but for money received from other sources, I should not have had enough to get along at all until now. If I had the 5 mo's pay due me—$650—I could pay all my debts & get along very handsomely—That from the U.S. is all safe, but I don't know when if ever, we will get our pay from the State. I drew up a letter to Gov. Morton[21] on the subject, which all of the officers signed; we have heard from him since, and he is trying to throw the responsibility of paying us on to the Federal Paymasters, & between the two I expect it will fall to the ground. We have also written to Mr. Colfax[22] at Washington about it, & I don't altogether despair of getting our rights from that quarter I suppose I shall get 2 mo's pay—$260—in a few days, & you may be sure every cent of it I can spare shall be sent home.

I think your letters have all been received—there was a time when we first came up here for two or three weeks, that the letters didn't find us, but since they have come with great regularity. I have rec'd 3 letters since I have written you, one with the pictures one a few days after, when I don't think you felt very well, and one a week ago tonight, just after you had got my letter mailed at Cairo & that was so dirty.

I sent that down to Hamburg landing by a strange wagonmaster, & gave him a half dollar to be sure & have it mailed there I suppose the chuckle-head forgot it till he got back to camp and then sent it down by some one going to Cairo

I am glad you are getting hopeful of a speedy termination of the war. God knows I am anxious to have it over & get back to my dear wife & babe. You cant tell how I feel sometimes, when I think I am losing the pleasure of seeing our darling beauty passing from infancy to childhood—to me it was always the most interesting period of a child's life & you know I am fond of children. Well I must close with this half sheet. I could write on all night, but my backless seat admonishes me it is time to quit. My dear Jeanie, you may be sure I will write just as often as I can, if you don't hear from me with regularity don't worry but write same as ever. I judge from your last that Nellie must have been confined by this time, if so, you doubtless have your hands full. Write soon & often & believe me as ever Yr aff. Husband, Edward

LETTER 18

Camp Cathcart,[23] 6 miles east of Corinth
June 25th 1862.

My dear wife,

Again it is a long time since I have written you, and again it has been nearly equally impossible that I should have written sooner. My last was written June 7th or 8th I think, from camp near Booneville nearly 30 miles south of Corinth, where we were then in our pursuit of the rebels.

At this point further pursuit seemed to be injudicious for many reasons, and a return to nearly our former position was resolved upon. Accordingly on the morning of the 11th our whole division took up the line of march towards Corinth in the hottest sun and thro' the dustiest road, it ever was my fortune to travel. We were to start at 5 A.M. to avoid the heat of the day, but as usual were delayed several hours, and so got the full benefit of the sun—We made 20 miles however, camping at nightfall on the bluffs of the Tuscumbia river—a not very large or clear stream but furnishing an excellent medium to dispose of the superabundant dust of our very dirty march—You never saw anything like the dust—the soil is very light and easily pulverizes when dry, into the finest of dust—every footfall starts a cloud of it—and in a still hot day it rises so as to stifle one with every breath. But as all things have an end, so our disagreable march came to one, about noon the next day, bringing us back to our old camp and tents, after an absence of ten days.

We remained there until Saturday the 14th when we started out prospecting for a new camp with the understanding that it was to be somewhat permanent. Saturday we established a very good camp, but we were not in our proper position in the Brigade, so Sunday orders came to move further to the left. The weather was excessively hot, and exertion of any kind was not pleasant, but about noon Sunday we moved again two or three miles to the left, only to rest on a succession of narrow ridges, with deep vallies between,—in fact an impossible ground for a camp—However we bivuaced Sunday night, and the next morning moved on for our present location—a very desirable one in many particulars. The country about here is quite uneven—not exactly what we would call hilly—for the road will wind for miles without a hill—but rather *ridgy*—and we are on one of the handsomest of these ridges—broad enough for our entire camp, but with steep declivities both in front & rear, running down to narrow vallies, to be succeeded in time by ridges. These ridges are covered with a rather sparse growth of oak and pine, and generally free from undergrowth. We are within a half mile of Clear creek—a fine stream for this country but one that sadly belies its name, in it's appearance—and have springs and wells of very good water in convenient distance

The location is considered a very healthy one, and what with rest and plenty of good water, the sanitary condition of the Regt has greatly improved in the last ten days. My own health has been excellent, my appetite is prodigious, nay almost alarming, but then my digestion is good. I sleep sound & regularly, and feel ready for any amount of duty. And I assure you we have plenty of it to do. The evils of idleness are too well understood by military men to allow their disastrous consequences to be entailed upon a camp—and so we are hard at work from daylight till dark. Here's our programme—Reveille, 4 A.M—that means "turn out," roll call, parade etc Police duty—cleaning up, *sweeping* the camp etc till 5. At 5.30 inspection of quarters, & then woe to the unlucky wight, whose blanket is not properly shaken & folded, and all whose equipments are not in regular order. At 6

A Barren Sceptre in Our Gripe

sick call & also breakfast 6.30 company drill till 7.30. 8.30 officer's recitation till 9.30. At 10. Officer's drill till 11. At 12. Dinner. At 1.30 pm. noncommissioned officer's drill till 2.30. At 3.30 officers recitation till 4.30. Supper at 5. Battallion or brigade drill from 5.30 to 7. Dress Parade at 7. Tattoo. (bedtime) 8½, & taps (lights out) at 9—

There, the few half hours left unoccupied in that programme, we have to ourselves to learn our lessons etc. Do you wonder that in getting settled into this routine, in this amazing hot weather, I should have felt little inclination to write in the week we have been here.

I have reproached myself with my negligence often & have made two three attempts that proved weak failures—but last night we almost had a thundershower, at least there was one not far off that sensibly cooled the air, and after a most invigorating cold bath this morning I seated myself cooly under my tentfly, and determined to give you the best part of the day—the hour before breakfast. I wish you could see how comfortably we are fixed, and I know you would be amused, to see out of what slender means, we contrive our little conveniences. For instance, my little round writing table, that looks as elegant as need be, with it's cheap spread, is formed of three stakes driven into the ground and a large sized cheese-box (!) that makes a symmetrical and servicable top. It is just the right size for a cardtable, but tho' Gibbons & I have threatened to have a whist party, we haven't found time yet. The sight and smell of breakfast cooking makes me think perhaps you would like to know how we live and what we find to eat. In the first place then we are almost entirely dependent for supplies upon the Commissary and the Sutler. The country is thinly settled & the inhabitants poverty-stricken at their best estate—you have doubtless seen the accounts of movements to send them supplies.[24] Occasionally a little milk, butter, corn meal, or rarely a fowl is all the addition to our larder to be had from the natives, & these always at fabulous prices Eggs we can usually get from the Sutler at 25 cts pr doz. Flour, ham coffee sugar, tea & everything that is issued to the soldier as part of his rations, we can buy of the Commissary at contract prices. Fresh beef we also get two or three times a week from the Quartermaster. Tommy makes an excellent soup from a beefbone and the dessicated vegetables that are put up for soldier's use (Get your dictionary, my dear, & look up that big word before vegetables) They are quite an institution and as you know my weakness for soup, you may be sure we have it whenever beef comes to camp. Ham however is our main reliance, it is convenient of carriage, always good & always at hand for a quick meal Boiled or fried it usually makes one of our meals for the day; dried beef, codfish & mackerel are about our only changes in the meat line from these standards. But here our troubles just begin—you can see from our slight stock of materials that it would be useless to attempt any lofty flights in cookery. Flour we have but how to convert it into bread is the problem with us yet unsolved. Tommy made a passable kind of flapjack, with sour milk eggs & saleratus,[25] but the milk is a very uncertain quantity. His biscuits are simply execrable,—is there any way that biscuit can be made with soda & cream tartar, or with saleratus, or with anything of that kind, without milk & be endurable, & if so, нow?—do send receipt, if such a thing is practicable. We have a baking kettle that answers a very good purpose—it bakes meat to a charm, & once when we had eggs & milk, I made a capital rice-pudding (now, laugh!) I forgot to mention rice as among our standards—in the absence of all other vegetables, we use it largely—Dried apples & peaches we get from the sutler, & condiments of every kind Just now we are luxuriating in a fine supply of blackberries. Tommy has attempted a pie or two, with but indifferent success,—somehow the crust won't shorten, & I prefer the berries in a natural state.

Well, well, with all this talk about eatables, Tommy thinks it is high time there should be some action, & besides his dish of fried liver & thickened gravy, flanked by a pan of mush looks very inviting & I must stop for breakfast

At night, in my tent. I have just read this long letter of trifles over, and thought how little there is in it, to ease the heart-ache of my dearest one at home, for I do know you are suffering greatly from this unnatural separation. God know the thought of it is overpowering to me, when I allow it to have full mastery of me, and I have a thousand cares & duties that occupy my mind, & so crowd out thoughts & feelings that otherwise would nearly drive me crazy. It is not natural, that my darling child should be growing out of her sweet babyhood away from the loving eyes of her father and it is not natural, that they whom God has joined should be so cruelly sundered, But He allows it for some good purpose, in his infinite pleasure.

I feel already in a measure some good growing out of this dire affliction in a deepened and higher appreciation of the rich blessing he has so unworthily bestowed upon me in my loving wife and sweet child—perhaps I needed this hard trial of separation for this very purpose, at any rate we are safe in saying that since God wills it, it must be for the best.

My dear Jeanie, we must try to cultivate this cheerful spirit, and avoid brooding over this hard, but present necessity. We must not gaze continually upon the dark & gloomy clouds that shroud the present, but lift up our eyes full of faith and confidence, and let them rest upon the rainbow hues of the bow of promise that spans the future.

It grieves me beyond measure to think that perhaps you are wearing your life away, by yeilding to feelings of despondency—Your letters do not say so but I know how keenly you feel this trial, and with how little else, you can occupy your mind. Do, my dearest, for my sake & the sake of our

A Barren Sceptre in Our Gripe

dear child try to put down such unpleasant thoughts to cultivate a spirit of cheerfulness & hopefulness for the future.

I cannot see my duty lying in any other direction than the present one I cannot honorably get out of the service if I would, and I do not think at present that I would if I could. A few months may make many changes. I have several reasons for desiring to remain in the service a few months longer, and then if my objects shall be accomplished and I can get out of the service honorably I would resign. I know you would not have me go out of it in any other way

We have not yet been paid for March & April—& are in hopes now that we will not be until after the 1st next month, when we will have 4 mo's pay due. I wish we could get it all at once, it would help me much. I guess you will be tired when you have got thro' this long letter, but this make up in quantity for the delay. Goodnight & God bless you every my dearest.

Yr Husband Edward

Chapter 4

A Fierce Wild Joy Exhilarated and Filled Me

The Battles of Iuka and Corinth, July–October 1862

After the evacuation of Corinth, Confederate forces consolidated around Tupelo, Mississippi. General Braxton Bragg replaced Beauregard in the command of the Rebel army in June 1862, and Confederate President Jefferson Davis gave him command over the territory east of the Mississippi River to Atlanta, as well as part of Tennessee. In late July and early August Bragg moved most of his force east to Chattanooga, Tennessee, to defend that vital spot, as well as to prepare to strike northward in an invasion of Tennessee and Kentucky. The remainder of Rebel forces in Mississippi came under the commands of Generals Sterling Price in northern Mississippi and Earl Van Dorn, who commanded the defenses of Vicksburg and Port Hudson. Bragg planned for Van Dorn to cooperate with Price to move north into western Tennessee while he and Major General Edmund Kirby Smith would march north from Chattanooga. In September, their orders from Bragg were to prevent Union forces around Corinth from reinforcing Major General Don Carlos Buell's army then in central Tennessee.[1] As a result, Price and Van Dorn advanced on Federal forces in northeastern Mississippi. Two hard-fought and bloody battles ensued at Iuka (September 19) and Corinth (October 3–4), where Union forces under Major General William S. Rosecrans succeeded in defending the important railroad crossroads. Rosecrans's subsequent pursuit of Price's broken army westward failed to catch the Rebel force.

Wood's brigade spent the summer months marching back and forth through northern Mississippi looking for the enemy. After the long exposure to camp diseases in Paducah, the fierce heat and drought-stricken conditions on these seemingly aimless long treks took a toll on the troops. The regiment was reduced to less than half its original strength even before they fought at Iuka and Corinth.

Wood was detailed to provost duty in Rienzi, Mississippi, and, to his chagrin, missed the battle of Iuka. The 48th Indiana's first action was a bloody baptism of fire, where it took the brunt of Sterling Price's fierce Confederate assault. Placed in support of an Ohio battery, the regiment drew the "murderous concentration" of fire from both the Rebel infantry and artillery. The 48th broke in panic and, amid the smoke and confusion of the battlefield, suffered "friendly fire" casualties inflicted by other Federal units. Later, the remnants of the regiment participated in a charge that drove back the Rebels and restored some sense of dignity to the unit. The regiment lost 100 of the 434 men who entered the battle.[2]

The Confederate army retreated southwest, while Rosecrans's forces moved back to Corinth within the strong defensive positions first built by Beauregard's army, strengthened the defenses further, and awaited reinforcements from U.S. Grant in western Tennessee. But in the last days of September and the beginning of October, Price and Van Dorn's Rebel forces marched north to the Tennessee line and then east to Corinth to cut off Federal forces and retake the vital railroad center. The Confederates attacked the defensive positions over two days, and fierce hand-to-hand combat occurred in the town itself.

Wood's division, on the right wing of Rosecrans's line, did not receive the brunt of the onslaught. Instead, the 48th Indiana and other Federal units on the right poured their fire into the flank of the Rebel assault on the Union center on the second day of the battle. Nonetheless, the regiment suffered several killed and wounded in the fighting.

As Wood was on duty away from his regiment during the battle of Iuka, he could not describe the battle. He dashed off a quick note to his wife during the pursuit of the Rebels after the battle of Corinth and did not have the time to pen an account of the battle. In his next letter, he attempted to rectify that omission: "I must . . . tell you the part the glorious 48th played therein." However, he was interrupted and never returned to the theme.

LETTER 19

Camp near Rienzi Miss
July 3rd 1862

My dear wife

Your last two delightful letters have been received, the one of June 24th just now, and I take this early opportunity to tell you how glad they have made me. Your other was received last Saturday night—June 29th—& I didn't expect another so soon, but in the absence of our P.M. Capt Wilson[3] & I went to Brigade HdQtrs on learning there was a mail, and brought that for the 48th over to camp, and assorted it. I was doubly grateful & fully repaid for trouble when I found one from my dear wife, and such a dear good cheerful letter too. I am so glad when I think you are enjoying yourself, and so miserable when I think you are worrying and unhappy—

I know it seems hard to us, but I do know, from a deep inward conviction that it is for the best good of both of us. I am glad you feel like uniting with the church, not that I think that or anything else could make you better & purer than you are, but more perhaps because it is in harmony with my earlier impressions, that all so good & true should be united by some visible bond. Your letter tonight was a rich treat, and so was the other received Saturday night, enclosing one from Mary for with it came one direct from her. I was glad indeed to hear from her—she is such a good correspondent, we must not lose her again—and don't you think we'll have a fine time, when we visit her at home. I don't indulge much in speculations for the future, but I think I would rather live in New York than anywhere else, & shouldn't wonder if we should settle down there after this war is over. If you want to do business—the motto is go where business is—& with my many friends & acquaintances there, I could command as much as Goshen ever afforded. Confidence & assurance are the main stock in trade in most businesses & if I had had more in my younger days I never would have turned westward. The army is a poor place to learn modesty, & I really have a notion to hang out a shingle in the metropolis—if sufficient encouragement should be given, after the war is over.

But all this sounds oddly enough away down here in Mississippi, 50 miles from any outlet even to civilization, for we have been on the march every day since I wrote you last untill today—and as I look out on the stirring camp scene, from my seat on the end of my cot, with the smell of the fragrant pines in my nostrils, and the beautiful new moon hanging out so clearly from a endless sky, it seems strange to think of life in the crowded city, amidst the whirl and excitement of busy thousands. As I said we have been on the march since Friday last. The order to cook three days rations & prepare for a light march came very unexpectedly, for we had made up our minds to spend some time in our old camp. We were ordered to go in the direction of Holly Springs, by the way of Ripley, and were making great calculations, on a visit to Holly. The first days march brought us a few miles west of this place, our direction to this point being Southward. The day was extremely hot & intolerably dusty. I never suffered so from heat & dust in my life and the march was most outrageously conducted—we marched from our camp to this place 16 miles, from 6 to 12 pm, with scarcely a decent halt. The men were greatly prostrated and not one half of those who started, stacked arms when we halted at noon. I could have kept up with the Regt but about a mile before they stopped I got mad at the manner we were being treated and went into a house, where after a good drink of buttermilk and a rest of an hour I joined the Regt. We rested till 5 p.m. by which time, most of the men had come up. The road was just lined with stragglers from every Regt—it was impossible to keep men in ranks, and I thought it was inhuman to do so, & didn't try very hard

Just before I left, the Col. rode up, & says "Why, Captain, what's the matter, we haven't got 300 men in the Regt." "No, sir" said I, "and if you keep them going this gait a half hour longer, you won't have 50." In the cool of the evening we marched a few miles further, & halted for the night. The next day was cool and cloudy, with a delightful summer rain, falling so cool and softly that it was a real pleasure to get wet by it. The road too was through a pleasanter country, with more signs of civilization, and under these combined cheering influences, the boys marched along at quickstep, singing the Hallelujah chorus; we made 15 miles westward toward Ripley easily by noon, and camped till morning in a fine open meadow, skirted by a pleasant belt of timber through which ran a fine clear stream. The men improved the afternoon in bathing, washing their clothes & picking blackberries, which best grow to perfection & in the greatest abundance all through this country. I have literally feasted on them every day since we started, and they have had an excellent effect on my bowels.—haven't had a touch of diarrhoea and have made the whole march on foot, without any sign of weakness, except being a little stiff and footsore last night.

Sunday found us again on the march making 10 miles and halting 2 miles this side of Ripley. Monday we moved on thro' Ripley, a pleasant county town of 1000 or 1500 inhabitants, to a point 3 miles beyond, where we halted and understood as it was the last day of the month, we were to be mustered for pay. But no sooner were we halted than Co. I. was detailed for grand guard & ordered to report to Genl Buford at once. We did so and were posted 2 miles in advance of the brigade, where we found 4 other companies, which with ours constituted the grand guard of the brigade. We have just got our arrangements all perfected, the different reliefs divided, our chain of sentinels posted, and Lieut. White of the 5th Iowa, & I being on the 3rd releif and having some time before duty, had settled down for a comfortable time, when the order came for the guard to return to camp. We remained however long enough to do justice to Tommy's excellent supper of chicken, new potatoes & onions, & then returned, much chagrined at the loss of our night of guard duty. Perhaps you have heard me speak of Carl. White[4]—the Lieut referred to,—he used to live in Goshen you must have heard Mrs. Barron speak of him,—he is an excellent & genial gentleman & companion & I must say with regret, these qualities, are rare among our officers, as far as my limited acquaintance goes. But if we were chagrined at the loss of guard duty, you may imagine what were the feelings of the Regt when word came in the morning that we were to retrace our steps, and that after all Holly Springs was not to be our destination. There were many long faces & hard words muttered as we turned backward—these citizen soldiers not liking the idea of being moved like puppets, but always wanting to understand the whys & wherefores When they did understand the reason—that our right under Genl Sherman had already occupied Holly, & there being no enemy there, we were not needed, they marched off again with alacrity, and inspired with the hope of spending the glorious Fourth in the old camp, actually made the same distance that had taken three days, on the outward trip, in a day & a half. But when we reached Rienzi and instead of turning Northward, toward the camp, kept on our way due east, the boys flagged again, and all sorts of queries & surmises as to our new destination arose. Well, here we halted last night, 3 miles east of the town, and all is yet a mystery as to our future movements. Some think we are to make a new camp near here, others that we are to go into North Alabama, & others affirm that we are to start for Holly again—I am inclined to the first opinion, but I have learned that in the military, "ignorance is bliss," and tormented as I am by a hundred questions, about which I know no more than the questioners, I have learned to be a first rate Knownothing,[5] and answer "don't know," with the greatest readiness

Don't you think I stand the roughing remarkably. Here we have made a march of 76 miles in 6 days,—no great marching to be sure—but in that time, tho' I have had a fly, have not once spread it—it being usually in the bottom of some wagon, and for the same reason I haven't taken out my cot, but have slept on the ground, under the blue sky or a canopy of leaves, and haven't felt a particle of inconvenience from it, but on the contrary have lain down tired and sore, and woke in the morning refreshed and invigorated and ready for another days work. One of the greatest nuisances that infest this wooded country, is a little insect, invisible to the naked eyes that covers every bush and leaf, and burys itself beneath the skin, causing an itching pain, compared to which the bite of a mosquito is pleasurable. They cover one by hundreds, & especially attack the breast & limbs—I suppose five hundred would be a small estimate of the number of blotches I have on me, caused by the depredation of the miserable little "chickers," or "jiggers" I don't know which the natives call them[6] Mosquitoes & other night insects are not as thick as with us. I haven't seen one of the former in the country, and tonight I have had a candle lit for some time, not a moth or miller or any other insect has singed his wings therein. I think sometimes when I have scribbled over so much paper, you must get tired of so many trifles, and I know any body else but you would—but they are all we have to write of, and I intend to write often enough to make my letters a sort of journal

Tonight we have rumors of the fall of Richmond, with great loss of life,—we hope the first is true & the other at least exaggerated God grant that George has come safely thro' the fight.[7]

My candle burns low, it is growing late & not one word yet in this long letter for papa's darling—not because he had forgotten her you may be sure for he carries her picture & wifey's in his pocket, and think of them a hundred times a day—The little dear one, how I would like to teach her little feet the way to walk God bless my darlings and keep them safe from harm, till in his own good time, he shall restore them to my arms, is the constant thought of Your devoted Husband

Edward

Many thanks for the postage stamps. I have thought for the last two or three letters, I would next time send a list of little things I would like to have you send me, but always forgot it till the last, so let it go this time. No pay yet, but we are still anxiously looking for the good time coming

LETTER 20

Camp near Jacinto, Miss

August 8th 1862

My dear wife,

I am ashamed of my long silence, of a month without any sufficient cause. My last was written I believe from near Rienzi, just after our return from Ripley, and I have received two letters from you since—the last one, acknowledging the receipt of my last. As I have said I have had no sufficient reason for not writing sooner, and no reason at all, save what could be found in the discharge of usual camp duties, and the oppressive and debilitating effects of the climate

You cannot imagine how hard it is to do anything not absolutely required of us, and with so much required, when that is performed, how readily one yeilds to the lazy influences of the climate.

I have made two or three efforts but have been interrupted or broken down before I could get fairly commenced. If perseverance is the great virtue it is reputed to be, I intend this effort to be a success, and I have more confidence that it will be, from the fact that we have made a march, and are not yet settled again in the routine of camp duties, and so have more leisure. I wrote you fully what those duties were, and you may be sure they are sufficiently onerous, to make any other effort even the most trifling, a labor indeed—We have moved our location 15 miles south of our old one, & as I have intimated are not settled yet. I think however, we are to go into camp some where near here, for the balance of the summer. It is impossible to do anything in military operations, while the present excessively hot weather continues. Our march the other day, conducted as it was with great care, prostrated a great many men & horses with the heat, several cases of sunstroke proving fatal. I dropped behind the Regiment, about a

A Fierce Wild Joy Exhilarated and Filled Me

mile before they halted for noon and went to a house some distance from the road for water. You recollect Bayard Taylor's descriptions of the fighting around the wells in the desert.[8] I could think of nothing else, as I came up and saw the frantic efforts of the soldiers—famishing for water, around this miserable little well of poor water—Such crowding and jamming around the [curb?], such thrusting forward of hands, eager to fill their tin cups, with the coveted fluid, and then when a dozen cups would reach the edge of the bucket at the same time, such contention, as to which one should have the first dip. I remonstrated with them as they hindering each other and spilling more water than they got, and soon succeeded in introducing a little system, by superintending the distribution of each bucket full standing there over an hour, before I got a taste myself. Just as I regained the road, I found my faithful Tommy prostrated with sun-stroke, close by the roadside and under the shade of a little clump of bushes. The dust from the road was intolerable but there was no other shade near, and I had to do what I could for him, where he lay—Fortunately, I had been reading a few days before, something of the treatment and gave him whiskey from my flask, and cold water application on his head. I was soon gratified to find my treatment successful—When I came up, he was insensible with no pulsation perceptible at the heart or wrists, but a violent throbbing in the jugular & at the temples. I pressed two or three stragglers to assist me and after half an hour's rubbing, with repeated inward stimulants, he revived so as to know & speak to me, but immediately dropped off again into a deep stupor. Afterwards, I hailed a surgeon belonging to a battery that was passing, & he made an examination of him and said I had done all that could be done for him, and we must let him lay until the stupor had passed off. We got him into an ambulance, and he lay until the next morning, in the same condition, when he revived and has continued to improve until he is nearly well. I really believe he would have died by the road, as some poor fellows did, had it not been for my timely assistance. I reached the Regt again about 4 P.M.—an hour before they started for the afternoon march. We passed through the little town of Jacinto, a pleasant looking place about sundown, but already occupied by Jeff. C. Davis' Brigade[9] and showing plainly the marks of military occupation, in deserted and ransacked buildings and in the guards pacing in front of those not already empty & destroyed. It is a sad sight to see these once flourishing little towns, depopulated and almost blotted out of existence by the ravages of war, but it is a sadder sight to see our brave boys who have cheerfully given themselves and their all for the defence of their country, standing guard over the property of men who are in arms against that country, and by whom, its existence and their own lives are imperiled. It would be a hard thing to burn and destroy all before, and it would not be done, but certainly, we ought to eat of the substance of the enemy, and cripple him in resources in every way possible, instead of putting guards over every cornfield and onion patch, thus keeping our soldiers from getting vegetables etc that would be of service to them & all for fear of exasperating the "Southern Confederacy"! I am glad to say such nonsense is about "played out," and on the last march, the boys foraged quite extensively—For the past few days, chicken, geese, ducks turkeys, peaches, green corn, potatoes, onion and other unwonted luxuries have been quite plenty in the camp.[10] You don't know how *ravenously*—such things are appreciated after a long enforced abstinence in camp. We haven't been able to get but few luxuries—nothing that would be called so at home—but I mean in the way of dried or canned fruits—& those only at exorbitant rates. I believe if the Gov't would only abolish the monopoly of Sutlers, and throw open the trade of the army to competition some men would be found, who would be willing to furnish the soldiers such comforts at reasonable rates. Every kind of fruit & berries, dried and canned, butter in 2 lb tin cans, peach & apple *butter* as the Hoosiers call it, put up in the same way & a hundred other such things would be of great service to the soldiers and would meet with the readiest kind of sale.

I have no doubt $5000 worth of such things could be sold in our Brigade in a week, especially just after pay-day—and a man could double his money on them, & then give good satisfaction. Why these licensed robbers of soldiers, sutlers, charge 300 & 400 per ct. where they are not restricted in price as in our Brigade And that makes one thing of a list of things that I wish you would send me.

—I have made it out once, as I would think of anything, but the list is mislaid & I must put down as I can think of them, what I want, and I don't know but I had better do it on another sheet for this one is most full, and I haven't half had my say out. Since I commenced writing, your dear welcome letter of the 30th has been received. It is such comfort to hear from you my dear wifey & to know that you and our darling are well, and then to look at the mailing only Aug 1st—it makes me feel as though you were not so far off after all. You have asked me several times about coming home this fall, and I have given you no definite answer and cannot yet. I cannot, with any consistency with my past course, or with my present convictions of duty, think of resigning now as long as my health continues good, and from the recent orders of the War Dep't, and the immense effort being made to get new recruits into the field for active operations at once,[11] I think a leave of abscense will be very difficult to obtain. Indeed it has been impossible to get one in this Division at any time, except upon a certificate from the Medical Director, that the applicant has been unfit for duty for so long a time, & that in order *"to save his life,* or prevent permanent disability," a change of climate, is absolutely necessary. I know you would rather not see me, than to have me come with such a certificate truthfully given. I know they are not always so given, & I know that some officers have gone home on them for the purpose of visiting, or attending to their private affairs and I suppose I could have had such a leave, anytime during the last month but I did not feel like asking for & obtaining a leave, under such false pretences

Since the new order, commanding every officer to report to his Regt by the 11th of this month, or be considered a deserter, I apprehend that few such leaves will be give, so you see the prospect for my getting home this fall is not very flattering—You may be sure tho' that I shall not let the first chance to get a leave of absence decently, pass unimproved. Of course, it is impossible to tell anything about our future destiny or destination, but if we should remain in this locality, without any more indications of a fight than we have had for two months past, I think I might perhaps get away some time next month,—but it will not do to build any castles on so airy a foundation. And now for the list, for if I run on much more, I shall fill this sheet too. *Imprimis,*[12] then I would like 2 sheets, and 2 pillow cases, & a slip or cover for my pillow of some dark stuff. Towels, or towelling stuff, coarse crash & finer, castile soap, tooth powder, Kathairon or cocoaine.[13] ½ doz. Pr merino socks, 2 merino undershirts, 2 pr drawers (light.) thread & buttons—1 Bottle good Brandy—& any other Knickknacks your can think of that would keep and come safely—I would like a good many little conveniences for cooking, such as a sauce pan, long handled spoon skimmer, dredger etc, but it seems ridiculous to send so far for such things, and I think I won't bother you with them. I would like too some books—some of the little blue & gold—Whittier, Lowell, & Bryant, also Burns,[14] and all the old magazines, that you think I may not have seen. I have seen some of the Atlantics & Harpers this summer, but not all,—don't buy any to send, but rather buy some cheap editions of new novels. Thackeray's "Phillip," will be issued now, & Bulwer's "Strange Story," and any of Trollope's new novels, except "Framley Parsonage." You know we read that in the Tribune. Trollope's other novels are "Brown, Jones & Robinson," "The Bertrams," "Dr Thome," "Castle Richmond" etc. Any of these or others that you may send, will be very acceptable.[15] The surest way to send, will be by the way of Goshen to the care of Lieut. Schaubel,[16] who is home on recruiting service & will probably return about the middle of next month. He may come sooner however, & you had better send as soon as you can. You must pardon the disconnected style of this letter—it has been written under most unfavorable circumstances seated on a camp stool, under a tree and with a dozen interruptions, of from ten minutes to an hour each, but as I wrote at first, if perseverance could accomplish the wonders told of it, I meant to make this letter a success—I am afraid it has proved so, only in its prodigious length. I certainly will try & not let such a long gap occur again in my letters. I am well, as usual and can only be too thankful for my continued good health. We have been very unfortunate in the Regt. Two of our Captains have died and of the other all but three have resigned.[17] So there have been a good many changes among our officers. I am now the 2nd Captain in rank, in the Regt & in case of any more changes by resignations or promotions will stand a good chance for promotion myself. I would like to be Major firstrate—it is a much pleasanter birth than Captain, with nothing like the work and responsibility. Isn't it strange in all ranks & professions, the higher one gets, the less work & better pay one gets,—but so the world wags.

Kiss our precious one for papa—how he would like to see her toddling around Ah-well-a-day, we will make up for all this sad time, if Providence kindly smiles upon us, and blesses us as I trust He will with long years of peace & contentment, to make up for this one year of separation.

I am so sorry you feel unpleasantly situated, & I know so little how to provide for you elsewhere. Could you not find some pleasant boarding-place, in a quiet respectable family—where you would not feel so crowded. I know it must be disagreable for you to feel that perhaps you are intruding, & I should feel much better, if you could find some such place as I have indicated. Write me what you think of it. Good-bye & God bless you, my dearest. Write often. Your Husband Edward

[On first page: "I am glad you got the money safely—send a bill of what you get for me, & I will pay it. I have a letter for you from Willie when I write next, I will send it—E. Oh! I want a portfolio & some good stationery that I quite forgot in my list."]

LETTER 21

Camp near Jacinto, Miss.
Tuesday, August 26th, 1862.

My dear wife,

Here it is again—more than two weeks since the date of my last—in spite of my better resolves for the future. I find two sheets in my trunk, that are evidences only of my good intention—one commenced a week ago last Sunday, wherein the determination is expressed not to let the day pass away unimproved, but preaching directly in rear of my tent interfered with the completion of that, and the other was but a feeble effort anyhow, commenced when I was not in the vein, as fell stillborn. Last Sunday I was out on grand guard and took paper & pencil along, confidently expecting to find time during the day to write, but the duties of the post were unusually numerous, & so you were cheated again.

Perhaps you wonder what grand guard is, my dearie. Well, you have heard of pickets, and doubtless know what they are—the sentinels posted in advance of a body of troops, to give notice of the approach of an enemy— A grand guard is simply composed of these pickets, and constitutes the guard for a corps, as Brigade, Regiment, etc. Our Brigade[18] is composed of 5 Regiments, and is at present, divided as to location—three of the Regts being some two miles to the right, and a little in advance of us—The whole front of a Brigade, and also the flanks, or sides, must be protected by the grand guard, so you see it makes quite an extensive line of pickets. The usual way of posting these, is by placing three men on a post, who remain on for 24 hours, taking turns, standing guard two hours at a time, and releiving each other. These posts are usually within sight of each other, so you see, that in a wooded country, it takes a large number of men to furnish pickets for such a long line. In addition to these posts, there are one or two reserves, composed of from ten to thirty men each according to the strength of the guard. The directions to pickets are, in case the enemy should approach in force, to fall back steadily upon these reserves, and the duty of the pickets & of the reserves, is to fire continually, annoying the enemy and keep him in check as long as possible, and so give our own forces warning and time to prepare for an attack.

The guard should, if possible, keep up the fire, retreating steadily until they reach their own camp—but in case of a sudden and furious onset by cavalry, they must fire as much as possible, and then, when unable longer to resist, they should disperse, and fall back towards camp, the best way they can. Upon the vigilance and good conduct of the guard often depends the safety of an entire command—For should pickets be negligent, or cowardly and neglect to engage the enemy when approaching, an attack might be made, as at Shiloh, before the men could get out of their tents.[19] Our guard last Sunday was composed of three companies all under my command. I found the guard that we releived, in some respects, very injudiciously posted, and all the morning was spent in modifying the line, and reposting the sentinels. I made the principal reserve where the Capt. of the Guard always remains in a new position, at the forks of two roads, where the pickets from each road could readily fall back on it and otherwise improved upon the old arrangements so that the General in his tour of inspection publicly thanked me for improving upon his work!—For the Genl commanding a Brigade, always locates the outer guard lines whenever there is a change of location, and I should not have dared change it, but for the existence of one or two glaring defects, that I knew must have been oversights, and while I had my hand, I thought I might as well make it to suit myself.

So much for guard duty—that I had no idea of stringing out so long—but when I commence to tell you anything,—it seems as if I must tell *all*. And it fills up paper so fast. I guess you would laugh if you had seen how fast without a pause the pen has run over the last sheet—for the writing materials are all good, and when all the other conditions are favorable, as at the present, writing is real fun.

I think you would be greatly surprised to see how comfortably we can and do live in our canvass houses. I believe I wrote you something of how nicely we were fixed up in our last camp, but that was nothing to the beauty & convenience of our present location. We moved our last camp at our leisure, making several trips with our waggon train, and so were able to bring everything with us, even to our tables & boards for floors—did you ever see a nicely–laid out camp? I expect not, unless in a picture—the tall, symmetrical Sibley tents all in rows with a wide street in front of each row, carefully *swept* each morning, the rows of co. officers tents in the rear, and still further back those of the field & staff officers, all the ground *swept* with brooms each morning, & the accumulated rubbish carried off in waggons—all this with the whiteness of the tents & the cleanliness of the ground, gives one an idea of neatness, that is a surprise here in the woods—& what underbrush there is, is always cleaned out—with its moving, busy population, and its every-varying aspect—I enjoy all this greatly, and if I could but go home to my wife and baby at night, I think I would like the life and business, as well as any I was ever engaged in—but there's the rub—when I do enjoy anything, I don't but half enjoy it, because my other half & truly my *better* half—does not share it with me—but when this cruel war is ended we will make up for all this. I think when we are together again, I can live with you more in one year, than perhaps I should in two, if we had never been separated, and so we shall regain this lost year,—for I really do not think the war can last many months longer—With the immense force now being brought into the field, it must be speedily terminated, by the annihilation of the rebellion. I fix the 1st of March as the outside limit for the duration of the war, for if we are not successful by that time, I am free to confess that I cannot see where it will end

The North has just commenced to get in earnest, & has for the first time, put forth an effort, that she has sensibly felt. In the South, however, there has been a strain upon every nerve of her social system, since the first inauguration of rebellion, and if we should defeat them now, there would be no elasticity or vital power left in them to recover from the disastrous effects of such a defeat.

I only fear that the new recruits & levies in the North may not get into the field in time to prevent the rebels from striking effective blows upon our scattered and weakened forces. No one knows, who is not in the army, how terribly our ranks have been thinned by death and disease. We all refrain from writing about it—for it would only publish our weakness to the enemy, & in private letters, it would only make our friends feel badly. I have refrained from writing anything of it, for I knew it would only unnecessarily distress you, and make you more anxious than you are for my safety.

But I am so unusually well and the worst part of the season has so nearly past that there can be no harm now in writing of it. Our Regt that started out 950 strong now musters only about 400 fit for duty, & that without having been in an action—the rest are dead, discharged, or sent to northern hospitals & sick in camp. My company which at one time numbered 103 is now reduced to 83, and of these less than 60 are present fit for duty, & yet I have the largest Co. in the Regt & have for two months turned out more men for duty than any other. Some do not average more than 25 or 30, the rest being included in the category above. While we thus have more men for duty than any other, we have most unfortunate in the number of deaths, a larger number—14—having died out of my company, than from any other. It has made me feel very sad, to see these brave boys stricken down by disease, and dying so far from loved ones at home, but cannot reproach myself with having neglected one, or having failed to render every assistance to their friends, to obtain the little mementoes of the lost ones, that are so precious. In two instances, the friends of the dead boys came for the remains, and I know they were more than satisfied with the attention I showed them.

But "let the dead past bury its dead."[20]—I am confident they have well served their day & generation, & no work of mine should bring them back, if it could—Our Colonel has been absent for the Regt on sick leave, and I am informed has just returned. I have not seen him, but am glad he has got back. Our Lt. Col. is *some* military but small potatoes *generally,* and we are glad to welcome our old Col. back again

I must have written you that Col. Hascall had resigned.[21] Maj Rugg is appointed Lt. Col. & Capt. Townsend Major. I don't [think?] I ought to allude to it, but Mrs. Hascall played me a shameless trick, that I shall not forget, but which I might have expected.

I wrote to Col. Hascall after his resignation fully of the affairs of the Regt as I conceived I had a right to—He had been second in command of it, & his relations & mine had been of the most friendly character, & we had often privately talked over the affairs of the Regt, discussing everything with the utmost freedom. I wrote him in the same spirit, and what was my surprise, in less than *two weeks,* to see my identical language quoted in a letter from Capt. Wilson's wife to him. Mrs. Hascall and she were both at Paducah together, and Mrs. H. had hastened to tell Mrs. W. who, by the way, is a very estimable & discreet woman—everything I had written to her husband. Isn't it abominable. I can't express my detestation of such conduct. Fortunately, it was nothing of importance—but you know how one feels about such things—when any thing is imparted under the implied veil of confidence & secrecy, how annoying it is, to find oneself made public property by untimely & unnecessary disclosures.[22]

Well the whole a/c is wiped out—there is no Debit or Credit a/c—in my books with the Hascall family—the Major is made. Capt. Townsend, the ranking Captain is Major, & I am the next in rank.[23] I shall continue to do my duty in my present position & have no fears after that is done, for the future.

I have written this last hurriedly & am called upon to command at Dress Parade, which will be on hand in a few moments. I wish my dearest one, that you could be present but for a moment, that I might see your loved form, and that you might satisfy yourself of my actual, living & stalwart (!) prescence.—for I reckon I can no longer be counted among the Lilliputians, or Fairbanks[24] and all being of his *scale,* must be counted liars.

Aug 31st—five days break, so near the close of this long letter. I had to drop my pen at the close of the last paragraph, & so leave the finishing until morning. But morning came & with it a detail for a foraging expedition under my command, lasting three days, & since my return I have been busily occupied in making out muster rolls, returns etc, that must be furnished the last of the month.

These I have just completed, and the muster & inspection of the Regt being over, I have a chance again to write. I was expecting a letter yesterday & today, but suppose you are busy perhaps, getting ready that box, with its multifarious contents. I expect you laughed over the incongruous list, but everything down in the bill, is not come-at-able here, & you will see, that most of them are prime necessities.

Lieut. Schauble has not yet returned, & I understand will not leave Goshen before the 10th prox, so I shall be sure to get the box You speak about my wearing calico shirts & say you would be afraid to have me take off my flannel. I know you would have given me a good scolding if you had seen me without undershirt or drawers, as I have been most of this summer. But you know I put up none but the heaviest of undergarments & no human flesh could have stood them thro' this scorching weather. We could get no other until lately—since I wrote you last—our Sutler brought on some thin gauze undershirts & cotton drawers, and as the nights are growing cooler, I have put on both. I commenced to tell you of my size & was about to brag of my huge dimensions, I find, when I left off the other day—Perfectly light—just in pants, shirt & slippers, the other day. I stepped on the scales & fixed the weight at the usual notch 120,—but greatly to my surprise & delight, the beam wouldn't rise till it indicated 132 pounds. My cheeks are full and round, & every body says, "how fat you're getting." I shave on the sides of my face, & that I think perhaps makes my cheeks look fuller.

I had a picture taken for you at the other camp in marching order—full length, with coat off, pants in boots, sword, canteen & haversack on, but it was so poor I concluded not to send it to you. But an opportunity offering I sent it to 'Gus Crane—if I have another opportunity I will try & have a better one taken.

Did I write you about the inspection at the other camp, when Co. I bore off the palm, for appearance drill etc?—We have had another today, with the same results. I am proud whenever I think of my Co. I had many misgivings of my ability to successfully command & take care of 100 men, & I am more

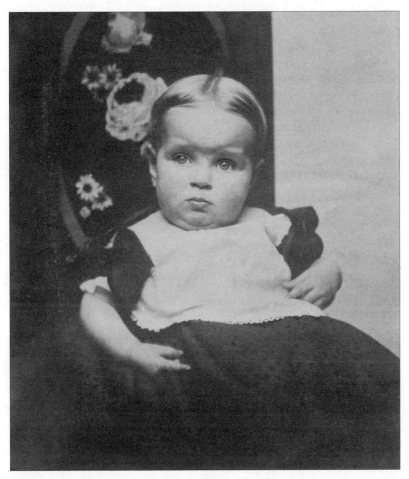

Marie Gautier Wood, Edward and Jane's infant daughter, during the war. Courtesy of Daniel Wood.

than gratified with my success, & I write this because I know it will please my Jeanie.

Papa has got his dear treasures, Jeanie & Marie, lying before him on the table—the dear, sweet, arch-looking little fairy-baby! Papa wishes he could clutch her to his heart—She must be toddling all about by this time & of course your hands are full.

I see no immediate prospect of getting leave of abscense—my looks would preclude all possibility of getting sick leave, & there's but slim chance for getting away, for any other cause. We have two months pay due again today, & as soon as we get it, I will send you some more money. I hope you have enough for present necessities—if you have not, write me, & I will send you some anyhow.

I shall be looking for a letter every day—til I get one—everything is quiet here. The enemy are not thought to be in force anywhere in our neighborhood—a few guerrilla parties are roaming about the edge of our lines, but they are very cautious how they approach too near. Write often, my dear wife, & I will try hereafter to divide my long letters into two. Kiss our darling pretty one for papa & remember me kindly to all. Goodbye my dear Jean, may God guard & protect you always is the prayer of

Your Husband, Edward

[In margin of first page] I enclose $10.00 as I can spare it—you may need it to replace what you have spent for me—send along the bill, little lady, & you shall have the bal.

LETTER 22

[*On stationery marked:* "Head Quarters, Department of the Mississippi. Office of the Chief of Artillery."]

Rienzi, Miss. Sept 16, 1862

My dear wife,

Ten day ago, we broke up our old camp near Jacinto, and moved to this place—9 miles west—& where you will recollect we have been twice before,—once on the march to Booneville, and once on the march to Ripley. We have been lying here ever since coming,—with rumor of an enemy in front in force, and with baggage trains sent to the rear, and everything ready to march or fight at a moment's notice[25]

Two days since, a reconnoisance in force to the front revealed the fact that we have nothing to fear from that quarter—the enemy having avoided us, making a circuit to the east of our old camp, and threatening an attack upon Corinth, or else with the design of crossing the Tennessee river, higher up, and engaging Buell who is marching North, to intercept the retreat of the rebels from before Cincinnatti & Louisville.[26]

It has been an exciting time, and I have had again, the responsible position of Provost Marshal of the town. Col. J. V. DuBois, Chief of Artillery of Genl Halleck's staff, has been in command, and I have been most intimately connected with him, in the administration of affairs here, acting as his Adjutant General and Provost Marshal also.[27] You may know I have been busy, but my health has been excellent, and I have enjoyed the whirl of business in a town full of soldiers, as an agreable contrast to the dull, quiet routine of camp life. We are again on the move tonight. Most of the infantry have already left. I have command of 80 picked men who are the last to leave, and whose business it is to see, that no depredations are committed upon property. Everything is carefully preserved—the men's wooden shelters, bunks etc, for we do not expect to abandon the place, but probably fall back on Corinth, and wait until the new recruits join us. We have some Two Hundred recruited at home, and all the Regts. are filling up finely at least those from Indiana.

Lieut Schauble had not yet returned. I suppose he is on his way, or will leave this week. I am getting very anxious to get my box—I meant to have told you to have a better picture of yourself taken to send me.—Have you seen these full-length card photographs? I think they are very neat and pretty—if convenient, I wish you would have one taken, and send soon, and now for the direction. I have neglected to send you any address, because your letters have generally come thro' with the greatest possible dispatch.

At Cairo they have a grand distributing office, where the letters for the Army are distributed for the different divisions. We are still designated as the Army of the Mississippi, under the general command of Genl Rosecrans.[28] Our immediate division commander is Genl. C. S. Hamilton,[29] & our Brigade comdr Genl Buford. So you may put as much or as little of this on as you please. "48th Ind. Hamilton's Divn Army of the Mississippi," will always reach us speedily, whether you add "Corinth Pittsburgh, Jacinto," or any other place.

I have been boarding in a very pleasant family since coming here—a Mr. Knight—a schoolteacher, formerly from Ohio, & about the only Union man in the town. They have three young children, & I have had delight in playing with them, and studying their cunning ways, and so calling up the image of our dear darling Mary—If you can, get her into a picture too, tho' I have no hope of getting a better one than the admirable one you sent me.

I have been expecting a letter for the last two or three days, but now we are to be on the march again, I don't know when I shall get one. I will write you as soon as we stop if possible, but don't feel worried if you should not hear again in a week or more, for it may be impossible for me to write. Keep up a good heart, my dear Jeanie, I know you are brave, & I believe you would rather your husband were here, however great the sacrifice, than that he should be poltroon and knave enough to refuse his aid to an almost ruined country

God bless you & our little one. Write often, Your Husband, Edward

LETTER 23

[*On stationery marked:* "Head Quarters. Department of the Mississippi. Office of the Chief of Artillery."]

Rienzi, Miss Sept 23rd 1862

My dear wife,

I wrote you a week ago, when I supposed we were about to start at once. After our Regt left, an order came, countermanding the previous one, &

Col. DuBois was retained here, in command of a small force remaining behind. He wanted me to stay with him, so I have been separated from the Regt. since that time.

I know you will be anxious to hear from me, especially as the Regt has been in a fight. I have heard nothing definite from them, except they were in the action at Iuka, where Price[30] was defeated, and behaved themselves well—there was a report that Lt. Col. Rugg was killed, but I think it must be a mistake.[31] I do not know what our loss was—the total loss in our Division (Hamilton's) was 75 killed and 250 wounded[32]—the enemy's loss was much heavier—I know you will be thankful that I am unhurt, but you can't imagine how chagrined I am, that I should be absent from the first fight our Regt has been in. However, I am consoled by the reflection, that I was doing my duty here under orders, and no one can impute any bad motive to me, in being away.[33]

I will write you again in a few days I have scribbled this to assure you of my safety, while the boy has been waiting with the mail bag. Excuse this dirty sheet, it is all I could find. Health still good—if anything better than ever. I ride horseback two or three hours every day & it agrees with me splendidly.

Goodby—God bless you my dear one, and keep you & Marie safe till papa comes home, is the prayer of your loving Husband

Edward

Please send me some postage stamps—I am *"played out"*—everybody is short of stamps in the army & I never can refuse to lend or give one away—for it's always the lastintheend [?]—Goodby—E—

LETTER 24

[*On letterhead marked:* "48th Regt. Ind. Vol. U.S.A., Col. Norman Eddy."]

[Camp] On the March
Rienzi, Oct 8th [18]62

My dear wife,

I send you a hurried line to assure you of my continued health & safety.

We went through the bloody storm of battle at Corinth last Friday & Saturday and thanks to a merciful God I came out harmless—Thanks to him too for a great & glorious victory—Price & his whole army are defeated with great slaughter, & for three days we have been following him in close pursuit—The whole road we have travelled was strewn with tents, guns baggage, camp equipage & everything that denotes the wreck of a great army We must inevitably catch him, for the prisoners represent that he is in a state of great destitution, men & horses completely worn out.[34]

We were in the fight two hours & twenty minutes but owing to the favorable position of the ground we occupied, our loss was small 4 killed & 23 wounded among the latter Lt Col. Rugg & Capt Spain.[35] I lost one killed— a poor boy shot through the head in the early part of the engagement. I can only say for myself that my feelings were indescribable—a fierce wild joy exhilarated & filled me. I thought we had been fighting about twenty minutes when the order to cease firing was given—You will be pleased to hear that your boy is well spoken of for his good conduct on the field & that a Major's straps are already talked of for him—Our Major is under arrest & will probably be cashiered, & am at present acting in his place—[36]

God bless you & baby my dear wife—Keep a good heart & don't worry for me. The hard fighting is done in this section for the present. When we catch Price I shall try for a leave of absence

Havent heard from you for a long time, but we have had no mail for 10 days

Good by Your Husband Edward

[Envelope addressed to "Mrs. Edward J. Wood care Jas S. Gillespie Syracuse N. York"]

LETTER 25

Corinth, Miss.
Oct 23rd 1862.

My dear Jeanie,

It seems a long time since I scrawled you a hurried letter from Rienzi while on our pursuit of Price. You have doubtless read how inaffectually that pursuit terminated. We marched over 100 miles in six days, and then found ourselves back in Corinth, without having bagged the enemy.

I have been expecting every day to hear from you, in reply to that scrawl, but am most afraid it may have miscarried. I could find no envelope but one that was directed, but scratched that direction out, and wrote in lead pencil your address, & gave it to a Captain who was coming to Corinth to be mailed by him, after redirecting—I am afraid it may have been neglected or the letter may have miscarried on account of the two directions, and I am much to blame for not having written before.

But the fact is, I came back from the chase, pretty well tired out. We had been for two days and nights before the fight, under arms, and then two days in the fight, and the subsequent march was a very hard one on us. The battle was on the 4th—on the 5th we started in pursuit of Price—on the 8th I wrote you from Rienzi after a round-about march of 50 miles. We continued the pursuit for two days, and then abandoned it as hopeless, and returned to Corinth on the 12th—a footsore and weary lot I assure you. Since then we have moved twice & have just got settled on the north side of the town, inside of the breastworks, and have, after the usual manner of soldiers, proceeded to make ourselves as comfortable as possible.

I have got a good floor in my tent, and—thanks to Tommy—a good fireplace & chimney—so I am bound, for a time at least, to be comfortable. For these cold nights & mornings have admonished us, that we must "poke the wood & make the fire burn," away down here in Dixie, as well as in more Northern latitudes

Your dear letter of the 5th enclosing one from Mary, was received about the 15th inst. And I essayed a reply to it, but was interrupted by one of our hasty changes of location. And besides as I wrote you, I have had a great deal of responsibility. Our Colonel was wounded at Iuka—our Lt. Col. at Corinth, & our Major resigned—so that in reality I have been, as senior Captain, in command of the Regiment. Lt. Col. Scott of the 59th Ind. was assigned to the command,[37] but he has rarely been here, and the chief responsibility has rested upon me. I did hope, when a season of tranquility came, that I could get home to see my loved wife and child, but it seemed impossible and I did not make the attempt.

I am afraid you did not get my letter from Rienzi, and tho' your last was written after news of the fight, and you were congratulating yourself that I had probably not moved, and so was not in the fight—I must undeceive you, and tell you the part the glorious 48th played therein.

Nov. 1st/62—A long break, & I know you must be feeling anxious about your boy before this time.—Your dear welcome letter had been rec'd & would have been acknowledged sooner, but I was interrupted just here, and for the last few days have not been feeling well. I caught a severe cold a week ago, with the sudden change of weather, that brought snow with it, & with agueish aches & pains. I have been truly "under the *weather*." But today I am quite well again—I assure you I have been homesick enough the last few days, and my darling ones have never been out of my thoughts. I certainly shall try to get a leave of absence when Col. Eddy comes back, which will be within the week

I hardly know what to advise you about accepting Aunt Mary's kind invitation. I can well imagine it would be much pleasanter for you this winter, but it seems such an undertaking for you to make such a long journey, with Mary at this season of the year—We have rec'd no pay since I sent you the money in July, & my finances are at low-water mark. We are expecting four month's pay soon, but it may not come before the middle or last of the month, & there is some talk that we may have to wait until Congress meets in Dec. & makes the appropriations, before we get away. That would make it too late to think of spending the winter, & so at present I don't know how to advise you. I hope I may see you before the month is out, & that we can fix it all. Don't count too much on it, for I may not be able to get away, but if it is in the range of possibilities, I will do so.

I am sorry I haven't time to write you a longer letter, but the mail is about to close, & I can't delay this another day—will write again soon. Remember me kindly to all & kiss the darling one. Am sorry I can't send the $10 this time, but if I can get it before I write next, will do so.

Goodbye, dearest. God bless & keep you safely.

Your affectionate husband
Edward

Chapter 5

Our Progress Is So Slow

The Advance South, November 1862–January 1863

Union forces in northern Mississippi began a southward pursuit of the defeated Confederate Army, now under the command of Lieutenant General John C. Pemberton, who was given the command of Mississippi and Louisiana east of the Mississippi River.[1] However, progress was slow, as guerrilla forces raided isolated units, destroyed bridges and railroad lines, and caused havoc. With several commands now consolidated into the Department of the Tennessee under the command of Major General U. S. Grant, the focus became the Rebel stronghold of Vicksburg, Mississippi, which controlled the Mississippi River. Union control of the river would split the Confederacy in two, leaving those states west of the river cut off from the more populous East, reinforcements, and supplies. Federal combined forces working their way northward from New Orleans and working southward from Memphis needed to subdue that significant fortress to achieve control over the river.[2]

Grant had originally planned to march south from Memphis to Jackson, Mississippi, and then attack Vicksburg from the east. But Grant's forces in Tennessee and northern Mississippi were halted on December 20, 1862, by a daring cavalry raid under General Van Dorn. The Rebel horsemen raided the Union army supplies at Holly Springs, Mississippi, destroying large amounts of equipment and rations for the advancing Federal armies.[3] The raid retarded the Federal advance, forced a large portion of the army to retreat, and part of that force (the 48th Indiana included) marched to Memphis to guard an immense wagon train of supplies.

Another Union setback came at the same time. Grant detached Major General William T. Sherman and his reinforced corps from Memphis and sent him down the Mississippi River from which his force attempted to steam up the Yazoo River to approach Vicksburg from the north. There Sherman's troops would land and attack the fortress. But the plan was flawed, the defenses sound, and the swamps nearly all impassable. The landing and assault on December 29 was a costly failure, and the expedition was canceled.[4]

Wood's enthusiasm for the war continued even after the bloody battles of Iuka and Corinth, and he lamented the slow progress of the Federal armies. Nonetheless, he settled back into the routines of marching and camp life, enjoying his promotion to major and his additional responsibilities.

LETTER 26

Camp near Moscow, Tenn.
Nov. 26th 1862.

My dear Jeanie,

I am afraid you are half worried to death by this time at not hearing from me again for so long, when I promised to write again in a few days in my last, which I believe was written from Corinth Nov. 1st. That very night we received marching orders, starting the next morning without baggage, and marching to Grand Junction Tenn. in three days. Our supposed destination was Holly Springs where the enemy were in force—Holly Springs being about 25 miles from Grand Junction—our force that moved from Corinth was about 15000 strong, and at the latter place we met Gen Grant's column from Bolivar & Jackson Tenn. of about equal force, so it really looked as if something was to be done in earnest.[5] We only went 8 or 10 miles however, toward H. Springs from the Junction, when the enemy having evacuated the former place at our approach, and fallen back 25 miles upon the lower bank of the Tallahatchie river, we were ordered back to Davis' Mills, ten miles south of the Junction. Here Col. Eddy joined us, and you may be sure it was a source of rejoicing to us all—we had been so long without a field officer, that it was a great relief to have our old Colonel with us again About this time too, our camp and baggage was ordered up from Corinth, and in a little over two weeks after leaving, we had the gratification of getting a change of clothing and of sleeping once more under a tent. I think of those two weeks, with feelings of unmitigated disgust. I don't think I ever endured so much discomfort in my life. Tommy was sick & had to be left behind—We had not a single waggon to carry cooking utensils or provisions—except the Division train that carried rations for the men, and officers had to fare the best way they could. I messed with a squad of my company, clear fat bacon, toasted on a stick, hard bread & coffee, composing the fare, except when the boys foraged on their own hook, and thus added fresh pork chickens & sweet potatoes to our larder. Everything seemed to go wrong with me, all that doleful time, and I suppose one reason of it was that I was not feeling very well, and small things worried me a great deal. I missed Tommy and his kind attentions more than anything else, especially when night came,

Colonel Norman Eddy, 1862. Courtesy of the Northern Indiana Center for History.

& I had to look about for a place to bunk. Well, Tommy & the teams finally came up, and the next day, the 17th, we were ordered to prepare for a march. We moved by the way of LaGrange, Tenn, and the next day made this place 10 miles west from LaGrange on the road running from Grand Junction to Memphis[6]—we are 15 miles west of the former place and 40 miles east of the latter, only one Division—Hamilton's old one now commanded by Genl Quimby[7]—is here, and how long we are to remain, or in what direction we will move next, is all matter of conjecture. Genl Grant & the main body of our forces are near LaGrange. I think the intention is to re-open the R.Rd to Memphis before any movement southward is made. Several miles of track were torn up near this place & two bridges burned, which are rapidly being repaired—it is the general impression, that we shall be moved when this is finished. Well so much for our general situation & prospects—As for myself, I am much better than when we left Corinth and as usual my health has improved with the march and change of location but I am dreadfully homesick. I do want to see you and Mary so much, and I had so confidently calculated on being with you before the close of this month, that I cannot get over the disappointment. If we had remained at Corinth until Col. Eddy's return, I have no doubt, I could have got a leave, but here in the field, in the midst of prospective active operations, it would be nearly worth a man's commission to ask for one, unless he was wholly disqualified for the service. I still live in hopes however—for if all accounts of this country during the winter season are true, we must soon go into winter quarters, & then a leave can more easily be obtained The rainy season may be expected to set in by the middle of next month, and from that time to the 1st of march at least the roads are impassable to infantry and artillery. So don't despair, my darling, I am in hopes the New Year will not dawn, before I can again clasp you in my arms. Col. E. has as much as said to me, that when Lt. Col. Rugg returns, he will interest himself to get me a leave of abscence. Col R. is expected now in a few days,—he was wounded you recollect at Corinth—

Well I suppose I am actually Major, tho' I have not received my commission. I saw the announcement the other day in a Cincinnatti paper, among a list of promotions telegraphed from Indianapolis, so I suppose there can be no doubt of it. I have been acting as such ever since the battle of Corinth, & most of the time have been in fact in command of the Reg't.[8] All this long talk about myself and not a word of your good long letter of Nov 3rd Although the first part was rather sad, I was glad to see a more cheerful vein towards the last. I know you must feel sad & lonely & I can't blame you at times for feeling *blue*. I know I am sometimes most "deeply, darkly, beautifully blue,"[9] when I am a little unwell especially—not fit for duty, and with no active employment on hand, then thought has free scope, & it seldom runs in pleasant channels

I don't wonder that you poor women at home, who sit dreary hours alone perhaps, with no occupation to prevent you from *thinking, thinking* all the time, should get lonesome and *blue*. I only wonder that more don't go crazy—I have worried a great deal because I could not send you the money I know you need so much. The way we are treated is shameful. Our Division has not been paid for five months, and this neglect too, just at the season of the year, when the families of the men need all they can send home, to prepare for the winter.

There is no money in our Regt I have tried in vain to borrow a small sum to send you, but all the officers are *strapped* or nearly so. The condition is so common throughout the Divn that an order has been issued, authorizing the Commissary to sell subsistence to officers on credit—formerly we had always to pay cash.

I was much obliged for your batch of Goshen news, but as I get the *"Times"* every week, and some of the boys get letters every few days, I keep pretty well posted. The only thing I have noticed lately that would interest you is the death of Mrs. McGary who died quite suddenly, a short time since.[10]

Mrs. Barron has never been paid, I am ashamed to say. I know you will send her the money as soon as you get it. I haven't got the box of things yet, and am almost discouraged about it. Capt Schauble wrote me when he received it at Goshen about the 1st Sept—since then it has travelled once or twice to Indianapolis from Goshen, started once for the Regt, got lost but turned up again & the last I heard of it, was left by Capt Schauble in the hands of some friends at Indianapolis. In the mean time, Schauble *don't* come, when he *does* perhaps the box will come with him. I believe I get all your letters—direct them hereafter to Quimby's Divn Army of West Tennessee,[11] LaGrange Tenn, or almost any other place—Army P.M.s only look at the Divn & Regt & at Cairo where all letters are restamped, they keep constantly informed as to the location of Divns. I have looked over a goodly number of your letters, but can't find out Mary Mackie's address. I think you are right however 97 Irving Place. There, my darling, have I answered *all* questions?—I was greatly pained to hear that Mary's health had been so poor. I do hope she has entirely recovered—she was such a dear plump baby, it seems strange that she should become puny. I hope it may prove only temporary, & when papa hugs here "mos' to death," she may be well & hearty again. I believe I wrote you all I could in my last about going to spend the winter with Aunt Mary. I think we must defer a decision until I come home

Tonight as I close, there are indications of an early move. I should not be surprised if we left in the morning. I hope our baggage will keep up—if it does & pen & paper are comeatable I will not let so long an interval elapse again in my writing

Good night, dearest. God guard & protect you is the earnest prayer of Your Husband Edward

LETTER 27

Camp near Oxford Miss
Dec 6th 1862.

My dear wife

Your dear & welcome letter of the 18th ult. was received last night, and it gave me many a pang to think that I should have raised such fond expectations in your breast only to meet with cruel disappointment

I certainly did think that as soon as Col. Eddy returned I could get away & if we had remained at Corinth, I doubtless could & would have been at home by the middle or last of the month, as Col. E. came back on the 9th— But when he came he found me with the Reg't. 60 miles from Corinth, on the road to Holly Springs, and as every one supposed in close chase of the enemy. It would have been fatal to any officers reputation to have asked for a leave then, except in case of downright sickness & utter inability to do duty

I wrote you something of our peregrinations since that time from Moscow Tenn. & intimated at the close I believe that there were indications of a movement on hand. We got the orders to march that night, and started the next morning, marching in the direction of Holly Springs. We made 22 miles & bivouacked near a small stream called Coldwater, 3 miles from H. Springs. The next morning we moved on thro' the town, halting a half hour near the public square Holly Springs was quite a handsome town of 3000 or 4,000 inhabitants before the war broke out, and still retains many traces of its beauty. The business part of the town, surrounds the square in which is a fine Court House, and the many fine private residences, with well laid out grounds filled with the holly & other evergreens, gave evidence of the wealth & refinement of their occupants

Many of the residents were in the street & I inquired after Mr. Failing, Mrs. Ferriss' brother—found a gentleman who knew him very well. He had moved to Memphis or near there some time ago.[12]

We continued our march about 8 miles further and then went into camp near a fine sheet of water formed entirely by springs and called the very romantic name of Lumpkins Mills Here we pitched tents a week ago today and stayed three days, waiting for the provision train to come up. Tuesday morning we moved ahead again about 12 miles to the famous Tallahatchie river where the rebels were to make a stand, & dispute the passage of the river. But the game had been gone so long, the scent was cold. Our cavalry were then chasing them beyond this place.[13]

We had to wait a couple of days here, to rebuild the bridge over the river so as to make it passable for our wagons & artillery. They were two regular rainy days, and a more dismal dreary set you never saw, than we were when we started out yesterday morning. However we made good time, marching 15 miles thro' clay of the worst kind, & passing through the town to our camping ground just beyond by the middle of the afternoon. Oxford is built on the same plan as Holly Springs, & with the exception that it is rather smaller, & with fewer pretentious residences, might pass with a stranger for the same place. There seems to be prospect of staying here a few days—tho' when or where we shall go is of course impossible to tell. The enemy are still retreating, & manage to keep out of the way of our infantry. Our large Cavalry force however in front is harassing them continually, and damaging them considerably[14]—They have taken over 1,000 prisoners since the flight of the rebels commenced, many of whom are confined here & many are being brought in every day—they are a saucy, impudent set, & don't seem to feel the least discouraged, or cowed down, tho' they are most thinly clad & with no blankets or those of the poorest quality. And by the way, speaking of prisoners reminds me that the same mail that brought your last, brought one from my half brother Robert J. Corley, a prisoner of war at Frankfort, Ky. He & a cousin Frank Phillips[15] were taken prisoners on the retreat of Bragg's army from Ky—they were sick & left behind. He wrote a very kind brotherly letter, with but little reference to existing trouble, beyond the hope expressed that they should not disturb the relations that bind us together. Mother was well when he left the South, he says, but does not say when that was—her great anxiety was about Willie and I.—He was expecting to be exchanged & was to leave for Vicksburg for that purpose the next day. He had been in the C.S. service nearly 2 years, but does not say in what Regt or corps or in what capacity. My commission as Major to date from October 21 also came in the same mail, so you can direct accordingly

There is a report to-night that the 1st Brigade (ours) is to be left behind at this place. I don't relish the idea of being in the rear, but I suppose wifey at home will be glad of it, as being a safer place. I can't say anything more definite about coming home, than I wrote you in my last. As soon as we *stop* anywhere, & it is evident the pursuit is up, or we are not to share in it, I shall make the attempt to get away. Col. Rugg's wound is worse again & he may not be here for a month or six weeks. Capt. Schauble has arrived with his recruits—he brought the box to within 7 miles of Holly Springs, where he was obliged to leave it & his own baggage on account of a break in the R.Rd. There was a guard left with & it may come up after a while. Well my sheet had run full and as it is late, & I have to go out in command of the Regt early tomorrow morning to a foraging train I must close. I do hope I shall have some money if only a small am't to send you when I write next. I have written to Goshen for some & expect it when Capt Wilson returns in a few days—Kiss the darling one all over for papa & may God guard & keep you both safely is the prayer of Your Husband Edward

LETTER 28

Camp on Okona River, Miss
Dec. 13th 1862.

My dear wife,

Two letters and *the* box all the same day! You may be sure I am a happy boy—so many reminders of my dear kind, thoughtful wifey, and so many things of real comfort and use. The underclothes are just the thing, much better for present wear, than what I sent for in the summer and all the articles are just what I wanted and needed badly. The two letters were dated Nov 25 & Dec 1.—our mails have been somewhat irregular lately & they both came together.

I had been out on the road all the morning, having charge of 300 men at work, making a roadway through a bad swamp, and came in for dinner, but I found the letters & the box, & Capt. Wilson had just returned from the North and I found it hard work to get back to my work. The men thought I had deserted them, but we spent the balance of the P.M. at it & did up a creditable job. Civil engineering talent is in great demand in the army, & since they have found out my qualifications in that direction, there is no bridge to build or road to repair, but I am detailed in charge. The distinction is flattering, but the work is not always so agreeable, I have to go out again tomorrow & as we will probably move the day after I couldn't tell when I might have a chance to acknowledge the receipt of all my goodies, unless I wrote tonight.

You don't know how often and how longingly I think of my absent treasures—my dearly loved wife and my little stranger darling. I never thought Fate could shape out such a strange destiny for me, and deny, even the common lot of men, & what would be to me the greatest of earthly pleasures to see my dear little one grow from infancy to childhood to watch with a father's pride & love her cunning ways, & note her gradually expanding perceptions

all this you know from my natural love for babies, would be the highest delight for me, & I can't help feeling that it is hard to be denied it. But philosophy does a good deal toward helping it & a confidence in the wisdom of Him who doeth all things well, goes a great ways further, & I try to be resigned.

I am thankful that you both continue so well, and have been spared any great sickness or calamity. I trust you may always remain so, & that we are all to be spared many years of usefulness and happiness. We are still crowding forward but the enemy are away out of sight and hearing. It is impossible to follow a flying enemy, as fast as he runs. Bridges are to be rebuilt, & roads made. Subsistence must be hauled up by wagons, & with a large army progress must be slow. We are now 7 miles south of Oxford where I wrote you last. We are ordered to draw 5 days rations tomorrow, & I think that indicates that our next stopping place will be Grenada 40 miles south. The rebels may stand at Jackson nearly 100 miles further South,—but I doubt it We are moving upon them with an immense army, & they haven't got the force to meet us.[16]

If the weather don't interfere, we shall make winter quarters at Jackson.—if it does, then we shall pull up this side somewhere, for I am more than ever satisfied that locomotion will be an impossibility,—when the heavens open & the rains descend, as we are told they do in this latitude. And when we do stop then look out for a boy pointing northward. The Col. has assured me it shall be so. I am well acquainted & I think not unpopular at the Genl's Head Quarters, & I have every confidence that I can get away. It is hard I know to counsel patience—for I find it hard enough to practice it, but it is the best that can be done. You know, my dear girl I will fly to you, the moment I can, & I know you will try to keep up a brave heart, and bear whatever fortune Fate may have in store for us. I shall start this northwards by Capt Spain, who have been compelled to resign[17] & you may get it before the last one I wrote from Oxford. Goodnight my dearest. Kiss baby & keep her in mind of that Papa, who certainly will come and treat his darling very gently till she gets used to his rough ways. God bless you. Your Husband Edward

LETTER 29

Camp on Yokona River, Miss
Dec 18th 1862

My dear wife,

Your welcome letter of the 8th is just received, and I am so glad you seem to bear our disappointment so patiently and hopefully—I was cruel to write you with so much certainty of my coming home from Corinth,—but the prospect certainly was flattering, and my own hopes doubtless made it look more so. Now it is a matter only of hope and conjecture—our progress is so slow, and the weather continues so horribly pleasant! No rain and no mud to speak of, and the oldest inhabitant declares that this condition of things is unprecedented. But still we seem to be loth to take advantage of this splendid weather. We are at the same camp I wrote you from last—our supply trains are all up, and why we don't move, is a mystery to small fry like myself.

I am anxious to penetrate as far as possible into the bowels of this land, find the enemy if he will stand, whip him if we can, and winding up this fall campaign, stop somewhere till the inevitable mud dries up, and so let me get to wife and baby—I am so glad Baby Mamie is well again. I was anxious about her for a while—she seemed to be getting so thin. Does she try to talk any, and has she learnt to make her Ma understand what she wants?

I'll warrant she has, and that her wants are neither few or feebly expressed. If she has her Pa's temper, as well as looks, she will not be slow to demand attention to her claims. I must have a new and good picture of you both, when you get some money.—if they are true we may be paid before we leave this camp. I would rather wait now two weeks longer & then we would have 6 months pay due—if they pay us now it will be for 4 months, & we should probably have to wait 4 mo's longer for another payment.

Yesterday I had a fine trip, 9 miles into the country, with the Regt, as guard to a forage train We started at daylight with 100 Gov't wagons—a great unwieldy train—made the 9 miles, loaded them all heavily with corn & fodder and got back to camp some time after dark. The day was delightful, and the whole trip, a complete success. The boys enjoy these excursions mightily, and indeed they are acceptable to officers as well—for we have a chance to forage for ourselves, as well as the horses & mules, & the opportunity is seldom lost I know our mess was the gainer this morning, by a fine shoat,[18] a sheep, and a quantity of sweet potatoes, the product of yesterday's excursion. They were paid for in Secesh money, of which there is any quantity—spurious & genuine—in the army. On this magnificent plantation, where we took so much corn, there is ten times as much left, and fully $20,000 worth of cotton, baled and ready for the market, and not a single white person on the place. The Negro cabins, 30 or 40 in number, are reasonably well filled with the poorer quality of this live stock—old men, women & children—but the white masters have deserted their fine mansion, taking their horses & mules, household furniture and the likeliest of Negroes. Today I understand we sent out & hauled in the cotton[19]—And this is the condition of all that part of Dixie, our army has passed thro'—We are met by finely-stocked plantations, deserted by their owners, and soon made a desert of in fact by the army. Truly the iron has entered into the soul of these people. We talk lightly & flippantly of the ravages & devastations of war, but no one who has not followed in the wake of an army or been part & parcel of it himself, can form any idea of what it means

Today, Col Eddy being Officer of the Day, I had the Regt. out on battalion drill. We had a fine plat of ground, & the afternoon being mild & pleasant & the boys in good health & spirits, I enjoyed showing off my Hoosiers, & "put them thro' their paces" in very lively time. Speaking of the weather, it seems hard to realize that you are having snow & ice & all the rigors of a Northern winter. With the exception of a few days, our weather has been very mild—I have not yet got an overcoat, partly because I could not find one to suit me, mostly in fact, because I have not seriously needed one. It is impossible to get any fine clothes, down here, & it would be folly to get them if it were possible I wear a pair of light blue cavalry pants, double-seated—such as Gov't furnishes the soldier, & I intend to get an overcoat of the same pattern—not double-seated I don't mean, but a cavalry overcoat. I wear my same old Captain's single breasted coat, & can't even get a pair of Major's straps to adorn the shoulders. I am only suffering for a pair of boots—the only pair of thick ones I have are the ones I started with from Goshen & none are to be had. Sutler's stocks soon run out on a march, & in fact they only carry tobacco, writing paper & a few indispensables of little weight

About the knit woollen cap. I have one that was given me last summer, by an officer going home, or you would have found that on my list. You don't know how much the contents of that little box add to my comfort. I am writing on the portfolio, seated in a chair (!) at the door of my tent, back to a huge log fire—for the nights are cool—candlestick formed of a stake in the ground, with a little iron piece on top, while Tommy sits on the end of the cot, mending & fixing, the pants aforesaid I enclose you a little scrap from the *"Times,"*[20] Geo. Copeland, editor,—it is pleasant to have friends and to have their kind wishes & it makes one anxious to try to be worthy of their expectations.

Well Tommy has waited a long time to put me to bed—for he never lets me go without tucking me up & making me as warm as even your good bed—but I would put cot & all on the fire in a minute at the prospect of exchanging it for that same bed—so I must bid you Goodnight a thousand miles away, trusting & hoping that the good God may soon bring us together again, and spare us from all harm till that good time shall come.

Your loving Husband
Edward

LETTER 30

Lafayette, Tenn.
Jan'y 2nd 1863

My dear wife,

I hardly recollect where I wrote you from last, but I think from the Yocona river, 5 miles south of Oxford, Miss

Since then, our travels have been many and devious. I have forgotten, too, the date of my last but since then, we marched ten miles south towards Grenada, Miss, but were suddenly stopped by the rebel raid into Holly Springs nearly fifty miles in our rear. The rebels destroyed here twenty days subsistence for our whole army, and then by cutting the R.Rd. 150 miles further up towards Columbus, KY, whence we [had] been getting all our supplies, necessitates a further falling back on our part.[21] Accordingly we took the back track, reaching Lumpkins Mills 7 miles south of H. Springs, on Christmas day.[22]

Our army at this time was in a bad fix—or at least seemed so—if the thousand and one rumors were to be credited—Price [*sic*, Pemberton] with the army we had been so gallantly chasing Gulfwards was now in turn closely pressing our rear.

Our supplies were cut off—we had on hand only ten days rations, and Bragg was reported to be in our front with 40,000 men.[23] One thing was evident, that supplies must be obtained at once, and the Mississippi river was the only channel of communication left open to us. An immense wagon train consisting of 1200 wagons was accordingly organized and our whole division, detailed as guard to go to Memphis 60 miles distant, for supplies. We started a week ago (Dec 26th), made the trip in three days, loaded in one, and returned to this point 30 miles, from Memphis last night. You can hardly understand all these journeyings without reference to the map. Here is a rough diagram.

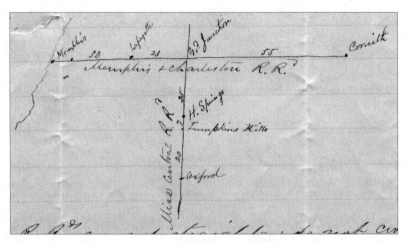

Wood's map of his troops' travels around Holly Springs, December 1862. Courtesy of the Indiana Historical Society.

Of course the R.Rds are not straight & do not cross each other so exactly at right angles, & the scale is not quite correct, but I think, if you regard the top of the plat North, you will have from the description, a pretty good idea of the directions & distances travelled in our Holiday march.

—xxxxx—Boonton Station, 5 miles east of Memphis Jan'y 3rd 1863. Just as I had got to the word diagram, on the other page, at precisely ¼ to 10, yesterday morning, orders came to march at 10 o'clock. Of course, slap went the portfolio & hurriedly my small kit was gathered together, tent struck horse saddled & mounted, and at 10 precisely the Regt took up its line of march towards Memphis again. We formed the rear guard of the Division train & were crowded through a distance of 23 miles by 9 at night. Men & horses completely tired out. This morning we moved forward 3 miles, & have gone into camp along the line of this R.Rd[24]—In fact our whole Division is scattered, a Regt in a place, all the way from Lafayette to Memphis, to guard this Road from the depredations of guerrillas who are unusually numerous & active in the section

Our Progress Is So Slow

The Regt itself is scattered over three miles of R.Rd—four Comps being encamped here at HdQrs, and three Comps a miles & a half in each direction. HdQuarters is magnificently located—we are actually in a house!—a poor negro cabin—but a house with three rooms & two fireplaces, so that we boast a bedroom, office & kitchen, and are living in fine style. Mind you, this splendid arrangement commenced at noon today, & is liable to terminate before noon tomorrow, but we have learned the soldier's philosophy & perhaps the true philosophy of life to make the most of present comforts & bear any fortune uncomplainingly

But it really looks as if this was to be our winter's occupation, and these our winter quarters. Acting upon this supposition, my application for a leave of absence will go in tomorrow. I am not very sanguine of its success, for I cannot plead sickness & most other grounds are ignored. I place my principal reliance upon the kind offices of my Col. & Brigade commander[25]—both of whom I think will do all they can for me. If the application passes the Divn commander approved, I think Genl Grant will not hesitate to endorse it. It will take some time to get the paper thro' the hands of all these functionaries, & you must be patient & don't look for me, till you hear I am on the road. I will try to give you notice—Our recent disaster at Vicksburg[26] may change the whole plan of operations in this Department & we may not have any winter quarters at all. The rainy season unusually late this year, appears to have just set in—we have had two days of incessant pouring rains & if they continue for a few days more, the roads must be impassable. It may be in anticipation of such a result that this disposition of our Divn has been made.

At Memphis, a longstanding order against trunks was rigidly enforced, & so I packed my most necessary articles in a valise & shipped the trunk to you by Adams Express. I enclose you the receipt. You need not present it or call for the trunk until you get some money to pay the charges. We are promised to be paid off at once, & now we are settled, I see nothing to prevent it. I had not a moment's time at Memphis to write a line. I hope you won't hear of the trunk before you get this.

We have had no mail since the rebels cut off communication about the 20th of Dec, so I am without later dates from you than the 7th ult. I have no doubt you have written, and hope you and Pet are still well. I know you felt gloomy when Christmas & New years came & went & still no Papa. I thought of you constantly all that week, and my longing to be with you, was only equaled by your own to have me there—I have just re-read your long good letter of the 7th ult. to see if I have omitted to answer any questions, for I find I am apt to be careless in that way—but I believe not this time—I am glad Geo. Ferriss is doing well—of course then Mary is happy & *well*—for I know not only her happiness but health depends upon his good conduct & prosperity.

Don't begin to expect me, Jeanie, for a month—it takes so long for these papers to go thro' all the official channels & return again, that I shall hardly expect to get my application back under two or three weeks & then too you know, it may be refused, so don't allow yourself to be too confident. I have written you fully just what I hope & expect, but you know we are disappointed before & something may occur again to thwart all our hopes.

Write often, dearest, & direct to Memphis, Quinby's Divn Good night & God bless you & and darling one is the prayer of

Your Husband Edward

CHAPTER 6

Disappointed, Sick, and Disgusted

Sick in Memphis, February–April 1863

Sometime in January or early February 1863 Wood's health deserted him. He languished in an officers' hospital in Memphis, suffering from a combination of flu, toothache, and a painful nerve disorder. His increasing eagerness to see his wife and child was requited in March 1863, when he received a medical leave. Departing Memphis he traveled north. Where and for how long he visited with his family is not clear. Soon enough he was back in Memphis, but still laid low by sickness. A long convalescence in an officers' hospital in that city made him restive and irritable. "How many vain regrets I have indulged in that I did not stay with you these long sick days!" he complained. "And everyone says how stupid!—to go home on a sick leave, & come back to stay in a hospital without having the leave renewed." Wood contemplated leaving the regiment for the Invalid Corps, or held out hope that consolidation of depleted regiments would make the 48th redundant.

While Wood was an invalid in Memphis, the 48th Indiana went down the Mississippi River to Grant's army north of Vicksburg in February. The Union general had been frustrated by both Rebel defenses and nature in his efforts to effect an assault on the fortress guarding the river. The regiment participated in the Yazoo Pass expedition, whereby troops and shallow draft steamboats under Major General William T. Sherman and Rear Admiral David Dixon Porter attempted to approach Vicksburg along the winding, narrow, and overgrown rivers north of the city. The force made excruciatingly slow progress through the maze of swamps and streams. However, the tree stumps, overhanging limbs, narrow channels, and harassment by Rebel forces halted the effort, and the expedition in early April retraced its painstaking way through the bayous back to open water.[1] Shortly thereafter the regiment crossed the Mississippi and went into camp at Milliken's Bend, Louisiana, where Wood was to rejoin them.

LETTER 31

My dearest Jeanie,

I hardly know what or how to write. I am so disappointed, sick and disgusted, and I have so long confidently hoped to send the good news that I was coming home, when I did write, that I know you must be alarmed at my long silence—And in truth I have been sick, not dangerously or seriously, but so as to unfit me for all duty, and I could not bear to write when I was feeling so ill. I thought it would alarm you more than no message at all, & I was in hopes with my recovery, would come the long looked for leave of abscense—but about a week ago, my papers came back from Division Head Quarters having lain there all this time, returned for a slight clerical informality. I had inquired for them there, was told they had been forwarded to Genl. Hamilton at Army Corps HdQrs—had been there for them—but they knew nothing about them, supposed they had been forwarded to Gen. Grant, and now to have them turn up, all this time been stuck away in some pigeon-hole at Division HdQrs for a mere clerical error, that a dash of the pen would have altered is too shameful, too outrageous.

I think I spoke my mind in very emphatic language, when I found out the facts, in the presence of the General & staff, & I was advised to make the application again. I have done so, this time based on a Medical Certificate, but just at this juncture I doubt whether it would succeed better than the other.

I would not have made an application now, if I had not felt so strong & insulted at the treatment the other received. It certainly requires no little patience to continue in a service where everything seems to be done to make it as disagreeable as possible. But a truce to grumbling—I don't think I often do it—but when I do see you, I am going to take a regular scold at all these vexatious things.

Your letter mailed the 7th inst. was duly received about a week since, & I have thought every day I would answer it, & have made one or two attempts, but I have really been quite miserable, & they all proved failures. I have had the old diarrhoea, with a low grade of fever that threatened to be typhoid, but by good care & treatment, that was happily avoided. I am feeling much better today, the fever has left me, & the discharges are less frequent & painful & I hope to be entirely well in a few days—but oh! You don't know how homesick I am I think the sight of wifey & baby, would do me a *"powerful sight"* of good. Col. Eddy is very sanguine that my second application will succeed but I am not going to let myself think so, until it comes back granted. Let us live in hopes!

I am so sorry you have suffered so with the toothache—I can truly sympathize with you—My attack commenced with toothache & neuralgia[2] in the face—I had the tooth out, but it didn't relieve the pain Your teeth need

Disappointed, Sick, and Disgusted

attending to very badly. I am ashamed that I have not been able to send you the money to have it done, but indeed it is not my fault. The government yet owes me for six months services—we were paid for two months only last Sunday—just think, we have not had any pay since last July, and for officers it is worse even than for the men, they have to board & clothe themselves, and as I sent home most of what I received before, I was in debt for most of my living, & many of my recent expenses, such as for horses, Major's coat etc. I have been unable to pay. I send you by Adams Express $100 I wish it was more, but must try to do the best you can with it for the present. If I should happen to get the leave, I should have to borrow money to get away on to Indianapolis at least, where I could doubtless get the balance of my pay.

Everybody thinks an officers pay is high, but when you take the extravagantly high prices he has to pay for everything, & his really necessary expenses, one sees that there can't be much saved.[3] I thought I would send this amount at once (for I know you much needed it) rather than to wait for the uncertain chance of taking it with me. You must have two pictures taken too & send them I can't wait a minute. I had a letter from Willie some days ago, and poor boy, he wants a dozen of my card photographs! to *circulate among his friends* He has improved in his writing, is living at a better place & seems contented. As soon as I can get a picture taken, I am going to write him & send him one.

Now my darling girl, don't worry because your boy has been a little under the weather—it is most remarkable that, I have escaped so well before, & really I am feeling quite well again. I will write you again in a few days, as I continue to improve, so that you need not feel anxious about me

I hope you and our darling Mamie continue well. God bless you both! won't we have a gay time when Papa comes home! I haven't time to tell you anything of our situation or prospects, but will write again soon.

You must have seen that my pen is a shocking one, & being a little weak & "*narvy*" myself, I am afraid this will prove hard to decipher

Good night dear one, write soon & often & hope with me, as strong as you dare hope, soon to see

Your devoted husband

Edward.

LETTER 32

Memphis, Tenn.
March 25th, 1863

My dear wife,

I reached here safely this morning about daylight, and shall go on down the river today or tomorrow. The Reg't is down the Yazoo Pass,[4] as I supposed, and communication is very uncertain and irregular. Indeed some of the officers who are here sick in Hospital say that there has not been a mail from the Regt since they went down the Pass on the 12th inst.

I found on reaching Indianapolis Saturday night, that I could not make connections thru to Cairo the next day, so I laid over there till Monday morning, arrived at Cairo Tuesday morn, & here this (Wednesday) morning.

I am not feeling very well, but I attribute it to the fatigue of the journey and hope soon to feel entirely well. I am stopping with four of our officers in the Convalescent Officers Hospital. They are very comfortably situated and it is much pleasanter and better fare than at the Hotels. I feel very much inclined to stay here a few days and get rested and doctored up, but then I am so anxious to get to the Reg't that I suppose I shall take the first boat down. The prospect is not an agreable one—you can't get a boat from here farther than Helena, Ark—a most miserable hole, & there you must wait and take your chances for a boat down the Pass. Since writing this I have picked up the Memphis Bulletin[5] for this morning & read that the Yazoo Pass expedition has been abandoned, and the troops returned to the Mississippi—but there are always so many unreliable rumors from below, that it is difficult to tell what to believe. I don't hardly credit the rumor, & expect to find the Regt as I have written.

I hope you did not feel as utterly desolate as I did in my long & lonesome ride to Cairo. I did not think it would be so hard to leave my dear ones again, & indeed I would not let myself think of it, till the bitter fact of separation forced the unwelcome conviction upon me that I was leaving a part of my own being behind me, and parting from those dearer than life itself.

I hear rumors of Regiments being consolidated—if this is done, many officers will be dispensed with, & I certainly shall try to be one of the number. I don't feel as if I could live away from you, & I know it is even more of a sacrifice for you to live so unsatisfactorily.

Milo[6] was quite unwell, suffering from cold etc He claimed one of my photographs & the boys here have taken four more, so you see they are apt to be gone soon. I found my pistol at Ind—$30 saved there—Miss Hudson is in this Hospital was just in to see me—most of the other nurses have gone back.[7] You must excuse this short letter my head is very thick, & I'm not very well myself.

Oh I went to the Express office & found where the trunk had been shipped on the 2nd Jan'y to Cincinnatti—the Agent promised to write & hunt it up.

Give all my love to all and Kiss papa's darling for him—does she miss him, I wonder? I think you had better get a dozen more photographs & send me what you do not want of them Good bye & God bless & protect you, my darling.

Your Husband Edward.

LETTER 33

Officer's Hospital
Memphis, Tenn. April 2nd 1863.

My dear wife,

I hardly thought when I wrote you on my arrival, that a week later, would still find me here. But so it is. I was unable to get a boat to the Regiment for several days, and when the opportunity offered I was really feeling too sick to go—so I thought I had better stay here awhile & try to get thoroughly well before I joined the Regiment. You know I was complaining of my head before I left home, especially at night. I don't think I ever suffered such pain, as I have every night for a week with my head & face. It is something on the neuralgia order, the Dr calls it *"tic doloreux"*[8]—it certainly is most *dolorous*, & whether to be had on *tick* or not, is a dear bargain. My old trouble has returned too, *in force,* and altogether I have been a poor miserable homesick body for the last week. Not the least of my grievances has been the impossibility of hearing from you. I know you would direct to the Reg't & I had no thought of being here so long when I wrote you. I suppose my only chance of hearing from you will be to get to my post as soon as possible. How many vain regrets I have indulged in that I did not stay with you these long sick days! And everybody says how stupid!—to go home on a sick leave, & come back to stay in hospital without having the leave renewed. It is provoking, but I don't see how it could have been avoided, and the only true philosophy now is to make the best of it.

I wonder often how you are getting on in your snug quarters, & how your plans for the future are shaping themselves, as time rolls along—for I think that *Time* the great disposer of things great & small, was to be left pretty much undisturbed, to determine for you all, what should be your situation for the Summer. I hope you won't leave the old home & I hardly think you will. If Henry & Myra go to housekeeping, you will doubtless make some arrangement that will be satisfactory to the remaining inmates. I am so anxious to hear how the matter is arranged. Let me know if there is any approach to a solution of the difficulty—The Dr thinks I had better not go to the Regt for a week or more yet, & I may possibly get a letter from you after this is rec'd, if you write at once, before I go down the river, at any rate, it would be forwarded to me if I am gone & it would be but little delayed.

I have had a suggestion made to me, that I might get on detached service at this post, if I desired it, but I hardly know what to think about it. It would be much pleasanter in many respects, but it would hardly be treating the old Colonel & the Regt right. If he was here & I could get his acquiescence, I should prefer to stay. The service would be as Deputy Provost Marshal—the Provost Marshal being a Colonel.[9]

I had a call this week from the Goshen ladies who are in the other hospitals here—there were eight in all, including those belonging here. I showed them my pictures & they all thought Mamie's was excellent. I am sorry we didn't have some photographs from it as you first proposed. How is the dear child & did she miss papa? Oh dear, it's weary work being away from wife & baby. I am more discontented I believe than before I went home. It will require a fresh installment of patriotism to keep me away from them many months longer. Don't worry about me, Jeanie. I am doing well here & now that I am under the Dr.'s care, I don't mean to leave him until he pronounces me fit.

Write soon, direct to Officers Hospital Memphis, Tenn, leaving off the Regt. & everything else. Remember me kindly to all. Kiss baby a thousand times for Papa and believe me

Your loving Husband

Edward

LETTER 34

Officer Hospital
Memphis Tenn. April 10th, 1863

My dear wife,

As you see by the date I am still in the Hospital, very much as I was when I wrote you last week, except that my complaints have been increased by the addition of a very severe cold, which the Dr. called old fashioned influenza—said complaint being among the most prevalent of the Memphis spring fashions, just at this writing. I hope it will mend so I can speak loud in a few days as I am anxious to get to the Regt. We have heard from them today for the first time in more than a week. After almost unheard of difficulties, with all the boats badly torn & broken up, the expedition has succeeded in returning to the Mississippi, and the Yazoo Pass route to the rear of Vicksburgh has been definitely abandoned.[10] Our Division is lying four miles below Helena Ark, which is 85 miles from here, so that it would be comparatively easy to join them now, & I should start to-day, but for my aggravated cold and sore throat.

I am greatly annoyed at this long enforced absence from the Regiment—the most so that communication has been impossible with them since I came here. I made two attempts to send the Medical Certificate of my disability for service, to the Regt, both of which were unsuccessful, and I suppose they have not heard from me since I left. Under these circumstances, I apprehend some trouble when I return—a Court of Inquiry & all that sort of thing, which will be annoying, if of no more serious consequence. You may imagine I haven't spent a delightful time here. I have worried over the necessity that kept me here, & the probable unpleasant consequences of it, and because

I haven't heard from you & a thousand minor inconveniences, until I believe I have become the most irritable, uncomfortable body in the world.[11]

Well, well. Patience is certainly a divine attribute & I don't know as we poor creatures are to be expected to have a large allowance of it. I do try to be patient, but it does seem as if just at present, I was having more than my share of aggravations—in perfect health, they would not seem so heavy probably, but as it is they have tried my temper sorely.

This is Friday—& it's three weeks ago today since I left you and no word from you yet. You must write me fully, whether you & the baby are perfectly well, & how your plans for the summer have been settled. I think I shall go down to the Regt the first of the week—say Tuesday or Wednesday. I do hope I may get a letter from you before I go.

I am unable yet to hear anything from the trunk, beyond that it was shipped from here Jan'y 2nd to Cincinnatti, & I haven't heard anything from the $300 I sent to Tiffany & Co. for a sword for the Col. on the 28th Feb'y nor has the box containing the articles come to hand.[12] I think they must be very careless with their Express matter down here—The weather is oppressively warm, and the shop windows & streets are gay with the most gauzy of summer fabrics I haven't changed my underclothing yet—partly on account of my cold, & partly because I wanted to have the benefit of the change when I went further south

You must excuse this short letter Jeanie, I am far from feeling in the mood, but I know you will feel easier to get this poor scrawl than nothing at all. I will write you again from here, just before I go down the river. I think you had better not direct more than one letter to the Hospital as I am quite certain in another week, I shall be with the Regiment.

Give my love to all the family. Kiss the darling one for Papa, and tell her she must be a good girl for her Mama, & then by and by Papa will come home, and love his dear little girl *so much!* Write often Jeanie, and tell me just exactly how you are getting along & I will try and write once a week whether I hear from you or not. Good bye, dearest. God bless & keep you & our darling child from all harm

Your Husband

Edward

LETTER 35

Officers Hospital
Memphis Tenn. April 21st 1863

My dear wife,

Your dear welcome letter was received day before yesterday and you may be sure I was glad to hear from you & to learn that you and the baby were well. I had been worrying about you for several days—more because

I had not heard from you since leaving home, and when the Steward came in with the letters Saturday afternoon & none for me, I was greatly disappointed, & as agreeably surprised when he made the rounds again, & gave me the welcome letter, which he had overlooked the first time

I am sorry you are not settled yet in your plans for the future. I was in hopes to hear that you were settled before I left here as communication will doubtless be very uncertain below—I am feeling very well again, and shall leave for the Regiment today. I had no idea of it, when I commenced writing, but a good opportunity offers to go on the Division Quartermaster's boat that will take us direct to the Regt, & so a number of convalescents from the Hospital are going down.

I am very much better than when I came here, and indeed with the exception of the remnant of a severe cold am feeling very well.

We are taking such a sudden start that I haven't time to write at all. I have a great deal to do to get ready—Transportation to be got, & I want to take down some Mess stores—they must be bought & permits got for shipping them etc, etc, so it will take me a good half day to get ready. Our Regt. is at Milliken's Bend, La, 14 miles above Vicksburgh—I suppose we shall reach them in two or three days, & then I will write you again.[13] My dear, you don't know how much good your long encouraging letter did me. Do write often and as much as you can—You must keep up a good brave heart, and trust in God, that all things will work together for our good.

Remember me to all kindly. Kiss our darling precious one—tell her she must be good to her Mama & comfort her a heap till Papa comes home. The two photographs were rec'd I suppose the others are at the Regiment—I have only the two you sent me left, & haven't got to the Regt yet. I expect I shall have to have some more—Goodbye my dearest. God bless & keep you and our darling from all harm is the prayer of

Your Husband—Edward

CHAPTER 7

They Have Seen Nothing Like It

The Vicksburg Campaign, April–July 1863

The campaign to capture Vicksburg was the most significant campaign of the war. It required the boldest generalship in the war and an unrelenting pressure on the Confederate defenders to succeed. Grant's efforts as Federal commander were sometimes wrongheaded, sometimes brilliant. At all times his army performed their tasks with alacrity and fortitude.

After the war Grant wrote in his *Memoirs*, "I had in contemplation the whole winter the movement by land to a point below Vicksburg from which to operate." The critical element was transportation across the Mississippi River. He informed Admiral David Dixon Porter of his idea, and "Porter fell in with the plan at once."[1] The plan necessitated running riverboats past the Rebels' guns overlooking the Mississippi at Vicksburg. The plan was enacted on the night of April 16, when a line of gunboats with army transport steamers fortified with cotton bales and loaded barges lashed to their sides steamed past guns. One transport was sunk, another severely damaged by the fire from the city's batteries, but the return fire from the gunboats impaired Rebel accuracy and allowed the other boats passage.[2] Once the boats were south of the city and its guns, troops from Grant's army marched south on the Louisiana (west) side of the river past Vicksburg to a point about twenty miles south of the city. On April 30, Union troops began to be ferried by the gunboats and transports across the Mississippi to the east side, and marched to Port Gibson where they repulsed Rebel forces.[3]

Wood's letters recounting the battles before Vicksburg are the climax of his Civil War writings. The driving spirit of Grant's army is apparent in each letter, and is nowhere surpassed than in his letter, number 39, of May 25. In the letter, Wood described in detail and stirring language the marches from the river crossing to south and east of Vicksburg; the battles of Raymond, Jackson, Champion Hill; and the frontal assault on the fortress works of May 22.

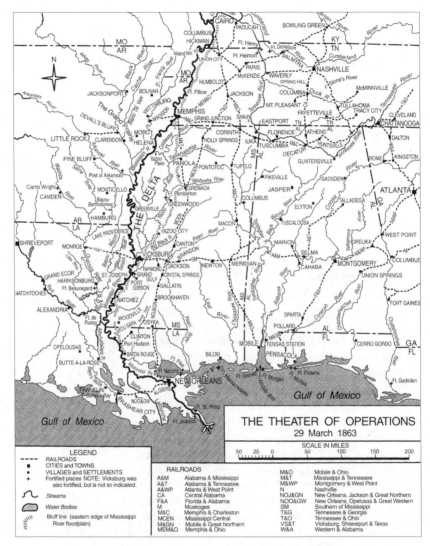

Theater of operations, Vicksburg, March 29, 1863. From Warren Grabau, Ninety-Eight Days: A Geographer's View of the Vicksburg Campaign *(Knoxville, 2000).*

LETTER 36

Milliken's Bend, La.
April 25th 1863.

My dear wife,

I arrived here yesterday and found the Regiment had left for Carthage, La,[4] some 30 miles distant, and about 15 miles below Vicksburg. I shall follow today and hope to catch up with them tomorrow.

I found much to my surprise that Lt. Col. Rugg had resigned and was about to start North as I got here—He has never entirely recovered from the effects of a wound received at Iuka in Sept. last, and latterly he has been so much worse that he felt compelled to resign.[5] I am very sorry to part with him, he was the most of a military man of any officer in the Regt, and we had all learned to rely greatly upon him. I suppose if everything goes right with me, I shall be promoted to fill the vacancy caused by his resignation.

I can't tell you anything of the prospect of things here—The new movement of troops to the south of Vicksburgh, looks as if it might be intended to cross the river at some point below to attack the stronghold from the south, but this is all conjecture.[6] My health continues good, with the exception of my cold, and that is improving.

I have only time to write these few lines as I am about to start with a wagon train which is waiting for me, while I write this. I send this North by Mr. Strong, our Sutler, as you will probably get it, about as soon as the one I wrote on the 21st from Memphis just before starting—I will write every opportunity that offers, & if you should not hear from me so regularly now that I am so far away down here, you must keep up a good heart, and try to think that all is well with your boy.

Write often—direct to Quinby's Divn,[7] near Vicksburgh—& be sure I shall write as often as possible. Give my love to all, and tell papa's little girl that she must think often of her dear papa, who is coming home to his darlings as soon as ever he can.

Goodbye dearest God bless you
Your Husband

Edward

LETTER 37

Black River, Miss.
22 miles from Vicksburg.
May 4th 1863.

My dear wife

I wrote you a hurried line from Milliken's Bend, just as I was starting to overtake the Regt. I came up with it on the march at about 9 o'clock that night, and took them by surprise. We continued our march every day thereafter on the Louisiana side till we reached a point 55 miles below Milliken's

Bend, and a few miles below Grand Gulf, Miss, a strongly fortified bluff on the opposite side, where we crossed the Mississippi by means of the gunboats & transports that had run the blockade.

You will doubtless see in the papers full accounts of the success of the enterprise. We crossed the river on the 1st and advanced rapidly into the country, striking for Port Gibson—but Genl McClernand's forces were in front of us, and after engaging the enemy severely all day forced him to retire, and took possession of the town on the night of the 1st.[8] We came up by noon of the next day, and advanced some 8 miles beyond the town, the enemy retiring slowly before us and occasionally stopping to throw shell at our advancing column—

Yesterday morning, soon after crossing the Little Black River,[9] over an iron suspension bridge, which the rebels had made ineffectual attempts to destroy, we were met by a furious fire of shot & shell, which made it seem probable that the rebels were determined to make a stand. We were delayed some two hours getting artillery in position & forming lines of battle, when it turned out that the enemy had left. About 3 miles further on the same thing was repeated, delaying us all the afternoon Our Regt was formed in line in an open field, & the enemy's shell burst over our heads, and struck all around us but fortunately none of us were injured—We pursued them as they retired, and chased them to the other side of Black River, where they are now in strong force.[10] This movement of ours compelled the rebels to evacuate Grand Gulf, which was the key to this river. Our gunboats can now come up here in the rear of Vicksburg & this river will probably be the base of our operations—But you will probably see much more of all this in the papers than I know. Our march of 90 odd miles has been a hard one—The weather has been extremely hot like our July, and the season seemed full as much advanced. We traveled for three days on the Louisiana side thro' the richest and most delightful country I ever saw. The road followed the course of a broad, swift bayou, abounding in excellent fish, and on the banks of which was a succession of broad rich plantations, upon which were most magnificent grounds and palatial residences. One of them I was told cost a quarter of a million of dollars! All of these fine residences were deserted by their owners, and I am sorry to say many of them were pillaged and the fine furniture, magnificent pier [?] glasses, pianos etc destroyed by our soldiers We have had no transportation with us since we were three days out, & consequently have no baggage, tents or in fact anything but blankets strapped to the saddle with us. My health has been pretty good, but I can't get rid of my obstinate cold & cough. I found two letters from you at the Regt, but both of older date than the one I got at the Hospital—the photographs came safely—I am very anxious to hear from you, as your last date is a month ago—but we have had no mail since leaving on this expedition. Don't fail to

They Have Seen Nothing Like It

write often. I do hope that you and Mamie continue well—I certainly think that if I am spared thro' this Vicksburgh campaign I shall resign & come home. By a recent order, Regts that are reduced below 520 are consolidated into five companies each, the Col & Major are mustered out of the service and the battalion left in command of the Lt. Col. I have asked the Col not to forward my recommendation for Lt. Col. for the present, in hopes to get the benefit of the muster out as Major

But we cant tell what the events of the next few months may be—we can only hope for the best—Kiss the dear one for papa—what a comfort she must be to you, and how I miss the sweet comfort of both of you I carry my album with me & it is a consolation. Remember me to all & believe me, my dearest

Your devoted Husband
Edward

LETTER 38

Camp on Big Black River, Miss.
May 8th 1863.

My dear wife

I wrote you a hurried pencil scrawl on the 4th I think, and on the 6th I received your dear long letter of the 19th ult. It was an unexpected treat, for I had hardly thought we should have a mail over the circuitous route we had travelled—but you may be sure it was none the less welcome. I am so glad you and Marie are well, and that you preserve such an equable & hopeful spirit, amidst all your trials & difficulties.

I don't wonder, my dear girl, that you should sometimes feel *blue,* but I know you have too much native strength of mind, assisted by true Christian faith to give way to feelings of despondency. God rules over all, and however hard and dark His ways may seem, He means that we should walk in them for His purposes, and for our own good. I hope before this you are pleasantly situated, where you will feel at home, and that thus one great source of annoyance to you will have been disposed of. It must have been hard indeed for you to give up the old homestead—it seems harder still for a man at father's time of life to sell his old home, and commence struggling with the world again—but perhaps it will all turn out for the best

Well, we are in the heart of Dixie, at last preparing for the grand assault upon the stronghold of Vicksburg and I think with a fair prospect of success. All the canal digging, passes & cutoffs by which it has been attempted for six months past to get in the rear of Vicksburgh have been abandoned, and the whole of Grant's army is being rapidly concentrated near this point by the route we came. There must be at least 80,000 men within a circle of a few miles here and more coming Owing to the limited means of crossing

the Mississippi—only a few gunboats and three or four transports that succeeded in running the batteries—the operation of crossing so large a force
is necessarily a slow one, and as men, artillery & ammunition are the most
essential for offensive operations, everything else has been left behind as of
secondary importance. Even rations have not been brought and for the last
week we have subsisted almost entirely on the country. Corn meal & fresh
meat, beef, pork & mutton have furnished our living, and pretty scant it has
been at that.[11] And yet our men do not complain—they are elated with the
successes that attended the landing on this side, the enemy have fallen back
before them, and they are eager to push forward to new victories. The temper of the army is admirable—officers from the Potomac say they have seen
nothing like it—They aver that it would have been impossible to have moved
the army of the Potomac as we have moved, a 100 miles crossed the largest
river of the continent, and without an ounce of baggage or rations, except
what the men have carried on their backs. Officers & men have alike slept
on the ground, with a single blanket & often none at all, and have marched
thro' a burning sun—the men carrying 100 rounds of cartridges besides
their guns & blankets—often 20 & 25 miles a day. The general health of the
army is excellent—I was much surprised to find the men looking so well,
after their severe trip down the Yazoo Pass—that was an infliction I was
very fortunate to escape—with a few days rest here, my health has much
improved—my cough is much easier, & I am in hopes soon to be rid of it. We
shall probably move 12 miles further up the river tomorrow, if our supplies
come up tonight as is expected—how long we shall remain in this vicinity
or when Gen. Grant will be ready to strike the decisive blow, of course it is
impossible to say.

I do not think however it can be long delayed, our route for supplies
from Milliken's Bend La, 15 miles above Vicksburg, is so long and can be so
easily cut, that I think it would be hazardous to remain here long, & then
it is so desirable to have the campaign wound up before extreme warm
weather, that it seems as if there would be as little delay as possible.

The letter you enclosed from Gus Crane, stated my trunk was at Goshen,
& wanted to know what to do with it. I have written to him to ship it to you
at Syracuse—so in the course of two or three months more it may reach you.
I expect the charges on it will be exorbitant—but as it has been through the
fault of the Express Co. that most of them have accrued I would not pay
more than the regular charges from Memphis to Syracuse.

I am glad there is a prospect of James' coming home.[12] I know Nell will
be so much better satisfied and he is so kind & good, it will be pleasanter
for you I expect from what you wrote that you will probably board with
Mrs. Van Vleck. I think it the best arrangement you could make, under the
circumstances—though I think perhaps you might have felt more indepen-

dent if you could have found a good place with entire strangers. You must try & be patient, my dear girl, till pa comes home, and will try again to have a little place to ourselves—won't that be nice? If my health keeps good & I am spared I think sometimes I would like to stay in the service until fall, to accumulate a few hundred dollars, after paying all debts, & then again when I feel sick in body & mind, I want to quit it right away & go home to my wife & baby. Time must alone determine what I shall do—if I am appointed Lt. Col. and the Col and Major are both mustered out, I would be left in command of the five companies—a very nice place—Do you think I had better accept the promotion?—the Col urges it on me—says he should feel easier at leaving the Regt in my hands etc, etc, but I have as yet refused to let him send forward my nomination. I want to try the effect of a month's campaigning on my health & abide the result of this impending battle— Well, my sheet is full—you must write often whether you hear from me or not—your letters do me a great deal of good. Take good care of yourself and our darling and may God keep you in this merciful keeping is the prayer of your Husband,

Edward

LETTER 39

In the rear of Vicksburgh, Miss
May 25th 1863

My dear wife

I know you will be waiting with intense anxiety for a word from your boy, long before this reaches you, but you will readily understand from the nature of our recent operations in this section, that communication with the North has been impossible. We have penetrated 100 miles into the enemy's country, leaving our rear and communication with the river unregarded, have subsisted for three weeks entirely upon the country, have made forced marches on *short* & on *no* rations, in five days from the 12th to the 16th inclusive, we fought three pitched battles, marching fifty miles, capturing Jackson, the State Capitol, more than fifty pieces of artillery, and over five thousand prisoners. I know that in the light of history, these achievements will be regarded as only preliminary to the grand struggle for the capture of Vicksburg, but to the actors they have been real victories in themselves, as well as important in the results to which we confidently expect they will lead.

I wrote you on the 7th I think from the Big Black river we moved in a few days in an easterly direction towards Jackson, and on the 12th near Raymond, Gen. Logan's division of our Corps[13] met the enemy strongly posted, 10,000 strong, & with several batteries in commanding positions. The engagement commenced about noon and lasted till sundown, the enemy retreating slowly to new positions for three miles. Our division was ordered up about 3 o'clock, and tho' not actively engaged was exposed to a severe fire of shell & grape, in which our Regt lost 2 killed & several wounded. Gen Logan's division is entitled to the credit of the day, although our arrival on the field at a time when he was closely pressed, was extremely opportune, & contributed to the success. The enemy lost in killed wounded & taken prisoners about 1500, while our loss was less than 500.[14] The next day we pressed on, striking the R.Rd between Vicksburg & Jackson at Clinton, 9 miles west of Jackson. We expected to meet the enemy before reaching the R.Rd, which we did not think they would surrender without a severe struggle. Meeting no opposition, however, we moved at an early hour of the next day, the 14th, from Clinton towards Jackson our Division being in front, & our Regt being the second Regt of the Division. About 9 o'clock & when within 4 miles of Jackson, the skirmishers of the 59th Ind—the leading Reg't met the enemy's pickets, & drove them a mile or so, to where their main force was posted. The skirmishers returned to their Reg't, and under one of the most drenching thunder storms I ever saw, our (1st) Brigade filed out of the road and formed line of battle, the 59th Ind being the extreme right of the line & the 48th next—the 2nd Brigade formed across the road, and the 3rd on the left. We formed in all a line three quarters of a mile long, stretching across the road from right to left, through newly ploughed cornfields heavy with recent rains, but with a gently undulating surface that afforded excellent protection from the shower of grape & canister which they poured at us, when we attempted to advance. We would advance slowly to the crest of a ridge, double-quick it into the valley, lie down & rest & then slowly climb the next hill. In this way, we had advanced to within less than a quarter of a mile of their batteries, without firing a gun, & with little loss from their fire, when the order was given to "fix bayonet," and advance the whole line at double quick. You should have heard the Hoosier *yell*, started on the right and taken up along the whole line, as our boys came out in full view of the enemy, with colors proudly flying, and seen the eagerness & steady determination, with which they rushed upon the enemy, under a most galling fire of musketry & grape at short range. Many a brave fellow bit the dust, but the line maintained an unbroken front of glittering steel, and before we had fairly opened fire, the dismayed rebels were fleeing in every direction and two batteries of eleven pieces were in our possession—To the Hoosier regiments, the 59th & 48th Ind, belong the exclusive glory of this last achievement. The charge was a most brilliant affair, and those who saw it in the distance describe it as grand in the extreme I only know it was glorious to be in it—every other sense & feeling was absorbed in the excitement of the onset & the glory of the result. Our artillery was rapidly brought to the front & played upon the retiring rebels, now thoroughly scattered through the fields & woods. We were still two miles from the city, so we advanced cau-

They Have Seen Nothing Like It

tiously through the country, in line of battle until we came within sight of their breastworks, with rows of guns mounted in position. We were expecting the fight to be renewed, when citizens came out with the white flag, offering to surrender the place, the enemy's troops having incontinently fled thro' the city![15]

We marched into the town about 3 P.M.—the 59th leading & the 48th next & the colors of the 59th were the first raised from the dome of the State Capitol—We stayed in town only overnight—in fact I scarcely saw the place, but I was told that with the exception of the Capitol & a few other fine public buildings it was a place of very insignificant appearance.

On the 15th, we started westward for Vicksburg, passing thro' Clinton and about 4 miles beyond that day[16]—On the 16th when but a few miles on the road, the now familiar sound of cannon greeted our ears—we were not looking for a fight so soon again, but it seemed as tho' we were in for it every other day, and as we slowly marched towards the scene of conflict, or were halted by the roadside by some of the many delays that always occur in moving a large column of troops from the highway to position in battle, it soon became evident that the work before us was no holiday employment. Two divisions, Gen's Hovey's[17] & Logan's, were hotly engaged before we came up, and our division was formed as a reserve—The 1st Brigade was posted on the extreme right, but we had hardly got position, when the word came that Gen Hovey was being sorely pressed, and that the left was giving way, & we were ordered at a double quick a mile or more, over hills & through ploughed fields to his support. It was now just past midday and the heat was extreme—some of our men dropped from sheer exhaustion & more from rebel bullets, before we went into the woods where the fire was hot. The ground was extremely broken & covered with a dense undergrowth that made it in places, almost impassable. I dismounted before going into the woods, & gave my horse to my boy to be kept just outside in a hollow under shelter We were fortunate in forming our Regt. partially in a ravine that afforded some protection and for three hours we held that position, under a hotter fire than I had ever before seen. When we were ordered into the fight, the emergency was so great, and fresh troops were so badly needed along the whole line, that our Brigade was split up, and each Regt went into action on its own hook. We did not know what troops were on our right or left, and after we had been engaged something over two hours, and Col Eddy saw the line on our left giving way, & the Regt falling back, he sent me to Col Sanborn, our Brigade Commdr, to inform him of it, and to ask for reinforcements. I went out of the woods, but could not find my horse, so I made my way on foot as quickly as possible a full half mile to Col S. & returned, but before I could get back the Regt, having expended their ammunition, had fallen back into the fields & formed behind the crest of a hill The rebels did not follow out of the woods, for they were being driven on the right and extreme left and soon the rout became general.[18] We had taken more or less prisoners all day, but now they began to pour in, till they numbered over 2000. The contest had lasted from 9 o'clock in the morning until sundown and for 3 or 4 hours in the afternoon had raged with great fury, the rebels sometimes gaining ground on us, and then being pressed back, obstinately contesting every inch of ground, and as night fell and our victorious hosts passed over the battle field, after the vanquished foe the ground thickly strewn with dead & dying, revealed the terrible nature of the struggle. I did not go over the battlefield only where my duty called me, as I have no penchant for such horrors. I was told that I did not see the worst portions of it, but I saw enough, & the recollection of which will suffice to send a chill thro' me to my latest day. The loss of the enemy was estimated at over 1,000 killed on the field & several thousand wounded—our own loss was very heavy but the proportion of killed was much less, owing to the fact that many of our wounded were from buckshot. We marched three or four miles beyond the battlefield, called since Champion Hills,[19] & bivouacked for the night. Two fresh divisions of ours, Osterhaus'[20] & Carr's,[21] however, pushed on closely up to the rebels, who made for the Big Black river, where they had strong entrenchments. Early in the morning (Sunday the 17th) cannonading commenced furiously and we were expecting a repetition of the day before, but fortunately the rebs. were so disheartened & demoralized by their previous defeat, that they made but feeble resistance, and our forces drove them from their works, taking 17 peices of cannon & 2500 prisoners, before 9 o'clock.[22] You may be sure we were all glad, when the splendid news came back & that the rebels were in full retreat. I don't think many of us had any stomach for a fight that morning & the rest that followed all that day in delightful shade on the banks of the river, was never more grateful to any tired mortals. Sunday night however we were on duty all night building a bridge of cotton bales (!) across the river—We were then 23 miles from Vicksburg—Monday morning we crossed & moved out about 3 miles when our Brigade was ordered to return, and guard the bridge until other troops came up—that night we passed in quiet. Tuesday, troops were passing all day and the rear, our 2nd Brigade brought reports that the enemy were advancing upon our rear in force.[23] So we went out again just at dusk, planted our batteries & lay in line until 11 o'clock, when no enemy appearing we quietly withdrew, crossed the river, destroyed our bridge, lay down at 1 o'clock for a few hours sleep, and at 4 in the morning were moving towards Vicksburg. And oh! such a 20 miles march as it was—most intolerably hot with not a breath of air stirring, and the dust six inches deep, rolling up in thick volumes from the slightest tread of man or horse, encircling & enveloping you filling your mouth, nose eyes & ears & permeating every pore of the skin, until you felt like one great sandbag

They Have Seen Nothing Like It

We reached our lines already formed around the outer works at Vicks-burg that night, and the next morning were assigned our position in the front of the attack[24]

On Friday, the unsuccessful assault upon the works, of which you have doubtless read, was made[25] We were remarkably fortunate in the morn-ing being assigned a position & ordered to charge a small fort, when our forces on the right were in possession of a large one—They never got pos-session, but on the contrary were repulsed with great slaughter, so we were not called upon to charge at all. But in the afternoon about 4 P.M. we were ordered to support Gen McClernand's corps on the left, who it was said had got a foothold on the works.[26] Our Regt—the Major in command—passed up a steep ravine, or watergulch, and as we came to the top of the hill, we found a few brave fellows, clinging to the edge of the parapet, the stars & stripes planted half way up on the breast work, and the little band themselves only saved from complete annihilation by the steady stream of fire which they poured over the top of the fort, making it extremely uncomfortable for any rebel to raise his head so as to fire over. Our Reg't was to relieve these brave boys, who had held their place, till their cartridges were gone and more than half of their number were lost.[27] We planted our colors by the side of theirs, and opened a steady fire, raking the top of the fort, and sweeping everything that appeared on it. We were only separated from the rebs. by a distance of thirty feet, & they under cover of their works, while we were exposed to all the fire they could get at us—yet we stayed there an hour and a half, & until the enemy had sallied out from their fort on our right pouring in a terrible cross-fire and threatening to outflank us and cut us off. I was ordered to withdraw the line, and then the danger of retreat, seemed greater than the danger of remaining. I knew that if we ceased firing at once, & undertook to go down the ravine as we came up, that the rebels would pour up over the fort and open a murderous fire upon us, so I ordered the Regt down a Company at a time, the others keeping up the fire, until only two companies were left on the fort when I ordered to cease firing & fall back as best they could. By this means I do not think we lost a man in getting again under shelter, where we reformed, when with anything like a general or precipitate retreat, we must have been badly cut up. As it was we were obliged to leave our dead & some of our wounded to fall in the hands of the enemy[28]—Well this was our last fight, and I hope it may be the last for sometime. We have lost killed & wounded in our Regt. since we crossed the Mississippi just one third of the whole number we started with. We left the river 420 strong, and have lost 141—& besides these some 50 are worn out & sick, so we have really only about 230 men fit for duty. I know you will thank the kind Providence which has so mercifully preserved me through so many perils and has granted me the health to stand so much fatigue & exposure. It is singular but my health has improved, my cough has entirely ceased, and I am feeling much better than I have in a long time. If you could see & know exactly what we have been through you would not think it possible. Marching often till late at night, too tired to eat when we stopped but glad to drop down anywhere, in the furrow of a corn field, or by the roadside, with only a rubber blanket to lie on, an overcoat or single blanket for cover, & the saddle for a pillow, then up again before day, a hurried cup of coffee & a peice of corncake for breakfast, & this continued for a week at a time, without a chance to get thoroughly rested it does seem remarkable that one should thrive on it.

Night before last, was the first time I had slept with my pants off & on a cot, since leaving Millikens Bend—just about a month, and the only way I got a change of clothes, was when we were laying on the Black river I took off my underclothes, had them washed & dried the same day. On the night of the 16th after the battle of Champion Hills, our teams came up for the first time since we crossed the river, & on the next day, we luxuriated in clean clothes better food, & a poor article of commissary whiskey—we had not had a particle of any stimulant thro' all this fatigue, & it really did us all good, officers & men to get the whiskey ration, that Uncle Sam allows his boys in cases of unusual fatigue & exposure.[29] Well I suppose you want to know some thing of our present situation & prospects—We have got the rebs. completely hemmed in, in their stronghold, our right & left resting on the Mississippi above an below Vicksburgh, and the center where we are up within within less than a mile of their works—within sight of us are seven of their forts, and our sharpshooters & skirmishers, lie on the hills within two hundred yards of them pouring a deadly fire into the embrasures of the forts, & completely preventing them from handling their guns, while from 150 peices of artillery in their rear and from the gunboats & mortar fleet on the river a continuous fire of shot & shell, day & night, is hurled against their fortifications. They are a plucky set of fellows, & every night repair a great deal of the damage done thro' the day, but I do not think they can stand it much longer, especially when we get our heavy seige guns in position. I do not think another attempt will be made to carry their works by storm, & if not, we shall be comparatively safe.

You must trust in the good God, who has preserved me thus far, that I shall come out unharmed. Yesterday I recd yours of the 7th inst., & today one of the 4th. I was so glad to hear that you were well, & that there was a prospect of your being soon settled. I think you & Nell can live as happily together as is possible for two [love lorn] widows, I do mean to quit the service if it is possible when this affair is over, tho' Gen. Grant has promised that this division shall have rest as soon as Vicksburg is taken, & if we should be sent to garrison some pleasant point up the river like Memphis or Paducah, I would like to stay in & have you & baby with me. The Col.

will resign as soon as the campaign ends, if his health does not compel him to before—he is very feeble, & was unable to be in the assault the other day—he threatens to resign tomorrow, if he does not feel better than he does today—that will leave me in command, in the direct line of promotion to the Colonelcy.

I have written a thoroughly *self*ish letter, but thought you would like to know all about what we had been doing, and really it has been so much that the difficulty has been to abbreviate & curtail, rather than a lack of matter to write about. If I had a decent place to write in I could have filled a dozen sheets, instead of these three, but the dust has blown in one steady cloud, across the sheet, & you must excuse the soiled appearance of the paper, & the poor writing. Don't fail to write me often, & give me all the news, & every particular about yourself & the dear child. I am glad she gets the fresh air so often, & that you have got some one to releive you of the constant care of her. I hope this summer will give her a ruddier cheek and make her stronger. I think she ought to run & roll in the dirt as much as she wants to I found letters from Tiffany & Co. in regard to the sword for the Col.—they had it all boxed & ready to ship but understood that goods were not allowed to come below St Louis, so they were holding it for orders. I wrote them to send it at once to Memphis where I suppose it now is. I send up by one of our wounded officers to have it sent to us by the first opportunity. We lost 6 officers killed & wounded Capt Schaubel of Goshen, badly wounded in the privates. Your other acquaintances I believe all escaped.

Write soon my dear girl. I will write as often as once a week when circumstance will permit, but when you don't hear from me, you must think it is simply impossible for me to get a letter off—

My love to all. I hope George came safely thro' the late terrible disasters to the Army of the east, & that he is now discharged & at home.[30] God bless & keep you ever my dearest.

Your Husband
Edward

[Envelope addressed to "Mrs. Edward J. Wood, care C.B. Williams Esq, Salina New York."]

LETTER 40

Snyder's Bluff, Miss
June 1st 1863.

My dear wife,

Since I wrote you last, a week ago, we have been on an expedition to disperse the enemy whom it was said was assembling in force in our rear, and have returned thus far towards Vicksburg—12 miles distance and are resting for a day.

The expedition consisted of six brigades, selected from each division of the several army corps, all under the command of Maj. Genl. F. P. Blair Jr. and left Vicksburg Tuesday night the 26th ult.[31] The order directing the movement, read that we were to "proceed to the country lying between the Yazoo and Big Black rivers, and disperse and drive out the enemy said to be collected there"—you will see by a reference to your *Herald* map,[32] that this would take us in a northeasterly direction from Vicksburg, and that at some forty miles distant from V. the two rivers are not far apart. We started Tuesday night at 10 P.M. and quietly, under cover of darkness, our Brigade, withdrew from their position in front of the enemy's works and marched out 8 miles. About 2 o'clock in the morning, we lay down for a few hours, to resume the march at an early hour. We made 12 miles on Wednesday, bivouacking for the night on the banks of a swift running stream, to the huge delight and comfort of men and beasts. I never saw horses suffer more with the heat & dust—my horse would seem to get completely stifled and I was afraid he would give out—you can judge what it must have been for men. The next day, we lay on this stream until the middle of the afternoon, and then moved on, making 9 miles very comfortably. Friday we began to hear of the enemy—our cavalry were skirmishing with them all day, and were once driven back upon the infantry and we went through all the preliminaries for giving them battle, but they soon retired and we pushed thro' the little town of Mechanicsburg where we expected the enemy would make a stand

We chased them till dark, five miles beyond the town, marching 15 miles in all, & were confident we should be able to engage them in the morning But lo! when morning came, there was no enemy to be heard of—they had industriously occupied the night in crossing the Big Black river, and thus put a formidable barrier in the way of further pursuit. Our mission however was accomplished—we had driven the rebels out of the country, between the two rivers—and on Saturday we started back by the Yazoo valley route, a much nearer and more pleasant road. We struck the Yazoo river, after marching 4 miles, at Satartia, which you will easily find on the map and following the river down, on yesterday (Sunday) about noon, reached Haines Bluff, celebrated as one of the rebel defenses to Vicksburg by which any attempt to get into the rear of V. by the Yazoo river has been prevented. Our recent movements compelled the evacuation of these works & huge seige guns, dismounted, spiked or burst, lay strewn about. Yesterday's march was a terrible one—the heat was more intense than ever, and men dropped out of ranks by the score—it was inhuman to think of keeping them in, and I did not try to do it. As usual somebody was to blame for trying to make men march when it was impossible, but in a confusion or misinterpretation of orders, it is impossible to tell more, than that somebody blundered, and the troops were marched five miles further than was intended. When we halted at 2 P.M. 64 men of the 48th stacked arms—the balance were strewn along the road—as the boys say, *"played out."* As a sort of atonement for this outrage, we have been allowed to rest today, & I assure you, it is greatly needed.

I suppose tonight or tomorrow morning we will move back to our old position in the rear of Vicksburg—when the seige is to terminate is impossible to tell, but if the rebs. don't get a large army in our rear, I think the place must fall within the next ten days.

I am feeling as well as could be expected from the trip we have taken, and when we get rested out, I shall feel well again. I am still however, no better satisfied, & am anxious to be with you again.

There is no change in the condition of the Regt.—the Col's health is some better, and during the last two day's he has been in command of the Regt. On the rest of the trip he was in the ambulance, & I was in command.

The heat is so intolerable, & I am feeling so little in the writing mood, you must excuse the appearance of this sheet, and I know you will—for I think you will be glad to get even this scrawl to assure you that I am still alive, and reasonably well. I haven't heard from you since May 7th I do hope you are quietly and pleasantly settled—write me often. I will redeem my promise to write once a week whenever I can send off a letter.

Kiss the dear one for her papa, and remember me kindly to all friends

Your Husband
Edward

LETTER 41

Camp near Vicksburg, Miss
June 7th 1863.

My dear wife,

I waited with some anxiety for the mail this morning hoping for a letter but not expecting one very confidently, but determined to write *anyhow,* some time during the beautiful Sabbath day

Your are a dear good wife to write so often—your long letter of the 20th was received a few days ago and this morning another welcome message of the 15th came to hand. I wrote you about the same date, but I am afraid you have not got it yet, as we started on the expedition of which I have written you, the next day, & I learned afterwards that our mail did not get off but was taken with us—so you must be without word from me for a long time. I am so sorry, for I wrote at the very first opportunity, and I know how distressed you must be at not hearing from me after the battles and heavy losses we have been having.

I wrote you a long account of the actions we have been in, about the 25th ult. and again about the 1st on our return from the Black River Expedition— I suppose you will get them both about the same time.

I am sorry to hear that Nell's health is so poor. I am afraid the house-keeping undertaking will be too much for her strength. I know you will help her all you can, but I am afraid the burden, divided between you, even with sisterly affection, will be too heavy for both of you. Whenever I think of it, I feel as if I must be with you, to lighten your load of care & responsibility yet I can see no way of doing so, until this seige is over, and perhaps not very speedily then. My general health is very good—I could hardly resign now on a Medical Certificate, as with the exception of the local difficulty that troubled me, when I was at home, I was never better in my life. I find it impossible to decide on anything at present—If we succeed in taking Vicksburg, I think the Colonel will resign at once—his health has been poor for a long time, and it is only a matter of pride that keeps him in the service until this campaign is over. What effect that will have on me, or what will become of the Regiment, I can't tell. We are very much reduced in numbers, and the Companies of the Regt may be consolidated & left under the command of the Lt. Col. or they may be consolidated with another Regiment.

I think it very unjust that the men who have served faithfully thro' one term of enlistment, should be liable to the draft, but it would be still more rank injustice to muster officers out of the service, because their ranks had dwindled away through sickness and the casualties of the battlefield, and *then, draft* them into the service as privates.

This will be the effect with any consolidation of Companies or Regiments—of course, there will be supernumerary officers who will be mustered out, & if they are citizens at the time of the draft, they will be liable to it. I want to avoid this contingency—in any event—if I *must* be in the service I much prefer to remain in my present position, and with my old Regiment, as long as there is a respectable squad of them left. So you see, "things are *mixed*," and so, without any certain opening for business, or plans for the future, when I leave the army, I suppose for the present I shall remain in it, unless my health or something in your situation should make it imperative on me to come home, when I suppose I can cut the Gordian Knot[33] by resigning unconditionally. I hope you have a little money left to meet expense—we shall not probably be paid till after the 1st July, & I am running quite low already

Considering the high price of everything & your nurse girl you ought to pay considerably more for board. I suppose you & Nell agree upon the terms, but be sure to make them liberal as she has the responsibility. It is a great comfort to me to think that you and baby are well. I hope when you get thoroughly settled and feel at home in your new location that you will have quiet easy times, and lay in a fresh stock of health & strength. Don't be afraid of letting Mamie go in the *dirt*, the wash woman's bills is a greater better one to pay than the doctor's—I am so glad she has a chance to be outdoors, & hope she will grow much stronger this summer.

We are back nearly in our old position before the enemy's works, camped in one of the thousand ravines by which this country is cut up. We have secured a tent, and by digging into the hillside have made level ground enough to pitch it, & by the aid of large arbors & booths are well protected from the sun. We have very good water by digging a few feet & altogether the Reg't is more comfortably situated than it has been since it left Memphis, the 1st March. We are quite as well prepared to stay here a month or two, as the rebels can be cooped up in their forts & besides we have not been subjected yet to the annoyance they must experience from the very careless manner in which our guns keep dropping shells amongst them. The place is very closely invested, our first lines being within a 100 yards of them, & still we creep closer every night, throwing up earthworks & running our cannon so as to look right down into their forts. The ground is admirably adapted for defense and for this kind of attack also—but from any charges or assaults—Good Lord deliver us!—I don't think another will be attempted.

Our only hope now is in starving them out, or in destroying their hopes of reinforcements, by whipping the army that may be sent to their assistance before they get here. Joe. Johnston is collecting a force in our rear,[34] but Gen Grant is preparing for him, and if he comes with less than 50,000 men, Grant will be apt to send him back, badly punished. Unless we have this battle in the rear, & defeat them, I am inclined to think the place will hold out a good while yet. From the best information we can get they have supplies of corn & beef—salt & fresh, for 3 or 4 months, & men buoyed up by the hope of succor, will live a good while on that.[35] Take that hope away from them by beating back their expected aid, & they would surrender at once. We live in a continual roar of artillery, & have become so accustomed to it that we only notice it, when their is a slight interruption—there is a rumor that we are to try the effect upon them of a 48 hours incessant bombardment—from all the guns on land & water. It would be magnificent to see, but they are so well protected it would have little more than the moral effect upon them.

Keep a good heart my dear one, and take good care of yourself & our Mamie Kiss the darling for her Papa, "way down in Dixie," & write often Goodbye & God bless you Your Husband Edward

Shall I continue to direct to you to father's care or do you go to the office yourself? I think Nell and you might ought to have a box. E.

I send you two little slips that will explain themselves—the writer in one most provokingly left out the names of the two Regts that did most of the work. Gen. Crocker[36] commanded our division—Gen Quinby being sick. E.

[clipping from unidentified newspaper]

LETTER 42

My dear wife,

Another week has rolled away, and another bright beautiful Sabbath morning blesses us with its grateful presence. Not that Sunday in camp, is much different from other days, but early impressions & old habits cling to one, and when the body is refreshed with a bath & clean clothes, the mind is also purified by the healthy action, and even the *face* of nature seems to be cleaner for the operation. Seated under an ample, thickly-shaded a[r]bor, in front of our neat, white tents, with a cooling breeze wafting the hidden perfumes of many flowers & the soft music of innumerable birds—even the sharp, constant *crack* of the sharpshooters in our front, and the continual *boom* of cannon of every size, far & near, are not enough to destroy the deep tranquility of the hour & the scene.

It is a most striking illustration of the power of habit that we no longer notice this universal hubbub, unless for a few moments, there is perfect silence, & we lay down at night, & sleep as regularly & soundly as if there was nothing to disturb the slumbers of an infant.

I have no change to report in our situation, and worse still, no letter to acknowledge the receipt of, since I wrote a week ago. I know you have been waiting to get one, tho,' & I am sorry you had to wait so long—I explained the reason in my last—Last Wednesday, we had a succession of heavy thunder showers, all day and the weather since has been delightful—each day however the heat increases, and I expect it would be found very uncomfortable in the sun today—I certainly don't mean to try it without a very good excuse—About once a week our Reg't goes on duty as sharpshooters on the front line, and aside from details for fatigue duty, working the trenches etc, at night, we have no duty to perform. The men enjoy the rest, but contrary to what you would think, they don't improve in health. I have had considerable opportunity for observing, & my experience is that the invariable result of laying in camp, is an increase of the sick list—and an equally invariable result, that every man who is able to start on a march & keep up for two or three days, continues to improve no matter how severe the marching or the exposure—and this result is only affected in a degree, by the sanitary conditions of the camp. The water may be good, & as a rule is much better than that obtained on marches, the location may be favorable, & the police of the camp well attended to, & still every day the sick list increases I can only account for it, by the lack of exercise—the strong food & stronger appetites of the men, requires hard work to facilitate digestion. The hot climate, with hearty living, induces all kinds of liver derangements, & although I have tried to control my appetite, I have not escaped entirely.

On the whole, I am much better than at this time last year, and I do not think my added experience of camplife has been thrown away upon me. The seige progresses slowly, but unless one is curious, or has duty that calls him to the front, he has little idea of what is going on. Yesterday, our Reg't was on as Sharpshooters, but the rebels were very quiet—we were much annoyed however by the premature bursting of shells from our own guns. Two of our men were severely wounded by fragments of shells that burst over us from our own guns—What *is* to be the end of all this turmoil and *when* it is to come, are questions of intense interest to the whole country, & most especially to the soldiers. I don't think the privates worry much about it—they never do about anything—Uncle Sam feeds & clothes them, & they obey orders & ask no questions—but to the intelligent officer, who has time and brains to think, this suspense is at times, agonizing—the momentous consequences involved in the prize for which we are struggling makes the long delay for the issue of the conflict seem insufferable, and many would be willing to risk all on the hazard of a *"die"*—"to take arms against" the rebel works, "and by" assaulting, "end them."[37]

I don't think however, that anything of the kind will be attempted— gradual approaches to their works by digging & starvation must be depended upon to reduce this rebel Gibraltar. I think Gen Grant is receiving large re-inforcements from Burnside's corps, & the troops in Missouri & Arkansas—he had already ordered all the troops in Northern Miss. & Tennessee in his Dep't here, & no apprehension is felt of a serious attack in the rear.[38] I still adhere to my previously expressed opinion that the rebels will hold out for a considerable time, unless this force of Johnston's in our rear, is met and *whipped*—with the hope of relief from him taken away from them they would surrender speedily. There is talk of an expedition to find Mr. Johnston—if Grant feels strong enough to organize a campaign against him, it would be the speediest method to insure the fall of Vicksburg—Milo has been relieved of his command—I haven't heard but little about it, & don't know whether he has any other or not. His offense was similar to Gen. Burnside's in suppressing the Chicago *Times*, & I think was committed under his instructions.[39]

I am strongly in hopes I shall get a letter when the mail comes today— your last was the 25th ult, & I certainly ought to get one of about the 7th inst. You are my only correspondent, & you will have to write the oftener to keep me supplied with even a private's rations of letters. My recommendation for Lt. Col. has been forwarded to the Governor, & I suppose in due course of time the Commission will come—it won't keep me in the service longer than I would otherwise stay—I promise you that, my dearest. How I long to see your dear face and our little prattling cherub's—my pictures are my only resource, & they are a great comfort. Do you write or hear from Mary Mackie? I wish you could. I am ashamed to.

I never had such splendid opportunities for writing as we have had here, but I have only written one letter—to Hale[40]—except those to you. Write as often as you can, remember me kindly to all friends. Kiss baby *lots* for papa, & believe me ever

> Your devoted Husband
> Edward

LETTER 43

> In the rear of Vicksburg, Miss
> June 21st 1863.

My dear wife,

Our correspondence seems to be getting very one-sided—this is the third letter I have written since I heard from you I suppose you must have written, and the letters have got *lodged* somewhere on the road, but I am really very anxious to hear from you again, & I trust a few days longer will free me from my anxiety.

Everything has jogged along in the same old channels since I wrote you last Sunday, except that we have had a little more guard duty to do. The Reg't was on the sharpshooter's line two days last week and goes on again tonight. Last Thursday I went down to the landing at Chickasaw Bayou, on the Yazoo river, where we get all our supplies. There were over fifty large steamboats at the landing—many of them are retained there as store-boats for commissary & Quartermaster supplies, some of them were unloading ammunition etc, but the finest one of all–the *"Luminary"* was steaming up—Northward—bound for Memphis! I believe I envied even the sick & (slightly) wounded officers, who were so luxuriously disposed about her cool & pleasant cabin, & who were very smilingly bidding a farewell to Dixie—many of them for aye, and all of them for these coming blistering months.

I would have gladly swapped places with the owner of many a bandaged limb—for wounds as honorably received and for the delicious reward of loving words & tender care from wife & loved ones at home—I *did* envy those brave fellows & couldn't help it. I couldn't tell whether they were most proud of their wounds or glad they were going home—altogether they were a very pleased lot of maimed & perforated fellows.

I met at the Landing Mark Tucker of Elkhart—I don't know whether you ever met him—he is Q.M of the 100th Ind. which lately came down the river. Heath is the Lt. Col. & I know a great many of the officers & men—they are at present up the Yazoo, at Snyder's Bluff, and on Friday Col Heath & Capt. Johnson of Goshen came over to see us.[41] They spent the day and were easily persuaded to stay all night, to see the effect of the shelling and cannonading after dark—but most unaccountably the mortar-boats did not

They Have Seen Nothing Like It

open, & the booming along our line was dull & irregular. About 9. p.m. we received a general order, which explains the unusual stillness. The order was to the effect that at 4 a.m. of the next day, every gun in position along the whole line, should open and until 10 a.m. pour a continuous fire "upon the city of Vicksburg."—A little after daylight accordingly they did open, it is estimated, from four hundred guns, and for more than three hours the fire did not slacken at all. The scene would have been terrible to an inexperienced person of weak nerves—the roar was incessant & deafening, & the very earth trembled as from an earthquake—of course we know nothing of the results, but such a terrible fire from so many guns, shooting every kind of destructive missile, must have damaged the enemy very materially. They evidently expected another assault, & their troops were plainly seen marching to the support of those already in their works. Our position remains unchanged—Gen. Logan, on our right, has dug up to one of their principal forts, & is digging away at the fort itself. We have no news of Johnston in our rear, and the greatest confidence is felt in Gen. Grant's ability to defeat him should he come. The army has been doubled by re-inforcements since the place was invested, and the defensible positions in our rear strongly fortified. The besieged hold out stubbornly, but every day diminishes their stock of provision, & available force, & increases the chances of our ultimate success—I suppose the anxiety for the fall of Vicksburg among all classes of people of the North must be great—occasionally it seems to us that we cannot endure the suspense—that's when we get the *"blues"*—but in the main, we are very cheerful & contented as can be—if we, in good camps with plenty of water & abundant supplies get desperate sometimes—what must be the feelings of the poor secesh, cooped up in narrow limits, on rations of corn meal, peas, & meat—& a one-quarter allowance of that, exposed to a continual artillery fire, and tormented with all the uncertainties of their position. It is no wonder they desert in such numbers. Gen. Sherman told me the other day, that they were coming in at the rate of a hundred a day[42]

Consolidation of regiments seems to be *"played out."* The Asst. Adjt. Genl. of Indiana[43] is here to find out the exact effective strength of the Ind. Regts, and says they are to be filled up by the draft. Many a poor fellow who had hopes of being mustered out as a supernumerary officer is doomed to disappointment

The Paymaster is around—our rolls are made out & handed in, & we shall probably be paid for two months—to the 1st May—soon—I don't know how we will dispose of our money, but the first opportunity that offers I will send you some.

I have just heard there was a large mail at the river for us yesterday, and have sent to Divn HdQrs to see if it has got there yet—if we get it I am sure there is a letter for me.

It is two weeks today since I got one, & that was dated May 25th almost a month. My health is good except a diarrhoea & that through the summer. I believe many are actually healthier for it, for when it is checked, jaundice or some other more serious form of bilious disease is apt to set in—Supper is announced and I must close, as we go on the picket line just after dark. Don't fail to write, my dear, all about yourself and our dear child. I do hope you both keep well, take care of yourself & her, and pray to our Merciful Father to take care of us all, & to help us bear patiently & without murmur, whatever his wisdom has appointed for us. My love to Nell & all the family & believe me ever

Your loving Husband

Edward.

LETTER 44

Camp near Vicksburg Miss
July 2nd 1863.

My dear wife,

Last Sunday was a terribly hot day & I felt such an unwonted degree of lassitude that the day slipped away, & I failed to carry out my resolution to write every Sunday. Monday we were on the front line as sharpshooters, and Tuesday I was Officer of the Day for the Army Corps, & was relieved yesterday morning, so used up as to be glad to rest all day. I am feeling quite well again this morning and embrace the first opportunity to acknowledge the receipt of your dear letter of the 16th *ult*. I am glad you got my two letters—there was a rumor that Grant had ordered all letters from the army stopped at Memphis, and I knew how great your anxiety would be, if you could hear nothing from me.

I don't think there will ever be so sweeping an order issued, tho' it is a fact that much contraband information as to the strength, situation etc of the army leaks out through the medium of private letters. Some foolish persons are so anxious to glorify themselves & their correspondence that they "rush into print," & violate every rule of propriety, by publishing private communications, without leave or license.[44]

The seige hangs fire terribly, and we are all getting heartily sick of it. I have fixed the time for surrender for the last time—July 5th—if they don't accommodate us with a surrender then, I shall give them over as incorrigible—When we first crossed the river, May 1st, I & everybody was sanguine of marching straight into Vicksburg. I said I would be satisfied if we were able to toast the Union on the 4th of July, inside the city, and here we are, preparing to give the rebs a national salute on that day from the outside. Over four hundred cannon are now in position, and the programme is to give them a salute of thirteen guns (from each cannon) at sunrise, thirty four at meridian, and one hundred at sundown. I don't imagine this tremendous cannonading has much effect, they are so well protected. The streets of the city run up from the river a steep bluff, and the cross streets are deep cuts—from these, huge caves have been cut, and the whole citizen population take to their holes, when the fire becomes furious. The soldiers also have such retreats in the hillsides toward us, and it is impossible to damage them much. We have worked up to several of their large works, undermined them, and blown great breaches in the earthworks, but every attempt to enter through these breaches, and occupy the forts, has been attended with disaster—our men have been driven out with heavy loss.[45] It seems impossible to take the place, except by close investment, and starvation of the garrison. Johnston's force in the rear has made no demonstration yet, & the impression is general, that they will be unable to collect & equip an army sufficient to raise the seige. What we lack everywhere is *men*. If Grant had an army of 100000 men here, in addition to his present force, he would be able to march out after Johnston, disperse or annihilate him, and come down on the flank or rear of Bragg in front of Rosecrans[46] and in three months, the rebellion in the Southwest, would be among the things that were. The same thing is true in the East. Lee is in Penn, Harrisburg is doubtless destroyed by this time.[47] Philadelphia, Baltimore & even Washington threatened because of the lack of men to oppose the rebel hordes. The weakness of the Administration affords most cause for alarm. With a most efficient Conscription law, now almost five months the law of the land, they have been deterred from putting it in force, by the blatherings of noisy traitorous demogogues,[48] and now they are resorting to the pitiable expedient of calling out 6 months volunteers, to be credited on the draft, when four months ago, they should have had three million of men enrolled, and a half a million, two months in the field. Hooker's army wouldn't then have been weakened by the discharge of the two years men,[49] and both in the east & the west the union army would have been in condition for a vigorous & final campaign against rebeldom. The six months men will be a failure—they will just begin to be efficient when their time will expire, the vast outlay for their equipment etc will be a dead loss, and at the end of their term of service the Government will be in the same strait for men as it is at present. It is almost incredible that the affairs of a nation should be managed with so little foresight Everybody knew when the time of the two years men would expire, & yet no means were employed to fill their places, till Lee with a largely reinforced army, comes thundering at the very gates of the Capital and then we are treated with a panicy call for 100,000 six months men! It is most disheartening that with three million of able bodied men at home, the rebels should always be able to outnumber us in the field, & that thro' the imbecility of the Administration, which dares not enforce its own laws.[50]

Well I'm afraid I've bored you with this long disquisition, but it's hard to stop or condense when I get started on this theme. We have been paid since I wrote you last, & I enclose you $50.00 I hope you will get it safely & that it will be enough for your present purposes, we are promised pay again in two or three weeks, & then I will send you a larger sum.

The Col's health still continues poor, & he will resign—or rather his resignation which is tendered, will be accepted, as soon as Vicksburg falls. My commission as Lt. Col. has not yet come, but I suppose it will soon, to be followed shortly by one as Colonel—that is if I get thro' the seige safely, & nothing happens to disturb present arrangements. I am sorry you had to pay so much for the old trunk—I don't believe it & its contents were worth the amount. The weather is most excruciatingly hot and it is an effort to do anything—you must therefore excuse the looks of this sheet. I wish you could go to see Mrs. Ferriss this summer—how long would it take you to go—when I send the next remittance you must be ready to start—it would be a change for you, & would do you & Mamie good—the dear child, how papa would like to see her fat brown cheeks. You must write often & keep up a good heart, don't app[r]ehend any trouble to me, till you hear it, & I will try to keep you informed often of my continued health & safety.

Remember me kindly to all, and believe me ever

Your loving Husband
Edward

LETTER 45

Vicksburg Miss.
July 12, 1863.

My dear wife

Ten stirring days have passed since I wrote you last—you recollect I gave the rebels till the 5th of July to surrender—they anticipated me by one day, and it was well for them that they did—you have doubtless seen full particulars of the surrender, before this, but you can have seen nothing that could do justice to the proud bearing of our troops, as on the 4th of July, they marched in to the captured city, with bands playing and colors flying—All other 4th of July celebrations sink into insignificance compared with this splendid victory, a fitting tribute to the glorious memories of the day.[51] I enclose you Genl. McPhersons congratulations order—it seems to me to exhaust the subject. The results of the capture are more important, than were at first expected. Thirty-one thousand & some hundreds prisoners were taken, over one hundred pieces of cannon, 75,000 stand of small arms—ammunition by the hundred tons immense quantities of Q.M's stores, such as clothing camp & garrison equipage, harness, saddlery etc, in fact, the beleagured garrison had everything to equip a large army, except

They Have Seen Nothing Like It

provisions. Of these, they were entirely destitute, in fact, they were reduced to the starvation point, and we were obliged to commence issuing rations to them, as soon as we were in possession of the city. Genl Grant lost no time in useless glorification over his victory, but immediately started the bulk of his army under command of Genl Sherman, after the rebel forces under Johnston that had been hanging on our rear, while only two divisions of our corps were retained to take charge of the prisoners, arms etc.[52] We have not been idle I assure you—Guards had to be kept along the entire line of rebel works, all the guns & stores to be picked up and taken care of, and all the prisoners to be paroled, each individual of them being furnished with a parole. Our Regiment has been on guard five days within the last week, and the other two on fatigue duty, so you can understand why I have not written before. Today I was anticipating a little rest, but this morning I found a detail for me as Officer of the Day, and I have been in the saddle all day—I have no regret tonight however, for I have been over the entire extent of the rebel fortifications and have seen what I probably never should have seen, unless in the line of duty. During the whole seige, I never had any of the foolish curiosity that cost many good officers their lives, to know what was going on, and the exact situation of the opposing forces. I knew where our skirmish line was, and what I have not dared to write you before—I have been on duty there for days, within a hundred yards of the rebel line, between our artillery and theirs, and where shells from both sides burst, and rained their fragments—and when off duty, I was in camp, where in one day we picked up & dug out of the bank, nearly forty six-pound solid shot, that had struck within fifty yards of our tents while Minie balls whistled overhead, cutting branch & cane constantly. I wish I could give you a correct idea of this country & our situation. Conceive a deep, narrow ravine, running nearly parallel with the rebel lines, with steep almost precipitous sides, all covered with trees and a literally impassable growth of cane, and you have a very good idea of the original appearance of our camping ground. Occasionally from the main ravine are short ones, a very few of which, men & horses can climb running at right angles to the main ravine, and these constituted our roads. On the hill-side next the enemy, our men burrowed, and in the bank of one of these smaller ravines, three regiments of our brigade made their Head Quarters—you can thus perhaps understand why so many shot passed over us, & yet lodging in the opposite bank of the ravine, struck so near us. I have my tent floor paved with six-pound shot, & yet not a man was hit by them—the only danger was from glancing shot, and those sometimes came uncomfortably close—But thank God! The seige is over, the mental wear & tear was greater even than the physical, and I believe I should have *collapsed,* but for the necessity of continued exertion, which this late duty has demanded. The last rebel prisoner passed the lines today,[53] & we shall probably soon subside into quiet.

June [*sic*] 16th 1863—A most provoking break, but it was unavoidable, and I hope the enclosed draft, will reconcile you to the delay. The Paymaster has been amongst us—we have had our nine months drafted men to muster out—five per cent of the Regt has been furloughed home. The Col. has been sick all the time, & the work & responsibility has fallen on me

The Col's resignation papers have not returned but we understand it is accepted, and he will probably start home next week—This morning we are moving our camp a half mile nearer the river, & of course are very busy. Of course, you are anxious to know our fate, now that Vicksburg has fallen—well, it seems to be to garrison the place. I am sorry we are not to go further North through the summer, but really the summer is half over, and we are all doing well. My own health is still good. If Nellie goes to Washington in September how would you like to come West to Indianapolis I could make arrangement to procure you good board there, and you could soon make some pleasant acquaintances. Perhaps I might get home to see you, & if I remain here with the Reg't after the hot weather is over you could come down here. I can't see how I am to leave the Reg't as long as my health keeps good, & I don't know how I could do as well pecuniarily at anything else. If I am promoted to Colonel, the pay will be the better—I have paid up all my debts, & I would like to stay in the service long enough to lay up something besides. The war will continue for some time yet, but great battles are over for a good while at least–the power of the rebellion is broken in the Southwest, & in the East, for the first time, it has suffered a damaging blow[54]—hereafter the fight will be confined to smaller forces—My chest is full, & my boy has been waiting some time to pack up my things—You had better go to see Mrs. Ferriss—it will do you & the dear child good—couldn't you get a photograph of the darling now. Oh! I forgot to tell you, among these rebels that we captured here, I found a Colonel of the 56th Georgia, who lives at Madison—was well acquainted with Mr. Walker, & had seen Mother, when he last heard from them, they were well.[55] I wrote a long letter to Mother—sent her my photograph & Mamie's baby picture She will be sure to get them, & I know will be greatly pleased. I could hear nothing of Robert. I suppose he must be with Bragg's army.

The check I send is for $150.00. You will have to sign your name to it on the back. Henry will show you how, & will probably get the money for you. I hope you got the $50. bill I sent in my last. Give my love to all Kiss our darling a hundred times for papa & write *often*. I will write again in a few days. I have seen notice of my appointment as Lt. Col in a Cincinnatti paper, but have not yet rec'd the commission.

Good-bye & God bless & keep you safely, my dear one.

Your Husband
Edward

CHAPTER 8

The Vicissitudes Attendant on a Soldier's Career

Vicksburg Idleness, August–September 1863

After their arduous campaign, many of the troops had an opportunity to rest and recuperate in and around Vicksburg. After the capitulation of Pemberton's army, Sherman's 15th Army Corps was sent east to engage Joe Johnston and chase him away. After forcing Johnston many miles east and retaking Jackson, Mississippi, Sherman's force returned to their camps near Vicksburg.[1] The 9th Corps returned to Kentucky. The 13th Corps was sent to Louisiana and still other troops to Arkansas. Major General James B. McPherson's 17th Corps, including the 48th Indiana, remained in Vicksburg as a garrison.

There, Wood occupied his time in courts-martial, hearing the backlog of cases accumulated during the campaign. Once Vicksburg was taken, Colonel Eddy felt free to resign his commission and command of the regiment. Wood assumed full command. His commission as colonel arrived during this time, but he lamented that attrition in the regiment and little likelihood of recruiting it back to requisite strength meant that he was not likely to be promoted to full colonel.

Wood obtained leave in September and traveled north to Syracuse to visit his wife and child. He also transacted regimental business at Indianapolis, obtained a number of new recruits for the 48th, and managed an interview with Governor Oliver P. Morton. Later, in his letter of October 16, 1863, Wood wrote nonchalantly, "I see my plan published as Gov. Morton's for filling the old regiments." It is evident that while in Indianapolis Wood communicated an idea to Morton that the governor was to embrace as his own. On October 7, Morton telegraphed to the War Department in Washington, D.C., a proposal to retain the veteran volunteer troops whose three-year enlistments were to expire in 1864.[2] Military and political leaders understood that it was vitally important to retain these veterans—

experienced, blooded, successful, and toughened—in the Federal armies as the core of the fighting force. Morton's—and Wood's—plan called for old regiments, "say one for each Congressional district," to return to their homes if three-fourths of the enlisted men reenlist for three years. The troops were to remain on furlough as long as necessary, as determined by the governors of their states, to recruit. Once strengthened by new recruits, the units would return to the field, and a new batch of depleted regiments would return to recruit. Morton opined that "the plan will take so few men from any one corps as not to materially weaken it." Veterans who agreed to reenlist would be granted a furlough and a reenlistment bonus totaling $502, a substantial sum. After consideration, and after hearing from other state executives on the same topic, some offering their own plans, the War Department accepted the idea with modifications—the furlough would be limited to one month at home—and instituted it immediately. The plan is credited for retaining three-fourths of the veterans in the Union Army in 1864.

LETTER 46

Vicksburg, Miss
August 2nd 1863.

My dear wife,

I wrote you on the 26th ult.[3] acknowledging the receipt of three letters, and I have now to thank you for another good long letter enclosing an admirable photograph of Jessie I was in hopes at first that it was a picture of our own sweet one—but I know you will send it as soon as you can. I am glad you got the $50 safely—the sum was so small I didn't like to send it by express, & I believe the mail is quicker and full as safe. I sent you on the 16th a draft for $150. which you have doubtless received before this. I believe you asked me once what you ought to pay for board but I forgot to tell in my answer. I suppose you have settled on an amount that is satisfactory before this, but at present war prices for living, you ought to pay $4 to $5. I am anxious to hear what arrangements you think advisable for the "*fall campaign.*" If Nell goes to Washington the 1st Sept, you will have no special inducements to keep you in Syracuse, and you would be much nearer the seat of war, to be out West. I mentioned Indianapolis in one of my letters to you, on account of its central location. I did not suppose you would like to board with any one in Goshen. I could think of, and I do not care about your going there any way, but I do feel, that if Nell breaks up housekeeping, it would be better for you to leave Syracuse. If you did not want to be encumbered with all your luggage, you could box & store it, and take

The Vicissitudes Attendant on a Soldier's Career

with you only personal baggage & such things as would be essential to your comfort—I hope by the middle of September to get a leave of abscence— and not much before. Col. Eddy as I wrote you, has gone home, and I am left in sole charge of the Reg't.[4] By a recent order, rec'd yesterday, all line (Company) officers but one to a Co. & all the Field officers but one to a Regt. are to be furloughed home, on half-pay, and accordingly all my offi- cers have sent up their applications for furlough. I am the only Field officer with the Reg't and must remain, but when their time expires, thirty days, I hope to be able to get away myself. Many of the officers have been twenty months away from home and I am willing and anxious they should have the full benefit of this order. There is something inexplicable in the delay of our Commissions—I saw the announcement of the appointments in the paper of July 2nd and we have never hear one word from the Adjt Genl. in reference to it. Capt Byrkit who has been acting as Major for four months past is especially aggrieved by this neglect of the State authorities.[5] I sup- pose I shall never wear the eagles of a Colonel, as by an order from the War Dep't all Regts below the *minimum,* are prohibited from having vacancies filled (of Colonel & Asst Surgeon) and all below half the maximum (520) the Colonel & Major are to be mustered out, and the Regiment consolidated into five companies. So unless the Regiment is filled by conscript, I have no possibility of reaching a higher grade than Lt. Col. The Regiment numbers only 540, very near the consolidation point, and whenever it reaches that, I am determined to resign I will never command such an awkward squad as that would be. I haven't much faith that the consolidation order will ever be carried into effect but something be done to fill up or re-organize these skeleton regiments, before they will ever be fit for another campaign. Our Court Martial is still in session, and is likely to run two or three weeks longer.[6] It keeps me very busy indeed. I leave camp every morning at 8 o'clock, and return generally between 2 & 3 P.M. We have a very pleasant court, and hold our sessions in the court room in the city—a large fine *cool* room overlooking the city and the river. I send you the order detailing the court, and McPherson's general order which I forgot to send before.

Our duties have materially lightened since I wrote you last. For nearly a month, the reg't was on duty every day. The city was in horrible condition— the secesh evidently pay little attention to the police of their camps, and the men are filthy in their personal habits and negligent of the laws of health and common decency to a degree beyond belief. As I would not want you to see, so I would not shock you with a description of the indecencies these fellows perpetrate, not singly and as individuals, but as a body, wherever they are congregated. Every house of respectable dimensions and with suit- able grounds is a hospital, and in these the disregard of the most common sanitary regulations is more palpable than elsewhere. As a consequence the

Major Barnet Byrkit, 48th Indiana. Courtesy of Dan Wood.

mortality among them is fearful, and yet the health of our troops, continues good. Good diet, plenty of work and strict attention to the cleanliness of the men and the camp have saved them from any unusual sickness Indeed I think the general health of the army is better than it was last summer in the vicinity of Corinth. The rebel prisoners in hospital are being sent off as fast as possible, and the debris of the camps and the accumulated filth of the fallen city have been removed, and we have no apprehension of plague or pestilence. It is definitely settled that our Corps—the 17th McPherson's—is to constitute the garrison of the place and I think it is also settled that there is to be no more campaigning from this place as a base. The army is to be quiet for the summer. Sherman's corps goes to Natchez, and any future operations of this army must be by way of the Gulf against Mobile and the interior of Alabama.[7]

I quite agree with you in disapproval of Gov. Seymour's temporizing course with the New York mob. His action was a base concession to a traitorous, inhuman, fiendish mob, with whom reason was but as idle wind, and fair words but gave them time to prepare for worse acts of diabolism. Grape and canister were the only arguments such fellows could appreciate and a more timely administration of the dose, would have saved many valuable lives and the city from the disgrace of five days mob rule.[8]

I am still well as you may surmise from this long letter without any allusion to my health—diarrhoea afflicts me more or less, but on the whole I am feeling quite well and am doing every day my full share of work. My dear girl you don't know how much every day I think of you, and how anxious I am to see you. I have been thinking since I commenced this long letter, that perhaps on the whole, you had better not determine on breaking up until I come home. I feel most certain that I shall be at home in six weeks, either on leave or resigned and I can better determine with you, and help you if we decide to move—This is my birth-day. I am 29—it seems very old, but it is hard for us to give up the idea that we are still young. My half sheet is filled and I think you will have enough of my lucubrations for one time. Write often, Jeanie, your letters are a great consolation to me, and you are a dear good girl to write so often. Give my love to Nellie and all enquiring friends. Kiss our darling a thousand times for papa & believe me ever Your devoted Husband. Edward

LETTER 47

Vicksburg, Miss
Aug. 9th 1863.

My dear wife,

Another week has passed quickly away—so quickly that I can't realize it is so long since I wrote you last—you would rightly infer that it had been a busy and a pleasant week with me. Our Court has been in session each day, and the genial companionship which has grown up between the members of it—hitherto strangers—has done much to alleviate the tedium of the trials. We dispose of three or four cases a day and have made a decided reputation with the Commanding General for our dispatch of business. If we could have got a boat the Court would have been on a pleasure trip to Natchez today and you would have been cheated out of this letter. I did not much regret it, for I hope after we have been in session two or three weeks longer, that Genl. McPherson will be pleased to be more gracious still, and give us all a thirty days furlough home.

In the regiment everything goes smoothly, for which I am much indebted to Capt. Byrkit who has had the chief control while I have been upon the Court. It is too bad that his Commission as Major does not come. He has obtained a twenty days leave of abscence but has been waiting several days in hopes the commission would come. I suppose he will leave tomorrow[9]—the Adjutant has already gone and *all* the Captains, so I will be left quite alone. I don't despair however of getting away after some of them return tho' I don't think I shall ever be positive again about anything in the army, after my experience of last spring. The weather for the past week has been delightful—the great bugbear of a summer residence in this latitude is fast passing away. I don't think I ever saw more pleasant weather in August anywhere

To-day as I sit under my thickly shaded bower a strong cool breeze blows thro' my retreat, and the air is comparatively pure. I don't think it quite equal to a good sea-breeze that smacks of salt marches and all the innumerable good things of the mighty deep, but it is infinitely preferable to the airs that wander over Indiana's flat wooded country, laden with enervating miasma.[10] I do so wish you could see our HdQuarters. I try sometimes to tell you exactly how we are situated but I fear I succeed but indifferently in re-producing the picture. Let us see now how we look. We are just at the edge of the city, the backyard & garden of the houses in town running nearly back to our tents. Three wall tents in line occupy the only available level space on top of a narrow grass-sward ridge, while in front a valley two hundred yards wide stretches to the slope of a gently-sloping hill upon which are the tents of the brigade—from there the prospect stretches to the top of the hill and the outer line of the rebel works where sentinels pace in bold relief against the sky.

The view is not grand or sublime or anything of that sort, yet under the light of a quiet Summer Sunday, with orderly rows of white tents dimpling the green sward, like stately ships under full sail and with white clouds flecking the blue above, to a cheerful, contented mind, the scene has a pleasing effect—a contented mind, I said, and I only want the prescence of my darlings to make mine one

Two days ago I received your letter of the 26th, and since I commence writing this, one of the 28th written after you got my letter of the 16th

I hope you have heard again before this time I was very busy when we first came in & did not write oftener than once in ten days, but I mean hereafter to write, once a week even if I have nothing particular to communicate. Col. Sanborn of the 4th Minnesota who has commanded our Brigade for a year past has resigned and the command falls on Col. Alexander of the 59th Ind.—It could not have fallen on a better man, and I suppose he will be made Brigadier before long.[11] You were right in supposing that Col R. Proctor of the 15th Vermont must be my old friend. I had not heard before of his promotion, but I know his abilities and am not surprised at it.[12] I had noticed Pres. Lord's resignation and also that Prof. Patterson, my old teacher in Connecticut was spoken of as likely to succeed him.[13] I hope he may—I missed our decennial class anniversary and indeed did not think of

Colonel Jesse I. Alexander. Courtesy of Daniel Wood.

it until it was too late, even to write—This afternoon I am going with Col. Alexander to review the 63rd Ill, a new Regiment which has been attached to our Brigade recently, and as it is nearly time to start I must close.

I expect within the next six weeks to see you, my dearest, and to clasp my darlings in my arms—don't look for me sooner, and try not to be disappointed if I don't come even then—I dare not write you how sanguine I am of coming or exactly when I expect to start, but in the course of a month you can commence to expect me in the language of the Almanacs "about—these—days." Kiss papa's darling for him, tell her that Papa thinks of his dear little girl every day, and that she must be good to her Mama and love her a heap, and Papa will love her so much the more. Goodbye Jeanie, write often—you may depend on me at least once a week. Ever your loving Husband

Edward

LETTER 48

Vicksburg, Miss.
August 16th 1863.

My dear wife,

Sunday finds me again writing you after a very lonesome week. I wrote you that most of my officers had gone home, but I had hardly had time to find out how much I missed them. Capt. Byrkit and the Adjutant particularly—they were always about Head Quarters, and when time hung heavy on our hands, were always ready to while away an hour or two at cards or chess. This week I have been absolutely alone, and when off the Court Martial have been most dismally blue. To make matters worse, the men have commenced getting sick—nothing serious, mostly ague, but a great many of them are reported off duty, and it makes my squad of effective men very small. I have commenced issuing rations of quinine & whiskey to them and hope soon to make an improvement in their condition. The weather has been gradually increasing in heat, until yesterday which was a boiling, blistering day, and to-day promises to be after the same sort. My general health continues good, tho' I have felt the effects of the late hot weather considerably—This morning—up to 10 o'clock—has been dreadfully hot & sultry but a little breeze is springing up now that I hope may last thro' the day—Even while I write this it dies away, and the shrill noise of the locust is the only sound that breaks the sultry stillness of the day.

I don't know what to write you about coming home I can't see how I can leave the Regiment before Byrkit gets back, which will be sometime between the 1st & 10th of September, and even then a twenty days furlough would do me no good. I couldn't have more than two or three days at home at best and that would hardly pay for the fatigue & expense of the journey. It is barely possible that the Court Martial may be furloughed home for thirty days from the 20th of this month, and in that case, I should get home about the same time with this letter. If I get away I must go to Goshen and that will use up two days at least. I want to be in Indianapolis after the 1st and I think I'll go straight to Goshen, if we get away this week, and stop at Indianapolis on my return. I am not sanguine however, that we will "*get to go*" as the Hoosiers say, at all, but I mean to make some desperate efforts after my officers return.

I have been looking for a letter all the morning but the boy has just returned from Division HdQrs with "*no mail,*" so I must wait for another boat. Communication up the river is quite regular now, and Vicksburg has settled down into a quiet, orderly, well-regulated city of the Union. I don't think I ever saw the life as effectually *squelched out* of a place, as it is here. Nothing lives, moves or has being that is not connected with the army. The *"best families"* are glad to have somebody's HdQrs established on their premises, even if it is a Surgeon of a Hospital, and all are eager to take Uncle Sam's postage stamps, for anything they have got to dispose of. A lady nearby, sends me word that she has peaches & tomatoes, I authorize one of the boys to investigate & procure the same. Behold the result, one dollar in greenback brings twenty dwarfish, rusty peaches and twice as many tomatoes as big as your thumb!

But by sending outside of the lines occasionally, we manage to live pretty well—this morning I had breakfast, boiled mackerel, stewed potatoes, tomatoes, fresh boiled eggs, milk toast, and all the iced milk I can drink, with a heaping saucer of most delicious *"sweet peaches & cream!"* I don't believe Salt Point can beat that [living?]

I don't believe I ever told you that one of our first captures after we crossed the Mississippi was a cow!—but it was—she made the campaign with us, and was in the neighborhood of a good many fights. She never actively engaged except at first in some sharp skirmishes with the Dutchman who milks her. Now the campaign is over she is quite docile & tractable & in return for her good keeping yields quite a bountiful supply of milk—since we have had it so abundantly I drink neither tea or coffee.

Well, the commissions have come at last, dated April 25th!—better late than never, is all the consolation we have. I am Lt. Col. and that's as high as I can ever get, unless by some unexpected means the Regiment should be filled up. The Regiment is decreasing in numbers very rapidly—all the men who have been unfit for duty for any considerable time are being discharged or transferred to the Invalid Corps,[14] and my Muster Rolls at the end of this month, will hardly show 500 men—the men too are being furloughed very extensively, in addition to the 5 per cent. allowed to be sent for good conduct—all those slightly unwell, & whom a thirty days furlough would restore to duty, are being sent home.

My dear girl, I hope this letter will reach you only a few days before I come myself, but do not be too confident of it. I shall only feel certain I am going, when the steamboat gets well under way. I know my Divn commander would not consent to my leaving the Reg't without a field officer & my only hope is in getting a general order including the whole Court from Genl. McPherson—there is nothing doing actually requiring my prescence here, and I should feel no hesitation in going on such an order. Kiss the darling child for Father, tell her to look out for a big frolic when Papa comes. Write me as usual, for if anything should happen that I could not come I don't want to miss your letters

Your Husband, Edward

LETTER 49

St. Louis, Sept 22nd 1863.

My dear wife,

I write in the greatest uncertainty imaginable. I telegraphed you yesterday not to start, as the Division had left Vicksburg, and afterwards rec'd your despatch that you would leave this morning. I immediately telegraphed George for fear my dispatch would not get through yesterday, and that you might leave this morning, not having rec'd it, and determined to wait to hear from him and if you had started to wait for you.

Our party has hurried off on news that our Divn was on the move, and I am waiting here, as I said in great uncertainty and very ill at ease. I hope you have not started, but I cannot contain myself any longer, and as now at 12 m. I have rec'd no certain intelligence I have determined to write you as if you were still at home.

I am disappointed beyond measure for myself that you are not able to go with me down the river, and sorely greived on account of the trouble and disappointment you must experience. But it is the fate of war and but one of the vicissitudes attendant on a soldier's career

The Division has come up the river to Helena, and it is said are to support Gen Steele, who is at Little Rock, in his campaign in Arkansas.[15] We know nothing outside of newspaper reports, but the Division was certainly at Helena on Saturday last. Col. Alexander took his wife with him to Memphis where more certain information can be obtained, but expected to have to send her back from there.

I shall wait till I get an answer from George expecting one every moment, but if I get none, shall wait till tomorrow night, when you would be due here. I am glad to say that I have nearly recovered from my cold, my cough has left me, & I am feeling very well—I reached Indianapolis Tuesday morning—a week ago, & I left there Friday night. I was successful in getting a good many men, & sent a Lieut. down along the Ohio river to pick up the men & meet me in Cairo. I am sorry I can't give you much encouragement that the Reg't will be ordered North. I had to wait at Indianapolis till Friday to see *Gov. Morton*. I succeeded in getting him interested to get the Reg't home, and he made application to the Sec'y of War, for that purpose, but at the same time did not give me much encouragement that it would be granted.[16]

I have had no letter from you, tho' I expected to find one here, & didn't know how you are situated or what arrangements James made at Binghampton. Of course I am much distressed and doubly so by the thought of the inconvenience I must have caused you, to get ready for the proposed trip. I did it honestly and nothing but the most unexpected movement of our Divn would have interfered with it.

I send you Dft for $100.00 which I suppose will be acceptable. I am unable to write anything of our future prospects or of the probable final disposition of the Reg't, till I get to them I will write you then fully & will also write from Memphis. I am sorry not to hear from you here, for I suppose I can't get a letter now till I get to the Reg't, & mails will doubtless be irregular with them. I hope you are well & as contented as possible and that our darling Mamie continues to thrive. Direct to me as usual at the Regiment.

God bless you my dearest & pray with me that we may be soon united and all these present trials & tribulations

Your devoted Husband

Edward

I send the Dft. Payable to the order of Father, so that if you have started, we can send word to him, and he can open the letter & use it. E.

LETTER 50

Memphis Tenn.

Oct 3rd 1863.

My dear wife,

I reached here last Sunday—nearly a week ago, after having been four days on the trip from Cairo down and have deferred writing from day to day in hopes I could give you some definite information as to our future destination

Our whole Division arrived here from Helena, Ark, where they had been laying for ten days, without tents, baggage or blankets, the whole having been left at Vicksburg, under the impression that they were only going on an expedition, and would return in a few days to Vicksburg.

They arrived here in the same destitute condition, and yesterday & today, the camp equipage has just begun to come up.

I have just heard that we are to take cars from here today, and rumor says we are to stop at Corinth. I don't credit it, and expect we will be pushed on to reinforce Rosecrans as fast as possible.[17]

There is universal complaint among officers & men at the shabby treatment the old fighting 7th receives, in being thus sent to the front again, while a choice Corps the 16th Army Corps—numbering 20,000 men—one-half of whom have never been in a severe engagement are retained here under command of Genl Hurlbut. Genl Sherman's Corps of veterans and our Division of McPherson's corps—men who made the campaign before Vicksburg, are called on again while these *dilettante* soldiers of the 16th Corps. remain in their comfortable quarters at Memphis, where they have been for nearly a year past, and continue to do fairey soldiering[18]

I never heard a word of grumbling or murmuring before, from an officer or man of the Division, even when they had no rations for ten days, and were undergoing all the hardships of the hardest campaign of the war, but now they feel that they are badly treated, and from the Brigade commanders down, complaint is universal. Our General, Smith, comes in for the heartiest curses, for it is well known that he was ordered to return from Helena to Vicksburg, when it was found that Gen. Steele did not need our assistance, but instead of that, he came to Memphis, procured the order revoked, and got ordered up here, away from our Corps, and it is generally supposed for the purpose of making some reputation for himself, as commander of a separate detachment.[19]

The old 7th Division has made three or four Major Generals, but they are not anxious to try their hands any more, especially with such material as Smith—they very much doubt if there is the timber there to make one.[20] I found the Regiment in most deplorable condition and it has taxed my every exertion to bring order out of disorder, & establish something like discipline again. Major Byrkitt has not yet joined the Reg't. He reached Vicksburg the day after the Reg't left, & under the supposition that they would return in a few days waited there for them. Since they left Helena, he has started for them, but I learn the boat is aground on a sandbar near Helena. The river is very low & navigation very tedious, we were aground on a bar 48 hours between here & Cairo, and every boat has more or less detention. We had a very pleasant time however, dancing every evening, and singing by an impromtu quartette club. Our party left as I wrote you on Tuesday morning, & I remained to hear from you. I rec'd your despatch that you would not start Tuesday afternoon, & left on the cars for Cairo Wednesday morning, overtaking the boat with our part on these. Tuesday afternoon & evening I had a most agreeable time—called on my old Classmate, Blood,[21] & he took me out into the suburbs of the city, with his fast nag. We visited among other pleasant places, the Botanical Garden, owned by a wealthy & eccentric old bachelor named Shaw, & by him donated to the city of St Louis when he dies.[22] I never saw so large a collection of hothouse plants & flowers, & though a little past the season, the wilderness of petunias & asters, with other rarer flowers, made the grounds look very gay. How I wished for you at every step, to share the pleasures of sight & smell! In the evening, I went with Blood to see his wife & the smartest little four year old girl you ever saw—Mrs. B. gave me a very cordial welcome—had a nice supper, & I felt as if I had been among lifetime friends when the evening was past. I learned many things about our old classmates & was able to tell many things in return, & altogether we had a fine time, as you may imagine. I haven't heard a word from you since I left & you may know, I am very anxious about you. I am so afraid you will have to break up & find a new place. I suppose our mail has gone on to Vicksburg, tho' we have stopped two or three there & hereafter they will be stopped—direct as usual except Vicksburg—don't

Brigadier General John E. Smith, division commander. Courtesy of Daniel Wood.

forget to send me Mamie's photograph if you have not done it—I rec'd all your letters—four—written while Mamie was sick. I am glad I did not get them before I should have been worried to death. I do hope she continues to improve & that you are both well. My own health is firstrate, have entirely recovered from cold & cough, & don't expect to have any more, till I come home, which I hope will be before long. If we should go to Corinth, as garrison for the winter would you come. I beleive Mrs. Alexander is going with the Colonel, with that expectation You may know this has been written very hurriedly & you must excuse appearances. I will write from our next stopping place, wherever that may be.

Write often, & then if some of your letters fail to reach me others may be more fortunate, & then I won't be so long without hearing from you. God bless you, my darling, and our dearest child & keep you from all harm

Your Husband
Edward

CHAPTER 9

The Grandest Military Movement of the War

The Chattanooga Campaign, October–December 1863

A sojourn of comparative idleness for Wood and the 48th Indiana was followed by a new, arduous campaign. After a campaign of maneuver in which a Rebel army was forced from Tennessee in the summer of 1863, Rosecrans and his Army of the Cumberland were poised in northwestern Georgia for further advances. But the Confederates under Braxton Bragg with reinforcements from Lieutenant General James Longstreet struck back savagely on Chickamauga Creek in late September 1863. Rosecrans's army collapsed under the onslaught, falling back to Chattanooga, Tennessee. There it was besieged by Bragg.[1]

Ulysses Grant, now promoted by President Lincoln to overall command of troops in the West, replaced Rosecrans at Chattanooga and orchestrated a comprehensive effort to overcome the Rebel siege.[2] Crucially important was the gathering of available Union forces. Federal forces clustered along the Mississippi River were ordered east to the aid of the beleaguered Army of the Cumberland. Sherman's 15th Corps and parts of other Federal units from the West, including Wood's "Old 7th Division" from the 17th Corps, began an exhausting trek more than 250 miles eastward across Mississippi, Alabama, and Tennessee, rebuilding railroads as they went. The march through the mountains of Tennessee witnessed great difficulties. Wood's descriptions of the men carrying their wagons up and down the mountains over the rocks are telling.

Reaching Chattanooga in mid-November, Sherman's forces remained north of the Tennessee River and out of sight of the Rebels. Grant planned a coordinated assault on Rebel positions south of the river that commanded the city. However, his plans mainly came to naught, as a series of unplanned, uncoordinated movements occurred. Major General Joe Hooker's corps, ordered to make only a demonstration against Lookout Mountain, instead succeeded in scaling the sheer cliffs under fire and seized the seemingly impregnable position on November 24 in the "Battle Above the Clouds." Crossing the river in boats under cover of darkness on the night of November 23, the 48th Indiana and Sherman's command participated in the assault on the north end of Missionary Ridge at Tunnel Hill on November 25 and, combined with Major General George Thomas's assault, succeeded in sweeping Rebel forces off the mountain and into retreat into Georgia. Chattanooga was relieved.

Wood grasped the central importance of the Chattanooga campaign. Chattanooga controlled the Rebel center, affecting the survival of the Confederacy in both the East and the West. Wood, now regimental commander, having grown in his military knowledge, displayed greater strategic thinking in his letters, seeing the role of his regiment more fully and placing their movements in the larger Union military scheme. His broadened worldview reflected the impressions that General Grant, writing years later in his *Memoirs*, voiced in reviewing the Vicksburg campaign: "A military education was acquired [by the army] which no other school could have given. Men who thought a company was quite enough for them to command properly at the beginning, would have made good regimental or brigade commanders; most of the brigade commanders were equal to the command of a division."[3]

LETTER 51

Glendale Miss. Oct. 7th 1863.

My dear wife

I wrote you last Saturday from Memphis, and as I have a chance to send a letter back to the confines of civilization today, I scrawl a few lines again.

We left Memphis Monday morning the 5th on the cars, reached Corinth that night after dark went into bivouac—which means lying on the ground with nothing to eat—and moved out here, twelve miles east on the R.Rd towards Chattanooga yesterday. To-day our tents etc, have come up, and we are arranging a camp, with a strong probability of breaking up tomorrow or next day and moving still further eastward. Genl Sherman's corps, the 15th Army Corps and our Division of the 17th Corps constitute the expedition—all under the command of Maj Gen Frank P. Blair for the present. What the object & purposes of this expedition may be is all a matter of surmise to us subordinates[4]—We are 180 miles from Chattanooga by rail, with the R.Rd most thoroughly destroyed. It would be impossible to move a larger army this distance without repairing the R.Rd to furnish us with supplies, & so some of us think that we are to be stretched along the road, guarding and repairing it as we go, and so establish communication from Memphis to Chattanooga, & then transfer nearly all of Grant's army by this route to the scene of the recent desperate battles.

It is the grandest military movement of the war, this massing of troops on the center—like movements on a chess-board, everything else has become subordinate to this grand attack on the enemy's centre at Chattanooga, which is in reality the Key to the whole position. When I say, whole position, I mean the whole line of our contending armies as they stretch from the Potomac to Texas, and so considered, the present movement for our armies toward the centre of such a line, is the grandest military movement of any age. If we are in time, we shall be able to overwhelm the rebel forces in our front and from Chattanooga, we are in position to knock loudly at the back-doors of Charleston & Richmond. I feel the natural ardor of a soldier & a patriot, in such a momentous undertaking and all merely personal things are for the moment lost sight of. I am encouraged a good deal about the Regiment—we have gained by arrivals from Vicksburg & furloughed men, until we number 230—only 50 less than we had one year ago, when we came back to Corinth from the pursuit of Price.

I hear nothing from you & am worried enough. I know you have written often & it is too bad I can't get them—from what I have written, you can imagine it will be some time before a mail reaches us. Don't fail to write all the oftener, and some of your letters may reach me.

I have kept the messenger, who goes to Corinth with mail waiting sometime & must close.

God bless you, dearest, and our darling Mamie, will write whenever possible.

Beleive me

Your devoted Husband
Edward

LETTER 52

Glendale, Miss.
Oct 16th 1863.

My dear wife,

Your dear letters of date Sept 26th & Oct 4th have been received and I am truly thankful you are well and under such discouraging circumstances, are likely to be so well situated. I don't like to be in a situation where I am compelled to be under obligations to any one, and for that reason I suggested trying to find a boarding place for you. You know why I did not. I supposed it was fixed that you & Nell were to remain where you were. You may imagine I was distressed when your letter of the 26th ult. arrived two days ago, & I read of your sore disappointment in not coming after all your arrangements were made, and of your still more deplorable condition, turned out into the street almost, & all uncertain where to go, and I was made glad again today to hear that Edward & Sarah had so kindly offered you a home with them. I forgot all about my unwillingness to incur obligation in my great joy that you were to be so nicely situated, and still I thought and still think that it is not right and that I must get home to make a home of my own for my loved ones. I have no words to express my thanks to Edward & Sarah for their kindness to you—though they may think there is no obligation conferred on *you, I* owe them a debt that I fear I can never repay. Let them know that I am not unappreciative of their kindness, & let us hope that the coming years may show that we were not undeserving of it. Today we have marching orders for Burnsville, 18 miles east on the road & as usual in the front. Our old Division has been tossed about from point to point, but always manages to turn up in the lead, where there is an advance to be made. I have suggested that the *Division* be *divided*—so as to give each Brigade a chance to be in the front. If one Brigade was put in front of Rosecrans & one in front of the Army of the Potomac, I think our troubles would be at an end—for we have always been in the front and *never* have been defeated.

Seriously, we are in for an arduous campaign. We are attached to Sherman's Corps and are to go thro' to Rosecrans or rather Grant, who has gone to take command[5] some 200 miles & whether we build the RRd as we go or not, the expedition will be a very severe one. Barring some rheumatic twinges, I am quite well, & feel able to make the trip. There are some indications that we may get home, but it will not be this fall. I see my plan published as Gov. Morton's plan for filling the old regiments, & I take it from that, that he has rec'd some encouragement from Washington that it would be adopted.[6]

I have written this in a great hurry, with many interruptions consequent in moving & you must overlook appearances. Write to Mary Mackie, she a dear good girl & I am glad you have heard from her. Send Mamie's picture if you have not done so & kiss the darling one for papa. Write often & beleive me ever

Your devoted Husband
Edward

LETTER 53

Dixon Station, Ala.
Oct. 25th 1863.

My dear wife,

It is some time since I have written you—the last I think was from Glendale, when we were about to move to Burnsville. We reached B. the same day, remained two days, marched for Iuka, the scene of the hard-fought battle of a year ago—stayed one day, and moved to this point ten miles distant, day before yesterday. The weather has been horrible—both the last days march, it rained steadily, a cold fall rain—The streams were all much swollen, and the roads fathom deep in mud, add to this that the country is much broken the road winding thro' deep valleys and now passing over the summits of precipitous hills and you may imagine, it was wearisome work for men, and a seeming impossibility for our immense wagon train, & heavy artillery to travel at all. But we all came up to the stopping place some time, the rear being often till midnight in getting up. We are now within ten miles of Tuscumbia Ala, and our advance will probably occupy that place today. We are making slow progress towards Chattanooga, if that be our destination, and there must be more activity displayed soon, or winter will set in, when campaigning will be impossible, before we have accomplished our purpose. We have not abandoned the R.Rd yet—trains run to Bear Creek 5 miles west of this station—where there is a large bridge burned, which is being rebuilt. The R.Rd is more thoroughly destroyed than I ever conceived it was possible to destroy one. The rebels have built fires at every point—that is where the rails come together—and the fire has not only burnt out the ties, but the heat, causing the iron to expand, has forced the rails together and bent them so as render them useless. This has been done, not occasionally, but continuously for miles, and nothing remains of the road, but the grading. I beleive it is intended to open the road to Tuscumbia, some 70 miles east from Corinth—if so, we will be in this vicinity two or three weeks, unless other troops move up to take our place. I regard this as more than likely, as it would be out of character to have this Division anywhere but in the front. We are getting a little more reconciled to our fate, as one that is inevitable, and the boys especially rejoice that we have left Corinth, Tishomingo county, and the whole desolate region of Northern Mississippi, and emerged into a fairer & more fruitful country, where no large army has yet passed to devour its whole substance.

We have fared sumptuously here on fresh beef, pork chickens sweet potatoes, butter etc an agreeable change from the army rations that had previously been our fare.

Your letter of the 11th was received several days since, in remarkably quick time. I am glad you are well & that Mamie is improving so fast. Do send me her photograph, if have not done so, & I wish you would get a half dozen more of mine at Lazier's. I have lost the card & forgotten the No. but they can find it by the date—somewhere between the 10th & 20th of March last. I have had to buy some undershirts at enormous prices $3.50! & am *sorry* I did not bring more from home. My health is firstrate, barring the diarrhoea, which continues about as usual. The talk about going home to recruit has about died out with us, tho' occasionally some word from there, or some stray paragraph in a newspaper, fans its almost dead hope into a feeble blaze. Resigning is out of the question just now—except to be resigned to your lot, and hope for better things. I hope you have agreed with Sarah on a price to be paid for your board and that it is liberal. I know the money small object with them, but still feel better satisfied if you pay a good price, as some thing of an equivalent

Give my love to them & to Henry & Myra, write me how Nell & James get on, & all the news. I couldn't do anything with the Expressmen at Memphis about my trunk, so we'll have to submit to a big swindle on a small scale. Write often, dearest, direct to Smith's (John E.) Division, Sherman's Corps, *via* Memphis

Kiss the darling one for her papa, and beleive me, as ever

Your devoted Husband
Edward

I had forgotten to mention that this is the anniversary of our wedding day, not because I had not thought of it for it was my earliest thought this morning. Four years! & half the time separated!—not much such a wedded life, I fancy, as we looked forward to four years ago. Let us pray God that the next four years may be spend together, in a peaceful land.

Marie Gautier Wood. Courtesy of Daniel Wood.

LETTER 54

Fayetteville Tenn.
Nov 9th 1863.

My dear wife,

I embrace the first opportunity to write you since my last of Oct 25th. Busy days, they have been with us since then. On the 29th, we broke up camp at Dixon, Ala., retraced our steps, moving in a Northwesterly direction, and striking the Tennessee River at Chicasaw near the Alabama & Mississippi line. On the 31st we cross the Tennessee after night on transports & gunboats, during a terribly cold rainstorm that had lasted all day. In the morning we moved out reaching Florence, Ala, the next day, thence east to Rogerville, 24 miles. Here we encountered the Elk river, swollen by rains & impassable and were obliged to make a detour to the north, entering Tennessee at Gilbertsboro, 35 miles north of Rogerville thence our course has been easterly to this place, & we are now within 30 miles of the Nashville & Chattanooga R.Rd tho' about 90 miles distant from the latter place. We have marched 157 miles in 8 days, making no day less than 15 miles, and several days more than twenty. And over such roads!—tho' not in the most mountainous region of Tenn, we have passed over a succession of hills that in any other than a mountainous country, would be called mountains, and certainly the roughest, most rocky roads I ever saw. It is astonishing how our wagons have held together over them. Our Regiment has been very fortunate—I think ours is the only one in the Division that has brought thro' every wagon safely. Today for the first time, we halt to let the Divisions in the rear catch up, and we are told that a mail is to be sent ahead to the R.Rd. Tents are unloaded for the first time, the boys are writing letters & washing their clothes, horses & mules are being shod & wagons repaired, and it is still a busy day with us. I rec'd your letter of the 12th ult. a few days after one of the 18th—you may be sure they were both very welcome. I am glad indeed you are so pleasantly situated, and I can never be too grateful to Sarah & Edward for their kindness to you. I think Sarah fixes the price of board too low, you ought at least to pay $5.00 & I shall insist upon it. I expect we will receive pay soon again & I will send you a remittance If you need any money now, write me & I will send some at once. It is hard to tell where we will be tho' I suppose we will go on to the R.Rd[7] & then strike in the direction of Chattanooga. I haven't seen a Northern paper in two weeks, & of course am quite in the dark as to the present military situation. Dr. Ellis[8] writes me, that he thinks when the present active fall campaign is over, that the Reg't will be ordered home. I haven't much confidence in it, nor do I think that any great battle will fought in this Department this fall. *We* are not strong enough, *men* is the great lack as usual, & I don't see that any effective means are being taken to supply the deficiency. I shall probably stay until these active operations are over, & then if there is no prospect of filling the Reg't, bring about a consolidation of it, that will leave me out.

I don't like to resign while I am well & able for the service as I am now, but if two regiments could be put together, and I could be mustered out as a superfluous officer, I would be glad of it.

The mail-boy is hurrying me up—we only had half an hour's notice & I had to put up my tent & get out my writing materials so you must excuse this poor scrawl of a letter. It will assure you at least that I am well, in fact, in excellent health & I will write again when we reach the R.Rd at Deckard. If you have a map you can find the station on the Nashville & Chatt. R.R. Remember me to all. Kiss papa's darling Mamie, "when this cruel war is over" she shall sing it for papa.[9] Goodbye & God bless you my darlings.

Your Husband
Edward

LETTER 55

Winchester, Tenn
Nov 12th 1863.

My dear wife,

I have time to write you but a few lines, as I promised to when we reached the R.Rd. We are still four miles from the main line of the Nashville & Chattanooga road, which we cross tomorrow and strike out over the mountains in the direction of Chattanooga.

Our destination is Bridgeport on the Tennessee river, about halfway between Stevenson & Chat. The road runs directly over & through the Cumberland Mountains, and I expect a pretty hard trip—the distance is not much over 30 miles and we expect to be four days making it.

The distance from Fayetteville to this place is 36 miles, and it is still four miles to Deckerd—making 40 miles instead of 20 as I wrote you from F.

We made it easily in two days, over very good roads except the last part of the first days march, where after dark our wagon train struck a peice of bad road, & more than twenty wagons were stuck fast at once. As usual, it was our luck to be rear-guard, & it was late night before we got into camp.

Today for the first time over two weeks we have heard from the States, & seen the papers—the news is cheering—New York has repudiated Seymour copperheadism, & Sedgwick has acheived a success on the Potomac. Arkansas is cleaned of armed rebels, & the people begin to show signs of returning to their senses & their allegiance.[10] When our armies can be brought in contact with the people of northern & western Texas—now essentially loyal—the business of the rebellion will be done for west of the Mississippi.

I had a long conversation today with Maj Genl Stanley, for a long time Chief of Cavalry in this Department & he is inclined to think that Bragg is falling back towards Dalton Ga.[11] If he is, or if he ever does, I suppose we shall follow him. I was long ago of the opinion that we should never conquer the rebellion, until we should occupy the sacred soil of every state in the Confederacy. Georgia, Alabama Texas, and So. Carolina, are all that remain to be occupied. Gilmore must soon be able to open the Charleston door into So. Carolina[12]—Texas is already open & it remains for this army to occupy Alabama & Georgia. I think—and this is the first time I have expressed an opinion or fixed a time for the war to end—but I think I see signs of the beginning of the end, and early summer will see the contest substantially ended as far as fight is concerned.

The grave political questions that will arise as to the *status* of the revolted states will not be readily determined, and will undoubtedly serve to prolong the strife and delay the return of the seceded states to harmonious action in the Union.[13]

But I have run into too long a disquisition for my small sheet, which was all the paper that was convenient. We found the 2nd Ind. Cavl'y here. Capt. Mitchell of Goshen, has a Company in it.[14] Many of the boys have visited us this afternoon

My health is very good, we have lived fine in our mess on the march, but we are now in a country which has been thoroughly exhausted of subsistence for either man or beast, & must depend again on the commissary

I will write again as soon as we reach Bridgeport—direct to Sherman's Corps, *via* Nashville. Oct 18th is the last date I have from you, write often & let me know everything about yourself and Mamie. God bless you both, darlings, & may He soon restore to you,

Your loving soldier boy
Edward

LETTER 56

Near Chattanooga Tenn
Nov 21st 1863.

My dear wife,

By favor of Col. Alexander, commanding our Brigade I have tent room & pen & paper to write you a few lines. I wrote you last from Winchester, & promised to write, from Bridgeport, Ala, but writing was out of the question. I thought I knew something of soldiering and had done some campaigning, but the last ten days has opened an entire new chapter of experiences. From Winchester, the first day we made sixteen miles, climbing a mountain over the roughest & rockiest road where the wagons had literally to be lifted by the men up steep pitches three or four feet high—on the top of the mountain, we traversed a table laced road for several miles, and on the next day after making seven miles we commenced the descent, more awful than the ascent. Fifteen men were detailed to each wagon & with ropes they held them back and lifted them down the worst places. I led my horse down steps where the men were obliged to catch hold of the bushes & scrubs to hold themselves back. Four days of such traveling brought us to Bridgeport Ala, a thriving town of one sawmill and an immense bridge across the Tennessee, which the rebels had partially destroyed, but which our men are rebuilding—Here we were ordered to leave tents & baggage and with five days rations to strike out for the seat of war. We crossed the Tennessee on the pontoon bridge, consisting of 163 boats about twenty feet apart, with stringers laid from each boat, & covered with planks. Our Division commenced crossing at 7 A.M. & our Regiment which as usual was rear guard of the rear Brigade crossed just at dark, we marched then miles after crossing and went into camp just at midnight. Moved the next morning at daylight marched & marched & marched till it seemed as tho' we would never stop, making 24 miles & stopping at just 12 o'clock at night, waited for the teams to come to get our blankets etc, had a fire built, got warmed & had just got stowed away, with the comfortable assurance, that we were not to move till 8 o'clock the next morning, when the order came to "fall in" immediately, that this command must cross the river at once, no teams to follow, 100 rounds of ammunition, and ambulances in rear of the brigade. We moved at 1 o'clock expecting a fight at daybreak.[15] Consider the discouraging circumstances. We had marched till midnight for two days, had just got comfortably asleep horses & mules had been for three days on half rations, & my horse had just got his last feed—about a quart of oats Battery horses were used up as well as the animals, & men, the noblest of all animals, with more powers of endurance than them all, were completely tired out, falling to sleep at the least halt, & had to be urged up whenever we stopped. I fell asleep in the saddle, and dropped down whenever there was a chance by the side of the road & napped it for a while. Finally just before sunrise we stopped in this little valley, where 3,000 men have been living since yesterday morning, without a tent to shelter them from the pouring rains that have fallen without intermission. Do you wonder that everybody feels mad, discouraged, disconsolate. If we could have met these confounded rebels, that are causing us all this trouble yesterday morning, I think every man of us would have been good for ten of them. We were all so tired, desperate in fact, that we would not have known when we were whipped

Sherman's corps of which we are the advance, is concentrating here, & in a day or two we expect to throw a pontoon or two across the river and try to dislodge the rebs in our front. Whenever there is a chance I will write you. In the meantime I know you are a true soldiers wife, with a brave heart, that fears no result, but is only anxious for the success of our arms, & the safety of your boy. We are in the midst of a horrible & desperate conflict. God grant it may be decided for us. Write me often. I have written in a great hurry & you must excuse all mistakes. Remember me to all friends & kiss the dear one for me & above all don't fail to write Your devoted Husband

Edward

P.S. Send some postage stamps

LETTER 57

Near Chattanooga, Tenn.
Dec 2nd 1863.

My dear wife

I seize the first opportunity since our return from the front, and from the pursuit of Bragg's flying rebels, to assure you of my continued safety & welfare. I tried to telegraph Edward this morning, but found it impossible to get the use of the line for private messages, and so you will have to wait for Uncle Sam's slow coach to bring you the good news that your boy has again escaped unharmed. Our Brigade was remarkably fortunate, not being hotly engaged at any time during the three days furious fighting, and the casualties are confined to wounds received on the skirmish line, and from the random bursting of rebel shells.

You have doubtless read with great interest, full accounts of our operations with their glorious result, in the papers, and I can only give you some idea of our part, in the struggle. The famous Chickamauga creek empties into the Tennessee river, a few miles above Chattanooga, which is situated on the south bank of the Tennessee, the river here running nearly east & west. Lookout Mountain is a long elevation of table land, stretching for 20 miles in a northeasterly direction from Trenton Ga to Chattanooga, where it terminates abruptly at an elevation of 2000 ft above the river—the valley of the river to its foot being 2 1/2 to 3 miles wide. Missionary Ridge is a similar elevation although not so high running parallel with the river & at about the same distance from it as Lookout, stretching from Chattanooga to the Chickamauga creek, which runs nearly north. We, that is, Sherman's corps and Davis'[16] division of the Army of the Cumberland were on the North side of the Tennessee, and nearly opposite the mouth of Chickamauga and were the extreme left of our line. Hooker on the right & Thomas in the centre were both on the south of the Tennessee.[17] We were ordered to cross the river in boats at midnight of the night of the 23rd ult, for which purpose 120 pontoon boats had been hauled several miles up the river, launched & manned by a brigade of the 2nd Division, who under cover of night, dropped quietly down the river to the mouth of Chickamauga, landed two Regiments just about, who surrounded & *"gobbled,"* the rebel pickets stationed there, without firing a gun. So far it was a complete success and now commenced the crossing in earnest and a lively & exciting time you may beleive it was.[18]

The boats held from 25 to 30 men each, the river was nearly a quarter of a mile wide, & the current rapid Yet despite all these difficulties, broad daylight found two Divisions (ours & Morgan L. Smith's[19]) across the river & securely *entrenched.* Talk about your tremendous engines of so many thousand horse-power! Ten thousand *man-power,* with spades & picks can accomplish wonders in a surprising short space of time We landed near a house and when day dawned the surprised owner of the land found his farm fenced in with a dirt fence, that will last for many a day.

The day broke slowly, with a heavy mist that did not roll away, so as to reveal the top of Missionary Ridge where the rebels were supposed to be posted till nearly 9 o'clock. In the meantime, daylight had showed us a more advantageous position, a quarter of a mile to the front & our line had been advanced and a second line of rifle pits dug. As soon as our division were over, the work of laying the pontoon bridge was commenced & finished about noon. The two other Divisions—Ewing's[20] of our corps, & Jeff. C. Davis' of Thomas'—with the artillery crossed rapidly, and by 1 P.M. we were ready to advance. All this time, the rebels made no sign, and many anxious and curious eyes were sweeping with glasses the sides and top of the Ridge, distant about 2 miles, in search of any indication of rebels, but without success. Ewings division had the right & advanced straight toward Tunnel Hill—we had the centre, with Morgan L. Smith on the left—his left resting on Chickamauga creek, with Davis in reserve. We advanced in close column, the front well covered by skirmishers, who advanced without opposition, till near the foot of the hill, when they became warmly engaged, the enemy's skirmishers however retired, over the first ridge, which we occupied without opposition. In the next ravine however their skirmishers made a decided stand, & it soon became evident that the enemy were in force on the next ridge. It being near night, we halted, & commenced to fortify our position. My Regiment relieved the 4th Minn who had been out as skirmishers at night, & we lay all night in the ravine between the two armies, within talking distance of the rebel pickets. If our men were busy strengthening their position the rebels were not idle, & we could hear, distinctly, their chopping of trees & moving artillery into position all night. At daylight, we were releived having had no wink of sleep for two nights—at the same time the rebs commenced a vigorous shelling of our position, which was warmly replied to by our guns. We were well sheltered however behind the crest of our ridge, & during the bombardment I caught a couple of hours of sleep. We occupied our old position till about noon, the battle raging fiercely on all sides of us—our 2nd & 3rd Brigades being hard at work—when my regiment & the 63rd Ill were ordered to the left to support a brigade of

Morgan L. Smith's, but we did not become actively engaged, & the balance of our brigade was equally fortunate.[21] At night we returned to our old position, & under cover of darkness the rebels left the ridge in our front which they had stubbornly held all day, against three desperate assaults. Ewings Divn & our two Brigades supporting it, suffered severely, the loss in officers was very heavy. Lieut Col Heath was severely wounded by a piece of shell, but is likely to recover.[22] The rebels had massed a very heavy force in our front to prevent their right flank from being turned, & to keep open their communications with Longstreet, who had gone off in the direction of Knoxville[23]

At daylight, on the 26th we moved back towards the river and crossed the Chickamauga on a pontoon near its mouth and pursued the enemy until the night of the 29th continually skirmishing with his rear-guard, capturing many prisoners and several caissons & wagons, which he was obliged to leave behind.[24]

Bridgeport, Ala, Dec 6/63—I had written all but the last three lines of the above, when the order came about nine o'clock, that we would be paid that night and move at daylight the next morning I dropped my letter to make some necessary arrangements, & was not able to take it up again & our baggage did not come up again till last night. I am very sorry there is such a delay in sending this letter, but it is unavoidable, & I hope you will feel easy before you get this.

If we had been engaged you would have seen accounts of it in the papers, as full particulars have doubtless been published before this. We made the march from our camp beyond Chattanooga to this place—40 miles—in two days, but as I said our teams did not get up till last night.

We have got our tents once more, & have a very pleasant camp. It seems quite like home to get back into a tent, with all the little conveniences about you, that go to make camp comfortable and soldiering tolerable. Tough experiences indeed, we have had since we left this place for Chattanooga. The men have been on half rations all the time, & horses have had literally nothing most of the time. Ten thousand dead mules & horses would be a low estimate for the number that lie on the road & around Chattanooga starved to death. And talking about horses, I must tell you a curious, almost romantic experience that befell my old favorite horse, Charlie. To premise, he is always mischievous, & hard to catch when he happens to get loose, until he has had his play out, but was never known to break away before. While we were in camp near Chattanooga, he was unusually restive—broke his halter once, & afterwards a chain, & made good his escape. Two days & nights my boy Mike, who is greatly attached to him, searched in vain for him, through camps, in batteries, and amongst the cavalry. On the third day, three miles out in the country, he heard of a horse answering the description, that had been taken up by a man living two miles further on. Following him up, he described the horse so accurately, including the blanket, surcingle[25] etc, that the man said he had no doubt he was our horse & gave him up. Now comes the remarkable part of the story. The horse was at his old home! The man who had him, had raised him till he was five years old as a stallion—had then sold him to a man in Chattanooga for $150 in gold, for the use of his wife as a saddlehorse—the horse proving too highstrung for the purpose, had been sold about two years ago to an officer in the rebel army. Our Quartermaster found the horse loose about Hamburg Landing, near Corinth in the spring of /62—If we admit all that is fairly inferable from all this, that the horse knew he was in the neighborhood of his old house, & broke loose to go to it, & *did* go to it, who will say that he had not at least *horse-sense.* He was evidently a great favorite with his former owner & his sons. The boys could turn him loose & call him by his old name, *"Moro,"* & he would come to them, & contrary to his usual manner suffer himself to be caught—So much for horses—

I am in your debt for two letters, one recd at Chattanooga of the 19th containing the eulogistic article on Gov. Morton, and one of the 24th rec'd last night. You are a good girl to write so often & nothing tends so much to console me in this hard service, as to hear that wife & baby are so well. I know you will not neglect writing at least once a week, & when you do not hear from me with the same regularity, you may be sure, it is because the exigencies of the service will not permit. I will send you by express tomorrow—to-day being Sunday—$100 & will write enclosing the receipt.

I despair of ever getting the Regiment home to recruit, & suppose we must continue the same small squad. We are ordered to send recruiting parties home, but I do not anticipate much from their labors. I am in very good health—was a little under the weather—agueish for two or three days, the effects of late exposure—but am feeling firstrate again. I have no idea where we are going or what is to be our fate for the winter—you can direct as usual. We have had some very severe weather—a great deal of cold rain, followed by cold winter weather, freezing the ground so that it hardly thawed out during the day. Some little articles that perhaps you might send by mail would be acceptable—two pr of merino socks, a stout pillow-case, & a few postage stamps

Have you written to Mary Mackie, don't neglect it. I haven't heard a word of Walter, in a long time I was glad to hear of Jo Woods promotion.[26] I saw Gen Hooker the other day—a splendid-looking man—he *looks* the General, more than any man I have seen.

We were reviewed the day before we left Chat. by Maj Gens Grant, Hunter[27] & Logan, & I was not ashamed of the appearance the old Division presented.

Dinner is announced, my favorite dish—bean soup—so I know you will pardon me if I draw this long letter to a close. Tell our little daughter how her papa loves her, & how he longs to see her. I was disappointed in her dark-colored card photograph, & if papa don't come home pretty soon he must have another from the original. God bless you both my dear, & keep you safely from all harm is the prayer of your devote Husband

Edward

Chapter 10

I Write by a Cheerful Coal Fire in a Grate

Alabama Sojourn, December 1863–January 1864

Union strategic thinking envisioned advances into eastern Tennessee, Georgia, and the deep south of Mississippi and Alabama in 1864. Secure transportation links were essential to the success of any advances into Rebel-held territory. General Grant, now commander of all Federal forces in the West, ordered Sherman to occupy northern Alabama and nearby parts of Tennessee all the way to Nashville. Sherman broached with Grant the possibility of a Mississippi campaign to "clear out" Rebel resistance in that state. This was seen as a preliminary measure before a campaign into eastern Tennessee and Virginia could be made.[1] Hence, the 48th Indiana and much of the 15th Corps settled down to guarding railroads in northern Alabama during the winter. The regiment obtained enviable quarters in Huntsville, "living in clover" during their stay. When the requisite three-fourths of the regiment reenlisted, Wood and his men prepared for the promised furlough as their reward. Their opportunity finally came, and they embarked for home, arriving in Indianapolis by train on February 6 where Wood gave a speech at the reception. The veterans shortly arrived in their northern Indiana home counties and partook in additional welcoming celebrations. It is not clear where Edward met Jane and resided during his furlough, but as Jane reported her safe arrival back in Syracuse and the Goshen press reported the colonel's presence in town, it is probable the family reunited there.[2]

LETTER 58

My dear wife

Your letter of the 30th ult. enclosing photographs & postage stamps is received this morning, and as I have an opportunity to send a letter North today by private hands, I write a few lines, hoping they may reach you a day or two sooner than through our regular mail

I also send by Capt Packard[3] who goes home on recruiting service $100. to be expressed from Louisville. I hope you will receive it in good season and that it may be enough for present wants. I am much obliged for the stamps & photos. I was just out of stamps & had written you for them in my last.

I have nothing new or interesting to write. We are in the same camp as when I last wrote, and are enjoying the rest, after our late arduous services. How long it will last of course as soldiers subject to orders we can't tell, but the impression is general that it will be of short duration.

Two of the Divisions only of this corps, are here—Osterhaus' & ours— the other two—Morgan L. Smith's & Ewing's, are still out in front, either towards Dalton Ga, where Braggs army is supposed to be, or else gone towards Knoxville, to releive Burnside.[4] We shall probably remain here till they return, when Gen Logan will assume command, and we shall go to Huntsville, Ala, some 60 miles west of this place, on the line of the Memphis & Charleston R.Rd

It is reported that Genl Sherman meditates a winter campaign against Mobile, to include all the forces in his Department. Our Corps—the 15th to start with thirty days rations of coffee, sugar, hard bread & *salt*, from Huntsville Ala, and traverse the whole length of the state, subsisting for meat, corn meal etc on the country.[5]

Another column composed of the 16th corps, Gen Hurlbut commanding, to start from Memphis while the 17th corps under Genl McPherson leaves Vicksburg, the whole representing an aggregate of 60,000 men to be concentrated near Mobile for the reduction of that point. The object is a good one, and the force is adequate, but the march of 250 miles across the country, and thro' the heart of the enemy's country does not appear to me, feasible. At least, the great water courses, the natural avenues of commerce, and the means by which we have penetrated the country so far, would seem to me to indicate the route to Mobile. In other words, the troops should proceed *via* the Mississippi river to some point not over 100 miles from Mobile, it may be to New Orleans, & thence by the Gulf to within striking distance. I don't claim any military ability, but I should think common sense, would indicate the absurdity of fitting out an expedition at Huntsville, the extreme northern point of the State, to operate against Mobile, the extreme southern.

The thirty days rations, of even the limited number of articles named, with the smallest possible amount of baggage, and camp equipage, would make an immense train, that would greatly impede our movements, besides the great annoyance that light bodies of the enemy's cavalry might cause by frequent attacks on it. Many other disadvantages readily occur to any one who has seen service, and I am only surprised that it should be seriously entertained, as I am reliably informed it is, at Head Quarters. With such a prospect before us, there is no chance for rest or home, for our poor old Regiment. It seems to be doomed to extinction, and I am getting indifferent as to how soon the hour of its dissolution comes. I have refused to make any more recommendations for promotion to fill vacancies as they occur, and unless the recruiting service turns out better, than I have any reason to expect, intend to consolidate the companies into five, and turn over the command to the Major.

I am notified that my recruiting squad are about starting, & I must close. I am so glad Mamie continues well, & to improve, she must be a great deal of comfort & company for you. Kiss the darling for papa, and may a kind Providence watch over & bless you and restore you again to your own

Edward

LETTER 59

Bridgeport, Ala.
Dec 20th 1863.

My dear wife,

It is some time since I wrote you last, but I have been waiting expecting every day to hear from you, and really the monotony of camplife has afforded nothing to write about. The last letter I had from you was dated Nov. 30th, and you will not wonder that I am anxious & impatient to hear again. I suppose tho' you hardly felt like writing while waiting to hear from me after the battle, and am very sorry I could not have written sooner.

It is fortunate we were not sent to Knoxville to releive Burnside, or I might now be writing my first letter, as the two Divisions of our corps that were sent, have just commenced returning. Ewing's division reached here yesterday, and Morgan L. Smith's is expected to-morrow. The Corps having thus got together again, the day after we take up our line of march westward—along the line of the Memphis and Charleston R.Rd. thro' Stevenson Ala, to Huntsville Ala, distant about 80 miles. It is understood that all thoughts of a winter campaign have been abandoned, and that our Corps is to go into winter quarters, along the line of this road. There are two R.Rds running in a southerly direction from Nashville—one nearly southeast to Stevenson—the road over which all our supplies have hitherto come—the other directly south to Decatur, something in this shape

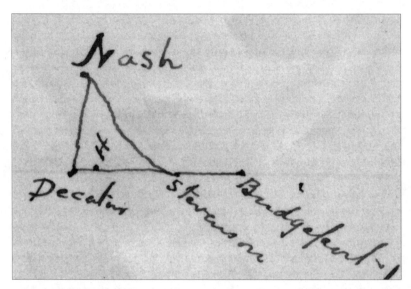

Wood's drawing of the Decatur, Alabama, area, December 20, 1863. Courtesy of the Indiana Historical Society.

the road is already open from Nashville to Decatur, we are to open & guard it from Decatur to Stevenson, thus giving two lines of communication from Nashville. With the immense armies that have been concentrated in this locality, such a measure became indispensable, as one road was found inadequate to supply the wants of the troops. We have been here just about long enough to get comfortably settled. We lived in all manner of discomfort until about a week ago—sitting over log fires in the smoke, when the weather would permit, and when the rain drove us inside, wrapped up in blankets, or sat shivering in our tents. About that time however, we concluded to build chimneys, and you would have laughed to have seen the Major and I tugging at the huge, rough stones, & puzzling our brains to get the rude pile into something like the shape of a fireplace & chimney. However, in two days, we succeeded in getting up two very respectable affairs not exactly ornamental, but very comfortable, and we are already repaid for our labor. The Regiment as usual, taking the hint, followed suit, and now every tent has some kind of a structure of stones, mud & sticks that answers the purpose of a fireplace. The weather has been very capricious—heavy rains have fallen, & been succeeded by clear cold weather that would do no discredit to a more Northern clime. This morning was unusually sharp—the ground was frozen hard, & at noon it has thawed but little. The other day, I received a very unexpected letter from an old classmate, Runnells, now a minister at Orford N.H.[6] It seems at the class meeting, last summer, he was chosen Secretary, & having heard of my whereabouts thro' Blood of St Louis, he addressed me to learn something of my life since leaving College. He proposed to publish a pamphlet in a few months, giving the personal history of each member of the class, since graduation, & I very gladly furnished him the few data necessary in my case. I am anticipating much pleasure from the perusal of the pamphlet.

The boys in the Reg't are talking strongly of re-enlisting as Veteran Volunteers—the chief inducement being the 30 days furlough home. If I can be assured that they can have it soon, I shall feel like advising them to it. They have a year yet to serve, & I don't think it possible that this miserable Confederacy can hold out longer than that—they would thus not increase their time of service, and would have the benefit of the large bounties, Gov't is paying. The bounty with the $100 bounty now due them, would am't to $502—admitting that they serve a year, this, with their pay would make $658—more than $50 per month for their years service. The inducement is very great, especially when you throw in the attraction of home even for 30 days. If we talk about starting, I will give you timely notice—if three-fourths of the Reg't re-enlist, we go in a body, & report to the Supt. of Recruiting in our state to reorganize & recruit. I think that will be my time to leave the service, & I shall try to get Col Eddy to take command again. I hope you have rec'd the $100 sent from Louisville—we shall soon have two months pay due again & I will send you more. Write often whether you hear from me or not—I will not wait again, but will write at least once a week, when possible. I ruined two of my photographs, by getting them wet, & am out again—when convenient send me a few more. Almost Christmas time again! how I wish I could be with you, or at least send you something for yourself & baby, but one is as impossible as the other. I wish you would send me some Magazines & occasionally an Illustrated paper. I haven't seen one or Harper or Atlantic since Oct.

Remember me kindly to all. Kiss our dear Mamie for papa, and tell her she must be a good girl to her mamma. Write often & tell me all about what you are doing, & don't forget the papers. Your devoted Husband

Edward

LETTER 60

Huntsville. Ala.
Dec 28th 1863.

My dear wife,

I received your welcome letter of the 10th inst. just after I had mailed my last of the 20th at Bridgeport, and was glad indeed to hear from you, but sorry that you should have been so long without tidings from me. Your anxiety must have been releived in a very few days after you wrote, by the receipt of my letter written after we returned to Bridgeport.

I wrote you we were expecting to leave B. for this place, in a few days. The order came very unexpectedly that night to move in the morning at daylight, without tents or baggage, & with ten days rations, to prepare for a rapid march on this place. Accordingly we started on time, leaving everything, trunks mess-chests etc, except our blankets, and pushed ahead, reaching here Friday night (Christmas), having made the distance—90 miles—in five days. Considering the season of the year & the state of the roads, we call it good marching—but then you know we are good campaigners, and to the boys that marched through from Memphis to Chattanooga, this march was a pastime. Not a man fell out by the way, & not a man sick in the whole Brigade when we reached here.

Indeed since we fairly got started from Memphis we have not lost a man in the Regiment by death, & the sick list has been very small. On the first day when 12 miles out, we came to a creek, impassable by reason of back water from the Tennessee. The men were sent across on the R.Rd bridge, while mounted men & the teams had to make a detour of 14 miles up the creek to a ford in the mountains. It was nearly night before we unwillingly determined that the creek was not fordable, & started for the upper ford. We had two companies of cavalry as escort which with all the field & staff officers & their attendants made quite a respectable mounted force, that galloped along right lively, making ten miles after dark that night and halting near the ford

Started at the first peep of the day the next morning and as we had to make the same distance back, & the infantry also moved at daylight, we did not overtake them till nearly night, after a day's hard riding of over thirty miles. The poor mules in the teams had the worst time of it—tho' they travelled all night, they had not reached the ford, when we left in the morning, & moving all the next day & next night, they came up with us about 9 o'clock in the morning of the third day out. We were very fortunate in having clear cold weather, not a drop of rain fell until the night we reached here, and then the heavens opened, & it has poured steadily ever since. The men are comfortably sheltered in the large R.Rd buildings here, machine shops etc, while all the Regimental HdQrs are in a fine large building, formerly used for offices for the R.Rd This was the HdQrs of the Memphis & Charleston R.Rd. & the President's Superintendent's & all the other officers of the road, were in this building. I write by a cheerful coal fire in a grate & we are preparing to take solid comfort, if we can only stay here. I beleive I haven't mentioned that our Brigade Col. Alexander comd'g, were the only troops that came thro' so hurriedly, the object being to relieve a cavalry force under Gen Crooks, that they might go in pursuit of the rebel Forrest who has been prowling about the neighborhood of Corinth and doing what damage he could to the R.Rd.[7] The other Brigades of our Division with the heavy trains & the camp equipage, left two days after us & yesterday were a little over halfway toiling thro' mud unspeakable. It is understood that the other Brigades are to stop at Larkinsville, 30 miles east, & we may have to rejoin them—tho' we all hope not. Col. Alexander has taken command of the post, the road will be open to Nashville via Decatur in ten days, & we can just live in the clover, here this winter.

The town is by far the handsomest one, I have seen in the South—had about 5,000 inhabitants before the war, & shows little marks of the ravages of war. The country round about is extremely rich & abounds in all manner of good living, and we are keeping the Holidays with some of the good cheer of home. Yesterday we had roast ducks, today a goose for dinner & I noticed this morning in our kitchen two fat turkies & half of a fine shoat—with plenty of good bread, butter, milk, eggs, & sweet potatoes in addition to our commissary supplies, we are feasting in a manner that becomes the season.

The Veteran Volunteer arrangement takes well with the boys, & I expect when we get settled & obtain the proper blanks for re-mustering them, all my Regiment will be ready to re-enlist. The understanding now is that we have 90 days at home, a 30 days furlough, & 60 days in the State to re-organize & recruit.[8] The Regiment will probably go back to South Bend, as the most central portion of the district in which it was recruited, & if it should happen that we should be there for 90 days, of course, Mrs. W. & the baby, would have to be with the Colonel. It is too early to make any arrangement, but if the Regt goes home for that length of time, I would come to Syracuse for you & I think we could have a fine time at South Bend for two or three months. I got some illustrated papers here for the first time—isn't the Christmas picture in Harper for Dec. 26th a fine one—I'm not quite as big as the soldier in the picture, & you won't have to reach as high as his eager little wife, but I thought I would like to try to represent the picture in a living tableau.[9]

I am admonished that it is time for the mail to close & must stop—Good bye dearest. God bless you & our darling & bring us soon together again. Write often, & I will write whenever we have a chance to send a mail.

Your loving Husband
Edward

LETTER 61

Huntsville, Ala.
Jan'y 4th [3] 1864

My dear wife,

I was glad to receive your letter of the 14th ult. the other day, conveying the assurance as it did, that you had heard from me, and that your dreadful anxiety had been relieved. I hope you will never have to endure such continued suspense again.

We remain just as we were when I wrote you about a week since—our comfortable quarters in the R.Rd building, with but little to do to pass away time. Guard duty is pretty heavy on the men and line officers, but as field officers have none of this to do, I am getting so lazy that it is an effort to do anything. Still as we have late breakfasts and dinner at 3 o'clock, these short days slip away quickly, without our having accomplished much. On the last of the month, I mustered the Regiment for pay, & took occasion to explain to them the orders on the subject of re-enlisting veteran volunteers. In consequence, three-fourths of the Regiment have been enrolled and are ready to be mustered in as veterans, provided they can have the benefit of the War Dep't orders and be furloughed home in a body, but in steps Maj Genl Logan commd'g our Corps, and says that only 25 per cent of the men can be furloughed at a time—whereupon the boys flare up and refuse to be mustered—so the veteran re-enlistment is at a dead-lock for the present. A few days will decide the matter, when I can write you with certainty about it—at this present writing the chances for getting home as a Regiment look pretty slim. It is a shame that we can't have the benefit of general orders from the War Dep't, which says explicitly, that when 3/4 of a Regiment or Company shall re-enlist as veterans they shall be furloughed in a body. I have telegraphed Gov. Morton that we are all ready, if we can be dealt by as other Regiments in other Corps' have been, and shan't despair altogether until I hear from him.[10] He is anxious to have the men re-enlist, so as to count them on the quota of the state before the draft, and may get an order direct from the Sec'y of War, sending us home. It is a pretty slim chance, as I said, but under Logan's orders, it is the only one.

The 59th Ind. which is in precisely similar condition, have about given the idea up, and I understand tonight that Col. Alexander, Lieut. Col Scott and several other officers have sent for their wives. It would be very pleasant to have you here if we were certain of staying two or three months, but I wouldn't think of asking you to make such a trip especially at this season of the year. The weather has been very cold for several days past. New Years morning, the thermometer stood at zero, with a piercing wind from the North that made it as uncomfortable to be out as any day I ever knew. The next day was but little milder, and today tho' the cold has moderated, there has been a fall of sleet, rain & snow, of as disagreable a variety as you can get up in Syracuse. There's a picture of the "sunny South" for you![11]

I didn't tell you in my last of my Christmas night experience. It was too bad every way—too bad because it was Christmas, & too bad because it might have been so easily avoided We marched without tents & had fine weather all the way thro'—within two miles of town, Christmas afternoon, we were halted & told to bivouac for the night, as usual. There was no appearance of rain & nobody thought it particularly hard, tho' we would all preferred coming into the town. For the first time since leaving Bridgeport we stretched a tent-fly that I had smuggled into the wagon making what we call a dog-tent—more as a protection from the wind than anything else, & it was lucky enough that we did—for about 11 o'clock it commenced to rain, and continued to pour all night. As it was, tho' the fly kept the rain from pouring down on us the water ran in & around & under us, soaking bedding & blankets, until about daylight we were fairly drowned out. To aggravate our discomfort the wind was variable, & would occasionally blow the smoke from our log fire so straight & steady into our dogtent, that we would have to leap out into the rain to avoid suffocation. On the whole, I think it was the roughest night I have seen in the service—and yet the men take such little grievances as a matter of course, & are ready to enlist for another three years!

It is a great comfort to know that Mary keeps so well—you must be more careful or perhaps less careful, about taking such dreadful colds. I am afraid you keep your room too hot, & keep too close indoors yourself—there is nothing like plenty of fresh air to keep off colds. You ought to go out every day, when it doesn't actually storm. You must tell me all about your Christmas doing. I warrant you had a famous dinner at Myra's & a good time afterwards. I learned today when it was too late to go, that there was service in the Episcopal church, which is still hung with the Christmas evergreens. Next Sunday if we are here, I shall attend—for by the way, my letter is dated a day ahead, I find, & this is Sunday night. To-morrow I go on a Court-Martial as President—we are to meet at the Huntsville Hotel—a large three-story brick, so I expect will have fine quarters. Gen Sherman's staff are here, & have made HdQrs in the same building—the Genl is expected in a few days. It is settled that our Brigade remains here for the winter, Col Alexander in command of the post—one regiment is to be sent out on the R.R. 10 miles to guard a bridge, & I only hope it may not be mine. I suppose you have rec'd the money before this. I have the express receipt dated Dec 12. I am very well, except the longing to see my wifey & baby, & I still have hopes that I am to be soon cured of that complaint. Write often, send the papers, and be sure to give the darling, three or four rousing kisses for her papa. Goodnight dearest & god bless you

Your own Husband
Edward

LETTER 62

Huntsville, Ala.
Jan'y 17th 1864.

My dear wife,

I have not written you in some time for a number of reasons. My time during the day for the past two weeks has been fully occupied on Court Martial, and when out of Court, matters connected with the re-enlistment of the Regiment as veterans have claimed my attention.

Then I have been made so sad, by the desponding tone of your letters, that the two attempts I made to write, were given up in despair, because I could not give you the consolation which I know you could derive alone from an assurance of my speedy release from the service. God knows it has been the hardest trial of my life, to give up for so long the sweet society of my wife and child, and to lose forever the delight of watching that dear God-given pledge of our mutual love, as she expanded from the promising little bud of infancy to the sweet flower of childhood. At times, the thought of the sacrifices I was making, while so many remained at home in "inglorious ease," has been full of almost insupportable bitterness,[12] and I have had no difficulty in convincing myself that I have discharged my duty to my country, and that the claims of my family should be paramount to any the country can now have on me. I need not say that I still feel so and tho' I feel a natural attachment to and pride in my Regiment, I would most joyfully hail any means that would honorably discharge me from the service and restore my loved ones to me. But while I am thus satisfied that my duty and inclination lie in the same direction, the obligation by which I am bound to serve the Government, is one not so easily sundered. It would be hard in a letter to explain all the difficulties in the way, but I can make some of the most obvious ones, apparent. Resignations tendered on any other ground than physical disability, accompanied by proper medical certificates—in many instances I am sorry to say, falsely made—have been for a long time in this Department "respectfully returned, not accepted" sometimes accompanied with the cheap compliment that the "service cannot afford to lose so valuable an officer etc." There have been no resignations accepted in our Division since Sept 1st and indeed but few tendered for the further reason I am about to state. I enclose you the War Dept order, recently republished by Genl Logan for the information of his command. You will see the original order bears date July 28th/62, and the procurement of these certificates is attended with so much difficulty & delay as to operate as an effectual bar to resignations. You may be sure that if it were not so, in a Division composed of 15 Regiments, we should have had some resignations in this time. I know men completely prostrated by disease, wholly unfit for the service and anxious to resign, who are yet kept in the service by the operation of this order, and I had a Lieutenant, who was sick at Vicksburg, tendered his resignation, and the very day I left for home in August last, after having been approved by Genl McPherson, it came back "not accepted" by Genl Grant, with a copy of this order requiring these certificates. The poor fellow who was not very sick, was so broken down by the disappointment, at not getting home in a reasonable time, that he rapidly grew worse and in two weeks, died. I have no doubt if his resignation had been accepted at once, & he could have gone home, he would have recovered. I mention this case, because it occurred in

I Write by a Cheerful Coal Fire in a Grate

my own Regiment, & because it is illustrative of the extreme harshness of the order.[13] I have a Captain who has been trying to procure these certificates since Sept, and altho' I know he is a very exact man, and have no doubt his accounts are all right, and altho' all the Government property for which he was responsible has been turned over to another officer proper receipts taken & his final account rendered, he has not yet received his certificates, and is detained with the Regiment, in a most anomalous position

The first Captains of the Regiment, who are so unfortunate as to remain with it—and there are only two—Maj Byrkit and myself, are in much worse situation than the second batch. They had the benefit of our experience to guide them, while we were ignorant and slow to learn the responsibilities that devolved upon us as Captains. I don't know as we were slower than most raw hands, but the requirements of the "Army Regulations" cannot be fulfilled without study *and* practical experiences and we were unfortunate in having a Colonel who was as ignorant as ourselves, of the requirements of the Regulations. In particular, this matter of Ordnance, about which these certificates are required, was managed very loosely in our Regiment. The Colonel never required receipts from his captains, when arms were issued to the Companies, never gave any in return, when a man was sent to Hospital, and his gun turned over to the Ordnance Sergt, and I never saw any of the Ordnance blanks upon which returns are now made, until after I ceased to be a Captain & never made any returns of Ordnance. By the Regulations, Company Commanders are made responsible for all guns, etc even to cartridges & *caps*, issued to the Co, and must account for every one on proper returns.

We exchanged guns while I was in command of the Company, & as I had given no receipt, I asked for none but took the new guns as before without receipt.[14] Now I am called upon to make all the returns required while I was in command, and you see at once if I charge myself with all the guns that were in my possession during the time, there is one set of guns for which I can show no voucher—but even if this could be done, I have no data to supply all the minutiae as to number of cartridges etc received no. expended in battle, no receipts to show for any turned over—nothing in fact from which to make out an Ordnance return for 1862, which would be as difficult with all the data before you, as a yearly balance-sheet of an immense business. It is only about a year since these blanks were received from the Ordnance Dept with full instructions for filling them & making the returns—since then by great care, company commanders have mostly kept their accounts straight, but there is not a resigned comd'g officer in our Reg't, who has not received notice to furnish returns to the Ordnance Dept for 1862 I have frankly & fully written them, that I can't do it—what the upshot of the matter will be, I can't say. One thing I think you will doubtless infer from this long explanation that if officers whose returns have been rendered cannot procure these certificates, it would be useless for me to apply for them. If my offence in not furnishing these returns, should be considered sufficiently heinous to procure my dismissal, though it is by no means a pleasant way of getting out the service, but as there seems to be but one other way, to die out. I think I should be disposed to take it philosophically and make the best of it. I don't apprehend any such result, but the Major & I are in the habit of joking one another about it. Col Eddy got out just in time—July 16th—to escape all this bother. I think this senseless & impracticable order must be modified before long, for it works as I have shown you to effectually prevent all resignations. So courage! my dear wife, as you truly say in your later letters we have *much, very much* to be thankful for—our lives have been spared—through many and great dangers, your dear boy has been shielded alike from the "pestilence that walketh by night, and the destruction which wasteth at noon-day"[15]—our darling Mary lives to bless us with her loving ways, and make us thank the Giver of all good for his precious boon to us, and my own true, loving, noble hearted wife lives to cheer her absent soldier boy with the assurance of her undying wifely love and constancy, and tho' at times she may feel that her burden is greater than she can bear, and repine at the hardness of her lot, I know she is too true a woman and too good a Christian, to let feelings of despondency gain the ascendency over her.

I am in receipt of your letters of Dec 24th & 28th and also of the last one enclosing photographs for which I am much obliged, as also for the "Atlantic" tho' I was so unlucky as to lose it before I had read it

I buttoned it in my coat, but it slipped out as I rode out to camp, when I did not notice—for you must know we have moved out of our fine buildings, and are once more dwellers in tents. I like the change and enjoy hugely my two miles ride to attend Court these sharp mornings. "Charlie" feels his recent good keeping & no work, and he is as "gay as a peacock." Well I suppose you want to know something about the veterans. I shall have a long story to tell you some time about the vexations delays & aggravated red-tapeism that have well nigh proved fatal to the veterans. Most of the difficulties appear now to be surmounted—we have made duplicate enlistment papers & a discharge for each man, 3 muster-out rolls, 3 muster & pay-rolls, 5 muster-in rolls for each Company, & are now making 8 consolidated receipt rolls—only 19 rolls to the company & 3 papers to each man! If no untoward event occurs, & we progress with the same remarkable speed we have made so far, we shall be ready to start home on our 30 days furlough in about two weeks

Don't be too sanguine tho'—you shall have due notice of our approach, & as we shall probably *boat it* from Nashville down the Cumberland to the

Ohio, we won't take any body by surprise. I wish you could be at Indianapolis when we reach there—I am expecting a warm reception for my war-worn veterans. At any rate, you had better direct your next letter after receipt of this, to "Bates House" Indianapolis as I shall want to know at the earliest moment, whether you are ready to come out & help me *recruit*, while we stay at home—The wind is blowing a perfect gale, & my writing table, which is fast to the tent pole, shakes with its every motion—it is worse than writing at sea, so you must excuse the appearance of this sheet. Kiss the darling one for me, and tell her papa hopes soon to do it for himself Goodnight & God bless you.

Your Husband
Edward

LETTER 63

[*Letterhead:* "Headquarters, First Brigade.
"3rd Division, 15th Army Corps."]

Jan'y 28th 1864.

My dear wife,

Your most welcome letter of the 19th inst. is just received, and I have concluded to drop you a line right here from Brigade Head Quarters while it is fresh, and to enclose you my old letter of Dec 28th which has just turned up in a most unaccountable manner.

Col. Alexander reports, that this, with a number of other letters written when there were no other troops here but our Brigade were found in the woods between here & Brownsboro,' the point to which the Railroad has been running until lately. Evidently somebody has been rifling the mails, and all the amends I can make, is to enclose the old letter. I am in a great hurry, as I am going out with Col Aleck to meet a flag of truce from the other side of the river, & while waiting for him, thought I would scrawl an acknowledgement of your letter, and enclose my old letter so singularly found.

I am sure you will be glad to hear that the veterans are progressing as well as could be expected and that we shall probably start north within a week.

We have had great trial & tribulation with our rolls, and tonight a new Paymaster orders us to make 8 new Payrolls to the Company—

The Colonel comes & I must say Good-bye. God bless you

Your loving Husband
Edward

Chapter 11

War for the Purification and Sanctification of the Nation

Huntsville Duty, March–June 1864

The return to duty was difficult for Wood and his men. A month of high living at home had made them "soft," so an overland march back to Alabama served as a tune-up for soldiering. Wood expected his regiment soon would be fighting in the front lines. Immediate on their return and thereafter during their stay at Huntsville, Wood and the 48th Indiana were called out to march to various points where reports placed Rebel raiders, most notably the feared cavalry commander General Nathan Bedford Forrest. The Confederates hoped to disrupt Federal supply and communication lines, and Union troops remained ever watchful for raids on the railroads and their positions.[1]

General Sherman's expedition into Rebel-held Mississippi from Vicksburg to Meridian in February 1864 had succeeded in destroying railroads, forage, and provisions that supported Rebel resistance and guerrilla activities. Rebel resistance under the command of General Leonidas Polk, who commanded a sizeable force, was slight. Polk's forces retreated into Alabama, and Sherman's troops retraced their route to Vicksburg, there to prepare for further advances into Rebel-occupied territory. Historian John Marszalek notes, "the Meridian expedition had demonstrated . . . a paucity of Confederate troops; much of the Confederacy was a hollow shell." The experience was an "important lesson" when the Federal general later considered his march to Savannah. Sherman "could wage successful war without having to slaughter thousands of soldiers in the process."[2]

In March 1864 Ulysses Grant was appointed general-in-chief of the entire U.S. Army, and Sherman was appointed his successor as commander of U.S. forces in the West, designated the Military Division of the Mississippi. Grant traveled east, and focused his attentions on the Army of the Potomac's almost stalemated duel with Robert E. Lee's Rebel Army of Northern Virginia. Sherman's preparations for attacking the Rebel Army of Tennessee, strongly entrenched in and around Dalton, Georgia, not far from Chattanooga, continued in earnest. Close coordination and cooperation between Grant and Sherman was the key. The latter general collected troops from all corners of his command, accumulating about one hundred thousand men, many of whom were strung out on the extensive transportation lines vital to the success of the campaign. The long-expected advance into Georgia began in early May, pushing back Rebel forces under Joseph Johnston. Sherman's strategy was to engage Rebel troops constantly but indirectly, often flanking Johnston's army to the right, forcing him to retreat, and not to allow the Rebel commander to detach any of his force of sixty-five thousand troops to Virginia to reinforce Lee (Grant would return the favor by constantly pressing Lee). A series of bloody battles, starting with the battle of Resaca on May 14–15 and continuing almost daily for the next five months, forced the Rebels slowly southward towards Atlanta.

Contrary to expectations, the 48th Indiana and its division under Brigadier General John E. Smith were ordered to remain in northern Alabama to guard the rail lines. Numerous attempts by Rebel cavalry to attack and break the lines were thwarted by the Federal garrisons distributed along the routes. While busy in fending off these incursions, Wood and his men were content to sit out the campaign in relative safety and comfort.

LETTER 64

Nashville Tenn. March 25th 1864

My dear wife,

We arrived here safely, yesterday (Thursday) morning, and this morning we leave on foot for Huntsville—a march of 120 miles. Transportation is so taken up with carrying supplies, that it is impossible to send troops by rail, and all regiments arriving here from the North, are ordered to march to their destination. Our men are *soft*, and we shall have to march slowly, and will probably be ten days making the trip. I have not yet succeeded in getting a horse, and the prospect is pretty slim for doing so. I don't fancy marching through a bit. Col. Alexander deserts me and goes thro' by rail, and as I am senior officer, I shall be in command of the two regiments. I don't like the responsibility—my rank isn't high enough to justify it

Later. The horses are secured and we start in half an hour. I have thought of you every hour since you left, and shall not feel easy until I hear that you got through all right. I hope you will not fail to write as soon as you get home, and very often thereafter

I miss you *so* much, and since I have learned to know our Mamie, I have a double regret every time I think of the hard fate that separates us—and a double inducement to get back to you as soon as possible—I returned Capt Allen's gloves to him tonight and he sends thanks for the mending.[3]

We shall not go by way of Stevenson, so I won't see Capt Wheeler & wife.[4] I have scrawled this line in great haste with many interruptions—I know tho' it will be welcome as an assurance of my safety & health. I am feeling firstrate, have got a tent & a cot, & will make the march without serious inconvenience. Don't fail to write often, tell me all about your trip and how you found everybody at home.

Kiss our darling Mamie—does she miss papa. I hope she will be a good girl—kind and obedient to her mama. Goodbye—will write as as we get to Huntsville

Your loving Husband
Edward

LETTER 65

Huntsville, Ala.
April 11th 1864

My dear wife,

I know you will have been anxiously looking for this letter for more than a week before you get it, and I am very sorry it has been so long delayed. The delay however, as you will learn has been almost unavoidable. To begin at Nashville where I wrote you last on the 24th ult. We expected to start thro' on that day, but delay in getting ammunition & rations, caused us to defer starting until the next day, Friday the 25th ult. We left Nashville about 9 o'clock and taking the turnpike running south, made an easy march of 11 miles, halting at 3 P.M. in a beautiful grove, and near a fine residence. I spent the evening very pleasantly with the owner, a Mrs. More and her son. The old lady was intelligent and very talkative, and when we parted at night, I was well posted in the genealogy of the More family. The next day marched 19 miles reaching Spring Hill, the place where about a year ago, the rebel General Van Dorn, was shot by Dr. Peters[5]—had excellent camping ground & fine water—Reached Columbia, a considerable county town and distant 10 miles, about noon the next day. Here we were delayed in crossing the Duck river—the bridge having been destroyed we were obliged to ferry the men over in a flat-boat. Here also we were to draw rations, having started with only a three days supply from Nashville—This occupied till the middle of the afternoon, and as the weather was threatening I concluded to be satisfied with a half days march and halt for the night at the edge of town where the men could get shelter in buildings. I was glad of it, for early in the evening we had a tremendous thundershower, that poured down for two or three hours. Major McNaught comd'g 59th Ind.[6] and myself, with our two

Adjutants, accepted the hospitality of a Mr. Webb & his wife—a very agree-able old couple. Mrs. Webb told us she was 76 years old—tho' she didn't look a day more than 50—and had lived on Duck river 45 years—This is the native town of James K. Polk,[7] whom the old lady had known from boy-hood, & with whom he was evidently a great favorite. I was most touched and pleased with the youthful tastes of the old lady—her flower-garden and canaries being her chief pride and delight. But when I walked with her in the garden in the early morning, pleasant after the evening rain, and as she plucked me a nosegay of fragrant hyacinths, told me of her daugh-ter, who had bloomed a spring ago as fair as those flowers, and with them had faded and died. I understood the affection of the old lady for her garden and canaries

We had been unable to get full rations of bread the day before, and I telegraphed to Nashville to have it sent to Columbia. The train came in in the morning without it, and as we were using up our supplies all the time, I determined to leave a man behind to bring up the bread by rail and push on to Pulaski, two days march distant and the next point at which we were to draw rations

Started at 10 o'clock and by 5 P.M. made Linnville 19 miles. Here we expected the bread would overtake us—sent to the Depot but nothing for us—the train had passed but no supplies for us—No bread in the morning and 14 miles to Pulaski. The boys, now getting used to marching, stepped off with a will and we reached Pulaski at noon. I had rode on in advance with the Quartermaster and made arrangement for the rations, so moving through the town, and 3 miles out, we found good water and a good camp-ing ground and halted for the day—An early start the next morning, and by half-past-ten, we were at Elkton, on the Elk river, and 30 miles from Huntsville. And the river, swollen by recent rains, presented an unexpected obstacle. We were told at Pulaski, that we would find an excellent ford at Elkton, but that morning, on the march I met teams returning who told me that the river was impassable. Not wishing to take hearsay evidence I moved the two regiments to the bank of the stream—now nearly a quarter of a mile wide—and called for a volunteer to ride a horse in and sound the bottom. A good swimmer having been selected from the many volunteers, I dismounted and let him have my horse—a large strong bay—Two min-utes decided the matter, the horse was swimming, and fording was out of the question.

I had already learned of a pontoon bridge across the Elk, at Prospect, 12 miles down the river, and immediately determined to make for it. Here we left the turnpike, and marched thro' a section of country never before vis-ited by troops, and on by-roads and no roads at all. However before night we had safely crossed on the pontoon & I felt much relieved. It rained this night all night, steady, pouring soaking rain, and in the morning every body felt miserable enough. We had to gain the main road again and after a march of 14 miles struck it still 25 miles from Huntsville. Marched 2 miles on this road, and as the neighborhood roads on which we had travelled thro' the day were very bad and the men tired, halted for the night

Started for Huntsville, the next morning Saturday April 2nd at daylight, and by hard marching reached our old camp 2 miles the other side of Huntsville about dark.

I found here your first letter, assuring me of your safe arrival, and tho' I was sorry you experienced so many detentions, I was glad that a soldier's wife met with such kind attention from a soldier. I am sorry you did not learn his name. I cannot tell his rank, as artillery officers wear the insignia you describe, called the Russian shoulder-knot, the same as infantry wear the *strap*—the designation of rank being the same in each case—plain for 2nd Lieut, one bar for 1st two bars for Captain, leaves for Major & Lt Col. etc—

Well, we reached here Saturday night, very much tired out and generally used up as you may imagine. The last two days our march had been thro' a country infested by guerrillas and as you may know I was considerably exercised for the safety of my command. Excitement kept me up, but when the reaction came, I was glad to keep still a few days. I knew I ought to write you immediately, and after taking a wash & the luxury of clean clothes, Sunday morning, & attempted it, but really felt so miserable I gave it up. So it run untill Wednesday—each day thinking I would write, but my time was completely taken up getting located in our new camp and the thousand things that you know occur to beset and worry a Regimental commander, that I had neglected it.

Suddenly about 3 o'clock Wednesday afternoon came an order to march my command without delay with two days rations & 60 rounds ammunition, on the Whitesburg road, leading to the Tennessee river. Enough of the 59th reported to me, to make my command 400 strong, and so about 5 P.M. we moved out. I haven't the heart to write the details of the disgusting performance. Enough to say, a Lt Col in command of a Regiment at Whitesburg on Tennessee river had got badly scared, expecting the rebels to come over and "gobble him," and had sent to Genl Smith for re-inforcements. We stayed with him, four days, and discovered his picket fires of the enemy to be old stumps burning in a field, and his heavy encampment of the enemy with new tents, to be plum & cherry trees in full blossom, and then last night returned.[8]

It was not a bad trip for us on the whole, the roads were good and the weather fine, so it was not bad soldiering, but it may serve to explain why I have not written sooner.

My health is full as good as it was at Indianapolis—if anything I think my diarrhoea is better. I don't anticipate a movement from this place for two or three weeks. I will write often and keep you advised of any changes. Your second letter I found here last night on my return. I hope you & Mamie have entirely recovered from your colds & fatigue. Don't neglect to have her vaccinated at once—small-pox is quite prevalent here. Write me often and tell me everything about your self and the darling. Papa takes great comfort in his pictures. I am so sorry for Myra. I hope she has recovered. Give my love to all and beleive me as ever Your loving Husband

Edward

LETTER 66

Huntsville, Ala.
April 17th 1864.

My dear wife,

Your dear long letter was received a few days since, but as I had written you only a day or two before, I have delayed answering it sooner.

I am glad you think of going to Binghampton so soon, and really hope you will find a good place to board. I know you will enjoy the sense of independence which the change will give you, and you must not be too fastidious about the rooms & furniture or price, if you can find a quiet, respectable boarding place. I shall be anxious to hear from you on your return—don't think of going to board with Nell, even if they should urge you, which is perhaps not likely—but I don't think I need to caution you, for I beleive you are sufficiently anxious to "set up" for yourself We have had one or two little events to disturb the monotony of the camp the past week.

On Monday our arms were inspected and condemned and to-morrow we are to draw new ones—which is a source of gratification to every one in the Regiment. On Tuesday, the camp & quarters of the men were inspected by Surgeon Kittoe, Medical Inspector of the Department, and he complimented us on our appearance.[9] Wednesday, we had a review of the Division by Generals McPherson & Logan—General Slocum was on the ground but did not review us.[10] He has been assigned to the command of the Defences & District of Vicksburg—I don't know whether he takes his Corps with him or not—but as the 17th McPherson's old Corps is on its way, it is quite likely he does. The review was no great affair for a Division—so many Regiments are away on furlough, and the duty is so hard on those that are here, that there were only five Regiments out. The 48th stole a march on most of them by appearing in white gloves!—and thus I suppose having attracted Gen. McPherson's attention, he was pleased the next day to speak of their soldierly appearance.

Wednesday night, just at tattoo, came a brief order from Genl. Smith, to fall in under arms and remain so until further orders—"then & there was hurrying to & fro"[11]—the long roll beat and my veterans were under arms in less time than it has taken to write these lines, and then of course all manner of startling rumors arose. "Forrest with 10,000 men was within 4 miles of the city, on the Elkton road."[12] "The enemy were crossing the Tennessee in large force—the 56th Ill. Taken prisoners, and the enemy marching from Whitesburg."—in a directly opposite direction from the reported coming of Forrest—and so we passed the night till daybreak, when we were ordered to quarters. Col Alexander was with us all night, but knew no more of the occasion of the alarm than I did. He was several times on the point of going to town to enquire of Gen Smith what it was all about, but as His Mysterious Highness (Smith) had not seen fit to communicate any particulars, I persuaded the Col. to stay & wait developments.[13]

About noon the next day, Col A. & I called on Genl McPherson, and learned that the excitement all grew out of false reports sent by Lt Col Hall commanding at Whitesburg—the same imbecile that I went down to assist, as I told you in my last.[14] I gave the General to understand plainly, that he could not attach any importance to reports from that quarter—not I know from any mean motive, but because we had been twice alarmed here by his scary reports, & I had seen what manner of man he was, and had satisfactorily tested his accuracy of observation & information.

Thursday was a very quiet day. I have had all the stumps grubbed out of my parade ground by offenders against discipline, and this day I commence ornamenting the grounds. The beautiful cedars of the adjacent mountains are being transplanted to the camp, and Head Quarters is already handsomely adorned—In front of each tent the cedars are planted in the form of a Z, and connected together thus

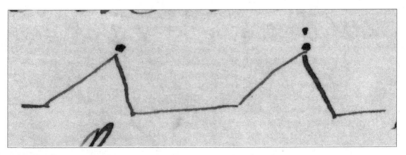

Wood's drawing of cedars at the Huntsville encampment, April 17, 1864. Courtesy of the Indiana Historical Society.

On Friday, I issued an order promising that the Company which should pass the best inspection on the 25th inst, for perfection of cooking arrangements, cleanliness & good order of tents, & general appearance of quarters, should be exempt from guard and fatigue duty for one week, and should be published in general orders. The Camp which before was in good condition, has since then been alive with men, busy to improve their grounds in any manner. Tents are being raised from the ground, bunks & kitchens built, every team is eagerly sought for each day to haul boards & cedars, and I think by the time the ten days is up, the 25th inst, I shall have the best camp in this neighborhood. The noble spirit of emulation as to "who shall best labor and who best agree"—the motto of Masonry—seems to have taken possession of the 48th & 59th, and the Major & I compare notes and brag on our commands every day.

I am expecting Major Byrkit with the rest of our recruits tonight—The train has just whistled and he will soon be here. They left Nashville Friday night, but an accident on the road delayed them, so I am certain they will be in tonight—and a wet gloomy night it is to come into camp. The weather has been very disagreeable ever since we have been here. A few pleasant days, but the season is unusually backward and cold. We have had fires every day, and generally throughout the day. Corn which is usually well out of the ground by this time, is just being planted.

Many thanks for the "*Atlantic*," it is an excellent number,—your appreciative pencil failed to mark the best thing in Mrs. Stowe's "*Home Papers.*"[15] You dear girl, didn't you know you sat for the portrait, when she described "that rare gift to man, a wife with the magic cestus of Venus."[16] "All that she touches falls at once into harmony & proportion." It seems as if she must have known the "veritable gift of good faerie," the "tact of beautifying and arranging," which my Jeanie has, or she could not so well have described it. Ah well, we will hope soon to put that tact into requisition, and try the "beauty of economy" for ourselves—we've got the picture to begin with, and you know how I admire the sunlight upon it—I am sorry I can't send you any money in this letter—in a few days, sometime this week, I have the promise of some, & will send at once. Don't make any definite arrangement about going to Binghampton till you receive it, as you might be disappointed. I am in hopes you can go before the middle of May—Inquire if James has learned anything more of Mr. Sessions—he was rather an uncouth mortal as a college boy, but I thought a diamond in the rough.[17]

"Where is my little puss?" all this time. Papa hasn't forgotten her, and Mamie mustn't forget her papa, who loves her more and more every day. She must be good and mind her Mama, and love her dear Papa & Mamma. Papa wishes he could play hide and seek and have a real frolic with his little girl tonight. I am glad Sarah liked the pictures—did you give Myra one? and did they like your dress. I'm as curious as a woman you see, but you know *me.* I would like to send Sarah a nice present—did you notice the advertisement of *"Daleth,"* Egypt Illustrated, on the back of the Atlantic[18]—Has Sarah got it, & do you think she would like it—I forgot to acknowledge the receipt of the pillowcase—it fits nicely and naturally as I lay my head on it, my last thoughts are of my dear wife—I sent Henry the other day a curious specimen of military red tape, as illustrative of some things I told him about the administration of affairs in the army—he will probably show it to you. And so George is to be married, and the day is fixed. I wish him all sorts of joy, and more particularly I wish that I "might be there to see"—you will of course remember the bride with a wedding gift.

I don't know but you will tire of these long rambling letters—whatever first popped into my head has popped out on these pages, and after all, that is the charm of a letter to me. Did you send pictures to Aunt Mackie? I know you will not forget to have Mamie vaccinated. I think Dr Rogers failed in not putting a plaster on her arm.

Nearly an hour has passed and the Major has not come, so I must give him up for tonight. I am disappointed & uneasy, for he should have been here last night My health as you may have inferred by my silence on the subject is firstrate—diarrhoea much better than at any time when at home. The sheet runs full and the hours grow late, and I must say Goodnight. Write me often and *everything* about yourself & Mamie

Goodnight & God bless you, my dear ones, and keep you safely always.

Your loving Husband
Edward

[*Envelope endorsed:* "Mrs Edward J. Wood, Care E. B. Judson Esq, Syracuse New York."]

LETTER 67

Huntsville, Ala
April 24th 1864.

My dear wife,

Your letter from Binghamton was received a few days since, and I was glad to hear you were enjoying your visit so much, tho' I infer, as much from what you did not say, as from what you wrote, that you are not likely to find a boarding place in B. I am sorry, for I was in hopes, you could find quarters where you would feel perfect freedom this summer. Understand me. I am not ungrateful to Sarah & Edward for their kindness to us, but to make the weight of obligation as light as possible, I would much preferred to have had you found a new home. Well, next fall we'll hope to find one.

Everything has moved on quietly here for the past week, but the indications are strong, that the quiet is to be of short duration. Orders preliminary to moving have been received from Gens Sherman & McPherson, and everything looks like an early start.[19] I suppose we shall cross the Tennessee, either at Decatur, where there is already a pontoon bridge, or at the mouth of Flint river, directly south of this place, where we should have to throw over a bridge—in either case I don't apprehend we should meet with much resistance

I beleive I told you of the spirit of emulation I had excited, between the different Companies, as to which should have the best quarters etc. After nearly ten days work, I can safely say that there is no camp in the vicinity that comes near equaling it It is the best camp we ever had—The parade-ground is a broad level space, running the whole length of the camp, from which every stump has been grubbed, and the ground smoothed, till it is as level as a floor. Each Company has a kitchen, built of boards or oak slabs, split out, with a brick cooking range—the chimney coming up outside of the building—the tables for eating are under bowers of cedars, and the whole camp looks like a forest of cedars. I think we must have hauled 100 wagon loads in the last ten days. Bowers & wreaths, and fancy letters of evergreen, abound everywhere. Around the Hospital however the most taste has been displayed. A thick-set hedge of cedars completely conceals it from view and the grounds inside are laid out with gravel walks lined with double rows of cedars, and in the centre is an octagonal summer house, where the convalescents take their meals.

Tomorrow we have inspection, and the Company which bears off the palm is to be published in general orders, and to be releived from guard & fatigue duty for one week. I looked though the different Companies this morning, & am glad I haven't got to decide. Our new chaplain gave us a sermon this afternoon for the first time—he did very well indeed—[20]

Wednesday morn. April 28th I was interrupted just here, Sunday night, and have hardly had a minute since, when I could resume—besides I have been delaying in hopes I should have some money to send you. The Army, especially the veteran portion of it, in this section is completely *strapped*. Our Mess, Major, Adjt, & self, are all dead broke, and have got to resolve ourselves into a Committee of the Whole on the state of the Exchequer, to devise ways & means to replenish our exhausted Commissary I never had known such a general lack of funds since I have been in the service—as a consequence the Sutler is doing nothing, and he, who is usually our last resort, is as short as everybody else. I am very sorry for I know you will greatly need money, if you move to Binghamton, but you must delay it a little longer, & you may be sure I will send you the first money I get. We are making Payrolls now, & I hope will soon be flush again

The inspection passed off finely. Gen Smith & staff and Col Alexander & staff were present and we got high encomiums from all Co. B, Lieut Collins comd'g were decided to have the best quarters, tho' there was little to chose between them & Cos I. & G. Col Alexander published a complimentary order, a copy of which I enclose[21]

As usual, I am detailed as Pres't of a Court Martial—it is very irksome & inconvenient at this time, when I have so many new recruits, & ought to devote my whole time to my Regiment. Our rolls show 160 recruits, pretty well done, considering we were so late in getting home. I have received my commission as Colonel, but might as well send it home, for there is hardly a chance of getting mustered on it

However, there is some slight prospect of getting some of those prisoners at Indianapolis, who are about to be released by the Gov't on taking the oath of allegiance. Of course, being citizens & not prisoners of war, there would be no trouble about enlisting them. If I could get 150 or 200 of them, as my boys write me there is a prospect of doing, I should apply to the War Dep't for a special order to be mustered, tho' I would not then have the required number 840, I have been expecting a letter for several days.[22] I am anxious to learn the result of your Binghamton trip. I hope you and Mamie both keep well. Papa intended to write his little girl a letter in answer to hers this time, but he will not have time this morning. You must write me all about yourselves. I have written this out-doors before breakfast so you may know we are having pleasant weather. It has been uncomfortably warm the last few days, & the trees are finally in full leaf. I enclose you a photo, of Gen McPherson, it is excellent, but hardly as good-looking as Mac is. I intend to get some others, Gen Sherman's, Logan's etc, and some views about town. Mrs. Alexander acknowledges the receipt of yours, & promises to reciprocate. Write often, will write soon again. There is some talk of an early move, if we go, will write before starting. Kiss the darling one for me, & tell her how much Papa loves her. Goodbye & God bless you my dear one.

Your loving Husband
Edward

Am in firstrate health—no trouble at all with the old complaint for two weeks.

E.

Head Quarters 1st Brigade
3rd Division, 15th Army Corps.
Huntsville Ala. April 25th 1864

General Orders
No 11

The Colonel commanding feels a just pride in the past glorious reputation of this Command, and takes this occasion to express his satisfaction at the elegant manner in which the Camps of the Brigade are being fitted up.

Follow the example of the *48th Indiana Veteran Volunteers,* and you will continue to be as you always have been, unequalled by any Brigade in Grant's old army.

By order of
Col Jesse I. Alexander
Comdg Brigade
(signed) John E. Simpson
Capt, & A.A.A. Genl.

LETTER 68

Huntsville, Ala.
May 13th 1864.

My dear wife,

I am in your debt for two glorious good letters, and have to acknowledge my own shortcomings again. Your dear long letter of the 27th ult was received nearly a week ago, and I commenced a reply immediately, but after writing two pages, was obliged to break off. Before I could resume, the half-finished letter mysteriously disappeared, I suppose whisked off the table by the wind, which scattered some other papers about, while I was up town attending Court Martial. Since then I haven't had the resolution to commence another, & have expected every day, that the half-written one would *"turn up."* I am consoled somewhat today for my negligence, by learning that no letters have been permitted to go North, since a week ago today, and as the Chaplain goes to Nashville tonight I shall try to smuggle this through, even tho' I may tell some contraband news—contraband or otherwise, I am sure it will be very welcome news to my little wifey.[23]

The forward movement has been made, as you are long ago aware, in this Department, and for a wonder, our Division, that never missed a march or a fight before, has been left behind.[24] The arrangement is considered permanent for the campaign. Col. Alexander has assumed command of the post, and we have moved our camp to a beautiful level greensward just at the edge of town. One Brigade has been sent west on the R.Rd to Decatur, and one east towards Stevenson, and our (1st) Brigade is the only one left in town. The duty is rather heavy, but the boys are so gratified with the idea of spending the summer in the delightful town of Huntsville, that they don't complain. Cols Alexander & Scott & several other officers of the 59th, have sent for their families—how I wish you could come, but I know it is out of the question, and I wouldn't feel at all easy to have you so far down in Dixie.[25] I am glad on the whole that you did not go to Binghamton. It would have been a serious undertaking for you to move there alone, and then you would have run the great risk of getting into unsuitable quarters, & been compelled to move again, or to have been annoyed & uncomfortable all summer. Edward & Sarah were right in their advice, and I am under renewed obligations to them for their kindness.

You can't tell how much good your long letter so full of your doings & "*thinkings*" did me—it was the next best thing to seeing you & Mamie, & having a long talk with you and a frolic with the darling. I could see her as well as if in a picture—from your description—as she hid under the bedclothes, and waited for her Papa to find his little girl. She is almost three years old—does it seem possible—and the best & dearest treasure in the world. Papa hopes she will continue to be a good girl, and always mind her Mamma and one of these fine days Papa will come home to live with her, & never go away any more—won't that be nice, Mamie? Papa thinks about his little Puss every day, & wishes he could toss her up high, and roly-loly her & have a regular frolic. I am glad you have had some pleasant days & find time to take her outdoors. We have had a few uncomfortably hot days, but the season is very backward, & all this week, fires have been necessary morning & night. The "*Atlantic*" has just come to hand tonight—your letter of the 1st was rec'd last night. I have just looked thro' the magazine & discovered the white violets—mute but eloquent tokens of spring in your frigid zone. I have looked over a magnificent boquet which stands me for something to reciprocate with, but the flowers are all too large for the purpose. Snowballs & double-roses, & verbenas with evergreens make up the collection—I send instead this time the photographs of two Major Generals—Rousseau[26] & Logan they are capital likenesses & good pictures. By the way, I want some more of my photos—that is, when I send the money for them, & a whole host of articles besides. I haven't decided on the list yet, but I want you to send me a small box with a few things. I lost my slippers somewhere, my shoes too would be handy in camp, am most out of collars & entirely out of tobacco—well, when your "*ship comes in*" you may expect an order for goods, with the remittance.

Rumors of Paymasters abound, but none have yet shown themselves. I suppose they will hardly venture south of Nashville, until Sherman has bagged Johnston. We have most cheering news from Dalton, everything is going on swimmingly. The brave old Grant more than holds his own on the Potomac,[27] & *we* know, that he has the gift of *tenacity* in a wonderful degree. He never lets go, when he had fastened on his victim, & tho' he may suffer delay, & perhaps temporary defeat, he will not fail of his purpose. The Major arrived in due time, sound & hearty as ever—we got 160 recruits, but are still a small Regiment. I hope to do something at Indianapolis as I wrote you. The Regiment is in fine condition, the recruits have got thro' the measles & mumps—perhaps you don't understand that—but they are the two diseases that always prevail, when recruits are first brought together, and we are having drill every afternoon

The chaplain warns me that it is most train time, & I must close. I won't let it be so long again before I write. Kiss Mamie for me, I wish I could celebrate her birthday with you. Write often

Your own Husband,
Edward

Will write to Willie tomorrow, shall send him your Indianapolis photo. I *don't* like it.

I am out of most everything, more particularly postage stamps—please send—that big blot was the fault of the blotting paper & not mine. E.

LETTER 69

Huntsville, Ala.
May 19th 1864.

My dear wife,

Your last welcome letter was received a few days since, in fact, the day after I had sent a letter by the Chaplain to be mailed at Nashville. I beleive the embargo on the mail has been removed, but as I have a chance to send Northwards again by the Sutler I avail myself of it, in hopes you will get the letter sooner. This is Thursday, and I wrote you last Friday. On Saturday, just after my Court adjourned, Col. Alexander invited me to make one of a fishing party, just about to start into the country. I sent to camp for my horse, & we were soon bowling along. Gen Crocker, who commanded our Division a year ago[28]—& by the way Saturday the 14th was the anniversary of the capture of Jackson, Miss—was of the party, & a right merry and successful party it was. We caught over *two bushels* of fish of all kinds, mostly bass & perch—had a party of Negroes along, who dressed them cooked & served them smoking hot from the pan, on a table spread on the grass, under thick shade, at the head of one of the beautiful springs common to the country. The day was delightful, and the absence of ladies was the only de*fish*iency in the feast—as for myself (after emptying the third plate-ful) I was fain to cry out, "suf*fish*ient!" which the General thought was horrible & should subject me to punishment, but when I disavowed any intention of taking liberties with the King's English, by exclaiming "no *pun*-ish-meant?" I was unanimously acquitted—Horrible, wasn't it?

Well, you may judge we had a nice time, and I thought as we rode back to town, it was the pleasantest day, I had seen in the service. Sunday was after the old hum-drum sort in camp, and Monday like unto it. But Tuesday morning about 8 or 9 o'clock we were roused by the sound of cannon and the familiar explosion of shell. The river is but ten miles distant, and a small gunboat is in the habit of patrolling it & occasionally shelling the opposite side, when rebs. appear, but it seemed to me before I left camp for court, that it was hardly in the right direction for the river, & sounded nearer. The morning however was rainy & the air therefore favorable for conveying sound, so I thought no more about it. There being no cases ready for trial, Court adjourned at once, & I sauntered into Post Hd Qrs (Col. Alexander's) and had hardly got seated, when a courier entered, breathless & in hot haste announced that Madison Station, 8 miles west on the R.Rd. had been attacked by rebels in heavy force, & that the small garrison were falling back on Huntsville. "Ah! then & there, was hurrying to and fro," and "mounting in hot haste"[29] too by orderlies carrying dispatches. I hurried to camp, the Reg't was ordered under arms, & every preparation made to give the rebs. a warm reception

About 11 o'clock, the 59th Lt. Col. Scott in command, was ordered to take the cars & proceed towards Madison, to cover the retreat of our men— the smoke had told us before that the rebels were in the town & had burned the stores. At 3 o'clock Col Scott sent word that the enemy were retreating towards the river, & that if he had artillery he could pursue them, with hope of capturing some. I was ordered to take my Regiment, with the 6th Wisconsin battery, & go to his support. It was nearly nine o'clock, when we had the artillery unloaded at Madison station, & were ready to move out. Taking the direct road to the river, towards Liana—I had forgotten to mention, that the rain had been pouring for three hours—we reached the river about midnight, but no signs of the 59th could be discovered. Our guide was as ignorant of the country as we were—we had evidently blundered, there were no signs of troops having marched on that road, so we marched towards the west, down the river, for two hours more, until we intersected with another road along which we learned from citizens that the rebs had passed. It was now 2 o'clock in the morning so I ordered a halt till daylight, when we learned that the 59th had returned to Madison station by this road the night before, the rebs. having made good their escape across the river, so there was nothing to do but to move back, which we did very slowly, the rain having made the red clay of the roads horrible traveling. We arrived here again on the train about 4 o'clock yesterday, having been absent less than twenty four hours, & marched including 16 miles by rail, over 40 miles. A used up community some of us were too, but to-day after getting full allowance of sleep, I am feeling well again.[30]

I send you some photographs—this time, Genl Sherman's & the Lookout are for Sarah—if you want duplicates will send them. I am sorry there isn't a decent picture of Grant in town. I have the promise of a large size one from Nashville, & will send it to Sarah. The other views I send are No 1 of the Spring & No 2 of the Country just below the Spring, No 3 is the Court House. The train has just come in, much earlier I expected, & I am warned that I must close. I had thought to write you a good long letter, but must close, you'll get more the next time. I am very well, my dear wife, and we are very pleasantly situated. Isn't it singular, that after all our service & fighting, we should be left behind for this battle summer, when the smoke from the field roll across the whole continent. Well, we deserve it, & are doing good service here, we are only afraid that the one hundred days men may relieve us and occupy our snug quarters.[31] Will write again soon—rumors of Paymasters, but none arrived. Good bye. Kiss the darling. Papa didn't forget her birthday—he would have written her a little letter if he had been in camp Write often. Your loving Husband

Edward.

[*Envelope endorsed:* "Mrs. Edward J. Wood, Care C.B. Williams Esq, Salina P.O., New York."]

LETTER 70

Huntsville, Ala.
May 24th 1864.

My dear wife,

Yours of the 16th inst. is received and I hasten to reply, to atone as far as possible my negligence when you were so anxiously waiting to hear from me, thinking we were on the march and probably engaged in the battle near Dalton.[32] I wrote you how the delay happened, but I didn't once think how concerned you would be at the prospect of a forward movement, & how anxious you would be to hear from me, or I would have found time & summoned resolution to write a few lines sooner. *We* knew we had escaped the hardships and dangers of the campaign & it was perhaps natural that we should feel easy, & think all our friends ought to, too. I won't be so thoughtless again.

Everything jogs along with us much as usual, and there is very little of interest to write about. The town has been made quite lively for the past few days by the arrival of the 17th Army Corps, under Frank P. Blair, about whose re-appointment as Major General, there has been so much stir in Congress.[33] It is our old Corps, you know, formerly commanded by Gen'l McPherson, and I have been renewing many pleasant acquaintances with the officers. All of our famous Court Martial at Vicksburg were from this Corps, and they have seemed glad to meet Col. Alexander & myself here. Col. Potts, 32nd Ohio, Col Davis, 23rd Ind, Col. Deimling, 10th Mo, Col. McCook, 31st Ill, Lt. Col. Smith, 17th Ills, & Capt. Pullen, Judge Advocate, all members of our old Court, have called on me yesterday and today.[34] An outsider can hardly appreciate the strength of the ties that bind men together, associated as we are in the army, sharers of common perils, & partakers of a common glory. There is, in addition a spirit of clan-ship, as strong as that of the Highlanders, fostered by the system of Corps distinctions, that tends in a high degree to attach men of the same Corps organization to each other.[35]

You know how keenly our Division felt the injustice of the act that separated them from the old 17th, and you can imagine how warmly we welcomed our old companions in arms. Col. Deimling I found was a resident of St. Louis, and a cousin of Charley Blood's wife, my old classmate with whom I spent such pleasant time last fall. Col. D. was at home this winter on recruiting service, & Blood happened to ask him if he knew Col. Wood of an Indiana regiment, hardly thinking it probable that he did, and the Colonel was as much astonished to learn that Charley & I were classmates.

There was a rumor afloat for a day or two that we were to be releived by a Division of the 17th Corps, but it had gradually died away. I beleive it originated from an assumption of command by Gen Blair, who is the personification of assurance—and who ordered Genl Smith to march at 6 o'clock last Saturday morning on 12 hours notice!—his Division being at that time scattered from Decatur to Stevenson—a distance of 80 miles Gen Smith refused to recognize the authority of Gen. Blair, then just arrived in town & on his way through to Chattanooga, & referred the matter by telegraph to Genl Sherman at Kingston Ga. Genl S. replied that the Division was left here by *his* orders, & would remain here until he ordered it away— so I think we are good for all summer, in spite of the machinations of Mr. Blair.[36] Mrs Alexander & Mrs. Rogers arrived last Saturday night. I have not called on them yet but understand they are well. Mrs. A. has three children with her. Mrs. Scott and several other ladies, wives of officers, came a few days before—so you see we are not going to lack for female society. I am afraid my sense of appreciation of the benefits thereof, is not keen enough to induce me to enjoy much of it.

I suppose you have been alarmed again, if you have seen the absurd telegraphic dispatch that Forrest & Roddy with 10,000 men were threatening Huntsville.[37] Don't beleive anything of the kind you may see—we have excellent fortifications, & our single Brigade would be able to take care of them, even with that number of men—but the fact is, they haven't got the half, and they will be very lucky if they cross the Tennessee river again and get back with any of their gang. The Paymaster is actually in town, in a few days, he will pay our Reg'ts—I am sure we all need it bad enough. I am so glad to hear such good accounts of Mamie—I pray that she may continue to enjoy such good health and gather roses on her cheek all the livelong summer. Papa has got two magnificent bouquets on his table—mostly roses, & the finest & handsomest I ever saw. Don't be jealous—they are not the gift of any fair feminine, but gathered—surreptitiously I reckon—by Jake. I learned how to cut a glass bottle in two the other day so as to make a *vase*. It takes *four* to perform the operation—one to hold the bottle firmly between the knees, then with a stout twine wrapped round it, two *saw* across it till the part of the glass where the *sawing* is performed becomes heated, when the fourth pours cold water on, when snap the bottle flies apart as smooth as if cut with a diamond. Simple, but very complete. I beleive I haven't alluded to my own health lately, simply because I had forgotten that I had such a commodity. I have not felt so thoroughly *well*, since I can't tell when, certainly not since I have been in the service. I attribute it much to diet. I have lost all relish for meat, especially the salt & fat meat, which forms most of the ration in the army. We get all kinds of vegetables in abundance—Lettuce, radishes, onions asparagus & peas, with such luscious strawberries, are brought to the camp every morning, by negro women from the country. Milk we have always, & occasionally fresh butter & eggs—so you see we are in no danger of starvation or scurvy. I don't know but you will think I am a *gourmand*, by such minute details of our living—no, I know you won't—soldier fare is good, the best conceivable for rough work, but in camp, all the accessories & additions that can be made to it are for the better.

The strains of the Brigade band reach me from town—probably serenading Mr. Blair, (he isn't a Major General & never ought to be) & I am reminded of what a fine Band we have. They number 22 members—have instruments that cost $1000, & play splendidly. Last night I am told they had a benefit at the theatre (!) and netted $150 towards paying for their instruments.[38] The theatre is an institution I never have visited—in fact, I haven't spent but one evening in town since we moved into the suburbs, and that at the lodge. Not that I haven't had invitations, but I have always found something that claimed my attention at camp. Soldiering and fulfilling the duties of a respectable citizen are hardly compatible—one or the other must be neglected, as you doubtless saw from your brief experience at Indianapolis. Dear old Bates House! I have already forgiven its manifold sins of omission & commission, for the sake of the happy hours I spent there with wifey & baby.

I don't think I told you I couldn't get a respectable picture of Grant for Sarah—am expecting one from Nashville. The situation looks critical for Grant in Virginia—if the Gov't only supports him, he is bound to succeed—he will do as he says, "fight it out on that line, if it takes all summer," and in that is the key to his character[39]

The music from the Band still falls on my ear, but the chime from the town clock also falls to the time of midnight, so I must close. I wish I could hand you one of my *millinery* roses, they are so full & fair & perfectly crimped they look more like the creations of a milliner's shop than of nature's

Goodnight & God bless you. I send a thousand kisses to my darlings. Your Husband Edward

LETTER 71
Send postage stamps

Huntsville, Ala.
May 25th 1864.

My dear wife,

I wrote you last night, and today we have unexpectedly got pay, so I send you enclosed Express receipt for $100. I hope it [*sic*] for your present necessities. I had to buy a horse at Nashville, "*Charlie*" was gone when I reached here—this, with the expenses of my home furlough, has made me short. In a month or six weeks, we shall receive pay again & then I can square up all around.

I send five dollars to Publishers of "*Daleth*," for Sarah—when it comes to hand, please say it is from me as a slight token of appreciation of her many acts of sisterly kindness.

I suppose you join in the Ladies Non-Importation Leagues, so you will hardly dare wear your new silk on the streets[40]—I am distressed to see in Frank Leslie's Ladies Magazine, that the Russian leather color will not be worn, in fact that it is tabooed, and that everybody is sick & tired of it. Poor dress, the wardrobe & closet are your appropriate sphere. I see also from the same undoubted authority that dresses only of an uncertain color, such as coffee with cream in it, a sandy shore, or perhaps I might be allowed to add, a dirty child's pinafore, indeterminately streaked with molasses will be worn. Well, well. I hope some good may come of the ladies dress reform movement—the reign of shoddy in this era of blood is terribly like the reign of a ghastly skeleton clothed in purple and fine linen.[41] This war is for the purification and sanctification of the nation, and the iron must enter the soul of the North, as it has entered the South, before its wise purposes can be accomplished. We may put off the evil day, devote ourselves to money-getting, and seem prosperous, but the end is not yet. The North has laid no sacrifices on the altar of Liberty commensurate with the magnitude of the interests [involved]. It is true, she has given her sons to battle and poured her treasures into the Government chests, but it has been at no sacrifice of material prosperity. On the contrary, the war has been a source of profit to every business man in the North, and the drain of armed men in the field, has scarcely been felt in our teeming population. If we had manifested one half the self-sacrificing spirit displayed by the South, where the one absorbing topic for two years with men, women & children has been the war, we should be much nearer the end, than we now are—Well, I didn't intend to write you such a Homily when I commenced, but simply to enclose you the receipt and to say that after all, we are probably about to be relieved and sent to the front, the troops at Nashville coming down to take our places, while the 100 days men fill theirs.

I hope it is not so, but that's the way it looks now. I will write you often & keep you advised of any changes. I wanted you to send me a box of things if we remained here, but it will hardly be worth while, till we learn something more definite. I enclose also two extracts from a letter of a private home—they were written just after our trial inspection. Send me the photographs & anything you may find good to read. I am disgusted at the ending of the "Small House at Allington" in Harper, & have been tempted to write the "Easy Chair" an indignant letter.[42] Kiss the darling Mamie with your sweetest kisses. Do write often—even a few lines are always acceptable. Your Husband

Edward

[*Clipping 1*][43]
We can, and feel proud to boast of a Colonel who is an officer of talent, pride and taste, as well as a hero of many hard fought battles; while a truer or braver soldier never commanded a battalion, either in time of peace or upon the field of battle. He is, and ever has been, interested in the welfare of his men, and could you witness the Regiment on "inspection" or "dress parade," it would no longer be a mystery why we enlisted. When it comes to battle with such officers as are those of the 48th, the men will stand by them, would die by them rather than flinch an inch without their command.

[*Clipping 2*]
Major Byrkit arrived here yesterday forenoon, looking as clever and good natured as ever, and every time I get a glimpse of him I feel proud to know that I am a member of his veteran regiment. He has the good will and best wishes of "all hands round," and long may he live to smote treason with that strong arm as in days of yore.

LETTER 72

Huntsville, Ala.
May 29th 1864

My dear wife,

I was just the least bit disappointed last night, when the mail brought me no letter—but I have no reason to complain—it is less than a week since your last was received—and I haven't been a good enough boy lately—to deserve one oftener. Still, tho' I haven't the excuse for writing which your letter would have afforded, I don't beleive you will feel very bad, because I am about to waive ceremony & write anyhow—especially when I tell you my many excellent reasons for so doing—and as this is Sunday, it would be well to divide this discourse into *heads*.

Firstly, then, my dearly beloved wife, the spirit moveth me to write unto you, because of the deep quiet and peaceful calmness of this beautiful

Sabbath morning. "What is so rare as a day in June? Then if every come *perfect* days." Read Lowell's beautiful poem & you will have a better description of the day than I can give you. Even his poetic soul attuned to such exquisite harmony with nature, would be satisfied with the complete perfectness of the scene and hours. Not a cloud marks the heavens, and yet the air is as mild and grateful to the senses, as any that e'er stole o'er lovers, at twilight on the Aegean shore. As I sit under my fragrant cedar bower, drinking in the wonderful melodies of the mocking-bird—the brilliant soprano in this universal harmony of nature—is it strange that my heart should turn towards my loved ones so far away, without whom, *all* days are very *imperfect*.

And yet ah! how little of peace & quietness there is. The deep booming of cannon drowns the pleasant song of birds all over the land, and the shrieks & moans of wounded & dying fill the air with a terrible chorus. The bad passions of man raise this infernal discord, and only with the millennium shall it cease in angel strains.

Secondly, My hearers, when the organ-grinder refused to *"move on,"* under less than a shilling, because he appreciated the value of "peace & quietness," he over-estimated the value of that commodity. There is a silence which is death-like, and a stillness which is of the tomb. Alexander Selkirk, imperial "monarch of all he surveyed," is at this moment an object of envy to me, for he never knew the dreary solitude of being left in camp without a man of the Regiment.[44]

On Friday last, the Major started with the Regiment to drive 2000 head of cattle through to Chattanooga—110 miles—I being on detached service as Pres't of a Court Martial remained behind, and thought I was lucky in being able to escape the trip, but I would rather march for a month than to endure a week of such lonesomeness. The Regiment is to return by rail, and they expect to be gone just about a week. I never stayed behind before, but the road is such a dismal one, and the purpose of the trip so peculiar, I thought I would give the Major the job, especially as he missed the march from Nashville here—in fact, I told him that I had just discovered what a Major's command was—2000 steers![45]

Thirdly, My hearers, as we pass through this vale of tears, how often are we reminded of the transitoriness of all earthly possessions. "Riches take unto themselves wings and fly away,"[46] and so even does the hard-earned small change of the soldier boy. Last Thursday night some nefarious individual not having the fear of Courts Martial before his eyes, and an evident irrespecter of rank & persons, surreptitiously and with malice aforethought, did enter my tent and feloniously take, steal and carry away, one pair of pants, one vest, one pair of boots, together with a large sum of money, to wit $150—the property of the deponent—It was the boldest robbery I ever knew committed—the Adjutant & myself were sleeping in the same tent, and the thief coolly took all our clothing outside, and helped himself to what he wanted—leaving our uniform coats & my *suspenders,* all the other clothing he carried off. The Adjutant fortunately had put his money under his hat—mine was in my pants pocket, & carelessly I must admit, hanging on a chair. I had been *strapped* so long that I didn't think about the money, or I might have been more careful. No clue has been obtained to the perpetrator of this bold villainy, and he will probably never be discovered. Experience is a dear school, but you know there's a class of men who never will learn in any other. I think I've learned my lesson this time thoroughly—

I don't think you need to have this discourse continued to sixteenthly & seventeenthly—cogent reasons enough for the production of this miscellaneous epistle have already been adduced—The robbery occurred on Thursday night—the Field & Staff officers having been paid a day or two before, in advance of the Regiment. There was great difficulty about procuring rolls for the use of the companies, and I managed to secure enough for my Regiment, in advance of the rest of the Brigade—in fact an officer had been sent to Nashville to procure rolls for the Brigade. Thro' friends in the Batteries & Cavalry organizations, outside of the Brigade, I borrowed rolls, and had them completed & handed in to the Paymaster by noon of Thursday. The Regiment was ordered Thursday afternoon to move at daylight Friday morning. I represented to General Smith the facts—that my Regiment alone of the Division had its rolls ready for the Paymaster, and asked a delay until noon of Friday that they might be paid, which was acceded to. Fifteen minutes after the last company was paid, they fell into line to take up the march, but before that time, Capt Green[47] came to me & handing an envelope said "that was the amount, that three companies sympathized with me in my loss," & then incontinently left. I opened the envelope, without mistrusting the nature of the contents & found $100 enclosed. My first impulse was to return it, but a few moments reflection convinced me that the kind feelings which prompted the gift would be hurt by such action, so I acknowledged its receipt, as handsomely as I knew how, and pocketed the envelope & contents.

The Paymaster happened to inquire if I was going with my Regiment, and learning that I was on detached service, offered to pay me for the month of May, on my order placing me on Court Martial, so I am decidedly in funds, despite the robbery.

I enclose Fifty Dollars herein, for it may be some time before we are paid again, and I shall be one month's pay short at that time, in consequence of the payment that had been made me for this month. I want some things from home very much particularly *boots,* but I hardly dare have you send them at present. I wish tho' you would order me a pair made from my old measure at Root's—I beleive was the name—it was the bootmakers under the Syracuse House, near Wilkinson's bank—not your patron—but the other one. My measure was taken there about 1st Sept last, and I have no doubt he can easily find it. I want them made just like those—double upper & double welt—and upon reflection, you had better send them at once. If we leave here, we shall always be in communication with this place, & I can send a man back for them. Well, let's see, what else—the shoes. I'll hardly need for campaigning—slippers I've bought—the woollen shirts you had better keep—Oh! four pounds best chewing tobacco from the Toledo tobacco store—D.C. Foote is agent I beleive—on Salina street, nearly opposite Yates. Next, anything that will make the hair grow on the tops of the head—my poor grey hairs are all falling out, & I want to save them—I can't think of anything else, because I hadn't thought of preparing a list. A small pair of shears or large pair of scissors would be acceptable. Yes, & a dark-coloured table cloth, small size. I suppose I could continue to think of little things, but it would hardly be worth while—Anything that you think would be acceptable to a soldier boy.

Everything indicates that we are to move soon—two Regiments of dismounted Cavalry, 12th & 13th Ind, have already reported here, and the programme is understood to be, that the 100 days men, and dismounted cavalry are to guard the R.Rds while all old troops are to be sent to the front.[48]

I will keep you duly advised of our movements I send accompanying this four photographs—three of them of scenes about Vicksburg. I beleive they are all sufficiently explained by the pencillings on the back. And for fear you wouldn't know what to do with so many pictures, I have ordered an Album for you, exclusively for military gentlemen & scenes.

May 31st. This long letter failed to get into the mail last night, so I am able to acknowledge the receipt of your welcome letter of the 22nd—and such a dear good letter. I can't pretend at the heels of this long scrambling letter to answer it. In a few days I will try to do it justice. In the meantime, I am glad you agree with me, in the estimate of your Indianapolis picture— have a good one taken *right away* Have Mamie's beads marked of course. It is such a comfort to think she is so well & hearty—Has she been vaccinated. I would not delay it, she can bear it easily now, and it is such a simple preventive of so horrible a disease

I am sorry you couldn't have been here all this pleasant time—if we had only known at Indianapolis, that the Reg't would remain here till 1st June, I think you would have travelled southwards & I am sure you would have had a pleasant glimpse of Dixie. The 59th ladies are all here, and seem disposed to make the most of their time. Picnics on the mountains, *"fish-fries,"* dancing parties for the juveniles with tea fights & suppers for the elders, have been the order of the day & night. Ten days more, I think, will see them on their way Northwards, & our old Division setting its face to the foe. Tell Mamie Papa don't love the naughty rebels, either, but he is getting most tired of fighting them, & wants to come home to his little girl. Give my love to Aunt Mary. I should like so much to see her—Sarah & Edward always have my warmest regard and as for you, my precious inestimable wife, you know you have the unchanging, unquestioning love, of your own Husband, Edward.

The proper address for a box, would be the same as for my letters. "48th Ind. John E. Smith's Division. Huntsville" I forgot to mention that the rascally thief stole my sleeve-buttons, with my portmonnais the other night. I would rather lost all the rest than the buttons—Adjt Branch of the 59th[49] gave me the neatest Masonic pin I ever saw, the other day—a small scarf-pin, the head round—with the keystone in black enamel & the enigmatical letters in minute characters on it Have the boots made, & box sent as soon as possible—it may be it will get here before we move Good bye again, dear wife God bless you. Your Husband Edward

LETTER 73

Huntsville, Ala.
June 10th 1864.

My dear wife,

I am real cross, disappointed lonesome and dismally blue tonight, and as by the happy provisions of the married state, you the natural sharer of all my joys & sorrows. I propose—after the manner of all respectable married men to make you the recipient of my dismal tale of sufferings. In the first place, to be a Colonel without a Regiment—two long weeks of dreary monotony, with nothing to do but imagine all sorts of evil surmisings in regard to my lost Regiment. I wrote you they had gone to Chattanooga to drive cattle—I wish the cattle had been possessed as the swine of old, and driven into the Tennessee[50]—they reached C. in seven days & would have been back the next day, but Genl. McPherson's Adjt. Genl. at Chat. coolly telegraphed to Genl Smith that he had ordered the Reg't to proceed to the front with the cattle, there being no Regt. there to releive them. The Major naturally indignant and outraged, sent me no word, & I have not heard a word directly or indirectly from them for more than a week—In the meantime the eternal Court Martial drags its slow length along, and I am refused to be relieved from it, as I have asked, to join my Reg't. Do you wonder that I am uneasy & chafe at the hard necessity that keeps me from my command—In the second place my little wife has forgotten her boy—or Uncle Sam has forgotten to bring him a letter—for more than ten days. I very confidently expected a letter tonight, and distributed the mail myself, certain that I should draw a prize—but tho' there were over two hundred, a blank fell to my lot, as it had every night this week. I begin to be afraid you have not received some of my letters—since I criminally let such a long time go by, without writing. I have written three or four letters, which I have not heard from. I sent one by the Chaplain, at a time when it was supposed there were restrictions on the mail—another shortly after—one by Mr. Strong, to be mailed at Louisville, one soon after enclosing Express receipt for $100, and one last week by Mr. Tyrrell, Strong's clerk,[51] to be mailed at Louisville, enclosing $50. I have send besides several envelopes, enclosing photographs—be sure to let me know what you have received. Of course, I feel uneasy about yours & Mamie's welfare, when with perfect mail facilities I don't hear from you for so long—I suppose it must be intended as a punishment for my long neglect in writing without sufficient reason

Again, I am annoyed by the uncertainty that prevails about our leaving here. Three days ago everything indicated an immediate movement—now, Genl. Smith says that we will not leave as soon as we expected—and that owl-like saying leaves us as much in the dark as ever. Many think—but perhaps the wish is father to the thought—that we will not leave at all. It does seem difficult to find troops to releive us—with the exception of Ohio, the hundred days men are responding slowly—and the Ohio troops have been mostly sent eastward. Indiana so far has raised but 8 Regts—where she promised 30—and those 8 have been distributed along the R.Rd. from Nashville towards Chattanooga—but one has got as far south as Stevenson. John Morgan is raiding it in Eastern Kentucky and all the troops intended to guard these lower lines of communication are being stopped in Ky to meet him.[52]

Yesterday, Forrest was reported crossing the Tennessee near Florence, with the evident intention of making a raid on the R.Rd. from Nashville to Decatur.[53] The guerrillas in our immediate neighborhood are growing daily bolder, and have already cut the road & burned a bridge between here & Stevenson On the whole, as Sherman don't need us, & we cannot well be spared from here, I think the chances are, we will remain.

But you see how in my case, all this uncertainty about leaving is aggravated by the absence of my Reg't 200 miles to the front—if we are to stay I want them back at once—if go, I want to know it, to telegraph them to remain, and so save making the march twice. I as confidently expected a messenger from them tonight as I did to hear from you, and can you wonder that my soul is disquieted within me.

Don't fail to have a good photo taken & send me. I am sorry you haven't heard from Mary Mackie. I suppose if your letter failed to reach her, one from me would hardly fare better. I am anticipating visiting Madison Ga. this summer, after Sherman takes Atlanta—it is only about 50 miles distant & is on the direct line to Charleston or Savannah.[54] Isn't it strange that in these days of terrific fighting, when in the east & in the west, men are slain by the thousand & tens of thousands, it should be our fortune to be out of the actual conflict. The end of this terrible contest undoubtedly approaches but it is farther deferred, than I once thought it would be. Nothing short of annihilation of two formidable rebel armies will gain us the victory—and to do that—as I have written you before, we must have more men. It would not surprise me now, if Grant's final victory was delayed until autumn, and then only obtained by reinforcements[55]—which the rebels will be unable to meet—The sheet runs over, and the hour will not admit of commencing a new one tonight. I need not say that I am well—all my old trouble has entirely disappeared, and I am sounder today than I ever expected to be, after the long seige with the most insidious & troublesome enemy of camp life—diarrhoea Kiss the darling child for Papa—he sends her all sorts of messages of love. Good night my dear one. God bless & keep you and our darling safely Your Husband Edward

[*Envelope endorsed:* "Mrs. Edward J. Wood, Care E. B. Judson Esqr, Syracuse, New York."]

LETTER 74

Huntsville, Ala.
June 17th 1864.

My dear wife,

I take it all back—all my last complaining, dismally blue letter. I am in receipt of your letter of May 30th, enclosing postage stamps and acknowledging receipt of photographs, also of letter of June 10th, acknowledging receipt of money—the very day I sent the last cerulean epistle above-mentioned. I received your letter of the 4th inst. so I am largely in your debt. I am glad you like the Album—it was ordered at a venture from N.Y. so I can claim no credit for its selection—I knew you needed one for your military pictures, which had over-run your other one.

Isn't it an admirable art, which so easily & so cheaply enables us to obtain perfect pictures of persons & scenes that will possess interest for us, while life lasts. I will try in the morning to get you pictures of Lookout Mt. and any others that may be of value. I am feeling particularly pleased tonight, at the receipt of the enclosed kind letter from my old friend Redfield.[56] He is at home yet, it seems, and if one may judge quite reconciled to remain with his growing family. How I wish we could accept his kind invitation to spend some pleasant time with him in his Green Mountain home this summer.

June 21st—My dear wife, this letter has lain by a long time and I must close it now hurriedly—I was interrupted by the visit of friends the other night, and put it away, thinking to finish in the morning—before I got at it, the Regiment arrived and I have been kept on the jump ever since. Marching orders came yesterday for tomorrow morning at 5 o'clock. I have of course been kept very busy.

We move towards Chattanooga & the front—Your letter enclosing express receipt was received today but the box has not yet come to hand. If you laugh at me for the rough looking letter, I shall send you back your last, for a signature Did you know how it ended—just with a notice that you enclosed receipt dated June 4th. I leave an order behind for the box, with Lieut Ellis[57] in charge of convalescents who is to join us at Chattanooga, so I will get it there. Will keep you advised of our movements—it is impossible to speculate upon them now with any certainty, tho' I think we are going with all dispatch to the front. I sent by express my overcoat & other things that I couldn't conveniently carry in a campaign—you have doubtless rec'd them ere this—that ugly blot is the result of a miserable pen, & my own fast & bad writing. Write me often if only a few lines, and send reading matter—much obliged for Atlantic for June, tho' Harper with Dicken's new story is far ahead.[58] Read the two numbers if you have not—I could not find pictures of Lookout here, but was told they could be had at Chattanooga— will try there. Good night my dear wife, the clock strikes twelve & reveille sounds at three, so I must stop. Write me all about yourself & Mamie—Papa thinks a thousand kisses is none too many for her & sends them again. Your Husband

Edward

[*Envelope endorsed:* "Mrs. Edward J. Wood, Care E. B. Judson Esq, Syracuse, New York."]

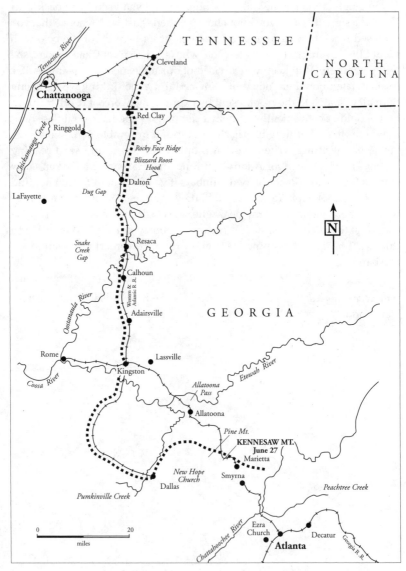

North Georgia Campaign. Adapted from C. Knight Aldrich, ed., Quest for a Star: The Civil War Letters of Colonel Francis T. Sherman of the 88th Illinois *(Knoxville, 2000).*

CHAPTER 12

The Best Soldiers in the World

Georgia on the Etowah, July–November 1864

Sherman's campaign of maneuver and incessant fighting continued into the hot Georgia summer. Federal forces launched themselves at the Rebels in a series of bloody engagements: Resaca, Cassville, New Hope Church, Pickett's Mill, Dallas, Kolb's Farm, Kennesaw Mountain. Nearing Atlanta, the fighting continued at Peachtree Creek, Bald Hill, Ezra Church, and Jonesboro, as Union troops besieged the city and artillery bombarded its inhabitants. Union troops finally entered Atlanta on September 1, continuing to pursue the Rebel army, now commanded by Lieutenant General John Bell Hood, which had withdrawn from the city after destroying their warehouses and munitions.[1]

The 48th Indiana's division received surprise orders to march toward the front in early July. Colonel Wood expected again that his unit would be placed in the front line of battle. But once more the division was ordered to positions in the rear, guarding important and vulnerable railroad bridges over the Etowah River along the thin strand of railroad tracks that supplied the Union Army.

Northern sentiment rebounded from the lows experienced earlier in the year, and Republican election victories in the state and presidential elections in October and November resulted. However, the Rebels had not been subdued. Confederate General Hood, by temperament rash and aggressive, succeeded Joseph Johnston in July 1864, and immediately instituted an offensive posture in an attempt to drive Sherman's forces from Georgia. After the fall of Atlanta, leading a force of thirty thousand, the remains of the Army of Tennessee, Hood marched west and north in an effort to threaten Federal supply lines and force Sherman to backtrack. Sherman tracked Hood to guard his supply line, but did not pursue the Rebel army. Hood's efforts to cut the rail lines with attacks at Resaca and Allatoona failed when determined defenders—veteran troops guarding the bridges and tracks—fended off multiple assaults.[2]

LETTER 75

Stevenson, Ala.
June 28th 1864.

My dear wife,

I finished very hurriedly a letter to you the day before we left Hunts-ville—then we expected to march through to Bridgeport, 15 miles beyond this, and then take the cars. Subsequently the orders were changed and we were ordered to take cars here. We camped on Crow Creek, three miles from the station, Sunday night, the 26th inst, after a tedious & most uncom-fortable march of four days. The heat is almost insupportable—men drop by the wayside unable to go further, and many cases of actual sunstroke have occurred. Fourteen deaths on the road are reported. I have not lost a man and had very few fall out, because I would not try to keep up with the column, but marched very slowly, and halted at every convenient shade, at least every mile. Arriving here, we found the arrangements for leaving on the cars, very incomplete, and hence the detention.[3] Our 3rd Brigade & one Battery got off last night and as I write the 2nd Brigade are load-ing—we shall probably leave tonight or in the morning. Gen Smith went on to Chattanooga day before yesterday, and Col. Alexander is in command of the Division.

I am writing in Capt Wheeler's private room at the Soldier's Home, a place doubtless familiar to Nettie—whose "gift of good faery" is sufficiently testified to, in the embellishments in the shape of *"New York Observers,"* with which the captain's room is papered.[4] It seems they went thro' Huntsville, when they went home and didn't know I was there. Captain Wheeler has been very kind to me, and all my friends, and I am under great obliga-tions to him. Col. Alex. has made Head Quarters here, and is much pleased with the Capt. You must be sure to tell Nettie, how much the Capt. has accommodated us. Our orders are to report to Kingston Ga. *probably to guard R.Rd.* from Chattanooga to Atlanta.[5] I am expecting the Regiment up from camp every moment & must close. Have heard from the box—it reached Huntsville the day after we left, & is in charge of Lieut Ellis who has gone on to Chattanooga.

Will write you again at the next stopping place. Have not heard from you since the letter enclosing receipt for box. We have had no mail since we left—understand it has gone on to Kingston. Don't fail to write *very* often I am in excellent health, and barring the discomforts of heat, & wood-ticks, am standing the march firstrate.

The column is just coming in sight. Good bye, my dear one. Kiss Mamie a *"good many"* times for Papa. Col. Alex. and Capt Wheeler desire to be re-membered the Col. pressed these little flowers which I enclose. I picked them on the way and he prepared them for sending This scrawling style is

The Best Soldiers in the World

not usual with me, but it is the only way this pen will write. Good bye again & God bless you. You devoted husband

Edward

LETTER 76

Kingston Ga.
July 10th 1864.

My dear wife,

It is a long time since I wrote you last from Stevenson, Ala, but it has not been my fault—we have been drifting about, until we are finally landed (or *stranded*, I dont know which) at the point, which was to have been our original destination. We reached here about a week since, were moved first North & then South on the R.Rd, and finally were perched on top of this high hill, overlooking the town & R.Rd, in the inside of a huge two acre fort, with the 6th Wisconsin Battery. When I say *fort*, you must not imagine high embattlements, or solid masonry with grim and threatening port-holes, but simply the circular crest of a hill enclosed with a breastwork of logs, to be hereafter covered with earth. The 48th seems in a fair way to do the latter business, and the establishment has already been christened Fort Wood. Really we have a pleasant location—the part of the *fort* we occupy, is well shaded, the elevation gives us every breeze that is stirring, and at the foot of the hill, are three good springs. Although we labored under a temporary inconvenience for want of tents, the boys soon remedied that. At Huntsville, where every-body had a safe-guard it was dangerous to touch a fence-board or a building—but here there are no such restraints and the lumber has literally walked into camp on the backs of 400 men. Capt Allen was telling me an amusing thing about one of his boys. I had noticed several old sheds and some deserted buildings near the camp, before we moved here, that I thought would make good shelter for the boys, and intended to tell them of it, but with the true soldier instinct, that finds anything to be appropriated as soon as you stop the boys got ahead of me, & were already *backing* it up the hill, when I went out to see if it was still there. I remarked to one of them, "I see you've found the old sheds," & passed on. Capt Allen says the man told him he never was so frightened in his life, he was bringing up a few boards, & met Col. Wood, he expected he would make him take them back and nail them on & punish him beside but he just said what I have written above. You've no idea how such a little thing flies in camp—in ten minutes, I dont think there were ten men in camp, & the sounds from the knocking off boards, in the valley below, were like continuous roll of musketry, soon they returned with the captured boards, & now are all comfortably housed—The box I received before leaving Stevenson but didn't have a chance to examine its contents fully, till a few days ago. What a dear thoughtful girl you are, everything just as I wanted it. The boots fit to perfection, the tobacco is superfine—the pocketbook was very acceptable, & so neat & convenient. The reading matter I have had no time to examine, but I know it will give me pleasure for many an idle hour—the little cravats I gave to Adjutant & the Doctor—all but one. I have so many ties, and they seemed to be tie-less. I haven't commenced the use of the Restorative yet, but mean to, as soon as I can get some good shampooing material—the collars fit to a nicety, & the mustard! Well, we lived on it four days, that is to say we had nothing to eat but bacon & hard bread for four days, & the mustard made it relish astonishingly.

I am in receipt also of your two letters June 20 & 28th—the latter with photographs for which I am grateful I am sorry Sarah is so unwell. I hope she will be able to take her summer trip—'twould do her so much good. You must try to persuade her to it.

I think every day how much reason I have to be thankful that you and Mamie are so well. I have had it brought nearer to me within the last few days, by the sad loss Col. Alexander has sustained. His oldest daughter, the one that was with them at Indianapolis last winter, died recently & the Col. has gone home. His little girl, about twelve years old was away at school, and was taken with brain fever, just as the term closed, and died in a few days. Mrs. A. reached home from Huntsville, only to hasten to her dying child.[6] Isn't it sad—the Col was quite broken down & as the anxiety & grief had made his wife sick, I advised him to go home at once.

There seems a probability that we shall stay here some time—we are 80 miles from Chattanooga, and 60 from Atlanta, and as there seems no doubt of Sherman's ability to enter Atlanta with his present force, we will doubtless continue here, to guard the R.Rd as was originally intended. Our Brigade, as at Huntsville, is all together, in & about the town, while the other two Brigades are scattered along the R.Rd. We thus have much better chance for resistance in case of an attack, and with the fort completed we could safely defy ten thousand rebs.

July 11, 1864. How vain are the expectations of man—especially when that man happens to be a soldier. I was writing last night so confidently of remaining here, and to-night we are under orders to march at 5 o'clock tomorrow morning with all baggage. The whole Division moves, & tho' I've learned no particulars, I suppose we go to the front, probably to join our Corps. I will write you whenever we halt long enough to do so & will try to write every few days, even if it is only a few lines. I still continue very well, the heat in the middle of the day, is most intolerable, & marching is decidedly tough business, but I suppose we shall all be salamanders, before the summer's business is over. The boys with Grant & Sherman have been doing heroic work under the same summer's sun and we claim to be their equals,

& can do our share of it. We must be up by three o'clock, & I must close. Don't fail to write often. I have received your last letters very promptly.

Write me everything about yourself & Mamie. Poor child! she hardly knows her loving Papa yet—if she only keeps well & hearty, & her papa gets safely out of this cruel business, we will get better acquainted Papa sends a "great many" kisses to his dear little girl Is she any more tractable than formerly, or does she show her *spunk* still. Write me everything Good night & God bless & preserve you from harm my best of wives, is the prayer of

Your loving Husband
Edward.

All the postage stamps thankfully rec'd & a good many given to the needy, whenever convenient put in a few

[*Enveloped endorsed:* "Mrs. Edward J. Wood, Care E. B. Judson Esq, Syracuse, New York." *On reverse:* "Answered July 24th 1864."]

LETTER 77

Camp on Etowah River, Ga.
July 15th 1864.

My dear wife,

I wrote you from Kingston, the first of the week, & promised to write again as soon as we stopped long enough. Our march was unexpectedly short—only 14 miles to this place, where there is an important R.Rd bridge over the Etowah. Two regiments of our Brigade and a Battery were sent 7 miles further on to Altoona, where there is another bridge. Our Division is now stretched along the R.Rd from Resaca to Altoona, a distance of 50 miles.

Gen. Smith makes his Hd Qrs at Cartersville, a little town two miles back on the Road towards Kingston. We found board shanties built here by the troops whom we releived, so the men were able to find comfortable quarters at once. My own quarters are, with those of the Brigade, in a fort, and very comfortable we have made them in the few days we've been here. The fort is one of two, located on each side of the R.Rd overlooking the river, and commanding the bridge. The other fort is occupied by the 6th Wis. Bat'y, with the 59th Ind. for supports—while the 63rd Ill. & my Reg't are camped just outside of the one we are in.

The ground inside has been made as level as a floor, and numerous board buildings, furnish us with an Adjt's office, kitchen & dining rooms so that with our tents, we have lots of room. The country seems more productive than any we have seen before, this side of Huntsville. There are many large wheat & corn fields, while hay & oats have been cut in considerable quantities. We have also had the first of vegetables since leaving Huntsville—the people, that is, the women & children who are left behind, are destitute in the extreme, and very gladly exchange their *"garden truck"* for meat, sugar, salt, & coffee. You were right in thinking we were in the midst of the blackberry season—for two weeks, we have had them every meal and the quantity brought in for sale is enormous

We get no fresh meat except occasionally chickens, and have got so tired of salt meat, that we live almost entirely on vegetables. There is a mill close by in running order, where we have flour ground out of new wheat— our baker supplies us with the best of bread, and this morning if you had stepped in to breakfast, we would have given you fresh bread & butter, a cup of coffee, or a glass of milk, new potatoes, cucumbers & onions, and a heaping saucer of blackberries & milk, & for substantials nice ham & eggs. All these little things, that we have so common at home, as to be no matter of thought, become cause of great satisfaction to the soldier, whenever he is fortunate enough to get them—I am in receipt of two letters from you, since writing last, one rec'd just as we were leaving Kingston, & the other written July 3rd, day before yesterday—don't you think the mails come regularly, considering the distance, & the unsettled state of the country.

I am sorry to hear you are feeling so unwell—you must take medical advice, the symptoms you mention make me feel uneasy—if you don't get better right away, you ought to consult a physician. I noticed you complained of weakness & languor, in a former letter, but I thought it was only temporary—don't fail to write me exactly how you feel. It is a great comfort to me, that you & Mamie have been well so long, and that she continues to do so well, but my little wife mustn't get sick, if it can be prevented. My patriotism, of which you are pleased to think I have a large share would ooze rapidly away, if I thought you were seriously unwell, and I should leave the service at any cost. I feel as though I must come home this fall, & shall make the effort to resign—at any rate, they cannot keep me longer than January, three years from the date of the original muster of the Regiment. I have no decided plans for the future, & it seems hard to make any. Goshen is the only *home* I've got, but I know your objections to it, & yet it will be hard work to find remunerative business in a new place, or in fact, anywhere. Law business is at a stand-still—the lawyers at Goshen are hardly earning their salt, & I would prefer a more active business—well, we'll not borrow trouble about it—in the mean time, I will see what can be done in business in Goshen or elsewhere.

My health is firstrate, never has been better since I was in the service, we have a fine, airy location, & with huge bowers each side of the tents, managed to keep shady & cool. Mamie mustn't forget to write Papa a letter, & he will be sure to answer it. I enclose Col. Deimling's photo—he is Charley Blood's friend from St Louis of whom I have written you—the picture hardly does him justice. I think I'll write my little girl a letter just so she will have no excuse for not writing to me Don't fail to write often. Goodnight & God bless you my dear wife. Your Husband

E. J. Wood

That signature got down before I thought, while the boys were talking & I came near adding "Lt Col. comdg 48th Ind. Vol."

LETTER 78

Camp on Etowah River, Ga.
July 27th 1864.

My dear wife,

It is more than a week since I wrote you last, and a good deal more than a week, since I heard from you. Do you know the last letter I had was dated July 3rd & do you wonder that I am anxious to hear from my dear ones. I try to think that the mail must be at fault, but every one else receives letters regularly, and I am almost constrained to think you are sick. The last few days I have been waiting with feverish anxiety, and when I tore open the mail tonight to search it once more in vain, I couldn't wait any longer, but must write just to tell you how bad I feel.

As you see by the date, we are still where we were, when I wrote you last. We have been here now, a little over two weeks, and as usual, when we are stationary so long, are very nicely fixed—I beleive I wrote you before of the camp & its location—we have been at work on it ever since & it is much improved—the board shanties which were of all sizes & shapes have been pulled down, and uniform regular barracks for each company built with kitchen and dining tables under roofs.

It is a great pleasure to me to see how the Regiment has improved in this respect—if I have never been of any other advantage to them I can fairly claim that I have educated them to appreciate the value of neatness & clean-liness. I say educated them to it, for it has not been accomplished without persistent efforts, and now they have acquired habits of good order & neat-ness, it is no trouble at all to keep them up to the mark. In this camp, while the other regiments occupied the old shanties as they found them, my men of their own accord, went to pulling down & re-building. I superintended the erection of one set of quarters, and without an order or a word, except of advice when it was asked, the other companies built them to correspond.

The duty here is not hard—the men go on guard once in six or seven days & have no fatigue duty, such as work on fortifications, handling stores, etc, so we have very easy times. We have been improving the leisure time by *drilling* at a furious rate—two hours company drill in the morning, and two hours Battalion drill in the afternoon—the weather has been admirable for this purpose—cool nights & mornings with frequent showers, and even in the middle of the day the heat has not been oppressive.

Two recitations a day for the officers, in Tactics, with the drills & other usual duties, fill up my time very pleasantly

Last Saturday, a deep gloom was thrown over the camp by the news that the body of Genl. McPherson was on the train going toward Chattanooga. The army could not have sustained a severer loss, and the country has but one or two Generals, who could be so illy spared. Brave as a lion, chivalrous as a Knight of old, modest, unassuming, warm & generous in his praise of others, a courteous gentleman in all the relations of life, he was the idol of his soldiers—the most *beloved* of all the Generals in the army. Such terrible losses but embitter the feelings of our men—it seems to us that the sacrifice of the whole rebel army would scarcely atone for the death of McPherson.[7]

I can write you no war news from this section—the veil seemed to lift a few days ago, & we were cheered by the official announcement "Atlanta taken" only to be overwhelmed the next day by intelligence of bloody disaster, & the town not in our possession yet. It greatly surprises everybody to find the place so strongly fortified—the seige guns are described as of great caliber & very numerous—when we find our two great armies thus checked it is enough to make one despair.[8]

Col. Alexander has returned—his wife was better when he left, but still feeble. I think he will soon resign—I wrote Mamie a letter, the last time I wrote you. I hope she was pleased with it. I am so anxious about you both, that I can't take any comfort, but then I think if anything was the matter, some of the friends would write.

Remember me kindly to all, and kiss Papa's little girl for him. I send Col Lane's photograph—he belongs to a N.Y City Regiment I've forgotten which one.[9] I met him at Stevenson, where he was staying with Capt. Wheeler. Write often, my dear wife, there may be some irregularity in the mail, & when I lose a letter or two, as I am trying to think I have now, it seems a long time *between letters.* Goodnight my dear one

Your loving Husband
Edward

The *Atlantic* has not been received—I have Harper for August would still like the Atlantic for July & August—was much pleased with your selection of books in the box. "*Notice to Quit*" was very good[10]—the tobacco still holds out, tho' it has had many patrons. E.

[*Envelope endorsed:* "Mrs. Edward J. Wood, Care E. B. Judson Esqr, Syracuse, New York." On reverse: "Answered Augst 6th 1864."]

LETTER 79

Camp on Etowah River, Ga.
August 9th 1864.

My dear wife,

I am in your debt largely for many recent favors, and I apologize humbly for my last grumbling letter.

You good long letter detailing the trials & tribulations of housekeeping, experienced by Aunt Mary and yourself, was received a few days after my last was written, and I assure you it releived my mind wonderfully. I had been conjuring up all sorts of chimeras dire, because I had not heard from you for three weeks, and it was with more than usual pleasure that I read your interesting letter, assuring me of your continued health and the highly prosperous condition of our chubby little darling. I was somewhat surprised to hear that you had decided to keep house during Edward's & Sarah's absence, but think it was the best thing you could do. It must have been quite an effort for you to overcome your nervousness at the idea of living alone, in so large a house and I think my little wife deserves credit for her bravery—however, I don't think there is any actual danger, and the advantages you enjoy, more than compensates for the unpleasantness of being alone. I hope Nettie Wheeler accepted your invitation—it would be pleasant for both of you, and Capt Park was very kind to me and all my friends, at Stevenson.[11] You never mentioned receiving my letter from Stevenson, giving a fully account of all his kindness, so I am uncertain you knew of it. You can say to Nett. that the Captain won golden opinions from all my friends and Col. Alexander & others often speak of him in the highest terms

I was again agreeably surprised the other day by receipt of your long letter of the 24th ult. enclosing letters from Walter & Mary Mackie—they were welcome indeed and revived the old associations of boyhood with which my dear cousins were so intimately connected. Walter is a dear boy, and I fully reciprocate all his fraternal feeling. I shall write to Mary and enclose a letter to Walter.

Well we are still on the Etowah, with little prospect of moving. Our armies seem to be at a stand-still. Grant has his hands full, apparently unable to make any successful demonstration against Lee,[12] and Sherman seems more intent on destroying the rebel army in his front, than capturing Atlanta—that he could have easily done, when he first cross the Chattahoocie, but an officer from the front told me yesterday, that Sherman says this campaign will be ended when the army under Hood is broken up, and its power for mischief destroyed, and not before.[13] I have lost faith in all prognostications as to the end of the war, and hardly dare form an opinion myself—of one thing I am sure, that I have fully performed my share of the work, and that my next & present highest duty is to my dear ones at home. I shall tender my resignation at once, probably to-day, and I hope it may be accepted. I am much pleased that Henry has had so good an offer on the Pacific R.Rd—it has all along been my thought that there would be the proper opening for me, when the war closed, or I should be out of the service—if Henry accepts, I should like a situation under him, & I think he knows my abilities well enough, to give me a prominent & valuable one. Of one thing I am determined to leave the service if possible. I have had a Colonel's commission over a year old—have been in command of a regiment all the time, & yet have been unable to be mustered into the rank or get the pay, to which my position entitles me. Col. Alexander has been in command of a brigade under similar circumstances for more than a year, has not rec'd the promotion to Brigadier to which he is eminently entitled, and has tendered his resignation with a fair prospect of having it accepted.[14] I hope in a month to be at home, a free man, the bondage of the service voluntarily assumed has become irksome to me—the Government itself does not treat its officers with the consideration to which they are entitled or even with common fairness.

You recollect I never obtained any compensation for time & money spent in recruiting a company, being two months time & $300 in money—well, of this payment comes a stoppage against me of $80 because I was mustered in and received pay as a Captain, before I had a full company—the stoppage was made against the first Paymaster who paid us, and here the other day, it was collected out of the month's pay due me, by the Paymaster who paid us. Isn't it a shame when I had never asked the gov't for the am't expended in recruiting, that it should stop nearly a month's pay as Captain, when I was mustered in, & had two-thirds of a Company in Camp. I am disgusted with such treatment—every original officer had stoppages against him, but against the men who have resigned it is impossible to collect it, while the men who have borne the burden & heat of the conflict are to be curtailed of their barely sufficient wages.

We have been having very easy times since stationed here—recently by the removal of the 63rd Ill. To Cartersville, the duty has become a little harder—we have 180 men on guard every other day, which brings every man on once in four days—which is nothing to the duty we had to do at Huntsville, or to what it would be at the front. I think we ought to be very thankful that we have been spared the dangers and hardships of this hard campaign. The body of Myron Baker of Goshen, Lt Col of the 74th Ind. passed here day before yesterday. He was killed by a sharpshooter of the enemy, while sitting in our rifle pits, quietly chatting with the officer in command, and unsuspecting danger. The ball struck him in the forehead, passed straight thro' his head—he gave a little gasp, fell over backward & died instantly. He was a noble fellow—before the war, honestly a Pro-Slavery Democrat, but when he was brought face to face, with the iniquities

& enormities of this Slavery rebellion he was as honestly and thoroughly a practical Abolitionist. His bold utterances for freedom have had their effect at home, but his dead body speaks more forcibly, than could his eloquent voice, in denunciation of the mad conspirators who have well nigh destroyed our beloved country.[15]

I send you enclosed some samples of home made stuff for women's wear, about which there is no smell of the African.[16] These stuffs were made by a poor white family named Davis—the boys planted, hoed & picked the cotton, the girls carded, spun, dyed & wove it, into its present shape, and the dyes were obtained from the woods, with the exception of the Turkey red.

The sweet gum furnishes the drab, the hickory the green, etc etc. I think these specimens are great curiosities—tho' produced by hard toil they are cheaper than common ginghams with us and you would be surprised to see how neat & becoming they are. It is no use to talk about subjugating a people who are so soon made self-reliant & independent. Four years ago they never thought of wearing any cotton goods but those manufactured at the North—four years ago they were in fact dependent upon the North for all but the coarsest of manufactured good, now every plantation has its own factory & all the material resources of the South have been greatly developed.[17]

Just as I write, your good long letter of the 31st ult. is handed to me. I fear I must be getting behindhand, for I find myself answering three of your letters in one—however I can't do justice to your last in this, for Col. Alexander is hurrying me up for an expedition into the country. Genl Smith has just returned three resignations tendered by officers of my regiment *disapproved*, and I am discouraged about my own. I shall sound him before I offer it. Write me if Henry accepts position with the Pacific—if he does not perhaps he could recommend me to a position. I am determined to get out of service, & want immediate employment—I am sorry you have had so much trouble in your housekeeping arrangements—I hope you are settled down again in comparative quiet. I am going to write once a week certain, & I hope next time I write that I can tell you of a prospect of coming home. Kiss Papa's darling girl. Papa will whip the naughty man, and then he will let him come home. Good-bye, dearest & may God bless you always.

Your loving Husband
Edward

LETTER 80

Camp on Etowah River, Ga.
August 20th 1864.

My dear wife,

I omitted writing you last Sunday, on account of the reported raid on the road by Wheeler, and the consequent interruption of communication with Chattanooga.

On Monday, my Regiment embarked on the cars with three days rations and 100 rounds of ammunition, for Resaca, 10 miles from Dalton, which place had been unsuccessfully attacked by Wheeler the day before.[18] Eight regiments of infantry, beside a brigade of McCook's cavalry[19] were concentrated at Resaca, Gen Smith commanding, for the purpose of dispersing a large body of the raider, who had been quietly resting at Spring Place, 18 miles east of the road at Resaca, for a day or two. They were variously reported at from 6000 to 12,000 strong, and it was necessary to approach them with due circumspection. After waiting at Resaca a day, for Major Genl Steedman[20] to concentrate a co-operating force at Dalton, on Wednesday morning we moved out at daylight—or rather the main body of the column did. The 48th had been lying quietly all day Tuesday in the woods near the town—the heat being too intense to permit unnecessary locomotion—and thro' somebody's blunder, the marching orders were not sent to us. I became aware that the troops were moving just as the last of the infantry were leaving town, and saddled my horse in haste, hurried to Head Quarters to learn why we were so slighted. Gen Smith had left, the Commander of the Post could not be found, so I reported to Gen. McCook, who ordered me to join the column at once. In half an hour we were on the road, & two miles from town caught up with the rear. Seven miles out Gen Smith sent me word that there was a heavy body of the enemy on our left—a half mile from the road, cautioning me to be prepared for an attack on our rear. We were in rear of the wagon train, and this caution rendered it necessary that we should keep well closed up with it to prevent a sudden dash between us & the train. Marching behind a train is hard work at any time, but when you have to keep the head of your regiment close up to the rear wagon, it is very laborious. The heat was intense, and the next eight miles was terrible marching, yet, as I had specially ordered in the morning that there must be no falling out, the men kept up, and at 1 o'clock when we halted, tho' the men were completely exhausted they were *all* in ranks. We halted two miles from Spring Place, the cavalry advancing through the town, to find the enemy flown. We rested till night, and then by the light of the full moon marched back to Resaca, arriving at midnight, having marched thirty miles, and every body well used up. Took the cars next morning for home, and reached our old camp about night, well pleased to be back. We left Mr. Wheeler making for the Knoxville road, and it was reported that he had attacked and captured Cleveland. He is reported to have a very heavy force, and as the guards are very light along the R.Rd above Stevenson, I would not be surprised if he did serious mischief[21]

My resignation was not tendered as I wrote you I thought of doing in my last—Genl Smith told me he should disapprove, and I knew there was no chance of getting it accepted, with his disapproval. If Atlanta ever is taken,

& this campaign comes to an end, I have his promise that he will approve it, and I am fully determined to resign, when there is any *"showing"* (as these Georgians say) of its successful issue. I am only a little lost to know what to do, & am very anxious Henry should accept the Pacific R.Rd appointment

My health is very good—never has been so good in the summer, & if I get through next month as well, I shall be well satisfied. Col. Alexander rec'd his papers—his resignation having been accepted to take effect Sept 1st—so he will be with us but a few days longer. I received yours enclosing Mamie's nice little letter, & also yours of *July 7th,* a few days ago. Our mail carriers are outrageously careless—almost every mail of ours is carried by to the front & then it goes the rounds of the army, till in the course of a week or so, somebody discovers where we are

Tell Mamie Papa will answer her nice letter next time. Kiss the darling one all over for Papa—he hopes to kiss her himself before long. Will write again in a few days. Good bye Your loving Husband

Edward.

LETTER 81

Camp on Etowah River, Ga.
Sept 10th 1864.

My dear wife,

I learn that there is a probability of a renewal of communication with the civilized world again today, by way of Nashville, and although I am expecting to start for Atlanta as soon as the train comes, I improve the few moments to write a line, for I know how anxious you must be to hear. I suppose however you know through the papers what mischief Wheeler has been playing with our communications, and so can account for the want of letters. I should be much more anxious, if I did not know of the embargo that Mr. Wheeler has laid for the last month nearly, on our mail matter—as it is, I can not feel easy, when I haven't heard from you for so long—your last date is nearly a month ago. I wrote you on the 20th ult. I hope that letter got through before the road was torn up. I wrote again Sept 1st by Col. Alexander—but as he was still Rail-road-bound at Huntsville, yesterday, I don't suppose you will get it much before this. Everything has gone on much as usual here, no alarms, & no encounters with the enemy except with the guerrillas who harass our forage trains. Yesterday one of the orderlies at Brigade head Quarters, returning in advance of a forage train, was killed by bushwackers, and three comrades captured. A cavalry squad was immediately started in pursuit, and threatened to burn & lay waste the whole country, if the captured men were not returned. Tho' they were not successful in capturing the bushwackers, they frightened them out of the prisoners, who returned to camp this morning, paroled. The 59th Ind. in company with four other regiments of the Division, are up the road towards Nashville—at present at Tullahoma—the great Wheeler raid seems to be over, but as the 100 days men have gone home & there are no troops to supply their place, it is probable that these regiments will remain along the Railroad to guard, until the drafted men get into the field. Col. Alexander as I wrote you in my last, has gone home, having had his resignation accepted to take effect Sept 1st

The Brigade is at present commanded by Col McCown, 63rd Ill, a weak, inefficient man—who has never been able to command his own Regiment, but assumes command of the Brigade by virtue of seniority of rank. Capt Simpson, former Adjutant General, has been detailed at Division Hd Qrs, and a Captain of the 63rd Ill. wholly ignorant of the duties of the office, takes his place.[22] You may imagine I am not well pleased with the change, and that it has not lessened my desire to get out of the service.

I have got Gen'l Smith's permission to visit Atlanta, having some business (legitimate) as an excuse, but really my object is to see Col. Clark (Howard's Adjt. Genl) in reference to the acceptance of my resignation.[23] I expect to see Milo too, who has tendered his resignation & I am afraid will get off home, before I see him.[24]

I enclose you a letter from brother Robert recently received,[25] altho' dated in May last—it would seem that Capt Franklin, into whose hands it fell, did not know my full address, & some one else has added "*Huntsville Ala*" which accounts for the length of time it has been in reaching me. Robert, you see, is a full-blooded Southerner, & determined to die in the last ditch—his rebuke to me, from his stand-point—is well-conceived & expressed. Politics have agitated the Regiment for the last few days, & I am able to announce the political complexion as returned to me by the Company commanders Lincoln 410, Morton 425, McClellan 15 McDonald 6—You understand Morton & McDonald are rival candidates for Governor in Indiana[26]—Judge Metcalfe—or Captain Metcalfe 129th Ind.[27] is stopping here over a train, on his way to the front to rejoin his Regiment—having gone to the rear sick about six weeks since. Did I write you he had lost his wife—she died in Iowa about two months ago. I am warned that the train is coming & must close. I do hope there will be a letter for me on it. I should enjoy my trip to Atlanta so much better, if I had the assurance, that you & Mamie were well. My own health is firstrate—our summer seems to be ended, & the health of the Regiment has improved under the influence of cool days & lots of work—the 59th Ind. being away makes our duty double—Will write again as soon as I return from Atlanta—4 or 5 days. Don't fail to write. I am living on the hope of a bunch of letters one of these days to pay for the long want of them Your Husband

Edward

LETTER 82

Camp on Etowah River, Ga.
Oct 9th 1864

My dear wife,

For the first time in more than two weeks, we have the welcome intelligence that a mail will go Northward, announced by circular from Division Head Quarters. It leaves in half an hour & I must necessarily be brief. I now reproach myself with not having written sooner so as to have a part of my news communicated. Two weeks ago to-day I wrote you by Lieut Warren[28] — ten days after he left we heard of him at Chattanooga, detained as were a host of officers, by the occupation of the Nashville road by Forrest[29] —indeed it is only within a few days that communication has been resumed with Nashville and during those few days the R Rd from here to Chattanooga has been rendered impassable by the carrying away of several bridges, caused by the unusually high water. On the 26th Sept. I made application for leave of absence to secure drafted men for the Regiment & confidently expected to have been with you right after our State election, which occurs day after tomorrow. Through an oversight of Gen'l Smith's Adjutant, my application was not forwarded in time & in a few days there were orders forbidding all leaves of absence, and countermanding those already granted, where the parties had not left the country. I can not get out of the service before January, and as there were many of the drafted men expressing their desire to come to the Regt. the officers of the regiment thought I ought to go home & try to secure them, and offered to bear my expenses if I would do so. Although I expect to leave the Reg't so soon, I could not reasonably refuse to do all in my power for it's interest, & I very suddenly determined to make the application which met with so untimely [a] fate. I don't think now I shall be able to get away before my term of service expires. I am very sorry for it, for I know how much you desire to change your present situation, & if I could be at home I could find you another location that would be endurable till I could come home to stay. The rebels are bent on mischief in this section—the whole of Hood's army has recrossed the Chattahocie,[30] and on Wednesday last, the 5th inst. a Division of the enemy 4,000 or 5,000 strong made an attack on Allatoona, five mile from here, and were most disastrously repulsed

The garrison consisted of three small regiments of our Brigade, 4th Minn, 18th Wis, & 93rd Ill. under command of Lieut. Col Tourtelotte of the 4th Minn., re-inforced by about 1,000 men under Gen'l Corse, just before the fight commenced, making the whole force about 2,200 men including a battery of six guns.[31] The fighting commenced at daylight on the 5th, and until 2 P.M. the roar of artillery & musketry was almost incessant. The enemy occupied the road between us & them, & we were thus cut off

from communication & could not tell how the battle waged. The position—
Allatoona Pass is a strong one by nature & had been well fortified, & as
we knew the character of our troops engaged, we felt confident the works
would not be carried without tremendous loss. We had a direct personal
interest in it for the Allatoona Pass was the key to 20 miles of this R.Rd &
once carried the victorious foe would have swept upon us, and scooped us
in with scarcely a struggle. You may imagine the breathless interest with
which we listened all day to the roar of the firing, & how when it slackened,
& we doubted the issue, we set our teeth, & determined to sell ourselves as
dearly as might be. But the rebels had already paid an enormous price, and
had not obtained the prize for which they struggled. After three desperate charges in which they came up to within fifteen feet of the works, and
attempted with their hands to wrench away the sharp-pointed stakes, set
in the ground by way of an abattis,[32] they were compelled to fall back, leaving the ground covered with their dead & wounded, and our little garrison
covered all over with glory—every man of them is a hero—there has been
no more gallant fighting during the war—but alas! it was not accomplished
but at the sacrifice of many noble & brave men[33]

The casualties among officers was immense—at one time a captain
was in command of three Reg'ts—Genl Corse, Col Tourtelotte of the 4th
Maj. Fish 93rd Ill Lieut. Amsden of the 12th Wis. Battery, poor fellow, since
dead,[34] all the field & staff officers of Genl Corse were wounded—but three
field officers of the whole command escaped, & last night by the "struggling
moon-beams misty light & the lantern dimly burning"[35] I assisted in bury-
ing six of the heroes. Our total loss was over 700—or 33 per ct. The rebel loss
can never be accurately know[n] as they took away most of their slightly
wounded—but over 500 dead lay upon the field, we have 200 prisoners, &
the wounded in our hands account to 700, so they have probably lost from
2000 to 2500.[36] Nothing but these figures could give an idea of the desperate
nature of the fighting. I didn't dare to commence on a new sheet of paper
& am told the mail is ready Good bye my dear wife I think of you more &
more each day & so long to see you, & our blessed child I have much more
to write & if the mail facilities continue open will write soon. Kiss Mamie
a thousand time—have heard directly from Mother, will write you particulars next time Again Good bye

Your loving Husband

Edward

[*Envelope endorsed:* "Mrs. Edward J. Wood, Care E. B. Judson Esq Syracuse
New York."]

LETTER 83

Camp on Etowah River, Ga.
Oct. 21st 1864

My dear wife,

Again we have a prospect of renewed communication with the North, and I avail myself of it, in hopes this letter may be started in a few days. Last night we have telegraphic communication with Chattanooga, and heard the results of the Ohio, Indiana & Penns. elections for the first time.[37] You are aware long before this that Hood with his whole army has moved up towards Chattanooga, threatening to plant himself on our line of communications & compel an evacuation of this hardly-won country. Gen. Sherman moved after him promptly, with most of his army, leaving the 20th Corps at Atlanta, and heavy guards along the R.Rd, thus showing no disposition to give up this region, even with the whole rebel army in his rear. The first demonstration of the rebels was made soon after crossing the Chattahoocie—they struck the R.Rd at Big Shanty, 30 miles south of here, captured the small garrisons along the road, & moving up in this direction destroyed the road completely to Allatoona, five miles from this point.[38] I wrote you of their desperate assault & terrible repulse at Allatoona in my last. Defeated in their design of capturing the place, with its two million rations, the attacking force drew off in a southwesterly direction towards Dallas, and united with the main rebel army. Sherman at this time was at Kenesaw Mt. 20 miles distant & crowding on after the rebels. He was signalling to Allatoona all the day of the fight "to hold out at all hazards," "he was coming to their relief etc," & most nobly & gallantly did they hold out, until the enemy fearful of being cut off by Sherman made a hasty retreat. The next few days were full of all sorts of rumors, the whole rebel army was within twenty miles of us their line running parallel with the R.Rd, & stretching from Marietta 20 miles below us to Kingston, 10 miles above—Their cavalry which covered their flank toward us, was constantly feeling of our pickets, and we had numberless alarms, but on the 10th the advance of Shermans army, the 23rd Corps, began to arrive & we felt safe—23rd, 4th & 14th Corps. halted here for the night, the next day the 15th 16th & 17th passed thro'

You could have formed a better idea of what an army is & what it looks like in motion, if you could have stood in our fort for two days, & seen the apparently endless string of men & wagons, as they filed past. The men were in excellent condition & in prime spirits—I beleive they are the best soldiers in the world. Four months of incessant fighting & marching have made them invincible—they have the utmost confidence in Sherman & in themselves, and went by here at a killing pace, eager to meet the "Johnny Rebs," & "clean them out"—then came a few days of blank—we were in the rear of the army again, but in a much more ticklish position than ever.

Suppose Hood's movement was only a feint, & that when he found Sherman was following him on parallel roads, he should take the back track, strike for the R.Rd at Kingston above us & follow it down, cleaning it out, as he had done from the Chattahochie on his upward march, & finally locate himself in his former strong position at Kensaw Mt.

Gen'l Smith returned about this time, and resumed command of the Division, & we were kept under arms day & night. Once we had orders to be ready to march at a moments notice & it was expected we would join the main army & abandon the road. In spite of the hardships of campaigning, every man welcomed the order, for we felt we should be much safer with the army than in our present exposed condition The order was soon revoked, & we were set to work fortifying. The 59th & my regiment have built two strong forts, & with a battery of six guns, we feel very safe. News from the army, which is still North of us is scarce. But I am anticipating—

Three days after the army passed us, Resaca was invested—after two days seige & some sharp fighting the rebels abandoned the attempt & moved Northwards destroying the road to Dalton & Tunnel Hill.[39]

A few days ago, the rebels abandoned the road & we learn from Sherman that he headed them off at Lafayette, about 40 miles south of Chattanooga & that they are on the return Southward. I don't expect them to return to their old position, but think they are bound for Blue Mountain (Ala.), which is the terminus of a projected R.Rd running from Selma, Ala. northwards through Talledega & Jacksonville, Ala, & intended to connect with this line of road at Rome, Ga.—if you look at Mitchell's Atlas you will see that the rebels are thus in direct communication with their interior country, and that Rome, Ga. is the natural point at which an army would be massed to oppose them.[40]

Gen. Sherman has ordered a million rations sent to Rome, & we expect that will be the scene of operations for the fall campaign—at present, if doesn't look as if we were to participate in it, but it is pre-eminently true of the army, that you can not tell what a day will bring forth. Like all soldiers however, we are making ourselves as comfortable as possible. At our Headquarters, we have erected a spacious edifice, 48 by 12 feet divided into 4 compartments each 12 feet square I am writing in the Adjutant's house, which No. 1 "Hotel de Etowah," No 2 is occupied by Jake & Anton, our faithful boys, No. 3 is the dining-room & opening into it is No 4, the kitchen. All of these rooms are furnished with fire places—one at each end of the building, warming the Adjutant's room & the kitchen & a double chimney in the centre: warming the boys' room & the dining-room. The Major & I still stick to our tents, & after all there is nothing like them to live in. I have often speculated on what an independent, Bedouin life we could live in one, & how happy we could be where the requirements of society—the

great bug-a-boo of the world—are so little. One never knows but by experience, from what small & trivial things the mind draws comfort. Mungo
Park, in the desert, fainting & despairing, revived to life by the sight of a
sprig of moss, is a type of humanity thro' all conditions of existence[41]—so
here, under most adverse circumstances, without a home, away from wife
& child, depressed at times to the verge of despair, at the condition of the
country for which I have risked my life & sacrificed all that men hold most
dear, it is a merciful Providence, that the mind not only has employment
but is able to find some consolation in it. But you don't know how weary I
am of this existence—unless you measure it by your own weariness—I am
unfit to be a commander any more, because my soul is not in the business.
Not that I don't feel as patriotic as ever, & am not only anxious but certain
that the rebellion will be put down, but I feel as if my share of the work
was done, & it may be & probably is, a selfish feeling, but I want my Jeanie
& my baby. Nobody but a regular soldier, which I have no aspiration to be,
ought to stay away from wife & home longer than three years—a longer
term of service unfits him for anything else, and you will have noticed that
the kind of life has fascinations, that I have not entirely escaped. But I have
no idea of becoming an Arab, a dweller in tents, migratory & predatory
in habit, but I intend shortly to pitch my tent where my dear ones can be
sheltered with me.

I wrote you in my last that I had heard directly from Mother, & promised to give particulars. About the 1st Oct. under flag of truce, Mr. Joshua
Hill & N. G. Foster of Madison, Ga.[42]—the former the last member of Congress, who represented the Madison district in our Congress—came within
our lines—their ostensible object being to recover the body of Mr. Hill's son,
killed last spring, when the rebels were falling back through Kingston. I
heard of them first as rebel embassadors of peace from the State of Georgia,
of which you have doubtless seen something in the papers. Learning accidentally that they were from Madison, I sought them out & found that Mr.
Hill was Mother's nearest neighbor, that their plantations joined, their children went to the same school, & that he had seen her nearly every day for
the last three years. You may imagine how quick my heart beat as I asked
after her, and how rejoiced I was to learn that she still keeps her health, &
singular as it may appear, her youthful looks. Mr. Foster told me an amusing
mistake on his part in this connection. At some gathering last summer was
a newly-married couple & of course a young bride, who were the "principal
personages"—not being very well acquainted with the bride or mother, and
there being some resemblance, he addressed Mother by the bride's title as
"Mrs.____," much to the amusement of those present I spent a half day
with them very pleasantly—full & free converse with intelligent & *Union*
citizens of Dixie is not often to be had & after exhausting family topics (no

small job, for they both knew well Peter Guatier, my Grandfather, & Mr. Foster had served in the Florida war with Uncle Ned Wood, after whom I was named)[43]—I got from them a very clear idea of the condition of things in rebeldom. There is no way to a peace, but over the conquered armies of the South. Mr. Hill, who is a politician & a statesman, says there never was on the face of the globe so complete a military despotism, as Jeff. Davis has established. His word is law, & no man dare breathe against it.[44] Mr. Hill himself was the last man to quit the old Congress, & was conspicuous in the Peace Congress afterwards[45]—he has been overpowered by the force of the Davis administration, & has been let alone, only by holding his peace but his mission North was not only to recover the dead body of his son—it was to confer with leading men still true to the old Union in this part of Georgia & see what could be done towards bringing her back to her allegiance

They visited Rome & returned here only a few days since. I wrote a long letter to Mother, & sent by them on their return I hope ere this it has reached her in safety—I had written thus far in this diffuse & I fear tiresome letter, & was about to complain that I had no later dates from you than Sept. 25th, when most unexpectedly a mail was announced, (the first for two weeks) & writing was suspended until I could enjoy the reading of your letters of the 2nd & 10th inst. I was releived, as I always am, when I am so long without tidings of you, to hear that you & Mamie were so well, but pained that I should have been the innocent means of causing you so much grief. You know my dear Jeanie, that my dearest wish is to be with you once again, that I will sacrifice all but my honor to accomplish it. If the Gov't will not release me in Jan'y, I shall take such steps as will compel the acceptance of my resignation

I know how unpleasant your situation is, to your sensitive nature—it is no less so to me. I feel keenly the mortification that you were staying where perhaps they would a little rather you were not, & it shall not much longer be so. I am coming home, dear. I have good health & some abilities & we will have a home of our own. Try to keep a good heart, & don't *imagine* any evil thing, [until these things be?]

I dare not send any money & I have very little to send if I would. The break in the road above Resaca is not yet repaired, the mail we rec'd was brought around in wagons, and there is no express matter being sent. The first opportunity by private hand I will send you $20. I mean by that the first chance to send to Chattanooga, where it can be expressed which will be in a few days. Don't borrow if possible at present.

I am surprised at Mamie's pedestrian performances, she must be very well & hearty—with all our troubles & grievances can we every be sufficiently thankful to the Great Giver of all Good, for this gift to us of this

The Best Soldiers in the World

Marie Gautier Wood Walker, Edward J. Wood's mother, who lived in Georgia during the war. Courtesy of Daniel Wood.

darling one, & for her & our continued preservation, and can we not trust his goodness & kindness to take care of us in the future.

Oh such a long letter, but it seems as if I could never tire of writing—if the line keeps open you will hear from me oftener. Goodnight dearest, God bless you, & grant that we may soon meet never to be so long separated

Your loving Husband
Edward

LETTER 84

Camp on Etowah River, Ga.
Oct 30th 1864.

My dear wife,

I am in receipt of your letter of the 16th inst. and hasten to reply. You do not speak of receiving my letter of the 7th inst. giving an account of the attack upon Allatoona, and I fear it may have shared the fate of two others which you have not received. For more than two months past, our communications have been in a very disturbed condition, and while it has caused the army but little actual suffering, we have thought ourselves fortunate to get a mail once a week—sometimes the interval has been two & even three weeks, that we have not a letter or a word of news from the North. I wrote you a long letter about a week since, detailing the operations of the rebs, since Hood moved Northward. All of his depredations & destruction of the R.Rd have been repaired, and yesterday the first through train from Chattanooga to Atlanta passed here, bringing us a large mail, and many men who had been North on sick furlough. Train after train passed—as many as twenty during the day—loaded with stores & on the top of the cars, with returning soldiers, & drafted men.

Dr Bryson of my regiment,[46] and Charlie Warren, to whom you are indebted for the last letter from me that I have heard from, were among the arrivals, and moving tales of hair-breadth 'scapes, on this breakneck R.Rd they had to tell. Bryson was 17 days on the road. Warren 14 days. Bryson was three times run off the track, & train fired into by guerrillas, & once with the train standing still, run into, by a following train—the one Warren was on—fortunately they both escaped tho' Bryson was in the caboose, & Warren in the next car to the engine. Cars were smashed to peices—40 or 50 men killed & many more wounded—no words or description can do justice to the awful destruction, but war has made human life so cheap with us, that I doubt if the catastrophe even affords a newspaper paragraph.[47] You can't imagine the state of affairs on this R.Rd—Here we are 500 miles in an enemy's country—our sole dependence for supplies, a single slender line of R.Rd—the country along its whole length swarms with guerrillas— the longer you occupy the country, the bolder they get—deserters from the rebel army, all the loose ends of society, that in time of peace, are held in restraint by the force of law are let loose, and it is no wonder that, without civil law at home, with a merciless conscription that drafts all men into the rebel army & obstructs all peaceful avocations, that the whole remaining male population of these Southern States should turn into guerrillas. We persecute them, we hang them, burn their houses, & lay waste their arms but they stick & cling around us, till no man is safe a hundred yards outside the pickets, & they can eternally run trains off the track, fire upon the helpless passengers, & if strong enough, rob & plunder the train. I see no way to end the war, but by depopulating the whole country, and making it a wilderness & a waste. I think it must end in that, or in a complete disruption of the Union perhaps with civil war at home. I don't apprehend seriously, the latter result, but I do seriously fear that the former will be inevitable. I say fear, because all my dearest & most of my nearest blood relatives are in the

The Best Soldiers in the World

South. I enclose you a letter received a few days since from my Mother[48]—you can judge of the number of kin-folk, from it, and of the feelings with which I regard the ruthless ruin, which seems about to overwhelm them. I wrote you the particulars of my interview with Mr. Hill, in my last, and the descent made by Stoneman's raiders, & their robbery of my Mother's plantation.[49] To-day I see by the papers, that Genl. Asboth, has made a raid from Pensacola thro' Marianna, Fla,[50] the home of my Grandmother, Uncle Tom & Aunt Sue, to whom Mother alludes, and from the spoils enumerated as the results of the raid, that they have probably been despoiled of their property. My feelings have been most unpleasant, and at the same time peculiar. I feel that there is no other way to subdue these rebels, but by extermination & depopulation, but when this theory runs into practice against Mother & birthplace, natural ties claim to be heard on the defence, and the conflict is no easy one. I have always hoped that my dear old Grandmother would be spared the sound of actual conflict at her door and that the place from its very insignificance would escape the sad havoc of war. But now no relative of mine, but has felt heavily the stroke of this unholy war made by rebellious children upon the best Government the world ever saw.

I haven't faltered in my devotion to the Union, in whose sacred cause I have for three years periled my life, and sacrificed all those dear comforts of wife, & child & home without which life is a blank, and I haven't changed my conviction formed long ago, that the only way to peace lay through complete *subjugation,* but when the plough share of ruin runs through one's own flesh & blood, something of indignation at the perpetrators of needless injury, of sympathy for the despoiled, of deep, lasting ineffaceable regret that they were so circumstanced can be understood & pardoned.

Ah! well, that isn't the least of my troubles by a good deal. I want to come to you & Mamie, not altogether selfishly I hope, but because I know you & I could be better contented. We belong to each other, and are neither whole without the other. I confidently expect, I shall be at home in January, but I suppose it must be by resignation. I wrote you that Circular 75 permitted officers who had been in the service three years to be mustered out. I had not seen it, but thought the information was reliable—that was the body of the order, but it went on to say "Provided, he has not voluntarily been remustered for three years,"—as every officer is, who is promoted. My last muster dates Aug 12/63, & under the terms of the last order, I could not be mustered out, but when I have served my three years. I have good grounds to think my resignation will be accepted—if upon the first tender it should be refused, I shall send it up, in a way, that will compel its acceptance.

About location, I am favorably disposed to Chicago, or any business centre, where business is to be done. I have written to several friends in Chicago, but have as yet heard from none. I saw Milo as he went up, and could have made a good business arrangement with him, but the exact time of my getting out of the service, and your objections to Goshen no less strong than mine, prevented it.[51]

I have no fears for the future, if we can once get established together again. Our long, and cruel separation has only made us know how dear we were to each other, and has better fitted us for the long life of happiness, that I trust a kind Providence has in store for us—If there is any such thing as compensation in this life, for ills endured, we ought to have a large balance in bank to draw against—

I have looked anxiously for the last few days to send you some money, by safe hands, but no opportunity has presented itself. Tomorrow we are to be paid, and some one will doubtless be sent to Chattanooga to express money for the Regts & I will send. Hood is evidently on the rampage, & there are rumors of our movement.[52] I think however they are unfounded—direct as usual. I send Mamie a letter enclosed—the dear darling child, I can not think of her, without a fresh pang of anguish at our separation—and a tightening of the heartstrings that draw me home. I am coming soon. You will not be disappointed. Your Husband

Edward

Nov 1st—This letter has been detained two days by a break in the road, & I open it to add a line—No pay yet, tho' the Paymasters are at work around us, & our turn will soon come. Sherman is making great preparation for a big raid, probably towards Savannah—our chance for forming part of it seems to grow better every day. The weather has been very unpleasant for a few days past, but is now bright & beautiful again—I never have seen more perfectly delightful weather than we had during the whole month of October, glorious Indian summer without a drop of rain, or a rude gust of wind to break the calmness of these smoky, hazy days.

I think we may calculate on a month or six weeks of good weather yet, & the expedition or campaign can't well last longer. I haven't needed my overcoat yet, & shouldn't probably if we remain—if we go on a march, I will get a cavalry overcoat (blue). I know you will be pleased with the following extract from a letter from Col. Eddy to the Adjutant,[53] so I copy it for your benefit.

"You are not perhaps aware at Head Quarters, that I have had quite a correspondence with the rank & file of your Reg't xxxxx I mention one thing with pleasure—the concurrent testimony these letters bear to the respect & confidence reposed in their commanding officer—& this on their part entirely voluntary." I think that's pretty high praise—it is certainly very gratifying to me, that my men appreciate my humble labors in their behalf, and is a new incentive to use my best endeavors to deserve their continued

The Best Soldiers in the World

confidence—I send you a copy of our class memorial—it is rather crude, & has some mistakes in it, but is a very pleasant reminder of auld lang syne.[54] I wish you would send Mother's to Willie, & write to her, if you can learn how to direct to send by flag of truce boat. I think you enclose the letter, directed & with a Confed. Postage stamp on, in an envelope directed to our commissioner of Old Point Comfort, Va.—the inner envelope to be unsealed.

Good bye again my dear wife, will write when send money, which must be in a day or two. Your Husband, Edward

[*Envelope endorsed:* "Mrs. Edward J. Wood, Care E. B. Judson Esq, Syracuse, New York."]

LETTER 85

Camp on Etowah River, Ga.
Nov. 9th 1864.

My dear wife,

Day before yesterday, we were paid, and I send you $250. by the hands of Capt Buck of the 59th Ind.[55] to be expressed from Louisville or New Albany, Ind.

Yesterday I was on duty all day, and have not had time to write before—as my last letter indicated, we are on the eve of a move—in fact, all our surplus camp equipage is turned over, and we are under orders to be ready to move on the 12th inst. We are to go light, with two wagons to the Reg't, and our destination is understood to be Savannah.[56] I can't hardly say I like it, but if we have to move at all, I beleive I would rather go in that direction, than back towards Chattanooga & so on to Nashville—or perhaps to Corinth & the country we have marched & fought over so often. Gen. Sherman evidently intends to let Gen. Thomas look after Hood, who has moved into North Mississippi, & probably West Tennessee, occupying the same ground we held two years & in fact one year ago.[57]

We are to take 30 days rations from Atlanta—the distance being about 250 miles, we shall easily make it in that time. I do not apprehend any serious opposition to our movements. We shall have three Corps, 15th, 17th & 20th, amounting to 35,000 or 40,000 men, besides about 15000 cavalry—there is no large force of the enemy on our line of march, or any that can readily be sent there, & besides the annoyance that the Georgia militia may give us. I do not anticipate any trouble.

I am afraid you will be alarmed at news of this expedition, but I assure you it is attended with no more hazard, & indeed with not so much, as many we have already undertaken successfully and in fact, it involves no more peril than common camp life, as we have been having it for the past four months. From Atlanta we shall cut loose from all communications tho' there will doubtless be couriers returning & I shall embrace every opportunity, to write you.

Don't think that this is to interfere, with my resolution to come home early in the new year—on the contrary, after the successful accomplishment of this trip—there will be a lull and a calm in the tempest—that will be highly favorable to the acceptance of resignations.

I expect to take my Christmas dinner near Savannah, and wishing Uncle Sam a "Happy New Year," return to spend it with my dear Jean, who I know has stout heart enough, to contemplate cheerfully all the perils that may environ her soldier boy.

I am in fine health—have got two good horses—an extra wagon for Hdqrs—so that we carry our mess kit, cots, blankets, etc, and one tent— Campaigning under such circumstances has always been favorable to my health, and—and—well, to tell the truth, I'd rather sleep on the ground than in a Christian bed, unless I had my Jeanie by my side—Have heard again from Proctor—I mislaid his previous one, which I meant to send you—he is the same dear old Redfield with a heart full of noble impulses—for a time conscientiously in the service of his country—accidentally promoted so that he served his time out in a 9 mo's Reg't—he is quietly pursuing his profession at Rutland, Vt—only waiting for the exigency to arise when he can again better serve his country in arms.

I know the metal of which he is made, & tho he writes so quietly, I know the fires that burn beneath. I am coming home dear, as I have often, of late, written, and when I get there, you must "bind me over to keep the peace," or I shall be off to the wars again. It does seem so mean & ignoble for men who know the magnitude of the interests involved in this struggle to sneak out of all personal share in it; Why the war may last 10 or 15 years, who knows? how ashamed I should be to meet any man or child on the street, if he could say I had no part in it. I could not live at home, and endure a draft, without honoring it with personal service. I believe I have got in the habit of writing such long letters, that I can't "close up" on a single sheet. Your last letter rec'd was dated Oct 23, I think—a few days before our wedding day, five years ago. Small thought had we, of a three years separation in that time, and as we have been in such degree disappointed, it's not unreasonable to hope, that the coming years may more than compensate us for the trials & hardships of the past. Remember me kindly to all friends and enquirers. Give my love to Myra, our dear sister, & to sister Nellie too, when you write her. If you want to pay Nell a visit hadn't you better go this winter. When I come home, I want you all to myself.

Kiss our dear baby, Mamie, a thousand times for Papa, won't we have high times when Papa comes home.

Goodnight, my dear wife, direct as usual, tho' at the same time you might need a missive *via* Savannah to await your boy, who will be very anxious to hear from you.

Goodby again Jeanie

Your Husband

Edward

[*Envelope:* "Mrs Edward J. Wood/Care E. B. Judson Esq/Syracuse/New York."]

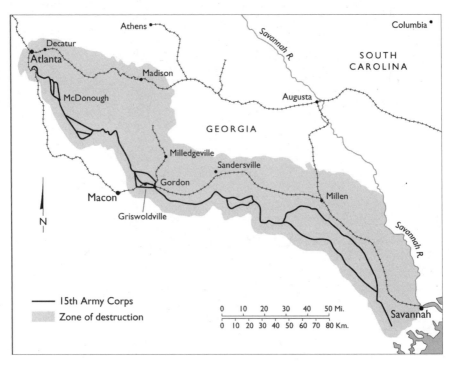

The 15th Army Corps in the context of Sherman's March to the Sea.

Chapter 13

My Cool Veterans

The March through Georgia, December 1864–February 1865

General Sherman reinforced Major General George Thomas in Tennessee and left him the task of subduing the army of Rebel General John B. Hood. Hood advanced into middle Tennessee with about forty thousand troops, and Thomas methodically prepared for him, building fortifications and organizing his forces in and around Nashville. Hood, having numerical superiority, attacked Major General John M. Schofield's well-entrenched troops first at Franklin (November 30, 1864), where the Confederate Army charged in waves repeatedly, were repeatedly repulsed, and suffered heavy losses. Following Thomas's orders, Schofield's forces withdrew in good order to join Thomas's in the defenses south of Nashville where they awaited the Rebels. General Grant, hundreds of miles away and fearing Thomas was too cautious, counseled him to attack Hood and almost relieved him. With Hood's forces just outside the city, Thomas ordered his army to attack in a well-coordinated maneuver. In fighting on December 15–16, the Federal troops drove the Rebels and crushed them. Hood retreated in disorder, and over the next days Thomas's troops rounded up thousands of Rebel prisoners. The Army of Tennessee effectively ceased to be. Thomas achieved what Sherman had originally intended but failed to do in the Atlanta campaign.[1]

Instead, in November, Sherman initiated a cross-country march, "cut loose from all communications," to the Atlantic Ocean coast, destroying all military and economic infrastructure en route in an effort to weaken the Confederacy. His army subsisted on the rations they could pack in haversacks and wagons, along with the normal foraging undertaken by the soldiers. The Union Army encountered limited resistance from Georgia militia and regular troops during the march, and reached the outskirts of Savannah in early December and surrounded the city. The garrison holding the city retreated into South Carolina on the night of December 20–21. Wood's prediction of spending Christmas in Savannah came true.[2]

Colonel Wood mustered out of his regiment in the New Year, his three years enlistment satisfied. He boarded ship for New York City, and soon was reunited with his wife and daughter. Shortly thereafter he traveled to Washington, D.C., to settle up regimental accounts and obtain pay. He also may have attempted to find work at the Capitol, as he now had to make the transition to peaceful employment.

The 48th Indiana continued under Sherman northward through South Carolina and North Carolina, participating in battles and skirmishes that destroyed Confederate resistance. The Rebel army in North Carolina under Joseph Johnston surrendered to Sherman on April 26, 1865. Marching from Richmond, Virginia, to Washington, D.C., the regiment marched in the Grand Review on May 24, and finally mustered out of service July 15, 1865.

LETTER 86

Near Savannah, Ga.
Dec. 17th 1864.

My dear wife,

We are just informed that our first mail will go North to-day, & I seize the opportunity to send you tidings of my continued health & safety—how welcome such tidings will be, and how anxiously expected they are, only poor wives at home, who have been waiting in painful suspense for more than a month can tell. I don't know how you stand it, when we, who have left our dear ones in comfort & comparative safety, are so much distressed at not hearing from them for so long. It has been reported that there is a large mail for us in the fleet, and there has been a state of feverish excitement about it, in the camp for the past two days. Today it seems probable that it will be landed and we hope to hear from home before night.

Well, I must despair of giving you my my connected account of our famous march as full as each day was of its special interest.

I commensed to keep a diary, but having no book, it was written on scraps of paper, some of which are lost, and sometimes paper could not got at for days at a time, so I finally abandoned it, & I have nothing but my memory to depend upon, for dates & places which I shall name, but I think they are generally correct. If you have any curiosity in tracing our route, you can readily do so, on Mitchell's Atlas—We left the Etowah River on Saturday, Nov. 12th, and at noon on Monday the 14th marched through Atlanta to the camp of our Corps, two miles beyond. The afternoon & night were spend in drawing clothing, of which the men were much in need. The weather was raw & blustering, with cold rain the next morning, & the men generally supplied themselves with overcoats. I got a pair of cavalry pants

& an overcoat, as my outfit. You have doubtless seen the general order of march in the papers, the 14th & 20th Corps, under Genl. Slocum, constituted one column, having the left and the 15th & 17th under Gen. Howard, another on the right—the 15th Corps was on the extreme right, and our Division was often on the right of the Corps. It fell to us to be rear-guard of the Division on leaving Atlanta, & so, tho' the head of the column started in the morning, it was 2 P.M. before we moved from camp on the 15th, & then owing to bad roads & the immense train of wagons in front of us, it was after dark before we got fairly started. But when the road got clear, we bowled along famously, making 19 miles before 1A.M. with only two halts, & stopping for the night near Jonesboro, on the Macon R.Rd. Kilpatrick's cavalry,[3] which was covering our right flank, had a sharp skirmish at the latter place, driving the enemy, & capturing two guns. Marched at 5 A.M. on the 16th, along neighborhood & by-roads, till we struck the main road leading from Jonesboro to McDonough, 8 miles from the latter place, which we reached about 4 P.M. having marched 18 miles. Here the Division passed in review before Genl Howard, & I was ordered to wheel my Reg't out of line & report in person to the General. I did so & found him a very agreeable, pleasant gentleman, received my orders from him, which were to quarter my Reg't in the Court House & yard, & to station two guards at each house, where families were residing—or rather where there were women & children, for men there were none, & I may as well remark here, that during the whole march, I have not seen a single able-bodied man at home—no male whites, except boys under 15, decrepid old men, & cripples—& very few of these. The stories told by the women of the impressments of tender youths & greyhaired men, fully justify Gen Grant's assertion that the rebels "have robbed the cradle & the grave" to fill their armies.[4] After my guards were stationed, I visited many of the houses, to learn something of the feelings of the inhabitants—among those who had been wealthy, & belonged to the higher classes, I found bitter malignant rebels, & no thanks for the kindness we were showing them in affording them protection for their persons & property—but among the poorer people, great disgust with the war, & immeasurable denunciations of the leaders, of their own section, generally the rich planters, who were able to shield themselves from actual service, & who had the means to move their families out of the line of march of a hostile army. I intended to make some general remarks on my impressions of the country & people as a whole, at the close of an account of the trip, but I find the impressions running into the diary, & I may as well indulge it— It might seem that there was some hope for a Union feeling among these poorer people, that would inure in time to our great advantage, but their ignorance is so profound, & so hopeless, that there is very little ground for encouragement. Through a large portion of the State which we traversed, not one family in ten can read or write—they know *nothing*, absolutely nothing, of the spirit of our free institutions, they are so besotted in ignorance, that they have no aspirations for any higher life, and when their natural protectors & providers, their husbands, & fathers & sons, are dragged by a merciless conscription into the army—to fight for they know not what, they have a dull, numb sense of injury inflicted, which they share with other animals, without knowing how to remedy it, in many cases, without thinking it could be otherwise. As an instance of ignorance, I inquired of a buxom good-looking young woman of twenty, & mother of two or three children, how far it was to the county-seat, distant about ten miles—she didn't know what I meant! I asked her how far to the next town—didn't know—what was it's name—didn't know, but said Milledgeville was a town, she beleived, it was 15 miles—we were then 40 miles S.E. from M, & were travelling away from it. Another woman said, if she was a man, she'd like to see *Jim* Davis keep *her* in the army—the right spirit, but what ignorance![5]

But I shall never get on in my narrative—We left McDonough at 5 A.M. on the 17th travelled through a fine country, passing thro' the county seat of Bibbs county, I beleive, Jackson, & camping for the night at Iron Springs, having made about 20 miles. At Jackson, Mr. Maxon,[6] my sutler, obtained a fine map of the State which was very convenient & interesting for reference during the rest of the trip. Our foraging parties got abundant supplies of sweet potatoes & fresh pork, & the cattle drivers increased their stocks largely, and indeed this was true of most of the march—Moved early the next morning, marched 7 miles, striking the Ocmulgee river at Planters Factory—where is—or was—a large cotton factory, & flour & grist mills. Our Reg't crossed first, in a large flat boat, that would hold 50 or 60 men—our brigade was crossed in this way & threw up rifle pits to protect the laying of the pontoons for the wagons & artillery, which was accomplished about 2 P.M.—as soon as the wagons commenced crossing we moved out to camp about 3 miles, having made 10 miles. Where we crossed the river we were 10 miles west of Monticello, & about 25 or 30 miles from my Mother's plantation in the south part of Morgan county. Monticello is where my Mother was born, & where my Grandfather, Peter Guatier, lived for many years. An old gentleman who lived a mile from the Ocmulgee, & where we halted before moving to camp, knew my Grandfather well, & related many anecdotes of him. I was in hopes we could go thro' Monticello, but from this point, our direction was South easterly, & we left M. to our left, probably not going nearer to it than where we crossed the river, but you must remember that we were the extreme right of the army & some of our troops did go through Monticello & Madison. I saw in a rebel paper, that the plantation of Hon Joshua Hill which joins Mr. Walker's was stripped of everything, & probably his shared the same fate.[7] Now as for the vandalism perpetrated on the march—of course, we lived on the country, & that necessarily takes

My Cool Veterans

all the provisions on the line of march, and for three or four miles each side of it—all cattle that could be found were driven along, all horses & mules were taken to replace the worn-out animals in the trains—all cotton was burned, as striking a blow at the credit of the Confederacy, which has pledged its cotton to secure foreign loans[8]—aside from this, very little destruction of private property took place. Of course, in so large an army, there are some pillagers and plunderers, but the orders against their acts were very severe—any one found pillaging a house, upon proof was to be shot on the spot, and everything that officers could do was done to protect outrages of all kinds.

19th This day the roads were very bad, made so by heavy rain in the night, & the clayey character of the soil, our progress was slow & laborious & it was long after dark when we camped near Hillsboro, where Stoneman & his command were captured on his raid from Atlanta[9]—we are now about 30 miles from Macon, & speculation is rife as to the probability of our going there. Marched 17 miles today—20th Marched to Clinton by noon, 15 miles, this is our nearest point to Macon, 15 miles distant, and our cavalry have sharp skirmishing with the enemy—the town is a county seat, & a pleasant little place—camped a mile beyond—rain at night & quite cold.

Our Division has been in advance on this road for several days—the 2nd Divn is to our left & the 1st & 4th in our rear, on the same road. At this point the last named Divisions take off to our right, sending their baggage train with us—the object being to secure the trains & for two Divisions to make an attempt on Macon—if found slightly defended to capture it & at any rate, to hold whatever force there may be at bay, till we can pass with the wagons beyond it. The 48th & 59th were in the rear on the 21st and were ordered to fall in behind the reserve ammunition wagons of the 1st & 4th Divisions, which did not get thro' passing till nearly night. Finally, after laying by the road-side a day, in a miserably cold rain, we got on the road, but had moved only about a mile, when heavy firing in our rear, in the direction of Clinton caused us to halt. Upon consultation, Col Scott & I determined to stop the train, corral it & then take up our position to defend it. These dispositions were barely completed when an orderly came back from Gen Hazen,[10] comdg the 2nd Divn ordering us back to the town, where there was one brigade of his Divn The rebels had forced his pickets back, & seemed determined to have a fight.

We got into line, covering one of the roads leading to Macon, about dark, by which time the firing entirely ceased. In the morning, 22nd started with the train to follow up the Division, roads bad, teams poor & heavily loaded, moved very slowly, marched till 10 P.M. & went into camp two miles from Gordon. 23rd Marched to Gordon, where we found the Divn had been since the night of the 21st, & where we also remained til the morning of the 25th

Gordon is on the Georgia Central R.Rd. running from Savannah to Macon—about 20 miles from the latter & 170 miles the former place—it is also the junction of the R.Rd running Northwards to Milledgeville. While we were at G. the left of our army—14th & 20th Corps—were at Milledgeville, & the extreme right of our Corps, 1st & 4th Divn, were on the R.Rd nearly up to Macon—the 1st Divn had a sharp fight near Macon, losing about 300 killed & wounded, & inflicting a loss of 300 killed & 1200 wounded on the enemy, who were driven into their works at Macon.[11] The R.Rd was thoroughly destroyed, about Gordon & indeed, from that on to Savannah it is a thorough wreck. 25th Marched to Irwinton, 17 miles fine weather & good roads, & this will apply to all our weather from this on. Perfect spring-like weather, & with the exception of the sand & slough of the pine lands good roads. I don't think I wore my overcoat a day after leaving Gordon. 26th marched 12 miles, to within 4 miles of the Oconee river. 27th Crossed the Oconee on pontoons took the wrong road, which I am bound to say, our Division commander was apt to do—about 4 miles out run into the 17th Corps, just as it was leaving camp & getting on to the road. Confusion confounded troops, wagons, artillery of two Divisions almost inextricably mixed. Took all the forenoon to get straightened out, & get back to our road camped at Irwin's Cross roads, marched 16 miles—28th Marched 18 miles thro' very monotonous country—narrow roads thro' woods with thick growth of underbrush; 29th Marched 4 miles, & came out upon a very fine, large plantation—have had some suffering among the men, foraging not good for two days before, was glad to find my Q.M. & foragers at this place, with 20 bushels sweet potatoes & some fine hogs—ran into the 17th Corps here & travelled on the same road with them, at the side of it—for several miles—when we turned off again to the right. Here we first struck the true *"piney woods"* of Georgia & Florida, so familiar to me in my youth, & henceforth to the coast, our course lay through them, only varied by the valleys of streams where the land is richer. 30th Marched 15 miles, to the little town of Somerville, not laid down on the maps, but it is on the road from Irwinton to Statesboro, the county seat of Emmanuel county.

The road was good, on the tough, wiry grass, just outside of the old wagon track, which was deep with sand, the sloughs however were very numerous & it took much time to corduroy them. Dec 1st Worse & worse, we have made but 7 miles & worked hard at that. We have been passing yesterday & to-day, along the head waters of all the thousand little streams that flow into the Oconee on the one side & the Ogeechee on the other, and have been through bogs & sloughs innumerable—the last one we crossed was a regular cypress swamp nearly ¼ mile long, & water breast deep in the road to a horse. The men had to take it the best way they could through the swamp, jumping from log to log, & very few I fancy got through with dry legs. Dec 2nd Marched 12 miles through similar country, though not so much infested with sloughs—3rd Lay in camp—the 15th Corps is in advance of the others—which are following more nearly the R.Rd Had inspection, & sent out two teams foraging with good success. Killed 15 sheep, as many hogs, & 3 beeves—sweet potatoes without end. 4th Marched 18 miles to Statesboro county seat of Emanuel—a decidedly *one horse* town, consisting of a very primitive Courthouse & jail, & two or three dwellings. 5th I am mistaken above, we marched 18—no, I was right we marched 18 miles, this day, & went into camp without incident. 6th Lay in camp, improved the time to scrub up, & have some washing done. All our rations are running short, soap entirely played out, used castile to wash clothes

7th Marched 11 miles, camping 3 miles from the Ogeechee river, which we are to cross near Station No. 2—2 miles from Savannah. 8th Lay in camp, waiting for the other Corps on our left, which are not yet up. 9th Crossed the Ogeechee on pontoons—a wide, noble river, marched 10 miles in a Southerly direction & at night, are 15 miles from Savannah, due west from it. Considerable skirmishing in our front, & heavy firing, cannonading & musketry three or four miles to our left, all day. Crossed the canal running from the Savannah to the Ogeechee river, near where it empties into the latter river & camped for the night.[12]

10th At an early hour, moved up the canal in the direction of Savannah. Keeping the tow-path—one wagon to a Reg't—the other corralled at our camp. Marched 8 miles in what seemed rather a precarious situation. Canal on our left, & impassable swamp on our right. Our only safety was in the fact that the enemy could not move where we could not

About 11 o'clock a halt, & infantry are ordered in advance of the artillery—a sure sign of work ahead to old soldiers. Our brigade was in advance, but my Reg't was in rear of the brigade, & before we could get by the battery on the narrow tow path the fire had opened hot & furious. Having cleared the battery, we took up the double-quick for half a mile, & filing to the right formed line of battle on the extreme right of the brigade The enemy's skirmishers, who had been in this neck of dry woods had been driven out across a swamp which subsequent examination proved to be impassable, except on the towpath. The enemy were strongly entrenched on the opposite side of the swamps, with three or four guns in position, which they opened upon us very savagely. Their shot & shell however flew high and but two or three men were wounded. Towards night, we commence to make breastworks, & the men went forward to get the rails from a fence—whew! What a shower of bullets they drew, but fortunately no one was hit and my cool veterans came leisurely back to the line, each one bearing his load of rails. Some Negroes in the Pioneer Corps,[13] who were at work in front fixing a place for a battery, stampeded as the first bullets whistled around, & I saw several of my men loaded with rails, stop, stoop down and pick up an axe, a spade or pick, dropped by the frightened contrabands. Afterwards the men went out & picked up implements enough to make the work of intrenching very light. Lay in line all night, and to add to our discomfort rain fell heavily. It was late however before I lay down, on a bundle of corn fodder, & as I was very tired, covered with rubber coat & blankets. I slept soundly, in spite of the rain, till I was called to coffee, at 4 A.M. Soon after daylight on the 11th the enemy opened fire briskly, & our batteries replied, but for some cause were unable to silence the rebel guns, a thorough examination of their position convinced Genl Howard that we could not carry it, & about 9 o'clock we fell back down the towpath about two miles to a road leading to the right where we lay all day. At night, under cover of darkness, for we had to pass with a quarter of a mile of two rebel batteries commanding the road for two miles, we moved on this right-hand road, running the blockade in safety, without awakening the suspicions of the rebels.

After passing the batteries, we struck a main road running Southwesterly from Savannah, & marching 4 or 5 miles on it, away from the city, halted for the night. The next morning, 12th moved a few miles further to the right, to our present position, which is the extreme right of the line. We are two miles from the rebel line (which is on the east side of the little Ogeechee) and are are [sic] near Station No. 1 on the Atlantic & gulf R.Rd, being between the little & big Ogeechee rivers—Our skirmishers are out well in our front, and except a little popping occasionally there, everything is very quiet. Since the taking of Fort McAllister, which occurred on the 14th, we have had communication with the fleet, and expect to get rations tomorrow[14]

The city is entirely surrounded by impassable cypress swamps & tidewater marshes, and the rebel fortifications are just the other side of these natural barriers. They have quite a large force, but can not have very abundant supplies—the place is closely invested, and I think, Genl Sherman means to reduce it by seige—Well, the long looked for mail has come, and I am in receipt of three long letters from you dates respectively Oct 31, Nov 7, & Nov 13th—not very late news, but very cheering to hear good news from my dear wifey & little one. I think I can say confidently, that if I am spared to the 16th of Jan'y, I shall be mustered out of the service, upon the expiration of my term of service. The term of service (original) of the Reg't expires at that date, and all officers who do not desire to be re-mustered for the new (veteran) term of service, which expires on the 1st Jan'y 1867, will be mustered out on their application. This is the present & latest interpretation of the orders from the War Dept. on this subject—if there is no change, you can reasonably expect me home about 1st Feb'y

I am sorry I have not been able to make any arrangements for business—it worries me a good deal, as I would like some employment, as soon as I get home. I shall write to Mr. Denny, my former guardian in New York today,[15] and ask him to be on the look-out for some business for me. His long residence & extensive business connections in the city, & throughout the country, will enable him I think to find some employment that will be suitable & lucrative.

I must close this long letter as the mail goes out soon I hope you have got the money I sent from the Etowah before this. The Adjt has heard from his that was sent by the same hands to be expressed at Louisville or New Albany, so I hope you rec'd it safely. Goodbye, my dear wife write often & direct as usual, except that you may say "near Savannah, Ga" instead of "Etowah River."

May our fond anticipations of meeting soon be realized, and until that happy time, may the good God who has preserved us so far, watch over over [sic] us all, and keep us from all harm is the prayer of
Your loving Husband
    Edward

[*Envelope endorsed:* "Mrs. Edward J. Wood, Care E. B. Judson Esq, Syracuse, New York"; "Answ'd Jan 6th 1865."]

LETTER 87

Near Savannah, Ga.
Dec 20th 1864

My dear wife,

Very unexpectedly I have an opportunity to send you a few hurried lines by the Adjutant and Mr. Maxon, who start North today. The Adjutant was mustered out of the service yesterday—he having been commissioned & mustered at the first attempt to raise the Reg't, and as I wrote you the other day, I see no reasonable doubt of my being mustered out on the 16th of Jan'y—three years from the date of the organization of the Reg't. I feel so confident of it, that I want you to send my overcoat to Mr. Maxon at the Merchant's Hotel, New York—if he starts back in time, he will bring it to me, if he don't I will find it at the Hotel when I get to New York. I expect to stop in the city a few days, and shall need my coat—it would be very extravagant to buy a new one when I have so good a one already.

I have only time to write this scrawl—the Adjt. didn't expect to go till to-morrow, & I intended to write to-night, but an excellent opportunity unexpectedly presented itself, and he is off at five minutes notice.

I am well, never better in my life the trip agreed with me firstrate—haven't been so entirely free from the camp scourge diarrhoea since I have been in the service

Goodbye. I must see you soon

Your aff. Husband

Edward

Maxon will telegraph you from New York to send the coat—E.

LETTER 88

Savannah, Ga.

Jan'y 1st 1865.

My dear wife,

A Happy, Happy New Year to you!—not as an empty compliment of the season, but from the fullness of my heart, for both our sakes. I hope the open of the new year may be the entrance upon a happier period than you have known for a long time.

I wrote you last a hurried scrawl about the 20th ult and sent it by Mr. Maxon, who with the Adjutant left for the North that day. They next morning, the 21st at daybreak, our pickets reported the rebel works in our front evacuated—we didn't know what to make of it—it might be a feint to draw us on across the salt marsh which separated the two hostile lines and it seemed improbable that it was a complete evacuation. Soon word came from the Corps commander that our whole front was evacuated, & to prepare for immediate movement. By noon we were on the move for the city, having learned by this time, that the city was completely evacuated.[16]

We camped at night just within the inner line of defences of the city, and the next morning moved to our present camp in the suburbs, and were ordered to fix up camp for a stay of several weeks duration.

I rode down into the city that morning & recognized many of the old buildings & landmarks of the city, which is indeed little changed in outward appearance since I was last here thirteen years ago—Isn't it frightfully suggestive of getting old, that one can remember so long back?—We have been very busy getting settled in camp, and getting up our back papers, reports, returns etc, for the months of November & December, which were necessarily delayed on the march, and it has added greatly to my inconvenience & labor, that I have had to break in a new Adjutant,[17] entirely unfamiliar with the papers & the routine of business in the office, & for fear I hadn't enough to do I suppose, I have been detailed on Courtmartial as usual, sitting six & eight hours a day, by order of Genl Smith, to clear up all the cases that have accumulated during the march. We are getting pretty well through, and I am hoping for a little respite before the 16th, when my official career will terminate. We have rec'd the Muster-out rolls from the Mustering officer, and have a full understanding with him that we are to be mustered out on the 16th—the only contingency I can think of to delay it, is a possible movement towards Charleston, but it is not probable that the army can be got

My Cool Veterans

ready by that time.[18] Supplies of all kinds are greatly needed & come in very slowly—we have suffered more for food since we came into the city, than at any time on the march—for six days, we had two days ration of hard bread, three of coffee, no sugar, one days salt meat, & three days of army beef—the cattle we have driven through on the march, & so poor that the boys say you can read fine print thro' the sides when it is hung up. We are doing better for the last few days, having drawn full rations, but no forage for the animals is furnished yet, and as the country for 30 miles around is exhausted, they are suffering greatly. Clothing also is much needed & Quartermaster's supplies of all kinds. The men too, who have four months' pay due, ought to be paid—at this season, unusually severe as it is at the North, their families stand in great need of the money—for all these reasons, I don't think a movement can be made in less than 30 days. Still I am not in Genl Sherman's councils, and we have had notice from Genl. Howard to prepare for a "short & decisive campaign." Supplies may be being accumulated at Hilton Head, which is on the road to Charleston, & much easier of access for vessels of large draught. The obstructions in the main channel of the Savannah river are very formidable, & no effort has been made to remove them. The few light draught steamers which have come up, have used the channel shallow & intricate, which the blockade-runner made use of.

So it is not impossible that I may make one more campaign, and you must not fix definitely on any time when you can expect me—you know I'll come as soon as I can possibly. All the troops have been reviewed by Genl Sherman by Corps, in the following order 15th 14th 17th & 20th, the latter made a splendid appearance. Gen Slocum & the 149th[19] are here but I haven't had time to hunt any one up that I know—haven't been to the city but once since we came in.

Last night I rec'd a letter from Willie in which he spoke of receiving your letter with yours & Mamie's photos—he didn't mention Mother's letter—did you send it. The "Class Memorial," which it seems you didn't get is quite a pamphlet. I have another copy which I shall keep. I am in receipt of your letter of the 8th ult. and am expecting by the next mail a week later news from you. How do you stand the dreadfully cold weather, that the papers say you are having—it sends the cold chills through me to think of the thermometer 20° & 30° below zero—the weather has been pretty cold here for the past few days but I have not needed a chimney & fireplace to my tent—a log-fire in front of the tent morning & night has answered so far. When we were outside & I wrote you such a long letter, the weather was decidedly warm & in the middle of the day the sun so hot as to make a coat uncomfortable

I wrote the whole of that letter outdoors in the shade of a building. I dread the change to the frozen region of the North at this season, but I shall be very careful, and as the Major says when we are about to start on a march without baggage, "put on all my shirts," and duplicate outside clothing as much as possible. I found Proctor's letter the other day & in it a sensitive plant, that I must have pressed for you when at Stevenson, last summer. You can form little idea of its beauty, from the withered specimen enclosed, it is a perfect ball in shape—& deep pink shading almost to white, with yellowish dust-like particles at the extremities of the petals I beleive you call them. I am sorry it isn't in a better state of preservation—Last Sunday being Christmas I attended St. John's Church—the building a large & handsome one, was crowded—the ladies turning out in force. I could not see that the blockade had interfered with their wardrobes—at least as far as the outside show of silks, velvet cloaks, Honiton[20] collar a foot deep, etc, etc was to be taken as an indication The citizens seem very well disposed toward the Yankees—officers are treated with every courtesy, & I am glad to say the feeling & treatment is reciprocal with the army. All this while I have been writing and not a word for my little daughter, but Papa has not forgotten her and thinks of her every day, won't he be glad when he can have a good frolic with her. Mama must tell that pretty soon Papa's coming home. I will write again in a week and keep you informed of the "situation." Goodbye a sweet kiss for Mamie right here {}

Your Husband
Edward

[*Envelope endorsed:* "Mrs. Edward J. Wood, Care E. B. Judson Eq., Syracuse, New York."]

LETTER 89

Savannah, Ga.
Jan'y 3rd 1865

My dear wife,

I wrote you Sunday, but having a spare half hour in the courtroom, looking over to-day's issue of the paper enclosed I thought you would like to see it.[21]

I have marked the resolutions adopted by the citizens, at a large meeting, composed of the most respectable & influential of the citizens. It is to be remarked from the closing resolutions, that these resolutions so honorable to the participants in the meeting, were not adopted under any military pressure, and that the citizens of Savannah are not ashamed or afraid to publish them to their fellow-citizens in Georgia and to the world, as their sentiments. This action on the part of so large & respectable a number of the inhabitants of Savannah, I regard as one of the most hopeful indications of the times. No other captured rebel city has so promptly & fully renounced allegiance to the bogus Confederacy, as soon as the restraint of the rebel army was removed, and so readily professed their willingness to return to its allegiance to the United States, in the manner and by the means prescribed by the lawful authorities—the Congress & President of the U.S.[22]

Nowhere has there been so much real Union sentiment as in this the chief commercial city of the Empire State of the South, and nowhere have our officers & soldiers been treated with so much courtesy—the good-looking young officers particularly say that the young ladies not only don't turn up their noses at the Yankees but actually lavish their smiles & blandishments upon them. The mutual goodfeeling is really astonishing—the army think they have never seen so fine a city, with its innumerable beautiful parks, & handsome monuments, nor certainly have they elsewhere found so friendly inhabitants—while the people are greatly surprised at the fine appearance & good behavior of the army. They had been told that the men were worn out & jaded, and naturally expected they would be ragged & dirty after their long march—but they were compelled to admit that the men were in better physical condition, & more tidy in appearance than their own men who had been doing garrison duty here all the fall.

Nothing new about the muster out—next Saturday the 7th inst. we are to be reviewed again by Gen Howard—so we shall stay till that time—one week after that is all I ask them to stay here, & I shall surely be free.

What do you think about meeting me in New York, it would be a good time to see Aunt Mackie & family & they would be delighted to see you—it may never be possible for them to see you again & I should like it very much—if you think favorably of it, get ready & I will telegraph you from New York & meet you at the cars. I shall stay there a day or two anyhow, & will telegraph you on my arrival—if you desire to come you can reply, stating when you will leave. Goodbye will write again next Sunday. Kiss the darling one for me. Papa don't mean to send many more paper kisses. Goodbye again. Your loving Husband

Edward

[*Envelope endorsed:* "Mrs. Edward J. Wood, Care E. B. Judson Esq., Syracuse, New York."]

LETTER 90

Washington, D.C.
Feb'y 27, 1865.

My dear wife,

I reached here Saturday morning, making but a stop of one day (Friday) in N.Y. I could find anything practical there, and so far don't meet with much success here—one thing is comfortable. I am in a fair way to get my troublesome accounts settled and expect to get through & get pay tomorrow. I think I shall leave here to-morrow night or Thursday morning, and shall try to get home Saturday night. Tho' if I should not, I will not come till Tuesday.

You will be glad to hear that I found my overcoat at the Express office at Sy. before I left. I left the cape at Ballard's, as I didn't have time to go round to the Bank.

The weather here is quite warm & spring-like, and an overcoat is superfluous except at night.

Mr. Kilbourne[23] is away, & Mr. Colfax & Mr. Nye,[24] I have not yet seen. It is toward the close of the session, & members are very busy—everybody is taken up with the coming Inauguration & the winding up of Congress, & such insignificant mortals as I obtain but little consideration[25]

I got into New York in the morning Friday & left that night, & as I was busy down town all day, I didn't go up to Aunt's or see Walter.[26]

I shall stop there on my return, & won't forget the rubbers. If you think of anything you want write me care of Thos Denny Wall St. I don't think on the whole, I shall leave N.Y. before Monday night, so if you write so as to go in the morning mail Saturday I shall get it. I hope Mamie's cold is entirely well. Kiss the darling for me, & remember me to Edward & Sarah.

Your affectionate Husband

E. J. Wood

[*Envelope endorsed:* "Mrs. Edward J. Wood, Care C. B. Williams Esq., Salina, New York."]

Postscript

Postwar Life in Goshen, 1865–1873

Readjustment to civilian life has often presented challenges to returning soldiers: becoming reacquainted with family and friends, finding work, confronting physical and mental challenges. These problems, classified and treated by medical and psychological therapists today, were not well understood in the nineteenth century. Yet many thousands of soldiers faced difficulties in making the transition from military duty to civilian life.[1] Some veterans were less than successful in coping with the aftermath of war. Evidence exists to suggest that Wood may have suffered from mental illness that prompted a decline into alcoholism. However, to state more than the basic facts in his case would be speculation.

Edward Jesup Wood faced his own set of problems when he left the army. He had no job, little money, and no certain prospects of obtaining either. Toward the end of his enlistment, Wood pondered in his letters to his wife what his future should be. Both he and Jane opposed returning to small-town life in Goshen, and sought new vistas for their future life together. But his inquiries with his former guardian, Wall Street businessman Thomas Denny, and his brother-in-law about employment in New York City and elsewhere produced no leads. Wood probably returned to Goshen with reluctance.

Wood's movements in early 1865 are not clearly known, but apart from his trip to Washington, D.C., on business (perhaps to inquire after suitable work as well), it is likely he remained in Syracuse with Jane, Marie, and her parents and siblings for the first few months. Those months served as a period of rest and recuperation from the stress of war and the responsibilities of leadership. The Goshen newspapers reported in February that he was expected to return soon, but his arrival only occurred in early April, greeted by his "numerous friends" with accolades for his "unflinching bravery" in the war. When the joyous news of the

Union occupation of Richmond, Virginia, reached Goshen, Wood was called on to address the celebratory rally.[2]

As the war ended Wood quickly turned to the business at hand: securing a living. Both newspapers in Goshen (the Republican Goshen *Times* and the Democratic *Goshen Democrat*) soon featured advertisements placed by Wood announcing his new practice as attorney and soldier's claims agent, his office in the Barns Block downtown. His practice was now a solitary one, without an elder and established mentor to guide him and funnel paying work his way. How his practice shaped up is not known, but, given his complaints about slow business in the town, it could not have been lucrative. Soon he was active in the public life of the town, participated in Masonic events and ceremonies, and returned to electoral politics. Cashing in on the popularity of the "soldier-boys," the county Republican Party leadership unanimously nominated Wood to be their party's candidate for clerk of the Elkhart Circuit Court. His Democratic opponent was also a veteran—an amputee no longer able to farm. During the campaign that summer and fall, Wood endured a crowded speaking schedule and the unkind cuts of the *Goshen Democrat*. Wood, it was insinuated, had had an easy time of it during the war and had escaped the struggle without a scratch. The *Democrat* accused Wood, called the "Negro Suffrage Candidate" or "Negro Equality Candidate," of "personal assaults" on the character of its candidate, a charge he denied in the pages of the *Times*. He denied that during the war when serving as provost marshal in Paducah, Kentucky, he used his office to protect the brothels in that town. The newspaper also launched the first of what became recurring salvos against Wood in his remaining years: that of being a drunkard. If the voters "want a whiskey guzzler, and professional billiard gamster [*sic*], they can have it by voting for" Wood. "All our citizens who have known Mr. Wood in years past, know, that we are warranted by the facts in saying this."[3]

Wood survived the character assassination to lead the county Republican ticket to victory in October 1865, winning with a 485-vote majority. Writing to Jane while she was in Syracuse and he was lodging with Chauncey Hascall and eating at the hotel, he cheerfully expected that the Clerk's office would pay two thousand dollars a year. However, he had no money with which to set up a household for wife and child. He contemplated borrowing from Edward Judson, Jane's brother-in-law Syracuse banker, or from her father. Wood secured a small house to rent for $150 a year and Judson came through with a loan. The rental was abandoned as Wood found a house to buy on terms that in the long run would be more economical. His letters in the fall of 1865 show great concern about the expenses of buying furnishings, carpets, and wood to keep the house warm in the winter. But his letters to Jane remained cheerful, lively, and full of expectation.[4]

Wood also wrote of learning the ropes of his new position. Legal business was still dull, and the paucity of suits and subsequent filings meant fewer fees for the clerk. However, he thought that five dollars a day in fees above the one dollar a day paid to his copyist would suffice to keep the family housed and fed adequately. In later months business continued to be slow. Beginning in 1867 he moonlighted as a fire insurance agent to supplement his official income. Wood mastered the functions of the clerk's office. In 1866 the editor of the *Democrat* found reason to complain that the clerk was steering legal advertising to the *Times*. But a call on the *Democrat* offices demonstrated no personal ill will on Wood's part.[5]

Life for the Wood family progressed. A son was born to Jane on July 20, 1868, and named Clarence Williams Wood. In that year Wood paid federal income tax on $1,458, not including over $1,000 that was exempted from taxation. The *Democrat* guessed that he earned $3,000 per annum as clerk. Wood was not poor by the standards of the day, but neither was he rich. He managed to support his growing family adequately.[6]

Wood continued to be active in politics in Goshen and northern Indiana. In 1868 he campaigned for Republican presidential candidate Ulysses S. Grant and vice presidential candidate Schuyler Colfax in the county and district, and attended the presidential convention at Chicago. However, his renomination to run for clerk was defeated in the county Republican convention. Why his bid failed is not clear. Nonetheless, he campaigned for his party, and his efforts helped produce Republican majorities in Elkhart County in the state elections and send Grant and Colfax to Washington.[7]

The *Goshen Democrat* in 1868 began to identify Wood as part of a Republican "clique" led by Goshen banker and businessman Milo S. Hascall, his friend and wartime comrade. The paper also reported Wood and Hascall drank bourbon after a Grant rally, pouring down fifteen-cent shots, and their names were frequently noted together in the press. Wood stood by his friend in 1870 when Hascall broke with the mainline Republicans and ran for the party nomination against the incumbent congressman, William Williams. Hascall, imperious, unforgiving, intemperate, and bombastic, had a talent for making enemies both in his own party and with the Democrats. The former general lost his bid soundly. Wood's alliance with Hascall may explain his being removed from the Republican ticket in 1868.[8]

Wood returned to private legal and business practice after his nomination defeat. During this period he had time to indulge in his pastimes of hunting and fishing with his circle of friends. Wood was praised for his leadership in the community in efforts to protect fish populations and restocking lakes in the area. In 1871 he accompanied Edmund R. Kerstetter in a monthlong trip to the northern Great Lakes, and was part of a group of sportsmen to fish on Lake Maxinkuckee in Marshall County in the following year. He also remained active in his local Masonic lodge, becoming chair in 1872. Sometime after the war Wood and his family managed a visit to Georgia to visit his mother, now Mrs. Walker. In 1866 she wrote to her son describing how her husband abused her. When Mr. Walker had slaves "that he would cuff & abuse about; I was let alone." But since the end of the rebellion and the abolition of slavery, she wrote, "if any one or anything frets him, I am the victim of his unholy wrath." To "say he is actually demented I could not tell the truth," she wrote, but "any one to be with him would take him for a lunatic." She thought that her husband would soon die, leaving her to the mercies of his grown children, who hated her for having a son who served in Sherman's army. "[I]f the worst came to the worst," she concluded, she hoped that she "could find home & protection with you." But matters did not come to the worst, and Mr. Walker lived on and mended his brutish ways.[9]

The Goshen newspapers reported on occasion that Wood was sick. In April 1869 the *Democrat* reported that he was recovering from a severe illness. In August 1871 the *Times* reported Wood's return from his Great Lakes trip and noted that his health was improved. However, the next month the paper reported that Wood was not able to work due to sickness.[10] What he suffered from was not mentioned.

Wood had opportunity to reenter public life in late 1870, after the elections. The judge of the Court of Common Pleas for the district containing Elkhart, St. Joseph, LaPorte, and Marshall Counties died in office, and Wood was nominated by the district bar to fill the judicial seat. Governor Conrad Baker, formerly colonel of the 1st Indiana Cavalry and acting assistant provost marshal general for Indiana, who ran on the Republican ticket for lieutenant governor with Governor Morton, duly appointed him to the position in November 1870. Wood immediately entered into the work, meriting praise in the newspapers for his hard work and energy in managing the case load and court business quickly and efficiently. The work entailed hearing a wide variety of cases in the four counties, including murder, incest, and other complicated legal matters. His work was not without controversy, as a ruling in a case heard early in his tenure was overruled by the Indiana Supreme Court. Nonetheless, the typically harshly critical *Goshen Democrat* commended his work as judge as "clear-headed and prompt."[11]

The judge's seat was up for election in the fall of 1872, and Wood renewed his efforts to secure his party's nomination. This time, Wood marched in step with the rest of his party. He was elected to the state Republican convention early in the year, and in June spoke in support of the renomination of President Grant, with Henry Wilson to replace the disgraced Colfax. In August he attacked the Liberal Republican/Democrat fusion that backed newspaperman Horace Greeley for president, a movement in reaction to the

Edward J. Wood, undated, probably after the war. Courtesy of Daniel Wood.

frequent reports of graft and corruption scandals emanating from the Grant administration in Washington. In this effort, he split from his alliance with Milo Hascall, who supported the Greeley bid. Wood was rewarded with the party nomination for the judgeship, and campaigned in the fall to retain his seat on the bench. Come election day in October, in a year that saw the Democrats secure the governor's office, Wood won the majority in Elkhart County by 167 votes, but lost in the four-county district by 70 votes.[12]

Once again out of public office, Wood returned to private legal practice. Little is known of his actions and fortunes in the next weeks, the last of his life. After reporting on his speech in the celebration over Grant's reelection in November, 1872, the Goshen press is silent as to his activities.[13] The next mention of Wood in the papers was the news of his death. Both the *Times* and the *Democrat* announced the sad news of Wood's death in an apparent suicide on April 9, 1873.[14]

According to newspaper reports and the findings of the coroner's inquest, Wood had traveled to Jackson, Michigan, by rail on Monday evening, April 7, planning to continue north the next day to Bay City to do legal work for the First National Bank of Goshen. The next day, April 8, Wood told hotel staff he was sick and remained in his room. A physician, a Dr. McLaughlin, visited him in the hotel. The Jackson *Daily Patriot* reported that Wood told McLaughlin that "on the journey thither he failed to make railroad connections at a certain point, and was delayed several hours, during which, in company with some of the passengers, he had drank [*sic*] rather freely, although not usually addicted to this habit." The doctor ascribed the symptoms to delirium tremens. Wood "seemed at times to be under the impression that strangers were present plotting against him, but assured the Doctor that he understood perfectly that it was all a delusion." The doctor visited him four times during the day. The last visit was around midnight, when Wood "seemed much better, and was very hopeful of resuming his journey in the morning." A hotel worker remained in Wood's room that night, during which he rested quietly, "but still entertained the idea that persons were conspiring against him."

In the morning, about seven o'clock, Wood "sprang up" from bed, found his revolver among his clothes, and began "searching for his invisible enemies," "looking through the keyholes of the doors in his room, imagining that some one was outside plotting against him." The hotel worker, Michael Schottenhoffer, tried to take the gun from him, but, according to the Jackson *Citizen*, "the distracted man threatened to shoot him with it if he did not let him alone." Schottenhoffer succeeded in calming Wood and getting him back in bed, but did not take the gun away. The worker then left Wood to go downstairs for breakfast, informing some co-workers, "but leaving no one with him."

According to the *Patriot*, another worker heard the sound "as of a revolver being snapped" three times in Wood's room, but the noises "did not occasion any comment." Dr. McLaughlin returned at eight o'clock only to find the door to Wood's room locked from the inside. The doctor put his ear to the keyhole and "could hear the breathing of his patient, which was unusually loud." He quickly found the housekeeper who had a passkey, who told him she had heard the "snapping caps" "but thought nothing of it as she supposed somebody was with" Wood. She also told the doctor that Wood had asked for whiskey, but the manager forbade it until the doctor arrived. The *Citizen* reported: "Upon entering the room they found Col. Wood alone, lying upon the bed upon his back, partially on his left side, with a bullet wound through the right temple, two bullet holes in the wall by his bedside, and his revolver lying by his right elbow on the bedclothes. He was bleeding profusely, but still breathing, and efforts were made to ligate the artery, but he died in about half an hour." The *Patriot* added that "some doubt has been expressed whether the fatal shot was intentional; but this, of course, no one can solve." The coroner's jury inquest ruled Wood's death to be from a "pistol shot, inflicted by his own hand."

The news shocked and saddened Goshen. His funeral was held in the Wood home on April 12, 1873. In addition to the reports from the Jackson newspapers, both Goshen papers featured detailed obituaries of Wood prepared by his Masonic colleagues. The eulogy in the *Times* added that he "had his fault, a grievous fault, with which he had struggled for a lifetime, but at such an hour as this let us remember only his virtues, and let him who has never sinned cast the first stone." The *Democrat*, now owned by his comrade from the 48th Indiana, Melvin B. Hascall, mourned his death, calling him "genial, high-toned and gentlemanly." However, newspapers from neighboring counties used Wood's death to attack Milo Hascall for drinking. Hascall shot back, "that the ashes of the noble dead, whose shoe buckles in life these miserable traducers were not worthy to unloose, have got to be dragged up in order to traduce me." "Intemperance is a crying evil," he wrote, but no one should "cram his bran-bread, total abstinence ideas" down people's throats.[15]

Jane Wood sold the Goshen house in May 1873 and moved back to Syracuse, New York, to live among her family and raise her two children. In 1891 she applied for and obtained a widow's pension paying eight dollars a month. Her brother George M. Williams, her brother-in-law Edward B. Judson, and Milo S. Hascall filed affidavits attesting to her status as a widow who had not remarried. Her kinsmen attested to her having no more than two thousand dollars worth of real estate, her house in Syracuse, and only her household furniture for personal property. She died in her home on April 14, 1892.[16]

Appendix A

Letters by Edward J. Wood Published in Goshen
Newspapers

From the Goshen Times • July 17, 1862

*"We make no apology for the publication of the following private letter from our
talented friend, Capt. Wood. It is written in his usual happy style and will be
perused with much interest by the friends of the gallant 48th."*

Camp near Rienzi, Miss.
July 4th, 1862

Friend George:[1]

Allow me to congratulate you upon again mounting the editorial tri-
pod—may it never prove the stool of repentance, but only serve to enable you
to reach higher the ascending rounds of the ladder of fame. I am indebted
for information of your accession to the corps editorial, to a copy of the
"Goshen *Times*," of the 19th ult., containing the valedictory of Stevens,[2] and
the melancholy letter of Warren Pease.[3] I hope you won't think his letter a
fair reflex of the sentiments of the 48th. The health of the Regiment is certainly not so good as could be wished, but I don't think worse than was to
have been expected, or worse, or indeed as bad, as many other Regiments.
As to looking forward gloomily to a campaign further South or in any direction where duty calls, there are no such feelings entertained by the officers
or men of 48th. Three resignations of officers have taken place. Col. Hascall's
from his position and qualities is more generally felt than any other. I do not
think the efficiency of the Reg. has been or will be impaired by the resignation of any more.

The last week has been a busy one for us. The order to cook three days
rations, and prepare for a light march in the direction of Holly Springs, *vis.*,
Ripley, came very unexpectedly upon us, in our old camp near Corinth,
where we had settled down into the routine of camp life, drilling recitations etc., and had made up our minds to tarry for a season. The order
embraced the whole left wing of the army of the Mississippi, formerly
Gen. Pope's army, now commanded by Gen. Rosecrans,—the left wing itself, commanded by Gen. C.S. Hamilton, is composed of three divisions

commanded respectively by Generals Buford, Sullivan[4] and Jeff. C. Davis. Each Division embraces two Brigades, composed of five regiments each, so that the left wing constitutes quite an army of itself. We are in Gen. Buford's Division—our Brigade, consisting of the 5th Iowa, 59th Ind. 26th Mo., 48th Ind and 4th Minn., being commanded by Col. Sanborn of the 4th Minn. I have been thus particular in giving you the composition of our wing, in hopes it may be of use to you in the future, in tracking us up, and judging of our share in the fight, if we should ever have one. Our first day's march was Southward, reaching the little town of Rienzi at noon, under a most scorching sun—and through an intolerable dust. (Col. Hascall can tell what that means.) The next day was cool and cloudy—with at intervals a gentle summer rain, that it was a real pleasure to get wet by. The country grew pleasanter with more signs of cultivation as we marched westward, and under these combined cheering influences, the boys took up the quick step, singing the "Hallelujah Chorus," and easily made their 14 miles by noon, when we were halted for the day in an open field, skirted by a fine growth of timber, through which ran the Hatchee river a sizable stream, and one that gave indications of being *some* in a freshet. The boys improved the afternoon in bathing, washing their clothes and picking black-berries, which last are to be found all thro' this country in the greatest abundance and of most excellent quality. Sunday the 29th, we were again on the march, making 14 miles, advancing two miles from Ripley. Monday we moved on 5 miles, passing thro' Ripley, a pleasant country town, of 1,000 or 1,500 inhabitants, but with no sign of life or business—all the stores being closed and but few of the natives showing themselves. Stopping a moment before the door of the principal Hotel for a drink of water, I found a brother and companion Mason in the landlord—an elderly gentleman who evinced more kindly and conciliatory feelings than I have yet found in Rebeldom. Tuesday morning, when we were yet distant 32 miles from holly Springs, the order came to retrace our steps, towards this place. Our citizen soldiers don't relish being moved about like puppets, but always want to know the whys and wherefores, so there were many long faces, and some hard words said over, when we first fell in, but when the boys came to understand that Sherman's division had already occupied Holly Springs, and the enemy having executed their favorite Skedaddle movement at his approach, and we were not needed, they marched with alacrity inspired with the thought of spending the glorious Fourth in our old camp.—but on the afternoon of the 2d, when we reached Rienzi, where our course would have been Northward for the old location, we marched straight thro' the town, crossing the Mobile & Ohio R.R., and halting at our present position 8 miles east of the town.

This morning there are rumors of rebels about in force, and Gen. Davis' Division has been passing, while I write this. I have not much faith in these rumors, but think we are about to remove our camp to this locality.

At noon to-day we were paraded, and a patriotic order from Gen. Rosecrans was read, which I enclose to show you we were not unmindful of the observances due the day.

July 5th—We are pained to hear today of the death of Capt. Roberts of South Bend, who died yesterday morning at camp, of typhoid fever, after an illness of several weeks. He was a brave and faithful officer, and we all feel deeply his loss. It is now settled that we are to remain here, the camp will be moved up as soon as possible.—My own health which was poor for a while, is now excellent, I have stood the marches much better than I expected to, lying on the ground most of the time and with no cover but the blue canopy of heaven or bower of leaves. George Gibbons is ailing and was left behind in camp, of which I understand he is now in command. Foljambe, Sam. Connell and the rest of the Goshen boys are generally well. Sam. has grown as fat as a seal, he is efficient and reliable in the discharge of his duties, and I don't know what I should do without him.

I notice with pleasure your list of officers in the Lodge for the coming year, you don't know how my heart goes out towards that old Hall and all its kindly associations, and how much I miss its friendly gatherings. Ah! well as our favorite song has it—

"We'll hope e'er life's best days shall cease,
　To meet in *peace* once more."

God grant it may be speedily, and that the peace may not be a peace only in in [*sic*] name—a hollow truce, an empty compromise—but an enduring peace whose foundation shall be laid deep in the principles of eternal right, and whose ultimate results shall reach above and beyond even the highest wishes of the patriot. In other words, a peace that shall cause the public mind to rest in the conviction, as old Abe has it, that Slavery and Rebellion, its outgrowth, are henceforth powerless for evil in the land. With such a peace, but a decade would elapse, before our enfranchised country, with her gigantic resources, would throw off the mighty burdens of war, and take her place unquestioned at the head of the Nations of the earth. The reverse of this picture is too sickening and disheartening to contemplate. My candle is on the last half inch, so I must close. I should be glad to hear from you all the news, of the day, of the Lodge, etc. Many thanks for your fine paper received today—its tone is admirable. With best wishes and kindest regards, I am your friend and Brother,

E. J. Wood

From the Goshen Democrat • *June 24, 1863*

"Through the kindness of Mr. H.G. Hale, we are enabled to make some interesting extracts from a private letter of Lieut. Col. Wood, of the 48th Ind. The letter was written to Mr. Hale, and not probably intended for publication; but the strong interest taken by this community in the fortunes and doings of the gallant 48th, (with whose brilliant achievements the writer is most prominently and honorably identified) will be our sufficient excuse, we doubt not, with the author, for placing it before the public:"

* * *

It is all a matter of history now, how Grant marched his army from Milliken's Bend to a point 60 miles below, on the river—how he crossed them, leaving every team and every owner of baggage behind, on gunboats, and three or four old perforated transports that still held together after running the blockade at Vicksburg; how he moved upon the enemy at once, defeating him at every point, capturing Port Gibson, Grand Gulf, Raymond and Jackson; how he confounded and struck terror into the enemy by the celerity of his movements—marching 50 miles, fighting three pitched battles within five days—from the 12th to the 16th ult.,—driving the enemy always, and capturing over 5,000 prisoners, and 70 pieces of artillery, and how in less than a month from the commencement of these brilliant achievement, he had possession of the strongholds Haine's Bluff and Warrenton, above and below the coveted prize Vicksburg, and the city itself as closely invested and beleaguered as was ever any fortress in ancient or modern times. All this, and much more, lo! is it not written in all the daily papers, and has it not passed into the current history of the country? But of the weary, dreary marches, at first through mud unspeakable, and after this heat and blinding dust, on half rations, and often with no rations, without baggage, without tents, with literally nothing but ammunition that the men did not carry on their backs—of the patient, nay, even cheerful endurance with which the troops bore all these privations; not an officer or a man of our regiment, and I suppose the same is true of most others, failing [falling] by the wayside, all buoyed up by the hope of meeting the enemy and whipping him, and then when we did meet him, of the noble heroism and unflinching steadiness with which these nameless officers and men of Grant's army advanced upon him, and by their cool determination made victory not only possible, but certain—of all this, the world knows but little. It is as yet unwritten history. But it lives, and is recorded in the memory of every participant in these glorious struggles. It is literally impossible to particularize events in the short space of a letter, but a few items may be of interest to show that the above is not meaningless talk.

Appendix A

On the 1st of May we crossed the Mississippi, and drew three days rations of hard bread and tea—no meal and no coffee—and we did not draw again until the 10th, and then only half rations of bread and quarter rations of coffee: after that, until we reached the river again, about the 20th, we did not draw regular rations of any kind. Of course, men must eat, and the country furnished us corn and bacon in plenty, and *corn coffee,* judiciously made, is not a bad drink, as I can testify. Nobody complained of the fare. I mixed much among the privates, and I did not hear one word of murmur— they all seemed to appreciate the magnificent stake for which we were contending, and willing to suffer anything for success. One instance of individual heroism and endurance may be taken as a type of the army: Capt. Jasper Packard, of LaPorte, commanding Co. B, was sick enough when we left Milliken's Bend, for anybody but a soldier to be in bed, yet he marched bravely at the head of his Co. until after we crossed the river, when becoming entirely prostrated, he was carried in an ambulance; while we were on the Big Black river for a few days, about the 10th of May, he was so feeble as to be helpless, yet in the action at Raymond, on the 12th, in the brilliant charge at Jackson, on the 14th, and in the bloody and hard fought battle of Champion's Hill, on the 16th, he was at the head of his company, doing valiant service; and again on the 22d, in the desperate and disastrous assault on the rebel works in our front, he led his men, remaining on the field till the regiment retired, though he received a severe wound in the face, that has disabled him for service.

Of such stuff the men are made, who have won these late victories, and who, with the blessing of God, propose to win more such, and thus do their share of the work in putting down this mad rebellion, by opening the Mississippi river.

I suppose it is impossible to write you news, as you doubtless will see later accounts from here than mine. The papers furnish very full, and in the main, correct reports of our operations, though, of course, it is impossible they should be exact in details; as for instance: our regiment has been mentioned as the 4th Ind., the 58th Ind., and the ___ Regiment. Not very flattering to our pride, but we console ourselves with the reflection that our name is known at army headquarters, and among the "pesky rebels." Our first day out as skirmishers, close up to the rebel forts, and within easy talking distance, we found the same Louisiana regiment who were in our front at Iuka and Corinth, and were also at Greenwood, on the Tallahatchie, and when they learned our regiment they seemed to be quite familiar with the name. I don't think any of them would ever confound it with others, as badly as the reporters have done. Only once have I seen the 48th mentioned in print, and then it was slandered scandalously by some scribbler in the Cincinnati *Commercial.* Of course we don't expect to see Indiana troops mentioned with credit in the Chicago papers—Illinois monopolizes all the glory as she does all the Generals; but the *Commercial* is usually ready to exalt the achievements of Indianians, and I noticed with pain this error: speaking of the assault on the 22d, the writer said that one of the forts of the left was "taken and held by the 16th Indiana[5] until relieved by the 48th Indiana, from whom it was taken by a *surprise* party of enemy!" Very much "surprised" indeed, would the enemy be, to read that paragraph. The facts are these: About 3 p.m., Gen. McClernand sent word that he had partial possession of three forts, and that if promptly reinforced he could take and hold them. Our whole division was moved from the center to the left to his support. Our regiment was ordered up a narrow, steep ravine, or water gulch, scarcely wide enough for two men to pass abreast, and at the top we found *three* regiments or parts of regiments at the very foot of one of the enemy's considerable forts, and within 30 feet of the rebels inside. We learned here for the first, time, that we were to *relieve* and not support these regiments, and they retired under cover of our fire as quickly as we were formed. The 48th maintained this position, their colors planted half way up the slope of the rebel fort, pouring a deadly fire over the top, and making it impossible for the enemy to show himself and live, for over two hours, suffering much during the latter part of the time from a severe cross fire of the enemy, until the rest of the Brigade being much exposed, and losing heavily, and night coming on, the order was given to withdraw the line. Then, and not till then, the 48th filed slowly down the ravine, a company at a time, the balance keeping up fire to prevent the rebels from mounting their works and pouring into us—and that's the way the outside of a fort was taken from the 48th by a surprise party of the enemy! I didn't think it would take half so long to tell this story, or mean to bore you with our petty grievances. They are petty, and we so regard them, but one likes among friends, to have full justice done.

Our Colonel has endeared himself to every man of his command, by his untiring devotion to their interests, his endurance under sickness and fatigue, and his splendid behavior on the battlefield, as he proudly said to his men, after the battle of Champion Hills: "You have shown that you are willing to die with me on the field, and I think I have shown that I am not afraid to die with you."

I suppose you have as little idea of a siege as I had, or as any one could have, without seeing it. Really, one who is not curious, has little idea of what is going on. Our regiment is pleasantly camped in one of the thousand ravines by which this country is intersected, and tho' within easy range of the rebel guns, are seldom disturbed by a hostile shot. Occasionally a bullet from a rebel sharpshooter rings through the air overhead, but our usual music through the day is the constant "peck, peck" of our skirmishers, with the undertone of the field pieces, until toward night the mortars join their thorough bass in the chorus, with most prodigious effect.

How the rebels are making it, of course we can't tell. We burn powder enough upon them each day to hoist the whole Confederacy, and some of it must tell. From the best information we can get they have three or four months supply of corn and beef—fresh and salt, and buoyed up by the hope of reinforcements, men can live a long time upon that. Johnson has some force in our rear, but if he attacks with less than 50,000 men, Grant will send him back with a sore head. I don't [believe] Vicksburg will surrender until we whip this force of Johnson's, or until they despair of receiving succor from him, and then I do not expect it before they have made a desperate attempt to break through our lines. But they are *treed,* and must come down. If they only have the sagacity of the coon, when Capt. Scott treed him, they will come down without any more shooting.

* * *

Ever your friend and brother,

E. J. Wood

Appendix B

Letter of Robert Corley to Edward J. Wood

May 15, 1864

Camp, 5th Fla. Regt.
Finley's Brig. Bates' Div. Hardie's Corps May 15, 1864

Brother Edward:

Actuated by a desire to relieve you of any anxiety you may entertain relative to the welfare of your family & friends in Dixie, I have determined to avail myself of the present possibility of getting a letter through to you. As you came upon us with such overwhelming numbers on yesterday, we have been compelled to "change our base" and I intend leaving this letter with some citizen and get him to mail it, should this part of the Empire state be desecrated with the presence of the Yankee mercenaries who seek to bury our nationality in oblivion, and their reputation in obloquy. It is not my purpose, however, to chide you for the ingratitude evinced in raising your arm to strike the bleeding bosom of the land which gave you birth, and which now contains a mother's home, and a sister's grave. Let the past be forgotten. Let not our political enmity [en]gender individual animosity, and should the fortunes of war bring us in contact on the field or elsewhere, let fraternal friendship over-rule all differences of opinion.

Mother continues well, and not much altered since the war began. Her heart yearns for her absent sons and their welfare is her constant wish. Aunts Ann & Sue, Uncles Tom & Wm together with their respective families are all well. Since the occupation of Beaufort, S.C. by the enemy, Aunt Ann has been a refugee from her home, and until a short time since was living with mother. She now resides near Charleston. Frank Philips is in the same Regiment with myself. Charley is an invalid suffering with chronic dysentery and threatened with consumption. In casting a retrospective glance at the past, how any heart swells with gratitude to our Heavenly Father for the greatness of His goodness in having guarded, guided & protected each member of our family both at home, in camp, and in battle and to-day after three long years of carnage when the Angel of Death has been in almost every house, and the spirit of mourning around every hearth, our has escaped, and each member alive. I have been in the Rebel Army since March, 1861 and should health continue & Providence permit, I intend to remain under its standard as long as an inch of ground or an hour of time remains.

When you write to Willie, give him Mother's love, and tell him to write to some member of the family, either by returning prisoners or the flag of truce via Fortress Monroe.

Mother rec'd your letter written from Mississippi last year, and I carried a letter she had written in answer in my pocket for some time, but could not get a chance to send it to you. I enclose 5 C.S. postage stamps thinking you might write sometime by flag of truce were it not for the impossibility of obtaining stamps. Farewell. Should we meet no more on earth, may we meet on that celestial shore where sin, sorrow, and soldiers never more intrude.

Your Brother, Robert Corley

NOTES

Introduction

1. Elizur Wood to A. M. Wood, August 15, 1829, in possession of Daniel Wood of Woolwich, Maine.

2. "Lines to My Husband," poem enclosed with letter of Marie E. Walker to Marie Gautier Wood, July 29, 1887, in possession of Daniel Wood.

3. Bessie Hovey to Marie Gautier Wood, March 30, 1892, in possession of Daniel Wood. When Union troops entered Savannah at the end of the famous March to the Sea, Edward Wood in January, 1865, alluded to having been in the city thirteen years previous. See letter number 88 of January 1, 1865.

4. See Edward J. Wood to Jane Wood, undated [1868], in possession of Daniel Wood.

5. J. W. Putnam to Thomas Denny, August 16, 1849, in possession of Daniel Wood.

6. *Dartmouth College Class Memorial of 1853,* comp. Moses T. Runnels, 245–46.

7. Speech, June 1856, and "Freedom & Fremont," in possession of Daniel Wood.

8. For studies of nineteenth-century American male behavior in marriage, see E. Anthony Rotundo, *American Manhood: Transformations in Masculinity from the Revolution to the Modern Era* (New York: BasicBooks, 1993), and Peter N. Stearns, *Be a Man! Males in Modern Society,* 2nd ed. (New York: Holmes & Meier, 1990). See also Reid Mitchell, *The Vacant Chair: The Northern Soldier Leaves Home* (New York: Oxford University Press, 1993), 71–87.

9. *Goshen Times,* September 19, October 10, and October 24, 1861; *Goshen Democrat,* November 13, 1861.

10. See letters of recommendation by E. W. H. Ellis for various officers in the 48th Indiana Volunteer Infantry regiment Regimental Correspondence, Indiana State Archives, Indiana Commission on Public Records, Indianapolis, Indiana (hereinafter cited Indiana State Archives).

11. For historical analyses of nineteenth-century American middle-class fatherhood, see James Marten, "Fatherhood in the Confederacy: Southern Soldiers and Their Children," *Journal of Southern History* 63 (May 1997): 269–92; Stephen M. Frank, *Life with Father: Parenthood and Masculinity in the Nineteenth-Century American North* (Baltimore: Johns Hopkins University Press, 1998); Shawn Johansen, *Family Men: Middle-Class Fatherhood in Early Industrializing America* (New York: Routledge, 2001); Robert L. Griswold, *Fatherhood in America: A History* (New York: BasicBooks, 1993); and Ralph LaRossa, *The Modernization of Fatherhood: A Social and Political History* (Chicago: University of Chicago Press, 1997).

12. For studies of soldiers' motivations for volunteering and fighting focusing on political ideology, see James M. McPherson, *For Cause and Comrades: Why Men*

Fought in the Civil War (New York: Oxford University Press, 1997); Joseph Allan Frank, *With Ballot and Bayonet: The Political Socialization of American Civil War Soldiers* (Athens: University of Georgia Press, 1998). See also Earl J. Hess, *Liberty, Virtue, and Progress: Northerners and Their War for the Union* (New York: New York University Press, 1988).

13. For Wood's letter of July 4, 1862, see appendix A.

14. For studies exploring the concept of duty to country, comrades, and family, see Mitchell, *The Vacant Chair,* 152, 166; Gerald F. Linderman, *Embattled Courage: The Experience of Combat in the American Civil War* (New York: Free Press, 1987); and Earl J. Hess, *The Union Soldier in Battle: Enduring the Ordeal of Battle* (Lawrence: University Press of Kansas, 1997).

15. Wood's outlook and "Brahmin" attitude to the enlisted men corresponds to that of Harvard College–educated officers of Massachusetts volunteer units. See Richard F. Miller, *Harvard's Civil War: A History of the 20th Massachusetts Volunteer Infantry* (Lebanon, N.H.: University Press of New England, 2005), and Carol Bundy, *The Nature of Sacrifice: A Biography of Charles Russell Lowell Jr., 1835–1864* (New York: Farrar, Straus, and Giroux, 2005). Wood mentions the names of enlisted men in his company in his letter intended for publication in the Goshen *Times.* See his letter of July 4, 1862, in appendix A.

16. Edward P. Stanfield to Thomas Stanfield, September 18, 1864, in Edward P. Stanfield Papers, SC 1135, Indiana Historical Society, Indianapolis.

Chapter 1

1. See Fred A. Shannon, *The Organization and Administration of the Union Army, 1861–1865,* 2 vols. (Cleveland: 1928; rpt. Gloucester, Mass.: Peter Smith, 1965). For Indiana, see Emma Lou Thornbrough, *The History of Indiana,* vol. 3, *Indiana in the Civil War Era, 1850–1880* (Indianapolis: Indiana Historical Society, 1965), 124ff., and W. H. H. Terrell, *Report of the Adjutant General of Indiana,* 8 vols. (Indianapolis, 1865–69), especially vol. 1.

2. Named after Erastus Winter Hewitt Ellis, a New York native, former auditor of state, delegate to the peace conference in 1861, and editor of the Goshen *Times,* the town's Republican newspaper. Ellis was instrumental in the formation of the 48th Indiana and the appointment of its officers. See E. W. H. Ellis, "Autobiography of a Noted Pioneer," *Indiana Magazine of History* 10 (March 1914): 63–73.

3. Augustus E. Crane, a Goshen resident.

4. The 44th Indiana Volunteer Infantry regiment was based at Fort Wayne, and recruited in the 10th and 11th congressional districts. See Julie A. Doyle, John David Smith, and Richard M. McMurry, eds., *This Wilderness of War: The Civil War Letters of George W. Squier, Hoosier Volunteer* (Knoxville: University of Tennessee Press, 1998), xvi.

5. Volunteer companies commonly elected their officers at the organization of the companies, and state governors typically heeded the views of the enlisted men in offering commissions to the elected. This practice often resulted in men with good political skills but no military abilities taking command.

6. For corroboration of Wood's impression, see Thomas E. Rodgers, "Republicans and Drifters: Political Affiliation and Union Army Volunteers in West-Central Indiana," *Indiana Magazine of History* 92 (December 1996): 321–45.

7. Nettie Bissell may have been Ann M. Bissell, a New York native, wife of Henry W. Bissell, a farmer in Elkhart Township.

8. Edmund R. Kerstetter, formerly a bank clerk, was adjutant of the 17th Indiana Volunteer Infantry regiment. Milo S. Hascall, attorney, businessman, and politician, United States Military Academy graduate in the class of 1852, resided in Goshen since 1847, and was a member of one of Goshen's most prominent families. He was commissioned colonel of the 17th Indiana Volunteer Infantry regiment in June 1861. See Stephen E. Towne, ed., "West Point Letters of Cadet Milo S. Hascall, 1848–1850," *Indiana Magazine of History* 90 (September 1994): 278–94.

9. George P. Copeland, a New York native, was a Goshen attorney and at the time the letter was written editor of the Goshen *Times,* the town's Republican newspaper.

10. Located off the strategically important Louisville and Nashville Railroad, Union forces concentrated at Bardstown, about thirty miles south of Louisville, to organize and drill.

11. Abraham S. Fisher, a druggist in Ligonier, Noble County, was born in Ohio. George W. Gibbon was a Michigan-born cabinet-maker and resident of Goshen.

12. James S. Gillespie, of Syracuse, New York, was husband of Jane's sister Nellie.

13. Cory Foster, born in England, was an Episcopal clergyman and served the St. James parish in Goshen.

Chapter 2

1. See Benjamin Franklin Cooling, *Forts Henry and Donelson: The Key to the Confederate Heartland* (Knoxville: University of Tennessee Press, 1987), and Stephen D. Engle, *The Struggle for the Heartland: The Campaigns from Fort Henry to Corinth* (Lincoln and London: University of Nebraska Press, 2001).

2. The 48th Indiana embarked from Cairo on the riverboat steamer *Empress.* See *Goshen Democrat,* February 26, 1862, and *The War of the Rebellion: A Compilation of the Official Records of the Union and Confederate Armies,* ser. 1, vol. 7: 597 (hereinafter cited *OR*).

3. The capture of Fort Henry occurred February 6, 1862, when Union forces under Brigadier General Ulysses S. Grant and United States Navy Flag Officer Andrew H. Foote compelled Rebel forces to surrender after a naval bombardment. See Cooling, *Forts Henry and Donelson,* 101–9, and Engle, *The Struggle for the Heartland,* 53–61. See also Rowena Reed, *Combined Operations in the Civil War* (Annapolis, Md.: Naval Institute Press, 1978), 64–96.

4. Major General Henry W. Halleck ordered reinforcements up the Cumberland River to meet Grant's forces marching overland from Fort Henry. Grant reported to Halleck that five gunboats and twelve troop transports arrived on February 14. See *OR,* ser. 1, vol. 7: 607–13.

5. Melvin B. Hascall, an older brother of Milo Hascall, was a prominent businessman in Goshen. A Democrat, he nonetheless vigorously supported the war effort in 1861 and was rewarded with a commission after recommendation by E. W. H. Ellis to Governor Oliver P. Morton. See Ellis to Morton, November 1, 1861, in 48th Indiana Volunteer Infantry regiment Regimental Correspondence, Indiana State Archives.

6. Fort Donelson on the Cumberland River in Tennessee fell to Union forces under General Grant and Flag Officer Foote on February 16, 1862. About fifteen thousand Confederate troops surrendered after a hard-fought battle (Cooling, *Forts Henry and Donelson,* 114–203).

7. The Sibley tent was a prewar design of U.S. Army officer Henry Hopkins Sibley, who later became a general in the Confederate service. The Enfield rifle was a much sought-after English design and imported into the United States in large quantities during the war. It was customary to equip the "flank" companies of a volunteer regiment—i.e., those on the ends in line of battle, Companies A, B, I, and K—lacking uniform armaments with the superior firearms.

8. William Hardee produced his *Rifle and Light Infantry Tactic: For the Exercising and Manoeuvres of Troops When Acting as Light Infantry or Riflemen* in 1855 after Mexican War service in the U.S. Army and study in Europe. Hardee's *Tactics* became the standard tactics manual for both armies in the Civil War. Hardee served as a general in the Confederate service. See Nathaniel Cheairs Hughes, *General William J. Hardee: Old Reliable* (Baton Rouge: Louisiana State University Press, 1992).

9. Major General Don Carlos Buell's Army of the Ohio took Nashville, Tennessee, on February 25, and a reinforced Grant planned to advance up the Tennessee River southward toward Corinth, Mississippi, not toward Memphis. See Benjamin Franklin Cooling, *Fort Donelson's Legacy: War and Society in Kentucky and Tennessee, 1862–1863* (Knoxville: University of Tennessee Press, 1997), 27–28, and Engle, *The Struggle for the Heartland,* 90–112.

10. Brigadier General William Tecumseh Sherman in February 1862 was posted to command the Department of Cairo, with his headquarters at Paducah. There he forwarded troops to General Grant and organized a division that soon would be part of Grant's army that fought at Shiloh. See John F. Marszalek, *Sherman: A Soldier's Passion for Order* (New York: Free Press, 1993), 169–73.

11. E. D. Richmond is not identified.

12. Freemasonry, a secret society of European origins, had established itself firmly in North America in the eighteenth century and played a significant role in American culture, so much so that in the early nineteenth century, politics and political parties organized around support of and opposition to the movement. See Steve C. Bullock, *Revolutionary Brotherhood: Freemasonry and the Transformation of the American Social Order, 1730–1840* (Chapel Hill: University of North Carolina Press, 1996), and William Preston Vaughn, "An Overview of Pre–and Post–Civil War Antimasonry," *Historian* 49 (1987): 494–507.

13. John N. Niglas of Peoria, Illinois, served as regimental surgeon of the 6th Illinois Cavalry Regiment.

14. "Contrabands of war" was a term coined in the early weeks of the war by Union General Benjamin F. Butler to refer to escaped or fugitive ex-slaves who had fled their Southern captors and sought asylum with Federal troops. Union forces employed many thousands of these ex-slaves throughout the war as laborers in and around camp. Cooling, *Fort Donelson's Legacy*, 18–19, and Mark Grimsley, *The Hard Hand of War: Union Military Policy toward Southern Civilians, 1861–1865* (Cambridge: Cambridge University Press, 1995), 48–52, 61–63.

15. William Shakespeare, *The Tragedy of Othello, The Moor of Venice,* act 3, sc. 1:

> Farewell the neighing steed and the shrill trump,
> The spirit stirring drum, the ear-piercing fife,
> The royal banner, and all quality,
> Pride, pomp, and circumstance of glorious war.

16. James Russell Lowell, *The Vision of Sir Launfal*. Prelude to Part First (1848):

> And what is so rare as a day in June?
> Then, if ever, comes perfect days;
> Then Heaven tries the earth if it be in tune,
> And over it softly he warm ear lays.

17. Platt Tracy enlisted in Company D, 12th Indiana Volunteer Infantry regiment, one year enlistment, in April 1861, and mustered out in May 1862. He subsequently enlisted in the 17th Indiana Light Artillery Battery and mustered out in June 1865. His brother, Wood's friend, is not identified.

18. "Col." Barron may have been Jonathan Barron, born in New Hampshire, a Goshen merchant. Martin Brown, born in New York and a prosperous Goshen merchant, was a partner in the firm Hascall, Alderman & Brown. He died October 10, 1862. Goshen teenager Alice Hawks, a cousin, recorded in her diary on that day, "Mart died this morning it seams as though it is a real blessing to him for he has suffered so much since he had been sick." See Virginia Mayberry and Dawn E. Bakken, eds., "The Civil War Homefront: Diary of a Young Girl, 1862–1863," *Indiana Magazine of History* 87 (March 1991): 57.

19. Mrs. Burnhans, wife of Frederick D. Burnhans, was the former Helen E. Barron.

20. 'Gus Crane married Nettie Case on March 20, 1862.

21. Sister Almira Williams married Henry Van Vleck, and sister Ellen married James Gillespie.

22. Lot Day, a LaPorte merchant, had previously been deputy warden of the Indiana State Prison–North, at Michigan City. Sutlers were private businessmen contracted by the army or state governors to sell goods to soldiers.

23. News of the battle of Shiloh, April 6–7, fought on the banks of the Tennessee River, evidently had not yet reached Paducah by the evening of April 7.

24. General Orders number 33, April 3, 1862, from the War Department stated: "The recruiting service for volunteers will be discontinued in every State from this date." *OR,* ser. 3, vol. 2: 2–3. In discussing this order after the war, wartime aide

to Governor Morton, W. H. H. Terrell, noted: "This was a most unfortunate step, but all efforts to have the order recalled were unavailing." See *Indiana in the War of the Rebellion: Report of the Adjutant General of Indiana.* (Indianapolis: 1869; rpt. Indianapolis: Indiana Historical Society, 1960), 22.

25. An undated letter written by Lieutenant Jasper Packard of Company D, published in the Plymouth *Marshall County Republican,* April 24, 1862, described how Wood trapped secession sympathizers at a Paducah horse auction. Packard wrote: "An incident occurred here a few days since which is worth mentioning. The whole country around here is filled with traitors at heart, even though they have not been active participants in the rebellion. They have talked treason and have been very fond of boasting that they would not take the oath of allegiance. Many of them have stayed away from Paducah ever since the Union forces came here, in order to avoid taking the oath, and it has been their boast that they had never acknowledged 'Lincoln's' rule. There was a picket guard around the place, and every person once inside the line could not get out without a pass from the Provost Marshall, on which the oath of allegiance was printed, which the bearer was required to take and subscribe. After the evacuation of Columbus [Kentucky] the picket guard was withdrawn, and then these gents jeered at their neighbors who were so foolish as to be 'caught.' These things came to the notice of Capt. Wood, and he determined to 'catch' them. There was a large public sale of horses by the Government soon to come off, and as was to be expected nearly everybody came, good horses being a very scarce article hereabouts, except those owned by the United States. After the sale had commenced and the buyers had all got in a picket Guard was quietly posted at the outskirts of the City, and every man was required to show his pass. Then there was some squirming, some little profanity was indulged in, but the oath was taken to be and remain good and loyal citizens. They will keep the oath outwardly. Fear is a great promoter of loyalty."

26. The battle of Shiloh, or Pittsburg Landing, fought April 6–7, 1862, was a Union victory notwithstanding heavy casualties and Rebel forces under General Albert Sidney Johnston surprising and overrunning the camp of Grant's army on the first day of battle. Union forces under Major General Don Carlos Buell arrived on the second day and forced a Rebel retreat. See James Lee McDonough, *Shiloh—In Hell before Night* (Knoxville: University of Tennessee Press, 1977).

27. Juliet Mackie and her daughter Mary Mackie resided in New York City.

28. Edward B. Judson, a prominent Syracuse banker, married Jane's sister Sarah.

Chapter 3

1. For biographies of Halleck, see Stephen Ambrose, *Halleck: Lincoln's Chief of Staff* (Baton Rouge: Louisiana State University Press, 1962), and John F. Marszalek, *Commander of All Lincoln's Armies: A Life of General Henry W. Halleck* (Cambridge, Mass.: Belknap Press, 2004).

2. George Gordon, Lord Byron, *The Corsair* (1814), canto one, stanza 3:

> She walks the waters like a thing of life,
> And seems to dare the elements to strife.

3. Major General John Pope served in Missouri and, most notably to date, on the Mississippi River in subduing Rebel forces at New Madrid and Island Number 10. After the bloody debacle of Shiloh, Halleck consolidated his forces and ordered Pope to command the Army of the Mississippi, part of the force advancing on Corinth. See Peter Cozzens, *General John Pope: A Life for the Nation* (Urbana and Chicago: University of Illinois Press, 2000), 65–66.

4. Fears of the climate of the Deep South and the diseases associated with it were widespread among civilians and soldiers of both the North and South. See Richard M. McMurry, "Marse Robert and the Fevers: A Note on the General as Strategist and on Medical Ideas as a Factor in Civil War Decision Making," *Civil War History* 35 (1989): 197–207.

5. Major General George B. McClellan, commander of the Army of the Potomac in the East, had begun his peninsular campaign for Richmond in northern Virginia. See Stephen W. Sears, *George B. McClellan: The Young Napoleon* (New York: Ticknor and Fields, 1988), 168–92. In addition, forces under Brigadier General Ambrose E. Burnside had successfully attacked and seized Confederate positions along the North Carolina coast. See William Marvel, *Burnside* (Chapel Hill: University of North Carolina Press, 1991), 41–96.

6. President Abraham Lincoln gave overall command of Union forces in the West to General Halleck. Halleck assumed field command in April 1862 (Marszalek, *Commander of All Lincoln's Armies*, 120–21).

7. Combined forces under U.S. Navy Captain David G. Farragut and Major General Benjamin F. Butler attacked and defeated the defenses around New Orleans and received the city's surrender on April 25, 1862. See Chester G. Hearn, *The Capture of New Orleans, 1862* (Baton Rouge and London: Louisiana State University Press, 1995).

8. *Frank Leslie's Illustrated Newspaper,* published in New York City, reached a wide readership in the North, competing with *Harper's Weekly.*

9. General Pierre Gustave Toutant Beauregard assumed command of Confederate forces at Shiloh after the death of General Albert Sidney Johnston. T. Harry Williams, *P. G. T. Beauregard: Napoleon in Gray* (Baton Rouge: Louisiana State University Press, 1955), 139ff.

10. Brigadier General Napoleon Bonaparte Buford had entered service as colonel of the 27th Illinois Volunteer Infantry regiment, and was promoted for his service at Union City, Tennessee. See Edward G. Longacre, *General John Buford* (Conshohocken, Pa.: Combined Books, 1995), 81–83.

11. Brayton Harris, *Blue & Gray in Black & White: Newspapers in the Civil War* (Washington and London: Brassey's, 1999), 157. Revised U.S. Army Regulations stated: "All correspondence and communication, verbally or by writing, printing, or telegraphing, respecting operations of the army or military movements on land or water, or respecting the troops, camps, arsenals, intrenchments, or military affairs, within the several military districts, by which intelligence shall be, directly or indirectly, given to the enemy, without the authority and sanction of the General in command, be and the same are absolutely prohibited, and persons violating this Regulation will be proceeded against under the 57th Article of War."

12. See *OR*, ser. 1, vol. 10, part 1: 804–8.

13. Milo S. Hascall was promoted Brigadier General of Volunteers on April 25, 1862, and commanded a brigade in Buell's Army of the Ohio (Mark M. Boatner, *The Civil War Dictionary* [New York: David McKay Company, 1959], 383).

14. Tommy Donahue does not appear in the rosters of the 48th Indiana.

15. Brigadier General Schuyler Hamilton, brother-in-law of General Henry Halleck, was highly thought of by General John Pope for his services in action at Island Number Ten on the Mississippi River. He resigned his commission in 1863 due to illness.

16. Lieutenant H. Seymour Burt served in the 63rd Ohio Volunteer Infantry regiment and as a staff officer for General Hamilton, who commended him in reports. See *OR* ser. 1, vol. 10, part 1: 725.

17. Robert R. Parrott of the West Point Foundry in New York invented and patented a design for heavy siege guns.

18. Shakespeare, *The Tragedy of MacBeth*, act 3, sc. 1:

> Upon my head they plac'd a fruitless crown,
> And put a barren scepter in my gripe,
> Thence to be wrenc'd with an unlineal hand,
> No son of mine succeeding.

19. Union forces were to employ Corinth's fortifications against the attack of Rebel troops in October. See Cozzens, *The Darkest Days of the War: The Battles of Iuka and Corinth* (Chapel Hill: University of North Carolina Press, 1997).

20. Army regulations based pay of officers and enlisted men on service from the date of muster-in. Indiana did not pay volunteer officers and enlisted men for time in service prior to their official muster into the U.S. Army.

21. Oliver P. Morton, Republican governor of Indiana, 1861–67, later served as U.S. senator from 1867 to his death in 1877. The letter is not in the correspondence of the 48th Indiana in the Indiana State Archives.

22. Schuyler Colfax, Republican U.S. representative from South Bend, became Speaker of the House of Representatives in 1863. He later served as vice president during Ulysses S. Grant's first term as president. Colfax's reputation was sullied by the *Credit Mobilier* scandal, and he was replaced on the Republican ticket in 1872. See Willard H. Smith, *Schuyler Colfax: The Changing Fortunes of a Political Idol*, Indiana Historical Collections, vol. 33 (Indianapolis: Indiana Historical Bureau, 1952).

23. Charles W. Cathcart, War Democrat from LaPorte, won elections to serve in the U.S. House of Representatives in 1845 and 1847, and briefly served in the U.S. Senate in 1852.

24. Reports of food shortages in Louisiana and Mississippi appeared in the *New York Times*. See issues of May 25, May 30, and June 10, 1862.

25. Baking soda.

Chapter 4

1. Steven E. Woodworth, *Jefferson Davis and His Generals: The Failure of Confederate Command in the West* (Lawrence: University Press of Kansas, 1990), 116, 128–37.

2. Cozzens, *The Darkest Days of the War,* 90–91, 106. See *OR,* ser. 1, vol. 17, part 1: 78, 94–98.

3. Captain Orrison Wilson of Company D, of LaPorte, resigned his commission in January 1863.

4. Carlos White, of the 5th Iowa Volunteer Infantry regiment, had formerly resided in Goshen. The 5th Iowa was brigaded with the 48th Indiana for several months. See Mark Grimsley and Todd D. Miller, eds., *The Union Must Stand: The Civil War Diary of John Quincy Adams Campbell, Fifth Iowa Volunteer Infantry* (Knoxville: University of Tennessee Press, 2000).

5. The Know Nothing Party attained significant power and influence in the North in the middle of the 1850s, running on an anti-immigrant, anti-Catholic, anti-slavery platform. It later merged with the precipitously declining Whig Party to form the Republican Party. See Tyler Anbinder, *Nativism and Slavery: The Northern Know Nothings and the Politics of the 1850s* (New York: Oxford University Press, 1992).

6. Chiggers, the larvae of the harvest mite, or *trombicula alfreddugesi.*

7. In a series of bloody battles outside Richmond, Virginia, called the Seven Days Battles, June 25–July 1, 1862, Confederate General Robert E. Lee, newly promoted to command of the Army of Northern Virginia when Joseph E. Johnston was wounded, attacked the Federal Army of the Potomac under Major General George B. McClellan and halted the Union advance outside Richmond. McClellan's months-long peninsular campaign climaxed and collapsed. The Union commander retreated in good order and ended the advance on the Rebel capital. See Stephen W. Sears, *George B. McClellan: The Young Napoleon* (New York: Ticknor and Field, 1988), 193–222; Sears, *To the Gates of Richmond: The Peninsula Campaign* (New York: Ticknor and Field, 1992), 179–345; and Kevin Dougherty and J. Michael Moore, *The Peninsula Campaign of 1862: A Military Analysis* (Jackson: University Press of Mississippi, 2005), 109–39. George M. Williams, Jane's youngest sibling, served in the 14th New York Volunteer Infantry regiment in the Army of the Potomac.

8. Bayard Taylor (1825–1870), noted American travel writer, described encountering a caravan at an Egyptian desert well: "The fierce Kababish were shouting and gesticulating on all sides as we rode up—some leading the camels to kneel and drink, some holding the water-skins, and other brandishing their spears and swords in angry contention. Under the hot sun, on the sandy plain, it was a picture truly mid-African in all its features."

See *A Journey to Central Africa* (New York: G. P. Putnam and Co., 1854; rpt. New York: Negro Universities Press, 1970), 417.

9. Brigadier General Jefferson C. Davis, a Clark County, Indiana, native, served in the Mexican War and parlayed his service into a regular army commission. A captain at the beginning of the Civil War, Indiana Governor Oliver P. Morton commissioned him colonel of the 22nd Indiana Volunteer Infantry regiment. See

Nathaniel Cheairs Hughes and Gordon D. Whitney, *Jefferson Davis in Blue: The Life of Sherman's Relentless Warrior* (Baton Rouge: Louisiana State University Press, 2002).

10. Federal military occupation of portions of the South in 1861 and 1862 had elicited a policy of conciliation toward Rebels in the hopes of undermining resistance to the federal government. Some Federal commanders, most notably Major Generals George B. McClellan and Don Carlos Buell, embraced this conciliatory attitude that corresponded with their more conservative, Democratic political ideologies. However, other commanders and political leaders with Republican ideological views chafed at these methods. Moreover, the enlisted men and officers in the field soon began to resent the "soft" policies towards the Rebels while Rebel guerrillas attacked Federal occupiers and isolated units. Commanders such as Buell came to be viewed by their men as sympathetic to the rebellion. The guarding of Rebel-owned property while Union troops suffered for want of rations enraged many. Mark Grimsley ascribed the collapse of conciliatory measures to the failure of McClellan's peninsula campaign, which demonstrated to Northern soldiers and civilians that the rebellion would not be suppressed soon, and that harsher measures were necessary to end the war. By August 1862 foraging by Union troops, already extensive, was officially encouraged by War Department instructions. See Grimsley, *The Hard Hand of War,* 63–100. See also Stephen D. Engle, *Don Carlos Buell: Most Promising of All* (Chapel Hill: University of North Carolina Press, 1999), 184–88, 190–92, 201–3.

11. In the spring of 1862, amid hopes of a quick end to rebellion, the War Department stopped recruiting. However, the defeats suffered in the East prompted the July 2, 1862, call for three hundred thousand volunteers. On August 4, 1862, the War Department called for an additional three hundred thousand troops, to be raised in part by conscription.

12. "In the first place."

13. Two commercial hair tonics.

14. American poets John Greenleaf Whittier, James Russell Lowell, and William Cullen Bryant, and Robert Burns, the Scots poet.

15. William Makepeace Thackeray, Sir Edward Bulwer-Lytton, and Anthony Trollope were three popular English novelists of the period. Many of their works appeared published serially in U.S. newspapers and magazines.

16. Lieutenant Gottlieb Schauble of Company H, a Goshen brewer born in Wurtemburg, Germany.

17. Captains Thomas B. Roberts, Company E, and Richard F. Mann, Company G, died of typhoid fever on July 4 and July 24, 1862, respectively. Captains David S. Snyder of Company K, David S. Crumpacker of Company C, and Gustavus Paulus of Company H resigned. Captain Benjamin D. Townsend, Company A, was promoted major when Dewitt C. Rugg was promoted to lieutenant colonel on the resignation of Melvin B. Hascall in June 1862 due to illness. Captain William H. Sutphen of Company B, and Captain Barnet Byrkit of Company F had seniority over Wood.

18. The brigade under Brigadier General Napoleon Bonaparte Buford consisted of the 48th Indiana, 59th Indiana, 5th Iowa, 4th Minnesota, and 26th Missouri

volunteer infantry regiments. The 11th Ohio Light Artillery Battery was attached to the brigade.

19. "The colonel of the Union forty-fourth Indiana probably spoke for much of the army when he declared that the general opinion of the regiment was that the rebel surprise attack on April 6 was 'the result of gross carelessness and an insufficient system of picketing.'" Much of the blame for the surprise attack on the Union camp at Shiloh fell on Sherman's shoulders. See McDonough, *Shiloh—In Hell before Night,* 223.

20. Henry Wadsworth Longfellow, "A Psalm of Life. What the Heart of the Young Man Said to the Psalmist" (1838):

> Trust no Future, howe'er pleasant!
> Let the dead Past bury its dead!
> Act,—act in the living Present!
> Heart within, and God o'erhead!

21. Lieutenant Colonel Melvin B. Hascall's resignation was accepted by the War Department July 4, 1862, to take effect June 16, 1862.

22. Elizabeth Horton married Melvin Hascall in 1851. Eliza Wilson resided in LaPorte.

23. Captain William Sutphen, Company B, resigned effective September 11, 1862.

24. E & T Fairbanks and Company of St. Johnsbury, Vermont, manufactured scales and advertised widely in newspapers and periodicals.

25. Following Braxton Bragg's orders to engage Federal troops in northern Mississippi to keep them from reinforcing Buell in Tennessee, Sterling Price's Army of the West advanced northward toward Rosecrans's force in early September. Cozzens, *The Darkest Days of the War,* 52–63.

26. Rebel General Braxton Bragg moved north into Kentucky in September, threatening supply lines to Federal forces in the South and both Cincinnati, Ohio, and Louisville, Kentucky, and forcing Union Major General Don Carlos Buell to follow in pursuit. See Kenneth W. Noe, *Perryville: This Grand Havoc of Battle* (Lexington: University Press of Kentucky, 2001), 53–68.

27. Colonel John Van Deusen Du Bois, a West Point graduate and captain in the regular army, was commissioned colonel of the 1st Missouri Light Artillery regiment. See Jared C. Lobdell, ed., "The Civil War Journal and Letters of Colonel John Van Deusen Du Bois, April 12, 1861 to October 16, 1862," *Missouri Historical Review* 60, no. 4 (July 1966): 436–59; *Missouri Historical Review* 61, no. 1 (October 1966): 21–50.

28. Major General William Starke Rosecrans led Union forces in western Virginia that drove Rebel General Robert E. Lee from the region. Rosecrans later transferred to Halleck's army in the West. See William M. Lamers, *The Edge of Glory: A Biography of General William S. Rosecrans, U.S.A.* (New York: Harcourt Brace, 1961; rpt. Baton Rouge: Louisiana State University Press, 1989).

29. Brigadier General Charles S. Hamilton served without distinction in the Army of the Potomac prior to transferring to the western theater.

30. General Sterling Price had formerly served as governor of Missouri. After success against Federal forces in Missouri in 1861, he was defeated at Pea Ridge in Arkansas in March 1862. He crossed the Mississippi River with his Missouri troops and assumed command of the Army of the West in Mississippi under Bragg's overall command. Confederate President Jefferson Davis had little use for him, but his political strength west of the Mississippi made him indispensable. Van Dorn also thought little of Price. Woodworth, *Jefferson Davis and His Generals*, 148–51; Cozzens, *The Darkest Days of the War*, 4–5, 43–46.

31. Lieutenant Colonel Rugg was severely wounded in the foot at Iuka.

32. Official casualty returns for Hamilton's division reported 132 killed, 614 wounded, and 32 missing, for a total of 778 losses. *OR*, ser. 1, vol. 17, part 1: 78. The 5th Iowa Volunteer Infantry regiment, next in the Union line to the 48th Indiana, bore the brunt of Price's assault and received 217 casualties.

33. The 48th Indiana entered the battle with 434 men and suffered 37 killed in action, 56 wounded, and 7 missing. Colonel Norman Eddy was among the wounded (ibid.).

34. By virtue of his higher rank, Van Dorn commanded his and Price's combined forces in the assaults on Corinth. Van Dorn's and Price's broken forces retreated to Holly Springs. Van Dorn's and Price's "campaign had been an unrelieved failure and had done nothing to further Bragg's effort in Kentucky" (Woodworth, *Jefferson Davis and His Generals*, 154–55).

35. General Charles S. Hamilton's division occupied the right of Rosecrans's defenses. The 48th Indiana was on the left end of General Buford's brigade, and was the "most actively engaged" unit in the brigade (*OR*, ser. 1, vol. 17, part 1: 216–17). Lieutenant James W. Archer of the 59th Indiana Volunteer Infantry regiment, who assumed command of the regiment during the battle when Lieutenant Colonel Rugg was wounded, wrote the 48th's after-action report (*OR*, ser, 1, vol. 17, part 1: 218).

36. General Charles S. Hamilton wrote to Governor Morton that Major Townsend "was so drunk on the field of Corinth as to be worthless. He will either resign or be dismissed" (Hamilton to Morton, October 12, 1862, 48th Indiana Volunteer Infantry regiment correspondence, Indiana State Archives). Townsend resigned on October 20, 1862.

37. Lieutenant Colonel Jefferson K. Scott of the 59th Indiana assumed command of the 48th Indiana on October 5, 1862, and led the regiment during the pursuit of Van Dorn until the return of Colonel Eddy.

Chapter 5

1. Woodworth, *Jefferson Davis and His Generals*, 169, 173.

2. Reed, *Combined Operations in the Civil War*, 215ff.

3. See Arthur B. Carter, *The Tarnished Cavalier: Major General Earl Van Dorn, C.S.A.* (Knoxville: University of Tennessee Press, 1999), 127–46.

4. Reed, *Combined Operations in the Civil War*, 234–40. Much of the reason for the failure was U.S. Navy Rear Admiral David Dixon Porter's misplaced confidence

that his naval forces could clear the Yazoo and land the troops safely north of Vicksburg. See Chester G. Hearn, *Admiral David Dixon Porter* (Annapolis, Md.: Naval Institute Press, 1996), 158–65.

5. Major General Grant, having been given command of the Department of the Tennessee on October 24, 1862, planned to take the initiative against Rebel Lieutenant General John C. Pemberton, who commanded in Mississippi. Grant planned a multipronged attack, one assault overland to reach Vicksburg from the east, and another assault via the Mississippi and Yazoo rivers north of the city. Pemberton, believing his forces to be outnumbered by Grant's overland army alone, retreated slowly southward toward the citadel. Woodworth, *Jefferson Davis and His Generals,* 181; Ulysses S. Grant, *Personal Memoirs of U. S. Grant* (Hartford, Conn.: C. T. Webster, 1885; rpt. Lincoln: University of Nebraska Press, 1996), 250ff. See also Frank J. Welcher, *The Union Army, 1861–1865: Organization and Operations,* vol. 2, *The Western Theater* (Bloomington and Indianapolis: Indiana University Press, 1993), 235.

6. The Memphis and Charleston Railroad, a major east-west line.

7. Brigadier General Isaac F. Quinby, a West Point classmate of Grant, assumed command of the division.

8. In his report on the battle of Corinth, Brigadier General Napoleon B. Buford noted that his aide-de-camp, Lieutenant J. W. Archer of the 59th Indiana, "was asked by the [48th's] senior captain to command." The identity of the "senior captain" in question is not clear, though shortly after the battle Wood was the "ranking captain" present. Afterwards, Brigadier General Charles S. Hamilton recommended Archer to the 48th majority. Colonels Eddy and Rugg and E. W. H. Ellis sent Governor Morton letters of recommendation for Wood, praising his "high merit," "gallantry," sobriety, and intelligence as an officer. See *OR,* ser. 1, vol. 17, part 1: 217; Hamilton to Morton, October 12, 1862; Eddy to Morton, November 4, 1862; Rugg to Morton, November 4, 1862; and Ellis to Morton, November 25, 1862, all 48th Indiana Volunteer Infantry regiment correspondence, Indiana State Archives.

9. Byron, *Don Juan* (1819), canto 4, stanza 110:

> Oh! 'darkly, deeply, beautifully blue,'
> As some one somewhere sings about the sky,
> And I, ye learned ladies, say of you;
> They say your stockings are so (Heaven knows why
> I have examined few pairs of that hue);
> Blue as the garters which serenely lie
> Round the Patrician left-legs, which adorn
> The festal midnight, and the levee morn.

10. The *Goshen Times* of November 13, 1862, reported the death on November 9 of Mrs. Susan McGary, widow of William McGary, "after a short but painful illness."

11. The District of West Tennessee was folded and reorganized into the Department of the Tennessee on October 24, 1862. Quinby commanded the 7th Division, District of Corinth, in Grant's 13th Corps, which was also called the Army of the Tennessee. See Welcher, *The Union Army,* 220–21, 235.

12. The identity of Mr. Failing is not known.

13. "The Tallahatchie, which confronted me, was very high, the railroad bridge destroyed and Pemberton strongly fortified on the south side. A crossing would have been impossible in the presence of the enemy. I sent the cavalry higher up the stream and they secured a crossing. This caused the enemy to evacuate their position. . . . The enemy was followed as far south as Oxford by the main body of troops, and some seventeen miles farther by McPherson's command. Here the pursuit was halted to repair the railroad from the Tallahatchie northward, in order to bring up supplies" (Grant, *Memoirs*, 253–54).

14. Grant created a cavalry division of three brigades under the command of Colonel T. Lyle Dickey, 4th Illinois Cavalry, on November 26, 1862 (Welcher, *The Union Army*, 256).

15. Frank Philips was the son of Mary Gautier's sister. He served in the 6th Florida Volunteer Infantry regiment as adjutant, and was captured in Kentucky in September 1862, and exchanged. By war's end he was a division adjutant. See letter of Philips to Wood, February 2, 1867, in possession of Daniel Wood.

16. Grant had about thirty thousand troops in Mississippi, and Sherman's force operating from Memphis had about forty thousand. Pemberton had about thirty thousand men, while Lt. Gen. Joseph E. Johnston, newly appointed commander of Rebel forces from western North Carolina to the Mississippi River, had about eleven thousand men at his command.

17. Captain David F. Spain, Company E, resigned to date from December 3, 1862.

18. A newly weaned, young pig.

19. For a study of the politics and Union strategy of collecting the cotton crop in the occupied South, see Ludwell H. Johnson, *The Red River Campaign: Politics and Cotton in the Civil War* (Baltimore: Johns Hopkins University Press, 1958; rpt. Kent, Ohio: Kent State University Press, 1993).

20. Goshen *Times*, November 27, 1862: "Captain Edward J. Wood of the 48th Ind. Regt. has received the appointment of Major of that regiment in place of Major Townsend, resigned. We congratulate our friend Wood upon his promotion and feel confident he will fill the position with honor to himself and to the entire satisfaction of the regiment. Major Wood is a brave and talented officer and one whose *heart* is in the cause. He is a Union man without any "*ifs*" or "*buts*" and has long deserved the promotion he has just received. Long live our gallant soldier friend, Major Wood."

21. The Mississippi and Ohio Railroad connected Columbus, Kentucky, with northern Mississippi.

22. Confederate Major General Earl Van Dorn, commanding a large cavalry force, made a rapid raid on Holly Springs on December 20, 1862, destroying large quantities of stores and cutting Federal communications with the North.

23. Braxton Bragg and his Army of Tennessee were actually far away, encamped in and around Murfreesboro, Tennessee, twenty-five miles southeast of Nashville, where he would soon face the advancing Army of the Cumberland under Major General William S. Rosecrans in bloody battle. See Peter Cozzens, *No Better Place*

to Die: The Battle of Stones River (Urbana and Chicago: University of Illinois Press, 1990).

24. The Memphis and Charleston Railroad.

25. Colonel John B. Sanborn, 4th Minnesota Volunteer Infantry regiment, commanded the brigade. He briefly attended Dartmouth College in 1851. Wood's silence on the Dartmouth connection suggests he was unaware of it.

26. Major General William T. Sherman's attack on Vicksburg, Mississippi, defenses from the north, December 27, 1862–January 2, 1863, through the thick swamps of Chickasaw Bayou, failed to dislodge Rebel forces. See Marszalek, Sherman, 202–9.

Chapter 6

1. See Marszalek, Sherman, 214–16; Hearn, Admiral David Dixon Porter, 182ff.

2. A condition affecting nerve endings producing burning and painful sensations.

3. Including extra pay for equipment, fodder, and other expenses, U.S. Army captains received $115.50/month; majors received $169/month; lieutenant colonels received $181/month, and colonels $212/month (Boatner, The Civil War Dictionary, 624).

4. Beginning in late February 1863 Federal forces under General Grant and Rear Admiral David Dixon Porter embarked on gunboats and transports in an attempt to approach Vicksburg via the rain-swollen and tree-choked streams and bayous north of the city. The effort failed to reach the Yazoo River, more because of the difficult conditions than Southern resistance. The 48th Indiana traveled on the transport Lady Jackson. See Grant, Memoirs, 263–69; Wentworth, Jefferson Davis and His Generals, 201–2.

5. Formerly the Memphis Avalanche, a pro-Rebel newspaper, Federal authorities in the city renamed it the Bulletin. The newspaper did not fully toe the Federal line, opposing President Lincoln's Emancipation Proclamation. See John F. Marszalek, Sherman's Other War: The General and the Civil War Press (Kent, Ohio: Kent State University Press, 1999), 110, 122–23.

6. Major General Rosecrans wrote Governor Morton in February that "General [Milo S.] Hascall is not able to stand field service during this inclement season," and that he had ordered Hascall to superintend the roundup of deserters in Indiana, Ohio, and Illinois from the Army of the Cumberland, many thousands of whom had sneaked away from the army in Tennessee. Hascall's headquarters were in Indianapolis. There he cooperated with the governors of those states, and coordinated his efforts with the commanders of the Department of the Ohio, headquartered at Cincinnati. See Rosecrans to Morton, February 16, 1863, Adjutant General of Indiana Records, Box A4017 024596, folder 18, Indiana State Archives. Desertion was rampant in the Army of the Cumberland during the winter. Rosecrans complained that thirty thousand men were missing without leave from his army. See Ella Lonn, Desertion during the Civil War (Gloucester, Mass.: American Historical Association, 1928; Bison Books edition: Lincoln and London: University of Nebraska Press, 1998), 204. Hascall was transferred to Major General Ambrose E. Burnside's Department of the Ohio on May 12, 1863. See OR, ser. 1, vol. 23, part 2: 326.

7. Martha Hudson was one of several young women from Goshen who volunteered as nurses at the behest of Governor Morton in February 1863 to provide medical assistance for the impending battles for Vicksburg. See the Goshen *Times*, February 19, 1863.

8. Trigeminal neuralgia, affecting the trigeminal nerve in the face.

9. Wood's suggestion of detached service at Memphis predated the formal creation of the U.S. Army unit specifically designed to employ disabled soldiers. In April 1863 the War Department established the Invalid Corps, later renamed the Veteran Reserve Corps, to employ the many thousands of partially disabled soldiers who still wished to serve, thereby freeing many able-bodied veterans from rear-echelon duties. See Paul A. Cimbala, "Lining Up to Serve: Wounded and Sick Union Officers Join Veteran Reserve Corps during Civil War, Reconstruction," *Prologue* 35 (2003): 38–49; Cimbala, "Soldiering on the Home Front: The Veteran Reserve Corps and the Northern People," in Paul A. Cimbala and Randall M. Miller, eds., *Union Soldiers and the Northern Home Front: Wartime Experiences, Postwar Adjustments* (New York: Fordham University Press, 2002), 182–218; and Fred Pelka, ed., *The Civil War Letters of Colonel Charles F. Johnson, Invalid Corps* (Amherst: University of Massachusetts Press, 2004).

10. "The heavy, overhanging timber retarded progress very much, as did also the short turns in so narrow a stream. The gunboats, however, ploughed their way through without other damage than to their appearance. The transports did not fare so well although they followed behind. . . . The river steamers, with their tall smoke-stacks and light guards extending out, were so much impeded that the gunboats got far ahead" (Grant, *Memoirs*, 268).

11. There is no evidence to suggest that Wood faced disciplinary actions for being absent without leave.

12. Tiffany & Company, New York jewelers, produced ornate presentation swords.

13. The 48th Indiana went on the Yazoo Pass expedition from February 24 through April 8, 1863, and encamped at Millikin's Bend, Louisiana on April 13.

Chapter 7

1. Grant, *Memoirs*, 272. Chester Hearn notes that "Porter was lukewarm on the proposition, but he agreed to cooperate fully, warning Grant that once the gunboats got below Vicksburg, he had little hope of getting them back up" (Hearn, *Admiral David Dixon Porter*, 208).

2. Hearn, *Admiral David Dixon Porter,* 208–16.

3. Grant later wrote that when the first wave of his troops landed on the east shore of the Mississippi, "I felt a degree of relief scarcely ever equalled since" (Grant, *Memoirs*, 284).

4. New Carthage, Louisiana.

5. Rugg's resignation was dated April 24, 1863.

6. Union troops began to march south on the west side of the Mississippi River on April 25, 1863, the day that Wood wrote this letter.

7. Brigadier General Quinby was absent from the division on sick leave from April 14; Colonel Sanborn briefly commanded the division. Later, during the crossing of the Mississippi and the engagements east of the river, Brigadier General Marcellus M. Crocker assumed temporary command of the division.

8. Major General John A. McClernand, an Illinois politician, commanded the 13th Corps in Grant's army. The 13th Corps crossed the Mississippi River on April 30 and the next day encountered defensive positions near Port Gibson held by Southern troops under Brigadier General John S. Bowen. Major General James B. McPherson's 17th Corps followed immediately behind McClernand's force. Much of Sherman's corps stayed further north in order, in Grant's words, to "compel Pemberton to keep as much force about Vicksburg as I could" (Grant, *Memoirs*, 282; see also *OR*, ser. 1, vol. 24, part 1: 48–49).

9. Wood probably meant the Little Bayou Pierre, near Port Gibson. See *OR*, ser. 1, vol. 24, part 3: 267–69. See also Michael B. Ballard, *Vicksburg: The Campaign That Opened the Mississippi* (Chapel Hill: University of North Carolina Press, 2004), 243.

10. See map 34 in Warren E. Grabau, *Ninety-Eight Days: A Geographer's View of the Vicksburg Campaign* (Knoxville: University of Tennessee Press, 2000), 171–74.

11. See Grant, *Memoirs*, 288, 291.

12. New York raised a number of two-year enlistment units, the muster out of which occurred in the spring of 1863. James Gillespie's unit is not known.

13. Major General John A. Logan, an Illinois politician, commanded 3rd Division, 17th Corps.

14. See General McPherson's report in *OR* ser. 1, vol. 24, part 1: 704. The battle of Raymond provides an example of the frequent disparities in troop levels and casualties offered in eyewitness accounts. Wood believed that 10,000 troops under the command of Rebel Brigadier General John Gregg awaited Union forces. McPherson estimated Gregg's numbers to be 6,000 men. Gregg reported that 2,500 troops were actually engaged. Wood's estimate of casualties on both sides were excessive; Union losses totaled about 450, while Gregg reported just over 500 killed, wounded, and captured. See *OR*, ser. 1, vol. 24, part 1: 737–38, and Ballard, *Vicksburg*, 269.

15. *OR*, ser. 1, vol. 24, part 1: 50–51. Major General William T. Sherman's 15th Corps simultaneously attacked the Rebel defenses from the southwest. See *OR*, ser. 1, vol. 24, part 1: 753–54. Grant wrote, "Crocker moved his division forward, preceded by a strong skirmish line. These troops at once encountered the enemy's advance and drove it back on the main body, when they returned to their proper regiment and the whole division charged, routing the enemy completely and driving him into his main line" (Grant, *Memoirs*, 297). In describing the charge of Crocker's forces, another soldier of the 48th Indiana noted: "The order was given, we went with a Hoosier yell that was heard three miles. Cannon balls boomed through the air, shells screeched and bullets whistled, but on we went" (Ballard, *Vicksburg*, 278, 453).

16. General Grant ordered Major General James B. McPherson's 17th Corps to retrace their route to Clinton to defend against the likelihood that Pemberton's forces would attack from Vicksburg. See *OR*, ser. 1, vol. 24, part 1: 50–51. General Johnston, who commanded at Jackson on the 14th and who retreated away from

Union forces, desired Pemberton to venture out of Vicksburg to strike at Grant's rear. But Johnston had retired to Canton, Mississippi, too far away to be of help to Pemberton. Wentworth, *Jefferson Davis and His Generals*, 207–8, and Ballard, *Vicksburg*, 279–80.

17. Brigadier General Alvin P. Hovey, Indiana attorney, judge, and Democratic politician, entered the service as Colonel of the 24th Indiana. At Champion Hill he commanded the 12th Division of McClernand's 13th Corps. After the war he served as governor of Indiana from 1889 to 1891.

18. "During all this time, Hovey, reinforced as he was by a brigade from Logan and another from Crocker, and by Crocker gallantly coming up with two other brigades on his right, had made several assaults, the last one about the time the road was opened to the rear. The enemy fled precipitately" (Grant, *Memoirs*, 304).

19. Confederate losses at Champion Hill totaled about thirty-eight hundred killed, wounded, and missing; of those, about twenty-four hundred were prisoners or deserted. Union losses were about twenty-four hundred (Ballard, *Vicksburg*, 308). The 48th lost three killed and thirty-three wounded.

20. Brigadier General Peter J. Osterhaus was a Prussian Army officer who after participating in the 1848 revolution in Germany fled to the United States and settled in Illinois, moving later to St. Louis, Missouri. He commanded the 9th Division in McClernand's 13th Corps.

21. Brigadier General Eugene Asa Carr commanded the 14th Division in the 13th Corps during the Vicksburg campaign.

22. Pemberton's army retreated toward Vicksburg, away from Johnston's forces near Canton, and constructed a line of works east of the railroad bridge over the Big Black River. The engagement at Big Black River on May 17 involving McClernand's 13th Corps produced over seventeen hundred Southern prisoners, while Northern forces suffered less than three hundred casualties. The Rebels destroyed the railroad bridge behind them and made for Vicksburg's fortifications (Ballard, *Vicksburg*, 318). Grant wrote, "I have but little doubt that we should have followed the enemy so closely as to prevent his occupying his defenses around Vicksburg" (Grant, *Memoirs*, 308).

23. Johnston's forces still lurked northeast of Grant's army. Johnston had ordered Pemberton to evacuate Vicksburg, and positioned himself north and east of the city to assist the escape. However, Pemberton followed his instructions from Confederate President Davis to hold the city (Ballard, *Vicksburg*, 325–26; Wentworth, *Jefferson Davis and His Generals*, 210–11).

24. Grant ordered Sherman's corps to occupy the Union right, McPherson's corps in the center, and McClernand's corps on the left, encircling the city and its fortifications, with naval forces on the river (Grant, *Memoirs*, 309–10).

25. Wood refers to the assault of May 22. An assault was also made on May 19, involving troops of Sherman's and part of McPherson's corps, but it failed with nearly one thousand casualties. The 48th Indiana did not participate in that attack (Ballard, *Vicksburg*, 326–32).

26. McClernand reported to Grant during the assault of May 22 that his forces had seized two Rebel forts in the ring of fortifications, but needed reinforcements

to press past rifle pits in their rear. Grant ordered Quinby's division of McPherson's Corps to reinforce McClernand. See *OR*, ser. 1, vol. 24, part 1: 54–56. See also Ballard, *Vicksburg*, 343–44, 346–47. The 48th Indiana participated in the assault on the 2nd Texas Lunette fortification. See map 67 in Grabau, *Ninety-eight Days*.

27. The regiment that the 48th Indiana reinforced was a part of Brigadier General Stephen G. Burbridge's brigade, though which regiment is not clear. See Wood's letter published in the *Goshen Democrat* of June 24, 1863, in appendix A. Burbridge, whose brigade had been badly battered on the lunette, believed the reinforcements were actually to relieve his troops in the assault, a belief that Wood evidently shared. Burbridge withdrew his force (Ballard, *Vicksburg*, 347).

28. The 48th Indiana lost eight killed and twenty-four wounded in the frontal assault. No report for the 48th covering the assault appears in the *OR*. See Sanborn's report for his brigade in *OR*, ser. 1, vol. 24, part 1: 732–34. See also *OR*, ser. 1, vol. 24, part 2: 62. Grant blamed McClernand for misleading him into additional assaults on May 22, resulting in heavy casualties. See *OR*, ser. 1, vol. 24, part 1: 37–38.

29. The army served a whiskey ration to soldiers on work details until 1865. See Edward M. Coffman, *The Old Army: A Portrait of the American Army in Peacetime, 1784–1898* (New York: Oxford University Press, 1986), 443n.

30. The 14th New York Infantry, a two-year regiment, mustered out of the Army of the Potomac in May 1863. That army, under Major General Joseph Hooker, had been defeated in the bloody battle of Chancellorsville, May 2–3, 1863. See Stephen W. Sears, *Chancellorsville* (Boston: Houghton Mifflin, 1996), and Gary W. Gallagher, *Chancellorsville: The Battle and Its Aftermath* (Chapel Hill: University of North Carolina Press, 1996).

31. Major General Francis P. Blair Jr., son of a close friend of President Abraham Lincoln and brother of Lincoln's postmaster general, was a Missouri congressman at the start of the war and was soon appointed a general after recruiting several regiments. For information on the expedition, see *OR*, ser. 1, vol. 24, part 1: 40, and Ballard, *Vicksburg*, 361, 390–91.

32. *New York Herald*.

33. Alexander the Great, Macedonian king, during his conquest of Persia in 333 BCE reached Gordium, in present-day Turkey, and was presented with an intricately tied knot around the yoke of a chariot. Local belief was that the person who untied the knot would be the conqueror of Asia. After fumbling with the knot and failing to find its ends, Alexander chopped through it with his sword (Peter Green, *Alexander of Macedon, 356–323 b.c.: A Historical Biography* [Berkeley: University of California Press, 1991], 213–14).

34. Johnston had received reinforcements and now commanded about twenty-three thousand troops near Jackson and Canton, Mississippi. See Woodworth, *Jefferson Davis and His Generals*, 210–16, and Ballard, *Vicksburg*, 390; Craig L. Symonds, *Joseph E. Johnston: A Civil War Biography* (New York: Norton, 1992).

35. Confederate troops and civilians in Vicksburg suffered for want of food (Ballard, *Vicksburg*, 382–83).

36. Brigadier General Marcellus M. Crocker of Iowa commanded a division in the Vicksburg campaign.

37. A parody of Hamlet's famous act 3, sc. 1 soliloquy in William Shakespeare's play, *Hamlet*.

38. Grant received reinforcements from several points, including the 9th Corps from Major General Ambrose E. Burnside's Department of the Ohio.

39. Brigadier General Milo S. Hascall on April 22, 1863, was appointed commander of the military District of Indiana by General Burnside. In an effort to suppress antiadministration dissent in Indiana, the general promulgated a military order banning such speech. He then arrested several Democratic newspaper editors, shut down their newspapers, and threatened others if they continued to criticize the administration and the army. Indiana Governor Oliver P. Morton chafed at this military infringement into political matters, and successfully lobbied the Lincoln administration to pressure Burnside to remove him. This was done June 5, 1863. See Stephen E. Towne, "Killing the Serpent Speedily: Governor Morton, General Hascall, and the Suppression of the Democratic Press in Indiana, 1863," *Civil War History* 52 (March 2006): 41–65. Burnside had shut down the virulently anti-Lincoln Chicago *Times* on June 1, 1863, but rescinded his order shortly thereafter under political pressure. See Craig D. Tenney, "To Suppress or Not to Suppress: Abraham Lincoln and the Chicago Times," *Civil War History* 27 (September 1981): 248–59.

40. H. G. Hale resided in Goshen. Wood's letter to him was printed in the *Goshen Democrat* of June 24, 1863. See appendix A.

41. Quartermaster Mark Tucker, Lieutenant Colonel Albert Heath, and Captain Ruel M. Johnson, all of the 100th Indiana Volunteer Infantry regiment, arrived as part of the detachment of the 16th Corps sent as reinforcements from Memphis, Tennessee.

42. "Confederate desertions convinced Grant's men that victory was certain" (Ballard, *Vicksburg*, 381–82).

43. The identity of this person is unknown. Governor Morton in the course of the war dispatched agents in various capacities to the Indiana troops in the field, often to assess their medical and supply conditions, but also to communicate political and military information.

44. Thousands of letters of Union soldiers were published in Northern hometown newspapers during the Civil War. These letters contained information ranging from the mundane to graphic details of battlefield carnage and the specifics of troop movements. Many soldiers wrote directly to the newspaper, while many private letters written to family and friends found their way into print either *in toto* or excerpted. Wood's letter to his friend H. G. Hale was published in the *Goshen Democrat* in this fashion. See appendix A.

45. The most notable attempt to breach the fortifications was the explosion of a mine dug under the Rebel lines on June 25 and an assault by two regiments. After fierce hand-to-hand fighting the assault failed (Grant, *Memoirs*, 324–25, and Ballard, *Vicksburg*, 367–69).

46. General Rosecrans's Army of the Cumberland had days before begun his noted Tullahoma campaign of maneuver that forced General Bragg's Confederate Army of Tennessee to retreat southward into northern Georgia. See Lamers, *The Edge of Glory*, 270–91.

47. Confederate Lieutenant General Robert E. Lee had begun a foray into Pennsylvania in late June 1863, and threatened the state capital of Harrisburg.

48. Antiwar sentiment in the North surged in the spring and summer of 1863, as Union defeats and the rising toll of dead and wounded played on Northern sentiment already soured on the new Federal conscription law. Democratic Party leaders increased their calls for a negotiated settlement with the Rebel South. A leading voice in the Old Northwest for an end to the war was former Ohio Congressman Clement L. Vallandigham. Arrested by General Burnside for treasonable speech in Ohio and tried by military commission, he was sent over the lines to the South. He later ran for governor of Ohio from exile in Canada. See Frank L. Klement, *The Limits of Dissent: Clement L. Vallandigham and the Civil War* (Lexington: University Press of Kentucky, 1970).

49. Major General Joseph Hooker commanded the Army of the Potomac from January to late June 1863, during which time his army was defeated by Lee at Chancellorsville, Virginia, in May 1863. Hooker lost more than twenty thousand men from the Army of the Potomac when the nine-months and two-years enlistment men mustered out.

50. Congress passed an Enrollment Act in March 1863 to establish a federally run draft of able-bodied white men in the Northern states. However, draft enrollment officers in many states, including Indiana, encountered violent resistance from many unwilling to be enrolled and drafted, as well as from deserters. In the summer of 1863 the federal government hit upon the short-term expedient—one of several during the war—of raising a force of six-months regiments to augment the armies in the field. A number of regiments were raised that saw limited action in Burnside's East Tennessee campaign and others. See James W. Geary, *We Need Men: The Union Draft in the Civil War* (Dekalb: Northern Illinois University Press, 1991).

51. Confederate General Pemberton had consulted his generals about the possibility of fighting their way out of Vicksburg, but their answer was that it could not succeed. On July 3 he sent a message to General Grant to arrange terms for surrender. Grant insisted on "unconditional surrender," but allowed the captured Rebels to be released on parole, with officers retaining their side arms. Union troops marched into the city on the Fourth (Ballard, *Vicksburg*, 396–99; Grant, *Memoirs*, 327–33).

52. "On the third [of July], as soon as negotiations were commenced, I notified Sherman and directed him to be ready to take the offensive against Johnston, drive him out of the State and destroy his army if he could" (Grant, *Memoirs*, 333).

53. General Grant's release of the prisoners on parole was not looked on favorably by the War Department in Washington, and the general was ordered not to release them. However, the release was made before General Halleck's order was received (Grant, *Memoirs*, 336–37).

54. Lee's invasion of Pennsylvania ended in his defeat at Gettysburg and retreat to Virginia after a bloody three-day battle, July 1–3, 1863.

55. Colonel Elisha P. Watkins had entered Confederate service in June 1861, as quartermaster of the 9th Georgia Volunteer Infantry regiment. He was wounded at Champion Hill.

Chapter 8

1. Marszalek, *Sherman*, 227–31; Grant, *Memoirs*, 339–40; William Tecumseh Sherman, *Memoirs of General William T. Sherman* (New York: Library of America, 1990; based on second edition published in 1886), 354–58.

2. See Morton to Colonel James B. Fry, October 7, 1863, in Governor Oliver P. Morton Telegraphic Correspondence, vol. 5: 18–20, Indiana State Archives. The telegraph is reprinted in *OR*, ser. 3, vol. 3: 865–66.

3. The letter of July 26, 1863, is missing.

4. Colonel Eddy's resignation was dated July 11, 1863.

5. Captain Barnet Byrkit, Company F, of Mishawaka, was promoted to major on August 13, 1863, backdated to April 25, 1863.

6. Officers were appointed to serve as judges for trials of military personnel for various offenses.

7. Sherman's 15th Corps did not stay at Vicksburg, but pursued Johnston to the east and encamped about twenty miles east of the city to rest.

8. Riots occurred in New York City July 13–17, 1863, after the drawing of names for the Federal draft on the eleventh. Exacerbated by underemployment, inflation, ethnic tensions, and a fear that freed slaves were to take away employment at cut rates, workers attacked a draft office and other offices and people who symbolized the threat to labor. African Americans in the city became especial targets of violence by the largely Irish Catholic rioters. Troops from the Army of the Potomac and elsewhere arrived, and order gradually was restored. More than one hundred persons died in the riots. While New York Governor Horatio Seymour, a Democrat, generally supported President Lincoln's war measures, he spoke against the Emancipation Proclamation, military arrests of civilians, and the Federal draft as improper extensions of Federal power. Seymour made conciliatory gestures to the rioters, acts that provoked Republican newspapers to brand him a Copperhead traitor. See Iver Bernstein, *The New York City Draft Riots: Their Significance for American Society and Politics in the Age of the Civil War* (New York: Oxford University Press, 1990).

9. Byrkit left on leave August 11.

10. A prevalent view of disease transmission held that disease floated in the air, often released from the ground when the earth was disturbed by agriculture or other activities. See John Duffy, *The Sanitarians: A History of American Public Health* (Urbana: University of Illinois Press, 1990), 67–68.

11. John B. Sanborn was promoted to brigadier general in August 1863, and served in Missouri and Arkansas later in the war. Colonel Jesse I. Alexander, 59th Indiana Volunteer Infantry regiment, of Gosport, assumed command of the brigade.

12. Redfield Proctor, Dartmouth College class of 1851, was appointed colonel of the 15th Vermont Volunteer Infantry regiment, a nine-months-service unit. An owner of extensive marble mines in Vermont, he was governor of the state 1878–80, and was appointed secretary of war in President Benjamin Harrison's

administration. Afterwards, he served as U.S. senator from Vermont for seventeen years until his death in 1908.

13. Nathan Lord (1792–1870) served as president of Dartmouth College from 1828 to 1863. Professor James W. Patterson did not succeed him.

14. In 1863 the War Department authorized the formation of an Invalids Corps, composed of soldiers, either wounded or ill, who were considered unfit for active campaigning but able to do other service. Soldiers' misgivings about the name prompted the change to the Veteran Reserve Corps. See Paul A. Cimbala, "Soldiering on the Homefront: The Veteran Reserve Corps and the Northern People," in Cimbala and Miller, *Union Soldiers and the Northern Home Front*, 182–218.

15. Major General Frederick Steele served in the western theater during the war. After Vicksburg's fall, he commanded the Army of Arkansas and seized Little Rock on September 10, 1863. See *OR*, ser. 1, vol. 22, part 2: 432ff. See also Thomas A. DeBlack, *With Fire and Sword: Arkansas, 1861–1874* (Fayetteville: University of Arkansas Press, 2003), 91–99.

16. Morton's correspondence to the War Department regarding the 48th Indiana is not found.

17. After brilliantly maneuvering Rebel forces out of Tennessee in the Tullahoma campaign, Rosecrans's Army of the Cumberland suffered defeat in northwestern Georgia at the battle of Chickamauga, September 19–20, 1863, when Rebel forces under Braxton Bragg, reinforced with troops from Virginia, struck back. Rosecrans's army retreated to Chattanooga, Tennessee. Bragg besieged the Union Army there. See Lamers, *The Edge of Glory*, 318–61, and Peter Cozzens, *This Terrible Sound: The Battle of Chickamauga* (Urbana: University of Illinois Press, 1992).

18. Major General Stephen A. Hurlbut, a Republican politician from Illinois before the war, fought in the battles of Fort Donelson and Shiloh, and the Corinth campaign. He commanded at Memphis until April 1864. See Jeffrey N. Lash, *A Politician Turned General: The Civil War Career of Stephen Augustus Hurlbut* (Kent, Ohio: Kent State University Press, 2003), 128–31.

19. Brigadier General John E. Smith, an Illinois politician before the war and friend of Ulysses Grant from Galena, formerly colonel of the 45th Illinois. For Smith's orders to move his division to Helena and then to move to reinforce Rosecrans, see *OR* ser. 1, vol. 30, part 3: 621, 640, and 774.

20. The 7th Division was renumbered the 2nd Division on September 14 when it reported at Helena. When it later joined Sherman's 15th Corps it was renamed the 3rd Division. However, Wood continued to refer to it as the "Old 7th." See Welcher, *The Union Army*, 284, 306–7. Wood's reference to "making" major generals is not clear. Previous commanders of the division—Quinby, Crocker, and Smith—all served as brigadier generals, and either did not attain major general rank or did so after Wood's comment.

21. Charles S. Blood left Dartmouth in 1851 and entered business in St. Louis. He died of tuberculosis in 1867.

22. Henry Shaw (1800–1889), born in England and a longtime resident of St. Louis, opened the Missouri Botanical Gardens in 1859 outside the city. See William B.

Faherty, *Henry Shaw: His Life and Legacies* (Columbia: University of Missouri Press, 1987).

Chapter 9

1. See Peter Cozzens, *The Shipwreck of Their Hopes: The Battles for Chattanooga* (Urbana: University of Illinois Press, 1994).

2. Grant, *Memoirs,* 348.

3. Ibid., 337.

4. Sherman received orders from Grant to march to the relief of Chattanooga on September 27, 1863. See Grant, *Memoirs,* 343.

5. General Rosecrans was relieved of command of the besieged army in Chattanooga on October 28, 1863. Grant, now commander of all Union forces in the West, assumed command.

6. Morton to Colonel James B. Fry, October 7, 1873, Governor Oliver P. Morton Telegraph Books, vol. 5: 18–20, and *OR,* ser. 3, vol. 3: 865–66.

7. The Nashville and Chattanooga Railroad.

8. Erastus Winter Hewitt Ellis, of Goshen.

9. "Weeping, Sad and Lonely; or, When This Cruel War Is Over," words by Charles S. Sawyer and music by Henry Tucker, a popular song published in New York in 1863. The chorus of the song:

> Weeping, sad and lonely,
> Hopes and fears how vain!
> Yet praying when this cruel war is over,
> Praying that we meet again!

10. State elections on November 3, 1863, produced Republican victories around New York state, and a reduction of the Democratic majority in New York City. See *The New York Times,* November 4, 1863. Major General John Sedgwick, commanding two corps of the Army of the Potomac, won an inconclusive battle at Rappahannock Bridge on November 7, 1863. See *OR,* ser. 1, vol. 29, part 1: 574–75, and Freeman Cleaves, *Meade of Gettysburg* (Norman: University of Oklahoma Press, 1960, rpt. Dayton, Ohio: Morningside Bookshop, 1980), 203–4. In Arkansas, Union forces drove out Rebel troops from most of the state. Southwestern Arkansas later served as a base for Rebel raids north as far north as Missouri.

11. Major General David S. Stanley served as chief of cavalry in the Army of the Cumberland from November 1862 to shortly before the battles around Chattanooga, when he commanded an infantry division. With Union forces approaching and increasing in strength around Chattanooga, Bragg's subordinates advised him to withdraw from the area (Cozzens, *The Shipwreck of Their Hopes,* 104).

12. Brigadier General Quincy Adams Gillmore commanded the Department of the South and led efforts to capture the island forts guarding Charleston, South Carolina, in September 1863.

13. With significant portions of the Rebel states in Union control in 1863, President Lincoln and Congress were faced with the task of wartime reconstruction

of political life within the national union. Views as to the proper policy divided the majority Republican Party. For treatments of Reconstruction policy making, see John Hope Franklin, *Reconstruction after the Civil War* (Chicago: University of Chicago Press, 1961), and Eric Foner, *Reconstruction: America's Unfinished Revolution, 1863–1877* (New York: Harper and Row, 1988).

14. Captain Joseph A. S. Mitchell of Goshen commanded Company M.

15. "There was no organized force of the rebel army north of the Tennessee River, but the country was full of guerrillas" (Sherman, *Memoirs*, 385).

16. Jefferson C. Davis commanded the 2nd Division of the 14th Corps.

17. Joseph Hooker had been sent from the Army of the Potomac with the 11th and 12th Corps, totaling about fifteen thousand troops. He commanded the assault on Lookout Mountain on November 24, 1863 (Cozzens, *The Shipwreck of Their Hopes*, 18). Major General George H. Thomas commanded the Army of the Cumberland in Chattanooga, replacing Rosecrans. Thomas's leadership during the retreat after the battle of Chickamauga was largely responsible for maintaining order in the army that prevented a rout. See Cozzens, *This Terrible Sound*, 520–21.

18. See Sherman's official report of December 19, 1863, in *OR* ser, 1, v01,31, part 2: 572, also reprinted in his *Memoirs*, 400.

19. Brigadier General Morgan L. Smith, a New York native and one-time resident of Indiana, commanded the 2nd Division of the 15th Corps.

20. Brigadier General Hugh B. Ewing, brother-in-law of General Sherman, commanded the 4th Division of the 15th Corps.

21. Colonel Alexander's brigade, including the 48th Indiana, was part of Sherman's reserve force on the hill. See Sherman, *Memoirs*, 402.

22. Lieutenant Colonel Albert Heath of the 100th Indiana was in Ewing's 4th Division.

23. While Sherman's troops engaged the Rebels at the northern end of Missionary Ridge, Thomas's force marched out of Chattanooga and advanced up the side of the ridge, drawing Bragg's forces away from Sherman. "It was not until night closed in that I knew that the troops in Chattanooga had swept across Missionary Ridge and broken the enemy's centre. Of course, the victory was won, and pursuit was the next step" (Sherman, *Memoirs*, 404). Confederate Lieutenant General James Longstreet was ordered west with his corps of the Army of Northern Virginia to reinforce Bragg before the battle of Chickamauga. Prior to the battles around Chattanooga, he and his troops were sent away to besiege Union General Ambrose Burnside's Army of the Ohio at Knoxville, Tennessee. Peter Cozzens argues that "[h]ad President Davis not suggested and Bragg not acceded to sending Longstreet off on his quixotic expedition toward Knoxville, Bragg could have disposed his forces" to have a "strong, mobile reserve" that would have been able to stop Federal forces on Missionary Ridge. See Cozzens, *The Shipwreck of Their Hopes*, 390.

24. Sherman, *Memoirs*, 405.

25. The strap around a horse's belly to hold on a blanket or saddle.

26. Jo Wood's identity is not known.

27. Major General David Hunter, an avowed abolitionist, formerly commander of the occupied areas of Florida, Georgia, and South Carolina constituting the Department of the South, had surprised and outraged many in both North and South when in May 1862 he declared the emancipation of slaves under his jurisdiction. He also organized the first African American fighting unit. Lincoln relieved him of his command. See Grimsley, *The Hard Hand of War,* 127–28. Hunter performed inspection duties for more than a year thereafter until given a new command in 1864. See Edward A. Miller Jr., *Lincoln's Abolitionist General: The Biography of David Hunter* (Columbia: University of South Carolina Press, 1997), 157–61.

Chapter 10

1. See Grant, *Memoirs,* 399; Sherman, *Memoirs,* 413; and Marszalek, *Sherman,* 247–50.

2. Goshen *Times,* February 17 and March 3, 1864.

3. Captain Jasper Packard of LaPorte had formerly been first lieutenant of Company D, but in September 1862 was promoted to the captaincy of Company B. After being discharged for wounds received, in March 1864 he became lieutenant colonel of the 128th Indiana. After the war he served three terms in the U.S. House of Representatives.

4. Bragg's army took up defensive positions near Dalton, Georgia. Confederate President Jefferson Davis replaced Bragg with Joseph Johnston on December 27, 1863 (Wentworth, *Jefferson Davis and His Generals,* 256–59). After their success at Chattanooga, Grant had dispatched Sherman and part of his command to Knoxville to track Longstreet and relieve Burnside. Longstreet withdrew to the north, and Burnside pursued him. Sherman's troops then marched back to Chattanooga and distributed along the railroads between Nashville, northern Alabama, and Chattanooga (Sherman, *Memoirs,* 408–13; Marvel, *Burnside,* 281–334).

5. Sherman actually planned a march through Mississippi, a plan that was realized in the Meridian campaign of February–March 1864. See Marszalek, *Sherman,* 246–51. Grant had envisioned and proposed an offensive aimed at Mobile, Alabama, shortly after Vicksburg fell, but Washington turned it down. See Grant, *Memoirs,* 340–41.

6. Moses T. Runnels, Dartmouth class of 1853, was a Congregational pastor at Orford, New Hampshire.

7. Brigadier General George Crook commanded a cavalry division at Chickamauga. Confederate Major General Nathan Bedford Forrest was perhaps the Confederacy's most effective cavalry commander, winning many battles and tying down thousands of Union troops in garrisons in the occupied South. In December 1863 Forrest was operating behind Federal lines in western Tennessee, recruiting and obtaining livestock to feed Confederate troops. See Jack Hurst, *Nathan Bedford Forrest: A Biography* (New York: Knopf, 1994), 143–44.

8. Wood's understanding of the arrangements was incorrect. The thirty-day furlough would be the entirety of the troops' sojourn at home.

9. The 48th Indiana's Regimental Descriptive Book listed Wood at five-feet-eight-and-one-half-inches tall. The image in *Harper's Illustrated Weekly* depicts a large, burly, bearded soldier towering over a small woman.

10. Logan's edict was unilateral, and not supported by War Department instructions. Wood's telegram to Morton does not survive. Other Indiana commanders at Huntsville complained to Morton about Logan's order. See Colonel John T. Wilder to Morton, December 30, 1863; Governor Oliver P. Morton Telegraph Books, vol. 13: 3–5, Indiana State Archives.

11. A severe cold snap at the beginning of 1864 brought subzero temperatures throughout the eastern United States and the South.

12. Wood and many other soldiers in the Federal armies developed a strongly bitter antipathy to the civilians at home, especially antiwar Democrats who supported a peace settlement with the Confederacy and opposed the various war measures initiated by Congress and the Lincoln administration to put down the rebellion. Many soldiers acted out their anger toward the "fire in the rear" antiwar population with violence directed at Democrats, Democratic speakers, and Democratic newspapers. Violence against Democratic newspapers in Indiana during the war was done primarily by soldiers. Soldiers on furlough in the early months of 1864 were especially dangerous to newspapers. See Stephen E. Towne, "Works of Indiscretion: Violence Against the Democratic Press in Indiana during the Civil War," *Journalism History* 31 (Fall 2005): 138–49. For works on the ideological formation of Northern soldiers during the rebellion, see James M. McPherson, *For Cause and Comrades: Why Men Fought in the Civil War* (New York: Oxford University Press, 1997); Joseph Allan Frank, *With Ballot and Bayonet: The Political Socialization of American Civil War Soldiers* (Athens: University of Georgia Press, 1998); and Reid Mitchell, *The Vacant Chair: The Northern Soldiers Leaves Home* (New York: Oxford University Press, 1993).

13. No lieutenant on the rosters of the 48th Indiana died in the summer of 1863.

14. The 48th Indiana had been issued a combination of Enfield rifles and rifled muskets, "Whitney rifles," in November 1861 and February 1862. See Indiana Quartermaster General Ordnance Book, Indiana State Archives. In July 1862 the regiment exchanged arms with the 26th Missouri, another regiment in their brigade, and were then uniformly armed with Whitneys. In April 1864 the regiment handed in their worn-out Whitneys and received new Springfield rifles. See letter of "H.J.P." in the Goshen *Times*, May 19, 1864.

15. Psalm 91:6: "Nor for the pestilence that walketh in darkness; nor for the destruction that wasteth at noonday" (King James Version).

Chapter 11

1. Wentworth, *Jefferson Davis and His Generals*, 277–79.

2. Marszalek, *Sherman*, 255. The Meridian campaign was another outlet to exhibit what historian Michael Fellman argues were the more destructive impulses in Sherman's character. See Michael Fellman, *Citizen Sherman: A Life of William*

Tecumseh Sherman (New York: Random House, 1995), 173–74. See also Lee Kennett, *Sherman: A Soldier's Life* (New York: HarperCollins, 2001).

3. Captain Willard P. Allen of Elkhart, Company A.

4. Captain Park Wheeler of the 149th New York State Volunteer Infantry regiment.

5. Van Dorn, a noted philanderer, was shot by Dr. George B. Peters on May 6, 1863, for having an affair with his wife. Van Dorn died the following day. See Carter, *The Tarnished Cavalier,* 186–95.

6. Major Thomas A. McNaught of Spencer.

7. James K. Polk (1795–1849), eleventh president of the United States, 1845–49.

8. Confederate forces nearby were actively probing Federal defenses at this time. See *OR,* ser. 1, vol. 32, part 1: 657–58.

9. Lieutenant Colonel E. D. Kittoe of Galena, Illinois, formerly surgeon of the 45th Illinois.

10. Major General Henry W. Slocum commanded the 12th Corps.

11. Byron, *Childe Harold's Pilgrimage* (1818), canto 3, stanza 24: "Ah! Then and there was hurrying to and fro; / And gathering tears, and trembling distress, / And cheeks all pale, which but an hour ago / Blush'd at the praise of their own lovliness."

12. Forrest was at this time in western Tennessee and involved in his infamous attack on Fort Pillow, where the African American garrison were murdered after surrendering to the Rebels. See Hurst, *Nathan Bedford Forrest,* 165–79, and essays by David J. Coles and Albert Castel in Gregory J. W. Urwin, ed., *Black Flag over Dixie: Racial Atrocities and Reprisals in the Civil War* (Carbondale: Southern Illinois University Press, 2004).

13. See *OR,* ser. 1, vol. 32, part 3: 355–56.

14. Lieutenant Colonel John P. Hall, 56th Illinois Volunteer Infantry regiment.

15. Harriet Beecher Stowe published "House and Home Papers" serially in the *Atlantic Monthly* magazine beginning in 1864. The novel appeared in book form in 1869.

16. A cestus was a belt or girdle, often worn by a bride.

17. Gilman L. Sessions, Dartmouth College class of 1853, was an attorney in Binghamton, New York.

18. Edward L. Clark, *Daleth; or, the Homestead of the Nations, Egypt Illustrated,* was published in 1864.

19. Sherman, *Memoirs,* 493.

20. John W. Smith of Middlebury was the 48th Indiana's first and only chaplain, joining the regiment in March 1864.

21. First Lieutenant Thomas J. Collins of South Bend was soon promoted to captain. For another account of the camp beautification contest, see the letter of "H.J.P." in the Goshen *Times,* May 19, 1864.

22. Camp Morton in Indianapolis had since March 1862 held thousands of Rebel prisoners of war. Many of the prisoners swore oaths of allegiance and entered Fed-

eral service during the war. However, many subsequently deserted. See Richard Nelson Current, *Lincoln's Loyalists: Union Soldiers from the Confederacy* (New York: Oxford University Press, 1992), 111–32.

23. On the eve of advancing against Johnston's forces, General Sherman forbade disclosure of troop strength, organization, and movement information in private letters and the press in a vain attempt to keep military intelligence from the Rebels. See Marszalek, *Sherman's Other War*, 177–79.

24. Sherman's advance into Georgia against Confederate forces under Joseph Johnston began in the first days of May 1864.

25. Wood frequently considered bringing his wife (and child) to stay with him while posted for any duration at a given place. The practice of officers' wives joining their husbands was not uncommon. For a study of women's presence near the front lines, see Jane E. Schultz, *Women at the Front: Hospital Workers in Civil War America* (Chapel Hill: University of North Carolina Press, 2004).

26. Major General Lovell H. Rousseau.

27. Grant was promoted to lieutenant general and general-in-chief in March 1864. Moving east to direct Union efforts in Virginia, he initiated attacks in the Wilderness campaign in early May 1864.

28. Crocker commanded a division in the 17th Corps until May 1864, when his tuberculosis prompted him to resign. Sherman instead sent him to New Mexico to try to rally his health. He died in 1865.

29. Byron, *Childe Harold's Pilgrimage* (1818), canto 3, stanza 25: "And there was mounting in hot haste—the steed, / The mustering squadron, and the clattering car, / Went pouring forward with impetuous speed, / And swiftly forming in the rank of war."

30. See *OR*, ser. 1, vol. 38, part 3: 266–67, 271–72.

31. In a stopgap measure to raise troops when volunteer enlistments were lagging, the War Department authorized the raising of volunteer regiments with enlistments of just one hundred days. The regiments were raised with the object design of relieving veteran troops of rear-guard duties, freeing them to fight at the front. See Jim Leeke, ed., *A Hundred Days to Richmond: Ohio's "Hundred Days" Men in the Civil War* (Bloomington: Indiana University Press, 1999).

32. The battle of Resaca, May 14–15, 1864, was the first of the major engagements in the Atlanta campaign. McPherson's flanking movement around Johnston's left surprised the Rebels on the first day, but the Army of the Tennessee commander did not follow through before Johnston could adjust his forces. Johnston retreated, the first of many such retrograde moves in the coming three months (Marszalek, *Sherman,* 264–65; Albert Castel, *Decision in the West: The Atlanta Campaign of 1864* [Lawrence: University Press of Kansas, 1992], 154–85).

33. Frank Blair resigned his commission to take a seat in the U.S. House of Representatives, where in late February 1864 he gave a scathing speech against the presidential ambitions of Treasury Secretary Salmon P. Chase. Thereafter, Lincoln renominated Blair as a major general. See David E. Long, *The Jewel of Liberty: Abraham Lincoln's Re-election and the End of Slavery* (New York: Da Capo, 1997), 36–37, and

William E. Parrish, *Frank Blair: Lincoln's Conservative* (Columbia: University of Missouri Press, 1998), 186–91.

34. Colonel Benjamin F. Potts, 32nd Ohio; Lieutenant Colonel William P. Davis, 23rd Indiana; Colonel Francis C. Deimling, 10th Missouri; Colonel Edwin S. McCook, 31st Illinois; Lieutenant Colonel Francis M. Smith, 17th Illinois; and Captain J. O. Pullen.

35. The "system of Corps distinctions" was much more advanced in the Army of the Potomac, which during the war led a more sedentary existence than the western armies. Sherman recounted an anecdote during the Chattanooga campaign purporting to be the origin of the 15th Corps badge that highlighted this spirit. "As the men were trudging along the deeply-cut, muddy road, one cold, drizzly day, one of our Western soldiers left his ranks and joined a party of the Twelfth Corps [part of the reinforcements from the Army of the Potomac] at their camp-fire. They got into conversation, the Twelfth Corps men asking what troops we were, etc., etc. In turn, our fellow (who had never seen a corps-badge, and noticed that every thing was marked with a star) asked if they were all brigadier-generals. Of course they were not, but the star was the corps-badge, and every wagon, tent, hat, etc., had its star. Then the Twelfth Corps men inquired what corps he belonged to, and he answered, 'The Fifteenth Corps.' 'What is your badge?' 'Why," he said (and he was an Irishman), suiting the action to the word, 'forty rounds in the cartridge-box, and twenty in the pocket!' At that time Blair commanded the corps; but Logan succeeded soon after, and, hearing the story, adopted the cartridge-box and forty rounds as the corps-badge" (Sherman, *Memoirs*, 389). For enlisted men, the regiment often represented the primary source of identification. See Gerald J. Prokopowicz, *All for the Regiment: The Army of the Ohio, 1861–1862* (Chapel Hill: University of North Carolina Press, 2001).

36. See *OR* ser. 1, vol. 38, part 4: 269, 329, and 341.

37. Confederate Brigadier General Philip D. Roddey. Federal commanders feared a raid on their supply lines, prompting great activity to counteract it. Forrest was at the time in northern Alabama with twenty-two hundred cavalrymen en route to Mississippi (Hurst, *Nathan Bedford Forrest*, 183–85).

38. At the beginning of the war the War Department authorized volunteer regiment bands of up to twenty-four players. However, Congress shed them later in 1862 as an unnecessary expense, but authorized brigade bands of sixteen players. Many units maintained their bands at their own expense. See Richard C. Spicer, "'An Inspiration to All': New Hampshire's Third Regiment and Hilton Head Post Bands in Civil War South Carolina," in Bruce C. Kelley and Mark E. Snell, eds., *Bugle Resounding: Music and Musicians of the Civil War Era* (Columbia: University of Missouri Press, 2004), 74–75.

39. Grant's and Lee's armies had bludgeoned each other for several days in a series of running battles. Grant's famous quote occurred on May 11, 1864, after the battle of Spotsylvania Court House, in a letter to General Halleck that he knew would be given to the press (Grant, *Memoirs*, 473). See also Jean Edward Smith, *Grant* (New York: Simon and Shuster, 2001), 349.

40. On May 2, 1864, an assembly of women in Washington, D.C., formed an association called the Ladies National Covenant to promote the wearing of American-

made clothing and discourage the importation of foreign fabrics. See *New York Times,* May 5, 1864.

41. Shoddy was a common cloth widely available of poor quality. At the beginning of the war, northern clothing manufacturers filled military uniform orders with shoddy, which fell apart quickly in the course of heavy wear and tear. The term came to signify poor quality and poor workmanship. "There was a rich man who was dressed in purple and fine linen and lived in luxury every day" (Luke 16:19, King James Version). The line is the beginning of the story of Lazarus, the begger.

42. Anthony Trollope's novel *The Small House at Allington* first appeared serially in the *Cornhill* magazine in Great Britain in 1862, and in *Harper's Illustrated Weekly* shortly thereafter. The "Easy Chair" was the section of *Harper's* in which letters to the editor appeared.

43. The newspapers from which the clippings were taken are not known.

44. Alexander Selkirk (1676–1721), Scottish seaman, was put ashore on an uninhabited island four hundred miles off South America's western coast and lived there alone for five years until he was discovered by a passing English ship. His story inspired several writers, including Daniel Defoe, who produced *Robinson Crusoe* (1719), and William Cowper's poem, "Lines on Solitude," which began, "I am monarch of all I survey / My right there is none to dispute."

45. General Frank Blair had ordered troops who did not reenlist as veterans to drive the herd of cattle to Chattanooga, where they would then muster out. Blair reported: "No dissatisfaction was expressed until after I left Huntsville, when they mutinied, refusing to go. I telegraphed Brig. Gen. John E. Smith, commanding at Huntsville, to know the circumstances, in order that I might send back enough men to take the cattle through. He, however, telegraphed me that if the non-veterans would not go he would send a regiment from his command, which relieved me from further anxiety on the subject" (*OR* ser. 1, vol. 38, part 3: 540, and Parrish, *Frank Blair,* 196). Chattanooga was the railhead for supplies to be forwarded to Sherman's army in Georgia and a strategic railroad center for both the Rebel and Union causes. See Thomas Weber, *The Northern Railroads in the Civil War, 1861–1865* (New York: King's Crown Press, 1952; rpt. Bloomington: Indiana University Press, 1999), 196–97, and John E. Clark Jr., *Railroads in the Civil War: The Impact of Management on Victory and Defeat* (Baton Rouge: Louisiana State University Press, 2001), 199–200.

46. Proverbs 23:5: "Wilt thou set thine eyes upon that which is not? for riches certainly make themselves wings; they fly away as an eagle toward heaven" (King James Version).

47. Captain Adolphus H. Greene, Company D, of Rensselaer, was promoted to captain April 29, 1864.

48. The newly organized Indiana cavalry regiments had not yet received horses. The arrival of these troops and the one-hundred-days men allowed Sherman to order General John E. Smith's division to Georgia. See Albert Castel, *Decision in the West: The Atlanta Campaign of 1864* (Lawrence: University Press of Kansas, 1992), 213–14.

49. Adjutant John W. Branch of Lafayette.

50. "Now there was there nigh unto the mountains a great herd of swine feeding. And all the devils besought him, saying, Send us into the swine, that we may enter into them. And forthwith Jesus gave them leave. And the unclean spirits went out, and entered into the swine: and the herd ran violently down a steep place into the sea, (they were about two thousand;) and were choked in the sea"

(Mark 5:11–13, King James Version).

51. This may have been Hubert Tyrell, of Goshen, a clerk.

52. Confederate Brigadier General John H. Morgan, a daring cavalry commander, launched a swift raid into eastern Kentucky in May and June 1864. See James A. Ramage, *Rebel Raider: The Life of General John Hunt Morgan* (Lexington: University Press of Kentucky, 1986), 211–25.

53. The report was incorrect. Forrest was planning to attack Union forces in Mississippi, resulting in the battle at Brice's Cross Roads (Hurst, *Nathan Bedford Forrest*, 186–95).

54. Wood's mother, Mrs. Marie Walker, lived on a plantation near Madison.

55. Grant and the Army of the Potomac, true to the plan of keeping Lee engaged so as not to allow him to reinforce Johnston, had been engaged in savage fighting near Cold Harbor, Virginia, for several days. Both armies suffered very heavy casualties. See Ernest B. Furgurson, *Not War But Murder: Cold Harbor, 1864* (New York: Knopf, 2000).

56. Redfield Proctor.

57. Second Lieutenant William R. Ellis, Company I, of Goshen. He was the son of E. W. H. Ellis.

58. Charles Dickens's novel *Our Mutual Friend* was serialized in *Harper's Illustrated Weekly*.

Chapter 12

1. Castel, *Decision in the West*, 523–24. See also Jacob D. Cox, *Atlanta* (1882; rpt. as *Sherman's Battle for Atlanta* [New York: Da Capo, 1994]). Cox commanded a division in the 23rd Corps through most of the campaign.

2. John B. Hood, *Advance and Retreat: Personal Experiences in the United States and Confederate States Armies* (1880; rpt. Lincoln: University of Nebraska Press, 1996).

3. Stevenson, Alabama, was the intersection of the Nashville and Chattanooga and Memphis and Charleston railroads.

4. Park Wheeler of Company D, 149th New York State Volunteer Infantry regiment. After the war he resided in Salina and was Onondaga County treasurer. The 149th New York was one of the units from the Army of the Potomac sent to the relief of Chattanooga in the fall of 1863, and later participated in Sherman's Atlanta campaign and march to Savannah. The *New-York Observer* was a weekly Presbyterian Church newspaper of religious and general news and opinion.

5. "About this time came reports that a large cavalry force of the enemy had passed around our left flank, evidently to strike this very railroad somewhere below Chattanooga. I therefore reinforced the cavalry stationed from Resaca to

Cassville, and ordered forward from Huntsville, Alabama, the infantry division of General John E. Smith, to hold Kingston securely" (Sherman, *Memoirs,* 527). The Western and Atlantic Railroad was the sole source of supplies for Sherman's army during the campaign. Securing its safety was essential for success. "Sherman's campaign was the supreme test for the military railroad organization. . . . Defeat or victory might hinge on military strategy or tactics in actual battle, but adequate supply was necessary to the undertaking of an offensive campaign, and in the Atlanta campaign the sole means of transporting supplies was by railroad" (Weber, *The Northern Railroads in the Civil War,* 199–200).

6. Eliza Alexander, wife of Colonel Alexander. Their oldest daughter was Lelia Alexander. Brain fever could have been either encephalitis or meningitis.

7. Major General James B. McPherson, commander of the Army of the Tennessee, was killed by Rebel fire outside of Atlanta on July 22, 1864. His body was taken to Sherman's field headquarters shortly afterwards, where Sherman wept over it while still directing the battle (Sherman, *Memoirs,* 550–52; Cox, *Sherman's Battle for Atlanta,* 169–70). Sherman is reported to have said, "I expected something to happen to Grant and me, either the Rebels or the newspapers would kill us both, and I looked to McPherson as the man to follow us and finish the war" (Marszalek, *Sherman,* 277–78).

8. Confederate President Jefferson Davis lost confidence in Johnston's leadership, whose constant retreating in the face of Federal assaults frustrated Rebel leadership. Davis fired Johnston on July 17, and replaced him with Lieutenant General John Bell Hood, a corps commander and junior to other generals in the Army of Tennessee. However, Davis chose Hood on the basis of his well-known aggressiveness (Wentworth, *Jefferson Davis and His Generals,* 279–86). Hood immediately attacked Sherman's forces, and, in battles around Atlanta, held up the Union advance. Sherman thereupon besieged the city and fretted about losing troops to the end of their enlistments. Hood's aggression brought heavy casualties and severely weakened his army (Marszalek, *Sherman,* 280).

9. Colonel James C. Lane, 102nd New York Volunteer Infantry regiment. Lane and his regiment participated in the Chattanooga and Atlanta campaigns.

10. William G. Wills's novel *Notice to Quit* was published in London in 1861.

11. Captain Park Wheeler.

12. Grant's and Lee's armies, having slugged it out for three months, settled into trench warfare outside Richmond. An attempt to breach the Rebel lines by exploding a mine beneath their fortifications and charging through the gap failed miserably (later called the battle of the Crater) on July 30, resulting in thousands of Federal casualties (Grant, *Memoirs,* 524–27).

13. Grant had directed Sherman to destroy the Rebel army in Georgia. See T. Harry Williams, *Lincoln and His Generals* (New York: A. A. Knopf, 1952), 307, 337–40; Marszalek, *Sherman,* 263; Castel, *Decision in the West,* 68. However, when Union forces ultimately seized Atlanta in early September 1864, the Confederate Army now under Lieutenant General John B. Hood effectively escaped intact.

14. Colonel Alexander resigned August 12, 1864.

15. Lieutenant Colonel Myron Baker of the 74th Indiana Volunteer Infantry regiment was killed August 5, 1864. See the account of Baker's death in the *Goshen Democrat*, August 17, 1864.

16. Though an avowed abolitionist, Wood rarely commented on slavery and African Americans in his letters. This reference, though mainly pertaining to southern manufactures not produced by slave labor, suggests a racist attitude toward African Americans. This would be consistent with much of white northern abolitionist thought: that slavery was abhorrent not because African Americans were equal to whites but because it debased democratic government in the United States. See V. Jacque Voegeli, *Free but Not Equal: The Midwest and the Negro during the Civil War* (Chicago: University of Chicago Press, 1967).

17. During the Civil War, homespun clothing "became symbols of women's political commitment to the Southern cause." See Mark V. Wetherington, *Plain Folk's Fight: The Civil War and Reconstruction in Piney Woods Georgia* (Chapel Hill: University of North Carolina Press, 2005), 105–11.

18. Confederate cavalry commander Major General Joseph Wheeler left Atlanta on August 10, 1864, with over five thousand troopers on a raid to destroy the railroad line supplying Federal forces in Georgia. Hood, with the approval of Jefferson Davis, authorized the raid as the best chance to stop Sherman from taking Atlanta—that Wheeler's raid would "decide the fate of Atlanta." However, Wheeler inflicted relatively minor damage on the railroad line, which was repaired promptly. Supplies to the Federal army were uninterrupted (Castel, *Decision in the West*, 448–50, 452, 466, 484, 490; Sherman, *Memoirs*, 576).

19. Brigadier General Edward M. McCook commanded a cavalry division during the Atlanta campaign. He was one of the "fighting McCooks," an extended family from Ohio that supplied seventeen officers and several generals to the Union cause.

20. Major General James B. Steedman, an Ohio Democratic newspaperman before the war, commanded the District of Etowah during the Atlanta campaign.

21. Wheeler's raid failed to stop Sherman and force a retreat. Wheeler's force rode into Tennessee to raid supply lines there (Castel, *Decision in the West*, 538–39).

22. Colonel Joseph B. McCown.

23. Lieutenant Colonel William Clark had served as Adjutant General to General McPherson, and continued in that capacity with Major General Oliver O. Howard, who succeeded to the command of the Army of the Tennessee on July 27, 1864.

24. Brigadier General Milo Hascall very effectively commanded a division in the 23rd Corps throughout most of the Atlanta campaign, but resigned in disgust when he was passed over for promotion.

25. See appendix B.

26. Indiana law forbade its troops in the field to vote. Governor Morton tried to bring back many Indiana troops to vote in the October state elections and November's presidential election, but clashed with War Department officials and army commanders. Failing that, units polled themselves and announced the results in order to influence voters at home. Major General George B. McClellan, former commander of the Army of the Potomac, ran as the Democratic nominee for president.

Joseph E. McDonald, a prominent Indianapolis attorney, was the Democratic nominee for governor. See Kenneth M. Stampp, *Indiana Politics during the Civil War* (Indianapolis: Indiana Historical Bureau, 1949; rpt. Bloomington: Indiana University Press, 1978), 250–52; Emma Lou Thornbrough, *The History of Indiana*, vol. 3, *Indiana in the Civil War Era, 1850–1880* (Indianapolis: Indiana Historical Society, 1965), 219–23.

27. Captain Edward W. Metcalfe, Company E, 129th Indiana Volunteer Infantry regiment, of Goshen had formerly been judge of the Court of Common Pleas and Wood's law partner. His wife was Celestine Metcalfe.

28. The identity of Lieutenant Warren is unknown.

29. Hurst, *Nathan Bedford Forrest*, 220–21.

30. With Union forces securely in Atlanta, Hood soon concluded to continue on the offensive by trying to force Sherman to withdraw from Georgia by striking at his supply line. In late September 1864 Hood took his army west and north of the city to engage the weaker Federal garrisons guarding the Western and Atlantic Railroad line. Once in Atlanta, Sherman did not pursue Hood's retreating army aggressively, allowing it to escape and continue its own aggressive plans. Learning that Hood had moved around to the west of Atlanta, Sherman left one corps in the city and, with the rest of his army, set out after the Rebel army, reinforcing the railroad garrisons in the process (Hood, *Advance and Retreat*, 243–46; Marszalek, *Sherman*, 283, 290–91; Sherman, *Memoirs*, 618–22).

31. Lieutenant Colonel John Tourtellotte and Brigadier General John M. Corse.

32. An *abatis* is a belt of felled trees and limbs that forms a protective barrier against infantry and cavalry assaults.

33. Sherman, *Memoirs*, 622–25; Marszalek, *Sherman*, 291–92. Marszalek considers the Allatoona battle the "turning point" of Hood's campaign. See also Thomas P. Nanzig, ed., *The Badax Tigers: From Shiloh to the Surrender with the 18th Wisconsin Volunteers* (Lanham, Md.: Rowman and Littlefield, 2002), 281–88.

34. Major James M. Fisher and First Lieutenant Marcus Amsden.

35. Charles Wolfe, "The Burial of Sir John Moore at Corunna" (1817): "We buried him darkly at dead of night, / The sods with our bayonets turning; / By the struggling moonbeam's misty light / And the lantern dimly burning."

36. Casualties in Confederate Major General Samuel G. French's division of about thirty-three hundred men were about nine hundred.

37. The state and congressional elections of October 1864 produced resounding Republican victories. The victory margins for the Republicans were: Ohio: 54,771; Indiana: 20,883; Pennsylvania: 13,898 (Long, *The Jewel of Liberty*, 286).

38. Although Hood's troops destroyed several miles of the railroad, Sherman's army and engineers were able to repair the tracks and have them operating again within a week (Marszalek, *Sherman*, 292; Weber, *The Northern Railroads in the Civil War*, 203–4).

39. Hood, *Advance and Retreat*, 258–62; Sherman, *Memoirs*, 628–31.

40. Wood's speculation was incorrect. Sherman took another course, giving General George H. Thomas and his army the task of collaring Hood. Instead, Sherman

intended to initiate a march to the Atlantic Ocean at Savannah. See Castel, *Decision in the West*, 552–53; Sherman, *Memoirs*, 631–36. S. Augustus Mitchell (1792–1868) published several editions after 1860 of his *Mitchell's New General Atlas: Containing Maps of the Various Countries of the World.*

41. Mungo Park (1771–1806), Scottish explorer, explored the interior of Africa and wrote *Travels in the Interior Districts of Africa* (1799).

42. Joshua Hill, born in South Carolina, served in the U.S. House of Representatives from 1857 until his resignation in January 1861, representing his Georgia district as a member of the American Party. An opponent of secession, he ran unsuccessfully for governor in 1863. After the war he was an important Georgia unionist. Elected to the U.S. Senate in 1868, he took the oath of allegiance in 1871 and qualified for the office, serving until 1873. Nathaniel Green Foster also served in Congress from the American Party from 1855 to 1857. According to the Baptist pastor of the town during part of the war, Madison, Georgia, had a reputation for loose loyalty to the Confederacy, primarily owing to Hill's influence in the district. See J. R. Kendrick, "A Non-combatant's War Reminiscences," *Atlantic Monthly,* October 1889, 449–63. According to Sherman's *Memoirs,* Hill and Foster came to Atlanta in mid-September under a flag of truce to try to avoid further destruction and desolation in Georgia. They also discussed making overtures to the Confederate Governor Joe Brown to withdraw the state from the Confederacy. Hill's son Legare was killed in fighting near Kingston (Sherman, *Memoirs,* 612–16; Marszalek, *Sherman,* 289; Kennett, *Sherman,* 255–56; Kennett, *Marching through Georgia: The Story of Soldiers and Civilians during Sherman's Campaign* [New York: HarperCollins, 1995], 215). See also Lucien E. Roberts, "The Political Career of Joshua Hill, Georgia Unionist," *Georgia Historical Quarterly* 21 (March 1937): 50–72.

43. The Seminole Indians of Florida fought against the encroachment of European settlement in a series of bloody conflicts in the eighteenth and nineteenth centuries, the most destructive of which was the Seminole War of 1835–42.

44. For a study of civil liberties under the Confederacy, see Mark E. Neely Jr., *Southern Rights: Political Prisoners and the Myth of Confederate Constitutionalism* (Charlottesville: University Press of Virginia, 1999).

45. The Washington Peace Conference, February 4–27, 1861, a failed venture called by the Virginia legislature to revive compromise efforts during the secession crisis. See Robert G. Gunderson, *The Old Gentlemen's Convention: The Washington Peace Conference of 1861* (Madison: University of Wisconsin Press, 1961).

46. Frank T. Bryson of Middlebury, regimental surgeon.

47. Railroad accidents were commonplace during the war. One railroad historian suggested that accidents were few before the war, but that the heavy wear and tear brought about by military traffic prompted a precipitous rise in railroad accidents (Weber, *The Northern Railroads in the Civil War,* 44).

48. The letter does not survive.

49. Wood's letter of October 21, 1864, does not mention the cavalry raid of Federal Major General George H. Stoneman in late July 1864. The purpose of the raid was to destroy the railroad connecting Atlanta southward to Macon. The raid failed, and

Stoneman and much of his force were captured on July 31, 1864. See Castel, *Decision in the West*, 437–42. Other than the troopers burning cotton and the railroad in Madison, the Stoneman raid produced no depredations on the civilian population of the town. See Kendrick, "A Non-combatant's War Reminiscences," 458.

50. Brigadier General Alexander S. Asboth commanded the District of West Florida from headquarters in Pensacola. In the course of a cavalry raid to release Federal prisoners held at Marianna, his troopers fought a small but protracted battle against Marianna's militia on September 27, 1864. See *OR*, ser. 1, vol. 35, part 1: 444–45.

51. Hascall's resignation was dated October 27, 1864. He returned to Goshen to enter banking and other business endeavors.

52. Hood and his army were at the time in northern Alabama and contemplating an advance into Tennessee and Kentucky to recruit his forces. Sherman had turned over the task of dealing with Hood's army to Major General George H. Thomas, commander of the Army of the Cumberland, sending reinforcements to Nashville. Sherman also himself destroyed the railroad line between Chattanooga and Atlanta to cut his army off from a quick strike from Hood. Sherman's army would thereafter forage off the land (Hood, *Advance and Retreat*, 263–71; Sherman, *Memoirs*, 637–39; Marszalek, *Sherman*, 296–97).

53. Edward P. Stanfield of South Bend. His Civil War letters are to be found in the Indiana Historical Society, but the letter in question does not survive with them. Norman Eddy resumed his law practice in South Bend.

54. *Dartmouth College Class Memorial of 1853*, comp. Runnels.

55. Captain Philip Buck of Bloomfield, Indiana.

56. After much correspondence and serious misgivings, Grant gave his approval for Sherman's project to march to Savannah on November 2, 1864 (Sherman, *Memoirs*, 641; Grant, *Memoirs*, 549–52; Marszalek, *Sherman*, 294–96).

57. Hood's army reached Tuscumbia, Alabama, on October 31, 1864, poised to march north into Tennessee (Hood, *Advance and Retreat*, 271).

Chapter 13

1. See Richard O'Connor, *Thomas: Rock of Chickamauga* (New York: Prentice-Hall, 1948), 295–324, and James Lee McDonough, *Nashville: The Western Confederacy's Final Gamble* (Knoxville: University of Tennessee Press, 2004).

2. Marszalek, *Sherman*, 297–310; Sherman, *Memoirs*, 641–95; Fellman, *Citizen Sherman*, 213–22; Kennett, *Marching Through Georgia*.

3. Brigadier General Hugh Judson Kilpatrick commanded Sherman's cavalry during the march to the sea.

4. "They have robbed the cradle and the grave equally to get their present force" (Grant to Elihu B. Washburne, August 16, 1864, in John Y. Simon, ed., *The Papers of Ulysses S. Grant*, vol. 12 [Carbondale and Edwardsville: Southern Illinois University Press, 1986], 16). Part of Grant's letter was released to the press and widely quoted.

5. For discussions of Georgia home front conditions and political sentiments, see Wetherington, *Plain Folk's Fight*.

6. Mr. Maxon is not identified.

7. Troops of the 20th Corps under General Slocum passed through Madison. According to one source, Madison was spared destruction due to the intercession of Joshua Hill, who sought out the Union commander and arranged for protection for the town. See Kendrick, "A Non-combatant's War Reminiscences," 461. However, a study of the effect of the Federal troops' passage through Madison suggests Hill's plantation was pillaged or partially destroyed, as were the plantations of his neighbors. See Brian Melton, "'The Town That Sherman Wouldn't Burn': Sherman's March and Madison, Georgia, in History, Memory, and Legend," *Georgia Historical Quarterly* 86 (June 2002): 201–30. Soldiers passing through thought the town was beautiful. See Joseph T. Glatthaar, *The March to the Sea and Beyond: Sherman's Troops in the Savannah and Carolina Campaigns* (New York: New York University Press, 1985), 106.

8. See Frank L. Owsley, *King Cotton Diplomacy: Foreign Relations of the Confederate States of America* (Chicago: University of Chicago Press, 1959).

9. Marszalek, *Sherman*, 279–80.

10. Brigadier General William B. Hazen. See *OR* ser. 1, vol. 44: 109–10.

11. The battle of Griswoldville, November 22, 1864, was the sharpest fight during the march. Georgia militia units suffered nearly six hundred casualties to the Federal forces' one hundred. The Federal veterans were shocked to discover that the militia was manned by young boys and old men. See William H. Bragg, *Griswoldville* (Macon, Ga.: Mercer University Press, 2000), and Kennett, *Marching through Georgia*, 255.

12. Sherman, *Memoirs*, 670–71.

13. The Pioneer Corps were units that specialized in constructing defensive works, bridges, and fortifications. African American troops and selected men from regular volunteer units formed these units attached to their brigades or divisions.

14. Fort McAllister was stormed and taken on December 13, 1864, by Hazen's division (*OR*, ser. 1, vol. 44: 110–11; Sherman, *Memoirs*, 673–76).

15. Thomas Denny.

16. Confederate Lieutenant General William J. Hardee, commander at Savannah, was ordered to escape the siege and preserve his force of ten thousand men. His force slipped out of the city north into South Carolina on the night of December 20–21, 1864 (Marszalek, *Sherman*, 307–8; Kennett, *Marching through Georgia*, 308; Sherman, *Memoirs*, 692–95).

17. Lieutenant John A. LaPierre of South Bend.

18. General Grant, tied up with Lee in Virginia, communicated to Sherman in early December his wish to forego capturing Savannah and join him against the Army of Northern Virginia. Sherman did not heed the request, but took the city. However, he soon made plans to begin marching north into South Carolina (Sherman, *Memoirs*, 718ff.; Glatthaar, *The March to the Sea and Beyond*, 10–14).

19. The 149th Indiana Volunteer Infantry regiment was recruited from the same counties that formed the 48th.

20. Lace made in Honiton, Devonshire, England.

21. The newspaper clipping does not survive. Several newspapers were published in Savannah at the time.

22. Marszalek, *Sherman*, 309–11.

23. Hallet Kilbourne of Goshen obtained patronage appointments in the Republican-controlled bureaucracy, rising to become chief clerk in the Department of the Interior at war's end and later participating in District of Columbia real estate schemes. During the war he wrote letters published in the Goshen *Times* describing politics and the Washington scene.

24. Possibly James W. Nye, New York–born U.S. senator from Nevada, newly elected in 1864.

25. President Lincoln's second inauguration took place Saturday, March 4, 1865, at the Capitol. The 38th Congress adjourned on March 3, 1865; the Senate held a special session March 4–11, 1865.

26. Aunt Mackie and John Walter Mackie, Wood's cousin.

Postscript

1. For an important study of postwar psychological problems in Civil War soldiers, see Eric T. Dean Jr., *Shook Over Hell: Post-traumatic Stress, Vietnam, and the Civil War* (Cambridge, Mass.: Harvard University Press, 1997). Dean focuses much of his analysis on Civil War veterans who were patients at the Indiana Hospital for the Insane, the state mental hospital. See also James Marten, "Exempt from the Ordinary Rules of Life: Researching Postwar Adjustment Problems of Union Veterans," *Civil War History* 47 (March 2001): 57–70.

2. Goshen *Times*, February 9 and April 6, 1865; *Goshen Democrat*, April 5, 1865.

3. *Goshen Democrat*, April 12, July 26, September 13, and October 4, 1865; Goshen *Times*, May 25, July 27, October 5, and October 12, 1865.

4. Letters of Edward J. Wood to Jane Wood, October 25, November 3, November 4, November 14, November 29, and December 4, 1865, in possession of Daniel Wood. In his letter of October 25, Wood humorously told of hotel fare at the Violett House: "I was happy to recognize some old acquaintances at the Violett. The identical piece of their leathery steak fried in rancid butter that was so constant a visitor six months ago, still maintains its place on the table. I recognized it at the first glance & on a single taste I could have sworn to its identity."

5. Edward J. Wood to Jane Wood, July 18, 1866, in possession of Daniel Wood. Goshen *Times*, March 21, 1867; *Goshen Democrat*, February 7, 1866, and November 13, 1867.

6. Goshen *Times*, July 23, 1868; *Goshen Democrat*, August 5, 1868.

7. Goshen *Times*, February 13, May 28, and November 5, 1868.

8. *Goshen Democrat*, November 4, September 21, and October 19, 1870; Goshen *Times*, September 15, 1870.

9. *Goshen Democrat,* March 29 and August 16, 1871; Goshen *Times,* July 13, 1871, and November 14, 1872. See Edward J. Wood to Jane Wood, November 14, 1865, and October 21, 1867, in possession of Daniel Wood. See also Marie Gautier Walker to Jane Wood, March 6, 1874, and Marie Gautier Walker to Edward J. Wood, June 19, 1866, in possession of Daniel Wood.

10. *Goshen Democrat,* April 28, 1869; Goshen *Times,* August 17 and September 21, 1871.

11. Goshen *Times,* November 17 and 24, 1870; *Goshen Democrat,* January 5, February 2, and September 6, 1871.

12. Goshen *Times,* February 15, June 13, and October 11, 1872; *Goshen Democrat,* August 14 and October 9, 1872.

13. Goshen *Times,* November 14, 1872.

14. The *Goshen Democrat* of April 12, 1873, quoted extensively from the Jackson *Citizen* of April 9, 1873; the Goshen *Times* of April 17, 1873, quoted from the Jackson *Daily Patriot* of April 10, 1873.

15. Goshen *Times,* April 17 and 24, 1873, and *Goshen Democrat,* May 10 and June 6, 1873.

16. *Goshen Democrat,* May 6, 1873. See pension application of Jane A. Wood in National Archives, Washington, D.C.

Appendices

1. George P. Copeland, editor of the Goshen *Times.*

2. Charles W. Stevens, co-owner and editor of the Goshen *Times* from 1857 to 1862.

3. Corporal Warren H. Pease, Company G, wrote a letter dated June 7, 1862, that appeared in the June 19, 1862, issue of the *Times.* Pease highlighted the large sick roll and widespread homesickness and gloominess in the regiment as it passed the time away in drill and reading the newspapers.

4. Brigadier General Jeremiah Sullivan, a southern Indiana politician, formerly colonel of the 13th Indiana Volunteer Infantry regiment.

5. The 16th Indiana Volunteer Infantry regiment was part of Burbridge's brigade that assaulted the 2nd Texas Lunette on May 22. However, according to maps 66 and 67 in Grabau's analysis of the Vicksburg campaign, the 16th Indiana attacked the fort on the southeast side, whereas the 48th later attacked on the east side. According to the maps then, it would be safer to suggest that the 23rd Wisconsin was the unit the 48th Indiana "relieved" that day. See Grabau, *Ninety-Eight Days,* 378–79, and maps 66 and 67.

Index

104, 117, 156; returns to regiment, 68; wounded at Iuka, 64

Elk River, 162

Ellis, Erastus Winter Hewitt, xx, **xxi**, 135, 248n2, 238n57

Ellis, William R., Lieutenant, 185, 188

Etowah River, 187, 191–213, 216

Ewing, Hugh B., Brigadier General, 140, 146, 147, 271n20

Failing, Mr. 72

Farragut, David G., Captain, 253n7

Ferriss, George, 79

Ferriss, Mrs. 72, 112, 114

Fisher, Abraham S., Lieutenant, 6, 249n11

Fisher, James M., Major, 202

Flint River, 168

Florida, 209; Apalachicola, xiv–xv, Marianna, xiv; 209; Pensacola, 209

Florida military units: 5th Florida Volunteer Infantry regiment, 245; 6th Florida Volunteer Infantry regiment, 260n15

Foote, D. C., 181

foraging, 256, n10

Forrest, Nathan Bedford, General, 150, 159, 165, 175, 183, 201, 272n7, 274n12

Fort Donelson, battle and surrender of, 9, 12–13, 27, 249n4, 250n6

Fort Henry, surrender of, 9, 11, 249n3, 12–13

Fort McAllister, 222

Fort Sumter, firing on, xix

Fort Wood, Kingston, Georgia, 189

Foster, Cory, 7, 249n13

Foster, Nathaniel Green, 205–6

Frank Leslie's Illustrated Newspaper, 30, 253n8

Franklin, Tennessee, battle of, 215

Freemasonry, 7,19, 166, 182, 238, 239, 250n12

Frémont, John C., xvii

Gautier, Pierre (Peter), xiv, 206, 218

Georgia, xxv, 145; Atlanta, xxvii, 45, 183, 190, 199, 200, 216; Big Shanty, 203; Cartersville, 196; Clinton, 219; Dalton, 137, 146, 160, 174, 198, 203; Gordon, 219–20; Hillsboro, 219; Irwin's Crossroads, 220; Irwinton, 220; Jackson, 218; Jonesboro, 217; Kennesaw Mountain, 203; Kingston, 175, 188–91, 203; Lafayette, 203; Macon, 219–20; Madison, 114, 183, 205, 218, 284n7; McDonough, 217–18; Milledgeville, 218, 220; Monticello, xiv, 218; Planters Factory, 218; Resaca, 198; Rome, 203; Savannah, xiv, 159, 183, 216; Somerville, 220; Spring Place, 198; Statesboro, 220; Union sentiment in, 226–27

Georgia Central Railroad, 220

Georgia military units; 9th Georgia Volunteer Infantry regiment, 267n55; 56th Georgia Volunteer Infantry regiment, 114

Gettysburg, battle of, 114, 267n54

Gibbons, George W., Lieutenant, 6, 249n11, 13, 34, 41, 239

Gillespie, Ellen Williams, 20, 251n20, 39, 94, 99, 104, 114, 116, 131, 134, 164, 212

Gillespie, James, 20, 251n21, 31, 94, 124, 134, 166

Gillmore, John Quincy Adams, Brigadier General, 137

Gordon, George, Lord Byron, 252n2, 274n11, 275n29

Goshen Democrat, 235, 240–43, 265n27, 280n15

Goshen Times, xviii, xx, 1–2, 71, 77, 235, 237–39, 285n23

Grant, Ulysses S., Lieutenant General, xxiv, 24, 46, 67, 69, 79, 93, 99, 105, 107, 109, 110, 111, 113, 129–30, 142, 145, 154, 159, 171, 176, 184, 195, 215, 217, 231, 232

Greeley, Horace, 232–33

Greene, Adolphus H., Captain, 180

Gregg, John, Brigadier General, 263n14

Griswoldville, battle of, 284n11

63, 64, 96, 99, 101; building quarters, 148, 166, 168, 189, 193, 203; Carolina campaign, 216; cattle drive, 179, 182; commanded by officer of 59th Indiana, 64; drill, 1, 4, 15, 40, 76; election of officers, 2; foraging, 51–52, 76, 94, 95, 146, 218–19, 221, 238, 241; furlough, 116, 117, 123, 145, 149, 151, 152, 156, 159; Grand Review, 216; guarding railroads, 145, 147, 152–53, 160, 170, 187, 188 191; marching, 29–30, 39–40, 47–49, 50–51, 63–64, 72, 77–78, 91–92, 98, 99, 102–3, 129, 132–33, 135, 136, 137–38, 150, 160–61, 161–63, 188, 198, 216–24, 238; mortality in regiment, 54, 56–57; picket duty, 54–55; recruiting, 1–6, 115, 117, 124, 133, 142, 147, 151, 166, 169, 171, 201; reenlistment, 115–16, 124, 132, 135, 145, 149, 151, 152, 156; regimental band, 176; regimental cow, 123; regimental elections, 200; reviewed by generals, 142, 164, 168–69, 217, 225, 227; sharpshooter duty, 100, 106, 108, 241; sickness in regiment, 106, 122, 150, 171, 185, 200, 237, 286n3; singing *Hallelujah Chorus* on the march, 48, 238; sutler, 21, 251n22

—59th Indiana Volunteer Infantry regiment, xxv, 64, 96–97, 120, 152, 161–63, 166, 170, 173, 181, 191, 199–200, 203, 211, 219, 238, 256n18, 259n8
—74th Indiana Volunteer Infantry regiment, 196
—100th Indiana Volunteer Infantry regiment, 108
—128th Indiana Volunteer Infantry regiment, 272n3
—129th Indiana Volunteer Infantry regiment, 200
—149th Indiana Volunteer Infantry regiment, 225
Indiana State Prison-North at Michigan City, 251n22
insects, 49, 122, 255n6
Invalid Corps, 261n9, 269n14
Iowa, 200

Iowa military units: 5th Iowa Volunteer Infantry regiment, 48, 238, 255n4, 256n18
Iuka, battle of, 45, 62, 258n31–33

Jackson, Michigan, *Citizen*, 234
Jackson, Michigan, *Daily Patriot*, 234–35
Jackson, Mississippi, battle of, 95–97, 172, 240
Johnson, Ruel M., Captain, 108
Johnston, Albert Sidney, General, 253n9
Johnston, Joseph E., General, 105, 107, 109, 111, 113, 115, 160, 171, 182, 187, 216, 243, 255n7, 260n16
Judson, Edward B., 132, 135, 167, 171, 182, 195, 228, 230, 235
Judson, Sarah Williams, 132, 135, 139, 166–67, 171, 173, 176, 177, 190, 195, 228

Kansas, xvii
Kentucky, 115; Bardstown, 6, 249n10; Bowling Green, 11; Columbus, 11, 77; Louisville, 60, 183, 211; Paducah, xxiv, 9–28, 45, 99, 252n25
Kerstetter, Edmund R., 2, 231, 249n8
Kilbourne, Hallet, 228, 285n23
Kilpatrick, Hugh Judson, Brigadier General, 217
Kirby Smith, Edmund, General, 45
Kittoe, E. D., Lieutenant Colonel, 164
Knight, Mr., 61
Know Nothing Party, 255n5

Ladies' Non-importation League, 177
Lane, James C., Colonel, 194
Lee, Robert E., General, 111, 160, 195, 255n7, 257n28
Leslie's Ladies' Magazine, 177
Lincoln, Abraham, xix, 129, 200, 261n5, 265n31; administration, 111
Logan, John A., Major General, 95, 96, 109, 142, 146, 152, 154, 164, 171
Longfellow, Henry Wadsworth, 257n20

A Fierce, Wild Joy was designed and typeset on a Macintosh 10.4.10 computer system using InDesign CS software. The body text is set in 9/12 Palatino and display type is set in Journal Ultra Small Caps. This book was designed and typeset by Barbara Karwhite and manufactured by Thomson-Shore, Inc.